GENTRY

SOCIAL CHANGE IN JAVA:

THE TALE OF A FAMILY

National Library of Australia Cataloguing-in-Publication entry:

Author:	Umar Kayam (1932-2002)
Title:	*Gentry* (original title: *Para Priyayi*)
ISBN:	978-0-9874637-2-2
Notes:	Introduction; Translator's Foreword; Glossary; Note on Spelling; Contents
Subject:	A sociological novel translated from Indonesian into English
Translator:	Vladislav V Zhukov © 2014
Dewey Number:	899.22133

The translator gratefully acknowledges the permission of the author's family to render the Indonesian original of this novel into English. Any errors or inadequacies in this new edition are solely those of the translator.

Other translations by Vladislav Zhukov:

The Kim Vân Kieu of Nguyen Du (1765-1820), published in 2004 by Pandanus Books, the Australian National University. Second edition published in 2013 by Cornell University Southeast Asia Program Publications.
Old Hunting Grounds and Other Stories by Yuri Kazakov: 38 stories rendered from Russian and published in two volumes by the translator at Mount Wilson NSW in 2013.

Printed by CreateSpace, an Amazon.com company

GENTRY

SOCIAL CHANGE IN JAVA:

THE TALE OF A FAMILY

A NOVEL BY

UMAR KAYAM

Translated by Vladislav Zhukov

Published by the translator
at Mount Wilson, NSW
2014

CONTENTS

INTRODUCTION	vii
1. WANAGALIH: setting and referent	1
2. LANTIP: at the margin	9
3. SASTRODARSONO: the bearer of destiny	26
4. LANTIP: the hero resolves	98
5. HARDOJO: new lives, first variation: reach and withdrawal	115
6. NOEGROHO: second variation: reach to new limits	145
7. THE WIVES: marriage in transition	170
8. LANTIP: from side to centre	192
9. HARIMURTI: third variation: over-reach	213
10. LANTIP: end and succession	245

INTRODUCTION

THE AUTHOR AND NOVEL

Born in Ngawi, East Java, Umar Kayam (1932-2002) obtained his primary and lower-secondary schooling within the Dutch colonial educational system: respectively at a *Hollandsch Inlandsche School* and a *Meer Uitgebreid Lager Onderwijs* institution, two levels created by colonial policy for the purpose of raising an indigenous elite employable in certain categories of the Netherlands East Indies officialdom. His father was a teacher at the Mangkunegaran HIS in Solo when Kayam was a pupil there, and the boy completed high school in Yogyakarta during the transitional restructuring of education following independence. These may seem unexceptional particulars about a Javanese youngster's passage through schooling, but the significance of that experience is in its historical setting, as described in this book.

In brief, Java in the period covered by Kayam's fictional saga was far more than at present a rural society somewhat relieved by mostly minor urban centres. It was a time of population increase and diminishing holdings, when the immemorial difficulties of the peasantry were growing more than usually acute. (An account such as Clifford Geertz's *Agricultural Involution* will set the scene for the investigative reader, since Kayam leaves that constricting situation implicit.) Nevertheless, modern ways and ideas were seeping into the countryside, offering prospects of upward social mobility and a securer life. The key was education: the one bright portal of hope for the wretched of Java. A central focus of the novel *Para Priyayi* (translated here as *Gentry*) is the indispensability of literacy for any peasant villager seeking to escape the miseries of his class and achieve familial betterment by rising into the higher of colonial Java's essentially two-tier society. That higher, literate tier was the priyayi, a functionary-gentry shading in its upper levels into the traditional aristocracy and acting in most facets of life as an intermediary and cultural filter between the peasantry and the Dutch (who are essentially a detached, overseeing layer hardly visible in this story).

The author's own experience as a pupil and student provide realism and credence to his descriptions of what was often a heartbreaking and unsuccessful effort to obtain that essential schooling. Kayam's later sociological studies served to give him perspective on the socio-cultural conservatism of those who did so succeed, and subsequently on the revolutionary changes to Java's generationally-constant structures that began with the Japanese invasion in 1942 and accelerated dramatically during the succeeding twenty years of upheavals. Those initial tremors, and then convulsions, affected the role of the gentry, beginning their transformation in various directions, and ultimately bringing into question the very meaning and relevance of the term *priyayi* in a post-colonial context of rapidly widening and vertically-extending education.

Kayam started writing fiction while still at school and then as a tertiary student, and so the politico-literary issues of the 1960s, the furores around such things as *Manikebu*—the anti-communist Cultural Manifesto promulgated in 1964 and soon afterwards repealed (q.v.)—resonated personally with him, if from a distance, since he spent much of the decade 1955-1965 studying in America: initially extending in New York his earlier Indonesian pedagogical studies, and then obtaining a doctorate in sociology at Cornell University. After returning home he passed through a number of senior positions in broadcasting, films, cultural and general journalism, and was a senior lecturer and professor at various Indonesian universities, a member of the Jakarta Academy, and also of the Indonesian Academy of Science. At the time he wrote *Para Priyayi*, he was the Director of Gadjah Mada University's Centre for Cultural Studies and a senior professor in the School of Letters there. The novel was published in 1992. Among other of his works are a collection of short stories set in Manhattan (1972), two novellas (1975) and a volume of journal columns (1990).

TRANSLATOR'S FOREWORD

The aim in this translation of *Para Priyayi* has been to offer readers an English version which would not merely be mathematically identical to the Indonesian text, if that were possible, but one that made explicit the cultural, anthropological, historical, linguistic and psychological associations inherent in the story and subliminally understood by its original readership. Obviously, faithfulness to the core account has remained of the utmost importance to this translator, but he has nevertheless held that much of significance would be lost were there not some development and depiction of background, by borrowing colours from those five areas and others. If the objective here had been to present a social-scientific study of the Javanese in the late colonial

Introduction

and modernising period, then the usual commentary-by-footnotes would have served well enough to assist deeper understanding of a strictly dictionary-based, literal rendering. Those footnotes and their related superscripts would, unfortunately, have peppered and plagued virtually every page of this book. This is no such study, but an 'entertainment', in the old-fashioned literary sense of that term: hopefully an instructive and possibly for some an enlightening read, but above all a tale to be enjoyed, as Umar Kayam certainly meant it to be. Bothersome notes of a more or less technical nature distract the mind's eye, slow things down, interrupt and generally detract from aesthetic pleasure. The procedure here has been instead to—judiciously—incorporate significant explanatory information into the interstices of the writing, wherever that could be done in a natural way. That is, where to an Indonesian reader a single word or phrase conjures, and is meant to intuitively conjure, a world beyond itself, the aim here has been to at least touch on that world by some textual extensions which may not strictly appear in the pages of the original work. In a small number of cases, this input for the purpose of unfolding *Para Priyayi* to the foreign reader has gone beyond paraphrasing to actually interpreting the author's intention, where in certain passages that has been left a matter of conjecture. Kayam's rather original instruction to postgraduate students under his tutelage, that as an examiner he was unconcerned with the minutiae of spelling, punctuation and grammar—'stuff for typists to worry over, not doctorate candidates'—may also tell us something about his approach to literary composition, and possibly explains certain minor inconsistencies and hiatuses in *Para Priyayi*. A further reason for reading and translating this tale creatively is this: Bahasa Indonesia has developed rapidly to serve the needs of administration, economics, the military, and other technocratic fields; but it has a way yet to go before bourgeoning into a truly literary language. In Kayam's time it was still an incomplete palette for the capabilities of artists of his imagination. The challenge, and the gain, in that temporary inadequacy lies in the requirement that general readers and translators alike give more scope than usual in a work of fiction to their own imagination as they follow this story. Nevertheless, whatever the interventions, mental or on paper of such reading and translating, this of course remains Kayam's tale, and no one else could have created it.

A further test for translators, beyond the textual one of describing things with greater precision by seeming to wander from the simple and focused meaning of words, is to present a tale which follows literary norms familiar to readers from another culture, while at the same time conserving most of what presumably attracted those readers to sample the work in the first place: that is, the especial exotic flavours of the original. In the present case, there are passages which sometimes disregard or overlook Western critical norms. I refer, for instance, to the usual Aristotelian principle of structural integrity. Here loose ends dangle not infrequently. One may ask, for example, where was Uncle Noegroho's mother-in-law when his family drama unfolded in her house? What happened to Hari's twins after they had been used to so tragically kill off their mother? I can only hope that for the sake of Kayam's epic—for the just enjoyment of his broad design, and achievement—the balance adopted in this translation between adjusting and ignoring will be charitably acquiesced in by the Indonesia-aficionados who in their thousands visit those islands yearly, and to whom this rendering of his novel is dedicated.

V. V. Zh.

GLOSSARY

This is a tale of classes and hierarchies in a society which measures such divisions largely in familial terms, by which every individual is assigned his or her position vis-à-vis others through titles or designations that express a real or conventionalised status in a family framework. As used in these pages, the terms reflect the socio-familial/age position of both the person addressed and the speaker in any exchange. Certain other honorifics exist outside this framework, such as those designating high nobility, occupations, and foreigners: often by introduced words in the case of the latter. Although it is expected that present readers will master the usage quickly enough contextually, they may nevertheless need to make occasional reference to the following list—which, the translator hastens to explain, is not an exhaustive and technically infallible set of anthropological definitions, but should suffice for the needs of this book. Travellers in Indonesia, particularly to back-country Java, will have discovered themselves slotted into this 'kinship', and may find the glossary useful in understanding how they are perceived and why they are addressed in different ways by different people. Unless specified, terms are both of address and third-person reference. Where more than one term appears against the same signification (e.g., *Embok*; *Ibu*: Mother), this reflects the widespread coexistence of Javanese with Malay-Indonesian terms. Unmodified Dutch titles are indicated by (D).

Adik, Dik	Younger brother or sister.
Ajeng, Jeng	Polite reference to a female the same age as or younger than the speaker.

Introduction

Anak, Nak	Child; kindly-meant address to a junior, usually a young male.
Bagus	Title of Javanese nobility.
Bapak, Pak	Father.
Bapaké Tolé	Familiar term used by a wife to refer to her husband.
Bapakné	Familiar term of address to one's husband.
Budé	Aunt, older than one's parents.
Bulik, Lik	Aunt, younger than one's parents.
Buné	Familiar term of address to one's wife.
Bung	Brother; democratic equal.
Bupati	Regent.
Carik	Classifier for paper, etc.; by extension: a clerk.
Dalang	Puppeteer who conducts shadow plays.
Dimas	Polite address to a younger brother or subordinate.
Dukuh	Hamlet; by extension: a hamlet head.
Embah, Mbah	Grandparent; old person generally; teacher; mystic.
Embok, Mbok	Mother; older female of humble origin.
Eyang	Grandparent; an honorific address and reference to the respected elderly.
Genduk, Nduk	Lass; female servant.
Guru	Teacher.
Gus	Polite address and reference to boys and young men.
Haji	Title of a male who has done the Mecca pilgrimage.
Ibu, Bu	Mother; older female of humble origin
Jagabaya	Village guard.
Jaksa	Public prosecutor.
Kaji	Knowledge, especially religious; by extension: a Koranic catechist.
Kakang, Kang	Elder brother.
Kakung	Male, polite usage.
Kamas	Elder brother; older male or a superior
Kiai, Ki	Venerated scholar; mystic; Islamic teacher.
Lurah	Village head.
Mantri	Middle-rank professional with supervisory roles.
Mas	Brother; male contemporary.
Mbak, Mbakyu, Yu	Familiar female contemporary or one of lower status.
Meneer (D)	Sir; Mister.
Menir	Colloquial form of the above.
Nakmas	Polite, kindly term of address to a junior male.
Ndoro	Master or Mistress.
Nyai	Respectful term of reference to an older female.
Nyonya	Madam; Mistress.

Gentry

Opziener (D)	Overseer or superintendent.
Oom (D)	Uncle.
Pakdé	Uncle, older than one's parents.
Paklik, Lik	Uncle, younger than one's parents.
Pakné	Term of address to one's husband.
Polisi	Police; policeman.
Putri	Formally polite term of reference to a female.
Raden, Den	Designation of exceptional politeness; title of nobility: *Raden, Den Bagus* – Excellency; *Raden, Den Mas* – Radiance; *Raden, Den Ajeng* – female equivalent of *Raden, Den Mas*. Courtesy honorific applied to males of imprecise status.
Romo	Father, highly respectful.
Sepuh	Honourable elder.
Seten	Assistant district head.
Siti	Title awarded to highborn females, or prefixed to female names with an Arab association.
Tante (D)	Aunt.
Tolé, Lé	Lad; boy; young man.
Tuan	Mister; term of address/reference to Western and (occasionally) Westernised adult males.
Wedana	District head.
Wedok	Colloquially polite term of reference to a female.

Indonesian is prolific in acronyms, abbreviations, and casual borrowings that rapidly take on a life of their own and are an important source of new vocabulary for this emerging language. Although a sufficient explanation occurs where such terms are initially met in the text, the reader may like to have the following glossary as an additional aide-mémoire.

AMS	*Algemene Middelbare School.* Higher ('Comprehensive') Secondary School
Bulog	*Badan Urusan Logistik Nasional.* National Logistics Board
Bundan	Infantry Section in *Peta*, q.v.
Bundancho	Section Commander in *Peta*, q.v.
CGMI	*Central Gerakan Mahasiswa Indonesia.* Indonesian Student Movements' Central Directory.
Chudan	Infantry Company in *Peta*, q.v.
Chudancho	Company Commander in *Peta*, q.v.

Introduction

Daidan	Battalion in *Peta*, q.v.
van Deventer School/ Pan Depenter	Boarding schools for indigenous girls, named after the colonial reformer
ELS	*Europeesche Lagere School.* Elementary school for Dutch children and those of the indigenous elite
Gerwani	*Gerakan Wanita Indonesia.* Association of Indonesian Women
Gestapu	*Gerakan September Tiga Puluh.* Movement of September 30th: the 1965 coup attempt
Heiho	Indonesian labour units assisting the Japanese, 1942-45
HIK	*Hollands Inlandsche Kweekschool.* Dutch-language indigenous-teachers training school
HIS	*Hollandsch Inlandsche School.* Primary school for the children of indigenous gentry
HKS	*Hogere Kweekschool.* Higher trade-training college
HSI	*Himpunan Sarjana Indonesia.* Association of Indonesian Scholars
Kenpetai	Japanese military police
KNIL	*Koninklijk Nederlandsch-Indisch Leger.* Dutch Colonial Army
Kweekschool	Trade-training College
Lekra	*Lembaga Kebudayaan Rakyat.* People's Cultural Association
Lestra	*Lembaga Sastra Indonesia.* Indonesian Literary Institute
Manikebu	*Manifesto Kebudayaan.* The intellectual and cultural proclamation of 1964
MULO	*Meer Uitgebreid Lager Onderwijs.* Dutch-language lower secondary school
Normaalschool	Teacher-training College
OSVIA	*Opleidingsschool voor Inlandse Ambtenaren.* An institute for training indigenous civil servants
Pancasila	The 'Five Principles' containing the affirmations of the Indonesian constitution: belief in and adherence to one God, humanity, unity, democracy, and justice
Perwari	*Persatuan Wanita Republik Indonesia.* Association of Indonesian Women
Pesindo	*Pemuda Sosialis Indonesia.* Socialist Youth of Indonesia
Peta	*Pembela Tanah Air.* Indonesian auxiliary troops during the Japanese occupation
PKI	*Partai Komunis Indonesia.* Indonesian Communist Party
Pron Nasional	National Front

Schakel School/ Sekakel	Primary school 'linked' to further education or training by an additional two years
Schakel Particulier/ Partikelir	Unofficial *Schakel School*, q.v.
SMA	*Sekolah Menengah Atas.* Upper secondary school created after independence
Shodan	Platoon in *Peta*, q.v.
Shodancho	Platoon Commander in *Peta*, q.v.
STOVIA/ *Setopia*	*School tot Opleiding van Inlandse Artsen.* Institute for training indigenous doctors
SS	*Staatsspoorwegen.* State Railways in the Dutch period
TNI	*Tentara Nasional Indonesia.* National Army of Indonesia
TNI Masyarakat	The People's TNI, q.v.

A note on spelling. Certain vowel combinations appearing in most of the period dealt with in this book have followed Dutch orthography and were still found in publications up to 1947; a number of consonants similarly lasted into the 1960s, when a reformed Bahasa Indonesia came into use. It may be helpful as an aid to pronunciation to note those earlier forms and their modern equivalents. Thus, *oe* has in modern Indonesian been converted to *u* (pron. *oo*); *j* to *y*; *dj* to *j*; *tj* to *c* (pron. *ch*). Kayam is frequently anachronistic with his spelling: for instance, his *nyonya* would have occurred as *njonja* during the early years of his story. However, no such 'updating' could have been made consistently by him or anyone else in regard to proper names, since many Indonesians have chosen to retain the original Dutch form of their own; so that the pre-reform *oe*, *tj* and *j* (as *y*) in the names of characters in *Para Priyayi* must be accepted as found. 'Mansoer' does become 'Mansur' at some point in the story, but that appears to be an authorial oversight rather than a spelling revision, and to avoid confusion has been continued in its *oe* form throughout this translation. Place-names were a different matter, and so Jogja(karta) could by fiat and popular acceptance be re-branded Yogya(karta) after independence, which is the form thrown back by Kayam to the early-20th century beginning of the book and then so used throughout. This whole issue is a can of worms, and Kayam may well be excused his anachronisms, in

Introduction

addition to the slips in narrative alluded to above. His hybrid 'Cokrokoesoemo' illustrates his nonchalance in the matter: it should be 'Tjokrokoesoemo', because the name first appears in the colonial section of the book; while if the author had wanted to use a consistently modern spelling, then it ought to have been 'Cokrokusumo'.

1. WANAGALIH: setting and referent

Let me introduce Wanagalih, where in my recollection so much happened during those years, and yet so little it might also be said.

    The town is the capital of a Javanese regency, a provincial area termed a *kabupaten*, from the title of the regent: *bupati*. The place, despite its long-established administrative status since the middle years of the 19th century, will appear to the odd visitor who comes here as rather small and homely, with a sense about it of a dreaming, declining age, of having passed beyond any possibility of further growth or hope of a new blossoming. Certainly, the great leafy tamarinds that once lined each side of the main street bisecting Wanagalih—and the picture of them remains so clear in my mind from childhood—those are there no longer and have been replaced by more lithesome new acacias; and certainly, again, the central market has put on some of the trappings of a modern shopping mall, for it now has its circle of covered kiosks facing hopefully outwards, in recognition, no doubt, of the universality of today's clients; but within the ring of the market itself, behind those kiosks, folk still vend the same merchandise that was common in my youth. There are the familiar black short trousers made from glossy cotton fabric, tied at the waist by a dependable drawstring (a reassuring detail to our peasant wearers), rows of them hang beside pink and white and black camisoles; there are the same wide-waisted sashes on sale today, within which on each side of the buckle the country people stow their capital when coming to market. And, what else? One looks about and sees whips, broad conical hats, the usual vegetables, green jackfruit, chickens and ducks; there are the lines of food-sellers behind tables of snacks and drinks, salads of blanched greens spooned-over with peanut sauce, glasses of soupy *wedang cemoe*, that lemongrass infusion thickened with sweet bean-sauce; there are piled cubes of tofu caged in ribbons of banana-leaf; and in general all those kinds of wares and market delicacies remain unchanged. And the odours of the market—pungent, sour, foul, the smell of livestock's urine—those too remain the same.

    And yet, yes, one must also admit that on the southern edge of the town there is a moderately-large bus terminal now, able to accommodate coaches from Solo and Yogyakarta, Madiun and Surabaya, even from Denpasar, one or another rumbling in or out at most times of the day; and in some of the residential quarters we have just begun to see concrete buildings in the modern style. We see them, indeed, but the older houses still predominate, still are there in considerable numbers, wooden cottages that look to be slowly sinking into their foundations, drawn down by the black, friable soil of Wanagalih. People recall that because of this instability of the soil the colonial authorities in their time forbade the erection of concrete or masonry structures that were thought liable to sudden collapse. Well, wooden houses also succumb in due course to that relentless undermining, but their yielding goes on over many years, goes on undetectably. Be that as it may, it seems people nowadays make up their own minds about how they build, past concerns are not of much interest to them as once they were. Perhaps some new technology has been invented to defend us from our soil? Or is this new architecture another sign of our infatuation with the modern, the novel? Or is it a particularly reckless display of the new wealth we have acquired even in these parts over recent years? But probably such reflections only serve to reveal how stuffy I have grown, show my age perhaps, and my schooling in Dutch days. Well, there can be no question but that the latest buildings do make the neighbouring wooden cottages look pathetically worn and ordinary, almost amusing.

But one structure from the past still stands with a handsome and sturdy presence, the town square spreading before it. This is the old pendopo, the open-sided audience hall where regents used to meet the kabupaten's assembled dignitaries. It has undergone a few repairs over time, but as far as anybody remembers not one of its supporting columns has ever needed to be replaced, all stand staunch without any sign of fatigue or distortion. And there is a tale worth telling about this venerable building, a legend that may serve to contrast these new times with those almost mythical ones now gradually fading from our memory.

According to tradition, the timber from which the pendopo columns were milled was brought out of the oldest, most inner and eerie depths of the forest which then surrounded Wanagalih. The story goes that before being felled the chosen trees were invited to a discussion about what was proposed for them, this by a local shaman who was living then, a specialist in forest magic, a certain esteemed scholar called Jogosimo. Kiai Jogosimo was famous for his sanctity and arcane powers, and his own backyard was no more familiar to him than the furthest reaches of this forest, he being on the best of terms with and knowledgeable about both those green expanses and all creation dwelling in them. Tigers, monkeys, and other such creatures came to him and submitted to him, the very trees and stones honoured Kiai Jogo and displayed a filial respect towards him. He possessed this authority, legend says, by being endowed with the ability to converse with the beasts and the trees and the stones, and his name, 'Jogo-simo', which in its honorific permutations translates as 'Keeper of the Tigers', had been long settled on him for that reason.

'Yon Kiai Jogosimo now, he and the prophet Solomon—whose name be

1. Wanagalih

honoured—know what? Why, those two were one and the same! True!'

This example of country awe came to me from Kang Man the water-carrier, who had heard his grandparents recounting stories about the shaman.

As the tale continues, the candidate-supports for the roof of the pendopo were one by one approached by Klai Jogo, who was followed by a retinue burning incense and bearing offerings, and behind them by the high officialdom of the kabupaten come in their full sodality to witness the proceedings. The trees were asked by the kiai if they were content to be parted from their roots and leave their native surrounds to become the invulnerable supports of Wanagalih's seat of authority and dignity, where dwelled the paternal guardian of the kabupaten's people. As the dialogue between the shaman and the trees progressed, it was said that the forest atmosphere changed to one characterised by a great silence: the chatter of monkeys, the crowing of jungle fowl, the muted rumble of the spotted leopard, all in short order and together ceased; the leaves and the fronds of the forest stopped rustling; and the very winds and lower zephyrs of the air settled into an unresisting quietude, overcome by the power of the shaman's mantra. And then the chosen trees suddenly began to slowly bend, first to the left and then to the right, in movements resembling the supple contortions of *ronggeng* dancers; this while the surrounding trees which had not been chosen or spoken to remained upright and still.

'Those trees, you ken, Pak—pitching about, dancing and such—it was like a sign they agreed to what Kiai Jogo asked. And, well, naturally, when it's the prophet Solomon himself—glory to him—what he tells you, you can't gainsay that, can you?' Thus from Kang Man again.

While I happen to be on the subject, I might say too that this aptness for conversing with vegetation, with forest trees and so on, is by no means a monopoly of sages like Kiai Jogosimo. Our old people in the country always ask permission first of any plant before culling its leaves or shoots to be used in salads. And now that I think of it, I recall reading in my early maturity that in South Sulawesi the Bugis shipwrights who build those cargo boats called *pinisi* also make the same obeisance to the trees they fell for timber.

However, to continue: the trunks of the selected trees were without further ceremony sluiced-over with bucketfuls of water, and there in those forest depths a *selamatan*, an assortment of festive dishes, was laid out on the ground around their base, and Kiai Jogosimo, his retinue, and the worthies of the kabupaten sat down and all solemnity partook of the food. The trees were felled and the trunks were transported with great care to their destination: one to become the principal pillar of the Wanagalih pendopo, and the rest to serve as subsidiary supports and props. And so—no workaday wood this, but sanctified and permeated with mystic aura—those timbers have remained strong and straight to this day. There is a generally accepted claim that only such supports as the main and secondary columns of the Mangkunegaran pendopo, and those of the audience hall of the Kasununan palace—both in Solo—and the columns of the palace in Yogyakarta, are more spiritually potent and enduring. I might add, by the way, that the same claimants have nothing but disdain for the supports of halls constructed for the bupati of the colonial period. Why, you will hear them scoff, those mundane timbers, felled and wrought under an unhallowed gaze, will stand no comparison—their quality diminishes to total insignificance!

Kang Man in defence of Wanagalih's pendopo explains why it must necessarily yield place to the royal edifices mentioned: 'Well, you can't expect our pendopo to be more holy than those of Solo or Yogya, can you? Those are from the time of old Mataram! Bless me, 'twould bring ruin on our heads to just *think* about *them* being overmatched!'

I should say something too about the open square which stretches out so generously before the Wanagalih pendopo. The greenness of the lawn covering that space is evidence of careful, thoughtful maintenance, and the obvious health of the twin banyan trees in its centre—a truly arresting sight, big, leafy, and noble—indicate the same consideration by the townspeople. This square is the largest in East Java, and the pride of everyone from the bupati down to the humblest citizen; in fact, I might say that there is a common proprietorial feeling towards it. Local teams wanting to play football on it must hold their games according to a strict schedule, and even the pasturing of buffaloes, cows, and goats is monitored with a view to the continuing fertility of the ground. Towards evening, when Wanagalih's day lapses into coolness and peace, the square and its surrounds become very pleasant indeed. All sorts of folk, young men and girls, married couples, children and infants, arrive to sit on the grass, savour the fresh air, eat peanuts and sip glasses of *wedang cemoe*. There will be children running about, young people in their teens sitting more quietly and perhaps stealing looks towards each other, adults keeping an eye on their offspring or glancing away occasionally towards the shouts of a ball game: such is the scene.

And yet . . . and yet, this square—it now suddenly comes back to me with horror, with abhorrence—this square with all its gracious, serene atmosphere was once, in my boyhood, a setting for the slaughter of human beings—an arena whose ground was drenched with blood!

Yes, during those three months in 1948, after Muso's *Partai Komunis Indonesia* raised its rebellion in Madiun, this Wanagalih of ours was one of the towns that bore the succeeding storm! Then it was that the executioners sent out by the PKI, and subsequently other, counterpart executioners from the Siliwangi Division, took turn and turn about to butcher, first, local figures deemed allied with the government; then, those who were the followers of Muso! All Wanagalih was in the grip of terror during those months!

1. Wanagalih

I just cannot imagine when such events as were seen on that square might have occurred in our past. I have certainly heard stories of executions carried out in the old days, about the rare hanging of some robber, the leader of a gang, or of a prominent rebel; but this slaughter, these shootings, wholesale and conducted with such organisation—could *they* have ever happened once? Could such things have been done during that clamorous uprising by Prince Diponegoro, for instance? Or out of some other tumult in our history?

I thank God that such a brutal experience has not been repeated since. Or, I should say, at least not so publicly, on our square. Not even following the failed communist coup against the army in September 1965. What was seen then were corpses floating in rivers, sometimes headless, sometimes missing their hands or their feet. But, thankfully, at least *that* terrible, horrible event passed by Wanagalih quickly. Although one does still hear occasional talk, occasional recollections of such things. . . .

But, anyway, anyway . . . the square itself has returned to its old aspect: green as before, healthy, a place to which people may come once again to enjoy the peace of evenings in confidence. I sometimes think of that old square as a fat, good-natured giant, yes I do. He opens his maw wide, this giant, he gulps in such a variety of things passing by him, incorporates so many things, placidly, without discriminating; then, satisfied, he closes that maw of his, and a faint smile like some vaguely glimpsed design in a batik pattern returns to his face. . . .

But let me continue telling about this little town of ours. Ah, yes, its rivers. Those canals and rivers . . . was I musing about things drifting on their waters just now? . . . Actually, to be precise, there are no fewer than three significant rivers flowing past Wanagalih, busily eroding their way around the town's edges: two of those being the Madiun and the Solo, and they meet just below an outlying corner of the town. Now, such a juncture of rivers used to have a strategic importance once, economic and military, as witness the so-called 'Hidden Fort' raised at that point by the Dutch during Diponegoro's time. Even now, quite a few river-craft transport produce and merchandise upstream and downstream in the age-old way on those waters beneath the old battlements.

Those two rivers are known well enough; yet Wanagalih has one other, a modest stream by comparison, and that is the Ketangga. Its inconsiderable size will ever exclude it from serving as a serious medium of trade, and it is also so shallow that fish and crocodiles and turtles are quite absent from it, and therefore so are fishermen, and even children seldom come to swim there. Nevertheless, this minor watercourse has an importance that in one respect elevates it beyond other rivers: for the Kali Ketangga is recorded in the prophetic epic, *The Era of Joyoboyo*, as that holy stream which will give birth to the returning *Ratu Adil*, no less: yes, the future Just Ruler of Java!

Well, as for myself, I would not dare claim to know positively that the epic describes the true significance of our Ketangga, but there are many who believe it does, and during the night-hours of holy days, such as certain Tuesdays and Fridays of the Javanese five-day week, some among those so convinced come to submerge themselves in its water. Nor would I conjecture that each of those folk in doing so offers himself as the fit vessel for that divine inflow, absolutely not. However, I will say, for what it may be worth, that I have heard apparently knowledgeable people in certain other places affirm that the Kali Ketangga referred to by King Joyoboyo is not at all the river flowing by Wanagalih, but another of that name in East Java. And, moreover, these same scholars, be they genuine or self-styled, affirm, not without derision, that those who go dipping in Wanagalih's Ketangga know nothing about interpreting times and portents, nor do they correctly understand *The Era of Joyoboyo* itself, which is a tome especially replete with mystical symbolisms. Actually, I confess that I find it hard not to smile when I hear a debate warming up around this issue, and if I retain my self-control it is by reminding myself that a highly venerated elder uncle of my foster parents used to be just such a dipper. Each time his nephews and nieces waylaid him on the subject of his nightly aquatics it used to throw him into a frightful pique.

He would round on those sceptics and proceed to educate them on the finer points of the question: 'O what a generation we have among us—look at ye now! Married, with children, descendants—and as runny-nosed as any of 'em! When your uncle goes "a-dipping", as you call it, Tuesday nights—and I mean *our, Javanese*, Tuesdays!—when his teeth rattle in his head from the cold, it's got nothing to do with any ambition to become *Ratu*—dopes! Nothing to do with some mummer-king on a throne in a travelling show! That's not the drift of it at all, not what I'm after! Spiritual power, power to do good in this world, is what it's about! For the world's welfare; maybe it's salvation. D'you understand, there, young man? You, missy?'

Well, of course none of his audience accepted any of that seriously, those tirades of the old man, peppered as they often were with vigorous back-country expressions and replete with saws about the world's beauties and our duty to it as its inhabitants; and particularly not when in some contradiction with their sense the words were delivered in a bad temper. It was years later—by which time we heard that he had become the manager, the *bas*, of just such a travelling troupe dealing in old sagas and pseudo-history, had on one and the same day married two of the troupe's prima donnas—that we all began to have an inkling of what he meant. By then our world had seen no end of remaking, and everyone of us had moved on to more maturity. I have a picture of him in my mind as a thriving figure in his later days, even something of a substantial personage in local terms: three or four gold teeth in his mouth, a red velvet *peci* set at a gay angle on his head....

1. Wanagalih

Yes, of such was, and largely is, Wanagalih. The town's name speaks of its origins, combining as it does 'forest' (*wana*) and 'heartwood' (*galih*). Surrounded by jungle and then, as that retreated in the course of time, by remnant stands of teak, Wanagalih lives by its timber, or that was its main resource in the past. The complex of offices occupied by the Department of Forestry in Dutch times, the *Boschwezen* (or *Bosbesem*, as our native conversion went), are among the best old structures in the town, and all are built of teak of the highest quality. The head of the Department was held in great esteem, and at every important event or ceremonial occasion of kabupaten-wide significance was infallibly invited to attend and take a seat in the foremost row of spectators. When his position eventually passed to an indigenous official, that person too, as had been the habit, was invited to cards at the home of the bupati, to nights of gambling at Chinese *pei*.

But that detail largely belongs to Wanagalih's past, to the colonial period, up to and perhaps including the Japanese occupation. Now the town is looked on as little more than a transit stop in more important and wider commercial movements, diminishing in that ampler context to seem very ordinary, rather nondescript, even when its best efforts to show that it has not been totally left behind in the race to modernity are taken into account. The young people leave to seek work in Surabaya, Jakarta, or wherever they can, while those lucky enough to further their education go to any big city that has a suitable school or university. The people who remain have for some time now in large part been those of pension-age, living on in their weatherboard houses, in those outmoded old cottages tranquilly subsiding into Wanagalih's unique, black, uncohesive and consuming soil. Come each morning, after first prayers and with the arrival of dawn, the lanes and roads of Wanagalih grow slowly alive with the matutinal strolling of those oldsters, grow animated a little by the antics of dogs chasing one another around the scuffling feet. They come, those superannuated folk, from all corners of the town, walking together in pairs or in larger groups, the sound of their sandals a distinct *srek-srek*; they come coughing, their necks wound in scarves still known by the Dutch '*halsdoek*', an article characteristic of that generation and associated with this town. They approach the great square, meet by the enclosure surrounding the ancient banyans, remain a while beneath the spread of branches, perhaps until the beggars and vagrants who have overnighted under the two trees become too persistent, and then the strollers may transfer to the guard-booth outside the office of the kabupaten.

What themes, what questions enter into their conversations? No doubt the usual comparisons of each other's children and grandchildren, the usual happy lauding of their own progeny. And there will be reflections too on life in retirement, on life itself, on the world and on life beyond this world. Mild and bland are those conversations generally, at least as far as children and retirement are concerned; but on some fundamental issues the talk can turn quite sharp, our people do sometimes clash in their opinions about those. Stuttering and unsteady, those old voices do rise, amid coughs and pauses for the relief of phlegm. I know well enough about that side, because I often heard the teacher with whom I lived, Guru Sastrodarsono, returning from such morning meetings and still hot and provoked by some argument relieve his feelings on us in his house. Yet he still persisted in his dawn routine: prayers, the morning stroll, the gatherings.

With the brightening day, pedlars appear, carrying their various wares, following one another in an increasing throng towards the market; the *kring-kring-kring* of small horse-drawn buggies and the larger gharries reaches the ear more often; our pensioners disperse to their homes to have their coffee and morning snack of fried bananas or boiled cassava. A bucket or two of warm water tossed over the head and shoulders constitutes the morning ablution; and then it's off to doze away the hours in a rocking chair. And so Wanagalih's day will slowly revolve to the accompaniment of the *kring-kring-kring* of its horse carts, that tinkling perhaps punctuated at times by the rumble of a distant bus.

The sound of a locomotive has never been heard in this town. The railway never came to it.

2. LANTIP: at the margin

But I should introduce myself: my name is Lantip. No, actually that became my name when I began living with the Sastrodarsono family, on Setenan Road in Wanagalih. My name at birth, given to me by my mother, was Wagé, which is merely the Javanese for 'Saturday', the day I was born. Through our custom of receiving a new name at decisive stages in life—and being taken into Guru Sastrodarsono's house to be schooled was one such transformative moment—it was deemed that I would need something more appropriate to my raised condition, and the word '*lantip*' has connotations of 'cleverness' and 'learning'. I should explain that as a teacher my benefactor was of the gentry, a *priyayi*, a member of a much-striated upper class whose most generally shared feature has been its detachment from manual labour. On leaving my mother to come to Wanagalih and be educated I partook of that same status, and poor 'Wagé' was of course merely one of those typically 'village' names.

Before that move, I had lived with my mother in Wanalawas, a large hamlet a few kilometres from Wanagalih. According to tradition, Wanalawas was in a sense the founding source of Wanagalih. In the days of Mataram's dominion over much of Java, the river junction on which Wanagalih now stands was at some point identified as strategic, and the ruler of Madiun, then a local vassal of Mataram, received instructions to raise a substantial settlement at the confluence. This he did by simply uprooting the surrounding villages. In that cause, Wanalawas, up till then a reasonably large community, was by the forced relocation of most of its people left as little more than a *dukuh*, a hamlet. Among the few families still living there in my time was that of my mother and what remained of her line: just her own mother. It was a community of rice-growing peasants, who in addition raised some dry-season crops of one sort or another, a little tobacco and the like. I soon became aware that our life was hard, and according to what I heard from my mother had always been so: families barely subsisted on plots of no more than a hectare and a half, and there was the additional handicap that rice in this area depended on rainfall, the fields being some distance from any stream that might have been tapped to irrigate them. From as far back as we could trace it, our family had always supplemented farming by fermenting soybean curd to produce tempeh for sale in the Wanagalih market and on the town's roads.

Gentry

As for my father... well, what can I say? I just don't have any memory of him at all. Mother always used to tell me that he had gone a long way away on a *rantau*, in search of a living. It was only years later, during my stay with the Sastrodarsono family, and by then considered a member of it, that I was given at moments when the teacher in some fit of exasperation rebuked me a hint about the kind of person my father must have been. Guru Sastrodarsono, whom politeness required me to address as *Embah Kakung*, 'Grandfather', was in fact kind-hearted and just, but he could sometimes be impatient and waspish too, capable then of releasing quite a torrent of invective. It was at such times that I came to gather indirectly certain things about my parent. Embah Guru Kakung would explode at me such a series as: 'Ignorant monkey! Ape! Gangster's son! Issue of a robber band!...'

Volleys of that sort I was most apt to receive when he deemed me slow in carrying out some errand: such, for example, as running for more money to his wife when he was having a bad run at cards. Not that the teacher was addicted to serious gambling, not at all, cards being merely one of the habitual minor pleasures indulged in by the lower gentry of his circle, a pastime institutionalised in the word *kesukan*, or simply 'diversion'. Nonetheless, losing at the card table, big amounts or small, still means losing. Emotions seethe, frustrations rise like vapours into the brain, and a whole throng of passions mix together: annoyance, frustration, even bitterness, a desire for revenge, for redeeming all by a coup; and at the back of it all probably lurks a degree of shame as well. Then it was that Embah Guru Kakung, his habitual good humour gone, changed into another being altogether, into something frightening to the child I was then: 'Idi-ot! You've been told to get the money! Issue of a hooligan-scoundrel!'

Under the machinegun-delivery of such language I could do nothing other than sadly lower my head. So, then, I was the son of a thief? My father had been at the head of a band of robbers? Could that be true? But with whom might I follow up those accusations? My mother was unwilling to talk about my father and was short with my questioning. When she delivered me to the Sastrodarsono family I had just turned six, and the few details I had heard her repeat about my father were simply these: 'Your father, child, has gone away, far, far away. He left so that he could bring us back a lot of money one day; so that we could have a new house, a bigger, more fertile bit of land, and maybe a cow and a buffalo and many other things. You'll see, you'll be so happy when your bapak comes back....'

I stopped enquiring about my father when it grew clear to me that he would never come back. Adults in the hamlet whom I asked, also said that he had gone on a *rantau*, gone to some unspecified 'abroad', somewhere distant to seek his fortune; and as for what the playmates of my own age might have known—village children who were always comparing the merits of their own

2. Lantip

fathers—those strangely were silent about mine. Finally, as I said, I gave up and stopped asking and accepted my mother's explanation. And, after all, those later outbursts of Embah Guru Kakung were not all that frequent, they only occurred occasionally, when he lost at cards.

My mother's connection with the Sastrodarsono family seemingly began with her selling tempeh to them. In her rounds through the town, shouldering her basket, she one day approached the teacher's house on Setenan Road; and it appears that her tempeh found exceptional approval, the evidence being that from then on she had a standing order there. My mother's product, as I remember, was indeed especially good: solid, yet crumbling in the mouth, deliciously oily and salty at the same time. It was all a matter of not stinting in the choice and quantity of the soybeans. The villages surrounding Wanagalih have always been known for their tempeh, and to this day the town enjoys a modest fame for it in East Java.

While my mother went about her business through the town, I was left at home on my own. Well, not really alone, there was also my grandmother, Embah Wedok, a dowager of indeterminate but very advanced years as it then seemed to me, old and worn out; and I remember that her room was like the nest of some animal, a mess of shabby possessions. During my mother's absence in town I had the responsibility of serving Embah's meal to her. The food would be ready, my mother having cooked the rice and vegetables early that morning, at the same time as she prepared her batch of tempeh for that day's trade, and I only needed to ladle a plateful and carry it into Embah's lair. I could not at the time understand why the old woman never smiled at me, or at my mother either. She always wore a profoundly melancholic expression, and her deep-sunk eyes rested on me without affection. She accepted the food with no sign of satisfaction and with a sound like that of pain or a lament which I could never interpret, and I always hurried from her room after delivering the plate to her. I stayed out in the fields playing with the other children until my belly growled with hunger again or I became tired of playing, and then I would return to take our plates to the well to wash, throwing the remnant rice from my grandmother's plate to the fowls.

At about the time of the mid-afternoon prayer, my mother would return from her rounds, her face flushed with the heat and running with perspiration, her hair in disorder. This was the moment I most looked forward to each day. Apart from simply missing my mother I could always rely on her to bring something nice back from the market: *klepon*, for example, steamed-rice cakes with a centre of palm sugar; or *onde-onde*, balls of rice-flour filled with mung beans; or *nagasari*, those little cubes of rice-flour and minced banana wrapped in woven strips of banana leaf. To this day, and I have left my youth long ago, the pleasure of anticipating those humble delicacies remains with me still, and even now I ask my wife to keep a plate of such things on our table.

Then came the morning when Embah Wedok did not rise from her bed and we saw that she had passed away. Our corner of Wanalawas, consisting of only a few households in the tiny village, made its uncrowded visits of condolence, and I recall that the ceremony of burial was also minimal and quick. I followed on the heels of the adults who bore the corpse to the village cemetery and then followed them back. And I noted a strange thing after that: no sooner had the old woman died than the house took on a certain stillness. And yet, what had been the sound of her voice, what had we heard from her when she was alive? In my memory, she was silent for the most part, her expression never changing from one of deep gloom, and her eyes were often turned away into the distance; what noises did escape her lips were like whimpers or groans of uncertain meaning. The day after the funeral, and when our neighbours had ended their visits to our isolated dwelling, my mother, as I now remember clearly, spoke to me about my grandmother. She actually only uttered one or two sentences: 'Your Embah Wedok, child, saw many disappointments and her life was one of great sadness because she was abandoned by all those she loved.'

Although I understood this for my mother unusually long remark, what sense could a boy of six really make of it? I did not take the opportunity of asking her to explain, and she made no sign of wanting to add anything else on the subject. It might have been a passing comment, but thinking back years later I believe it was a true observation on the course of her own life as well as her mother's.

After my grandmother's death, my mother decided to take me with her on her rounds. This now meant that I had to help her prepare the day's stock of tempeh and then walk beside her or trot behind her as she traversed the town. It was both an enjoyment and exhausting. Fortunately, there was little need for me to call out our wares at the top of my voice, as other children did, since mostly we had a set sequence of customers to visit. My most vivid memory as we trekked through one street and alley after another was of the sun's bite, Wanagalih being a byword for its heat, and I know that I was frequently parched with thirst. On one early occasion I tried wheedling my mother into paying for a glass of iced syrup. She replied sharply: 'No. Stop that!' and I fell silent. I knew that my mother was kind, but she was thrifty, too, and could be firm. She thought that we might quench our thirst quite adequately at the public well on the corner of the square, or else there was always the hope that one or another of our clients would offer us some tea.

One such generous house was that of the Sastrodarsonos. Setenan Road was in the inner part of the town, a considerable distance from the other of my mother's clients, but for some reason she was prepared to walk that far

2. Lantip

to offer her tempeh there. By the time we arrived, we were tired and our faces would be flushed and shining with sweat, so perhaps our appearance touched the heart of those who saw us coming. At that time I naturally did not address the teacher as *Embah Guru* or *Embah Sastrodarsono*, but followed my mother in more respectfully using the title *Ndoro*, and towards his wife, *Ndoro Putri*, as befitted our distance from such town gentry. They might see us arriving, and the teacher would make some remark, in a tone which to me sounded so even and authoritative, using the polite *Mbak*, towards the peasant woman before him: 'So, Mbak, and you've brought your boy I see there, mm?'

My mother would hiss deferentially in acknowledgement: '*Inggih,* Ndoro. There is no one to look after him in our house.'

'H'm yes. A pity. A child so young, to be trailing all over the town in this heat.'

'Ah, Ndoro, how else could it be with us?'

I well remember the long pause during which the honourable couple regarded us. Of course, with my head bowed I dared do no more than catch a glimpse of whatever I could from the corner of an eye—how might a six-year-old village-boy, his mother a tempeh seller, recruit the courage to lift his gaze and examine the faces of such elevated folk? It would have been inconceivable, it would have been impossible. Therefore, in the most proper and indeed the most natural and unexceptional way in the presence of the two priyayi, I kept my head well lowered.

'Off with you to the back now, Mbak, to the kitchen; tell them to give you tea!'

From those early days on, their house on Setenan Road became an important juncture where we would break our rounds; and in time not just a place to shelter from the weather and slake our thirst, because our relations with the Sastrodarsono household grew continually more agreeable and habitual. The large weatherboard house, although a spot where we knew we could evade the sun or rain, became for us also practically a second home. But no, there I go too far—no such great and grand structure could be a second home to the likes of us, whose real home in Wanalawas was a mean thing made of panels of plaited bamboo! And it should be remembered that this apart from its grandeur was also the house of a priyayi family, whose head was the principal of a village school. At that time a headmaster was someone of considerable stature in the perception of the populace in and around Wanagalih, his status as a being of an elevated class was well embedded in everybody's consciousness: his education, official position, and regular salary unmistakably defining him as such. No indeed, when I say that we thought of the house on Setenan Road as 'a second home' I mean it only with the most humble intent and sense of gratitude. It became a shelter where we felt a sense of acceptance towards us and in which we had a place not far below that of the domestic servants.

Although gentry, the Sastrodarsono couple were after all not altogether distant in origin from our own class, as certain provincial aspects of their establishment showed, and so we were easily incorporated into it. Of course we infallibly addressed them as 'Ndoro', and remained village folk beneath them, we kept a respectful space between us and never overstepped the conditions of our visits. During that hour or two, we might rest a while on the sleeping platform in one of the rear buildings; then, having recovered, my mother regularly joined the servants in their various routines: washing dishes, sweeping floors, hulling rice, and so forth. As a young boy, I could contribute little to those activities and I just followed my mother about. What I liked most was to see Kang Trimo, one of the outside help, driving the buffalo back from the rice-field on the approach of afternoon prayers, when I would often be allowed to sit on the beast's back while it ambled on its way towards the stable. Or I joined another of the field hands, Jairan, in herding the ducks back into their pen. For Ndoro Guru, although a headmaster and a gentleman, was still involved in farming. Behind the house was a large backyard where grew a variety of plants such as bananas, sweet potatoes, cassava, and a sort of tuber called *uwi*, with a dark skin and winding tendrils by which it supported itself on tree branches. As with a typical farmyard, there were clumps of tall bamboo at the corners. Behind this extensive backyard, or dry-crop field, were some hectares of rice paddy. All this area of cultivation furnished the staples of life and supplemented the headmaster's wage. Eventually it would largely provide for him in his retirement.

He had a considerable family to run, too: for in addition to raising his own children Guru Sastrodarsono had in his care a number of nephews and a niece. In short, this was a typical household of the better-off Javanese, in which a paterfamilias stood as the central pillar of an extended clan, kin whose general expectation was that he would accommodate under his wing (if I may vary the figure) as many as possible of its less fortunate members. Such income and social standing as accrued to the teacher were not considered by him to be boons imparted by providence for mere personal enjoyment or aggrandisement; and I often heard him lecturing his children, and anyone else within hearing, on the high impropriety, indeed indecency, of any relative of a priyayi family falling or being allowed to fall by the wayside. To drift into disorder and vagrancy, to find no benefit in education, and to stray from the proper path of that class—why, such a scandalous priyayi, the teacher harangued his listeners, was a bad priyayi, was indeed no priyayi at all!

One afternoon, after returning from our usual visit to Setenan Road, my mother and I were sitting on the bamboo sleeping-platform in the porch of

2. Lantip

our house in Wanalawas. The day was ending gloriously, the western sky becoming suffused with a brassy-red glow that radiated strange shafts and gleams of light. In the gathering twilight our yard and the open fields beyond it grew steadily more beautiful and at the same time oddly unfamiliar. I had never before seen or been affected by such an atmosphere as was now enveloping our poor, unattractive and dilapidated surroundings. In a moment of apprehension I moved closer to my mother so that our bodies touched. She gave me a hug and stroked my hair. 'We call it *candikala*, dear, when the sunlight comes together like that, in sheafs. It happens just before dark.'

I nodded my head, but the explanation did not wholly allay that peculiar feeling.

'The old people say that this was how the sky looked when Nyai Roro Kidul stood with the ranks of an army around her. She was the queen of the Southern Ocean and the wife of the old Mataram kings.'

I nodded again and pressed against her. I felt that something weird and terrible might be about to happen, and when I looked up at my mother her face seemed at that moment quite beautiful. Perhaps it was because she was fresh from a cold wash, or perhaps it was through the reflections of the *candikala*. She stood me up before her.

'Wagé, my dear, my child, listen to me.'

I was startled to hear myself address like that.

'You're big now. You're six.'

I thought this strange again. We had both known for some time that I had reached that age.

'It's time for you to go away, to leave this small, pinched village. Do you hear me?'

'Leave, Mbok? Are we going to leave?'

'Not we, child. You alone.'

I felt suddenly very frightened, I felt something unimaginable and awful was about to occur.

'Where do I have to go, Mbok?'

'You're going to live with Ndoro Guru, to live in Setenan Road.'

'And where are you going, Mbok?'

'Oh, your mother will stay here, in Wanalawas. Now dear, don't cry.'

And I had, of course, begun to cry, imagining our parting.

'I just want to stay here with you, Mbok.'

'Come on now, dear, we'll see each other every day, won't we? I'll be passing through Setenan Road, won't I? You're going there to quickly learn how to be clever and be a scholar. Here there's no school, there's nothing. You see that, don't you? Well, then?'

I saw that my mother had made her decision and it was useless attempting to change it. Evidently she had already discussed it with the teacher and his wife. And so, next morning, after we had called at Setenan Road I did not return to Wanalawas. I may or may not have cried up to that moment, but I do remember that I parted with my mother in an unexpectedly short and casual way.

'That's it then, dear. Be good and work hard and do everything Ndoro Guru tells you.' With that, my mother bent quickly, set her remnant tempeh in order, shouldered her basket, and left me standing bewildered and holding a bundle with a shirt or two in it. I watched her figure diminish in the direction of the main road, and I still wonder that I did so dry-eyed.

I did not understand then why, but the teacher and his wife put me in a room inside the house, although indeed it was the rearmost one. I had hoped to go into one of the outbuildings at the back, by the free-standing kitchen, to be where the male servants lived, Kang Man and Kang Trimo; or at least with the maids, old Mbok Nem and her junior, Lik Paerah. Among the servants I thought I would feel less like a stranger, and at night I might listen to their gossip and to the old legends; and surely they would teach me our Javanese poetry, chanted to the beat of a gong, and to sing those marvellous old ballads. But I was separated from the servants and instead put into that inner room in the house.

There were four bedrooms, the biggest of course belonging to Ndoro Guru Kakung and Putri. In my eyes at that time their room seemed huge and luxurious, containing a large iron bed with a mattress, pillows, bolsters and a mosquito net of dazzling whiteness, crocheted around with a white pattern of flowers. This room was not a thoroughfare to the other rooms, but the last on the northern side of the house. The extent and beauty of its bed filled me with awe: it seemed alone a thing of majesty and almost of authority. Around it were other attractions: a large and fine teakwood wardrobe, an oval mirror hanging on the southern wall, a small cabinet where the teacher's krisses— the appurtenances of a priyayi—were stored, and in a corner leant his ceremonial spears. I came to know that room well, because Ndoro Guru Putri made it one of my Sunday duties to clean it. On other days, when I attended school, the lady herself and Lik Paerah did any necessary cleaning. As for the other rooms, there were two shared by the three Sastrodarsono adult children whenever they visited, while the last was a spare bedroom for overnight guests. Finally, there was a small storeroom where were kept the old belongings and playthings of the three children when they were young, as well as current ones left by their own children when those were brought to visit their grandparents at holiday times. A partition crossed this little room, one side of which became mine; and so I found myself sharing space with an assortment of mainly worn-out toys.

At the time I arrived to become a member of the Sastrodarsono family,

2. Lantip

the teacher's immediate children had already left to make their own lives in other towns and had started their own families. Compared to the average Javanese nuclear family, that of Ndoro Sastrodarsono, with only three children, would have been regarded as rather small. The eldest, Ndoro Noegroho, lived in Yogyakarta and taught in a *Hollandsch Inlandsche School*, or HIS: a primary school for the children of priyayi. The second, Ndoro Hardojo, chose to become a court functionary employed by the Mankunegaran palace in Solo, where he was concerned with village education in the principality, including adult instruction, and with raising the level of education of the younger priyayi on their way to the rank of *wedana*, or district chief. The youngest of the three was Ndoro Soemini, elevated to Ndoro Raden Ajeng by the relatively noble status of her husband, Raden Harjono Cokrokoesoemo, assistant wedana at Karangelo. The two rooms belonging to the now grown-up children were for the most part unused in my time, and it was only at school vacations or during the traditional holiday marking the end of the fasting month that the three adults and their children—the teacher's grandchildren—occupied them again. Then was it that those two rooms, which were usually silent, deserted, and spotless, became filled with the commotion and noise of the visiting generations.

Next to the house and somewhat behind it stood a modest pavilion consisting of two small rooms: the quarters of nephews and nieces of the teacher. When I began living on Setenan Road, this pavilion was occupied by Raden Ngadiman and his family. There had been other nephews and a niece there in the past, and those had to one extent or another been brought up by the Sastrodarsono family and then had dispersed to follow their own fates. Den Ngadiman, son of the teacher's first cousin, alone remained, and he worked as a clerk in the office of the kabupaten. He and his wife had two small children at the time when I first came to the house.

During my initial days, Ndoro Guru Putri taught me how to clean and tidy the various rooms and the manner of setting the dinner table. In fact, this was Lik Paerah's regular duty, but my hostess desired that I should learn at the earliest opportunity the ways of keeping a proper house in order. By becoming so proficient, said she, once I had completed my education in the village school I could become an independent worker; and, who knows, she went on, I might even get a position in a Madiun restaurant or boarding house. I lowered my head and nodded happily at the thought of such a wonderful if distant prospect; and in the following days, all eager and elated, I set myself to mastering the techniques of cleaning and maintaining a priyayi household. It seems that although a child I learned quickly. The lady of the house showed many signs of satisfaction, while Lik Paerah could hardly credit such progress: '*Wah*, a wee lad just out of the villages—well, you *are* quick, all right!'

And I remember, looking back, that cleaning and setting the table were not all I was assigned, for I had time to help Mbok Nem and Lik Paerah in the kitchen preparing rice, splitting and grating coconuts, pressing coconut shavings to extract the milk, and assisting to bring in what was needed from the vegetable garden. In addition, I was soon trusted to wash dishes and crockery, and towards evening I helped Kang Trimo with chores such as mowing grass with a sickle. At night I had a special duty: while both the Ndoro sat listening to a concert of gamelan music on the radio, I massaged and kneaded their feet. I had done that often enough for my mother, and even my grandmother, in Wanalawas, so it was something I already knew about; and evidently I did it now to the satisfaction of the couple, for they told me that my kneading was just right: not done too vigorously, yet leaving the limbs revived. For this they sometimes gave me half a cent or even a whole cent. If they had no need of me for that service, I would run out to the back of the house where I would sit listening engrossed to the talk of the servants, the old stories passing among them, and especially to hear Kang Trimo reciting folk versions of episodes from history. He knew many in the form of the six-line verses called *macapat*, which he had learned when attending village school for a time in his youth. Strangely, however, my benefactors, especially Ndoro Guru Kakung, were not altogether pleased to see me spend so much time in the servants' area, and I could not then understand this: for was I not also a peasant like those four?

My mother appeared content with the changes that were taking place in me on Setenan Road, and during her short visits she would watch me with innocent happiness while I was at my household duties, and like Lik Paerah would praise me with astonishment: '*Wah*, bless me, you'll soon know how to do just about everything!' And it was a great moment for her when in my presence one Sunday the teacher broached to her his wish that I should start going to school.

He began thus: 'The boy, mother, is growing; and we have noticed, too, how clever he is in his work here.'

'*Inggih*! And God be thanked for that,' my mother replied.

'Now then, it's like this. We think that the time has come for young Wagé to begin his schooling. Rather late, in fact: he is almost seven. What do you say to that, mother, would you like that?'

For a moment my mother stood silent, did not reply. Then I saw that a flush had appeared on her face, and now suddenly two tears trickled down her cheeks! I was stunned to see this. My mother was crying?

'*Wah*, Ndoro Guru Kakung, Ndoro Guru Putri, it would be a godsend, past anything our sort might pray for. A thousand thanks! Please forgive me if I cry like this. The boy and I indeed had hoped, but not really dared to expect such a gift, we were happy enough that your honour and your lady-wife had opened your hearts to give him a place in your home.'

'Now, now, dear woman, don't go crying. Were you not told that we intended this from the start? From tomorrow, your son will go with me to my own school in Karangdompol. While I still have a position there I can get him on the roll without much trouble. Once I retire, that could be harder: the *gupermen* is making difficulties these days, screening people.'

'*Inggih!* Ndoro. We are both in your hands. Thank you, again and again!'

'H'm, yes. But there is something else.'

'Oh, Ndoro, what else?'

'We will have to change your son's name. Wagé is an unsuitable name for someone who is going to become an educated person. I recommend that it should be changed to Lantip. *Lantip* means intelligent, a thinker, things of that kind. What do you say to that, mm?'

'I bow to your wishes, Ndoro.'

'And you, lad, what do you say? Would you like to be called Lantip? It's a far nicer name, much more elegant than Wagé.'

To tell the truth, I did not then altogether understand what this matter of names was about, nor was I sure of my feelings towards my new name; but I caught my mother's eye and I too bowed my head in acceptance.

'*Inggih!* Ndoro.'

'That's the way, boy. So, we all concur. Now, mother, go to the back and tell Nem and Paerah to make some rice porridge with palm sugar, and we will have a proper little *selamatan* to celebrate your son's new name.'

The household grew busy to fulfil Ndoro Sastrodarsono's order, and at four that afternoon everyone gathered in a circle in a side room to celebrate my name-change. It was a short function, led by the teacher inviting those present to witness that following this event I would no longer be called Wagé but Lantip. The fare of this small feast—two kinds of porridge, of white rice and of so-called 'red' rice—visibly signified that apparently superficial but distinguishing transition. Naturally, at that time I was not fully up to appreciating the solemnity of the ceremony—young as I was, the eminently edible rice of both kinds was what most held my attention—but I did glimpse something else: how my mother's eyes glistened with barely controlled tears; and once again I could not understand why she should be crying. Was not Wagé indeed characteristically 'village', a common, unpretty name? Why, she should be glad and even proud to see it supplanted by a genteel new one like Lantip! But, anyway, no sooner had those attending chorused their '*Inggih!* We witness!' than we all set ourselves to emptying the bowls. The white rice had a rather savoury taste and was thickened with coconut milk, while the red had been sweetened and coloured with a syrup of palm sugar.

Gentry

Next morning, a Monday, I found myself on the rear rack of Ndoro's shining Fongers bicycle, somehow holding my seat and clutching a school bag containing a slate, chalk, an exercise book and a pencil; and also a bundle in which was a thermos of hot, sweet tea and a packet of fried bananas: the teacher's refreshments at the midday interval. The village of Karangdompol, where the school was located, lies on the far side of the Madiun, and each day Ndoro Guru and I boarded a raft-like vessel on which we and many other passengers were ferried across.

I was big for my age, so at the school I was given a seat on a bench at the back of the first class where I would not obstruct others. There, I immediately became the object of over-the-shoulder stares and whispers from the other children, both boys and girls: 'New kid . . . new kid . . .'

Next, my lowly position in Guru Sastrodarsono's house did the rounds: 'Headmaster's servant . . . headmaster's servant . . .'

I heard those comments circling the room, because of course they were meant to be heard, and I said nothing. They stated the truth and it was pointless to deny it. My mother had impressed on me the need to be patient, to avoid taking offence at the gossip of other children, even their mocking, and especially not to be provoked by anything that might end in fights. Control yourself, dear, she had warned me, remember you are still the child of a tempeh seller, even if they have given you the name Lantip and you live on Setenan Road. The important thing now is to shine, to study until you become educated and clever! She had conveyed that instruction with such quiet passion that it sank deeply into my mind and became a brake on any act which might have compromised this wonderful opportunity granted me. I experienced the usual attempts to test the mettle of a new boy, but I resisted giving my annoyers any openings that would lead to further harassment, and I quickly learned how to distract their attention to other things. Fortunately, I soon managed to catch up on such schooling as I had missed, and in a short time I was able to read and write and count as well as anyone else there.

What with the confidence I gained by those quick advances in my studies, and thanks to my mother's advice, looking back now I seem at that time to have begun developing a general knack for getting along with people and managing difficult situations; with such effect, indeed, that the other children soon gave me the role of a facilitator or even of leader among them. To illustrate, I might recount the following.

The days approaching the end of the fasting month, when classes ceased, was always a special time at the school. Pupils decorated their classrooms with fronds, flowers, and fruit taken from the school garden. An important side to the celebrations consisted in a combined theatrical presentation on a platform erected in the schoolyard. I was in fourth class then, and our class was set the project of preparing some joint performance with the pupils of

2. Lantip

the class above us. Our teacher left it to our two classes to decide on a program, we met to discuss it, and as often happened my suggestions were adopted. The event should consist of a *panembromo*, a song of welcome; then there would be a dedicatory piece in the form of a chorale sung in Javanese; then a *standen*, or acrobatic pose by a troupe; then an episode of *pencak silat* stylised fighting; then another group song; and, finally, a *ketoprak*, or historical drama. Oh, and in our class we had a pair of comedians for whom space had to be found for a skit before the dramatic finale—which last would be a melodrama chosen to break the hearts of our parent-audience and leave none of them dry-eyed! Everyone was happy with this list.

I remember how exhausting it was to combine all those elements into a whole; but fortunately Ndoro Guru Kakung and Ndoro Putri were very understanding and I was allowed to stay late at school to organise it all. As usual with numerous individuals working together for an outcome of that sort, the road was marked by laughter and tears, often together. One girl, I remember, sulked because she had not been chosen for the *panembromo*. I learned new skills of persuasion to smooth that situation with her; and then it was touch and go, because while I was calming her, others in the group were hooting: 'But she's tone-deaf, Lantip! We'll sound like market beggars singing for scraps!' Anyway, I bought her off with a walk-on servant's role in our great drama finale; but *that* nearly fell through and she almost burst into tears again when some wit shouted that she would be perfect as the mute goddess Dewi Bisu! But in the end I convinced her of the significance of her part, and everything ended in smiles. (I might add that years later, and all of us well past our schooldays then, I met her again when she was the wife of a Jakarta official in *Bulog*, the National Logistics Board, and, wonder to tell, my little classmate still remembered that event!)

Ah yes, youth: who does not have such memories of their early years? But let me go on a little, just to sketch the nature of our innocent preoccupations in those times, and perhaps to correct the impression that the girls were the only ones hard to manage. In our class we had five small boys, small in terms of build, not age, each suited by his light frame to occupy the apex of our *standen*, which originally was envisaged to represent a cone-like shape. But that obviously meant only one of those boys could be that peak, and each of the five believed he should be the one to stand there, on the supporting framework of the arms and legs and backs of his schoolmates: he alone might deliver our class salute to the spectators. Each of them was determined to be up there and would not be denied. After some thought, I proposed we decide on a top more like a tiara, so that all five could be accommodated. Success! The five would stand supported in their individual poses, the composition looking indeed like a tiara or coronet. In the event, alas, barely did the praise and applause of the spectators begin, when this handsome construction of linked humanity crashed to the boards in a welter of bodies!

Still, that *standen* of ours was commended for its originality. As for our *panembromo*, despite all efforts to weed out the musically deaf, it still sounded oddly strained. The problem was with the accompanying gamelan being tuned so high that the singers were almost standing on tiptoe and stretching their necks like turkeys in an effort to lift their voices to its pitch. But the clown skit went well, it had the audience doubled up, although I would not now be able to say where the humour lay. And yet, when I think of it after such a long time, other things, like that girl who could not keep a tune and the five boys of the collapsing *standen*, do live on in my memory. There certainly are some queer files and drawers in our brains, and we store the most unexpected things in them.

Regarding the *ketoprak*, that event is definitely preserved in one of those drawers, perhaps because of the pretty girl who played the leading part, with whom I think I must have been a little in love—yes, Surtiyem was her name, I now remember—or it might be because the drama did attain its object of wringing our dear parents' hearts. The elements of it were a young, unfortunate, and long-suffering damsel, a malicious stepmother, and an uncaring father. She flees her home, then her fate reverses when she meets and is wooed by a gallant Prince Charming who happens to be rich as well. Naturally we thought the plot unique and our staging brilliant; Surtiyem played her role excellently, and a boy called Paiman made a very believable father. And then here also there was a somewhat strange sequels to that performance, played out half a lifetime later. While on an official trip to a small town in East Java I was astounded to find Surtiyem and Paiman there, acting together in a travelling *ketoprak* troupe! The very Surtiyem I had brought guavas to in school, for whom I had painted an image of the wayang heroine Wara Sembadra! And now she was the leading lady in a company of wandering players, and Paiman's wife! I was delighted, and invited them both to a restaurant; and the odd thing was that all the while we were there they kept calling me 'Bapak', as if I were not their contemporary and former schoolfellow but some old gentleman to be reverentially sir'd. And their conversation with me too was carried on in the most ceremonial Javanese. I did what I could to steer our little reunion to a more comradely footing; but no, Pak Lantip had become a lofty Jakarta priyayi, a university man, a *Doktorandus*, you see.

Anyway, that performance was something we talked about for days with immense satisfaction and pride. And if I have dwelled overlong on this vignette from my school days, it may be for certain consequences that were revealed in a distant future. From my view of it in later years, the task I took on myself of stage-managing that tricky event and its assorted conflicting egos—successfully managed, in its small way—eventually came

2. Lantip

to seem quite prophetic.

My patrons in Setenan Road were greatly pleased, and praised me as one who was certainly living up to his new name. No words were sweeter to my ears.

In due course I moved into fifth class and could see the end of my time at Karangdompol. Before long, the daily ride on the back of the Sastrodarsono bicycle, clutching school-bag, thermos and packet of fried bananas, would be no more. The raft-crossings of the Madiun—meeting each morning an assortment of peddlers, hawkers of medicinal teak leaves and whatnot who waited on the far side; and in the afternoon the same folk bringing back to their villages market-purchases of sugar, tobacco, and the obligatory sweets for the children—those too would finish. I could see ahead of me at the end of the year how I and my classmates would part and go our separate ways. Where would their road take them? They were rural children from the local district. I wondered if any among them might chance to continue their education at a *sekakel*, as we called them, a *schakelschool* or 'linking' school of seven years, where instruction in the upper levels was carried out in Dutch. But it was a school rarely open to children from the villages; and for myself, I had no vision of such a miracle falling to my lot. I felt grateful enough to have been given the chance to study at Karangdompol, with fees paid and a haven in Setenan Road. I would be further thankful if, next, I could get some work and a modest income by which I might return something to my mother, and perhaps even to Ndoro Guru Kakung and Putri. And the early commendation of Ndoro Putri came back to me: that I was talented enough to gain service in a restaurant or boarding house in Madiun. Perhaps this is what I would become: a paid domestic or something similar. But in any such event I would be satisfied. My mother always said that any work is good when it is done honestly, done well and conscientiously; and how could I not be affected by the example of her own life as a seller of tempeh? Was there ever a more honest, good-hearted, meticulous, and persevering person than my own dear mother?

Then, unexpectedly, the blow fell!

One afternoon, typically hot for Wanagalih, when the whole establishment on Setenan Road was at their siestas, and I lay sprawled in the shade of the jackfruit tree in the front yard, I looked up to see Pak Dukuh, the village head from Wanalawas, pedalling furiously towards us on his worn-out bicycle. The moment he spotted me he cried out loudly: 'Oh Allah, boy. Oh Allah. Your Mbok, boy! Your Mbok!'

For a moment my heart stopped beating. 'What is it? My mother? What's happened, Pak?'

Gentry

'Oh Allah, boy. Oh Allah! Where is your Ndoro? Where is your Ndoro?'

I hurriedly led Pak Dukuh to the front veranda and asked him to take a seat; and the old man, always polite and retiring, chose a chair in a corner, under the stuffed head of a deer mounted high on the weatherboard wall. It was only after I had awakened the teacher from a deep sleep, had brought him to Pak Dukuh, and listened to the latter's report, that I finally learned that my mother was dead, had died after eating a poisonous mushroom! Unbelievable—my mother, so full of health, so strong, undaunted by any kind of weather or hard work, killed by a mushroom! I burst into tears. But I cried in silence, suppressing my sobs, for I had already learned among the lessons of a priyayi upbringing that one must try to control emotion. But painful it felt in the depths of my breast, keeping that sorrow confined; and Ndoro Guru, always wise, understood that.

'Cry, boy. As hard as you want. No one forbids it. Go ahead and cry!'

For some moments I let my grief escape, and I cried, hard and noisily. I shrieked, wailed: 'Mother. Poor, dear Mother. Mbok, Mbo-ok! . . .'

After I had stopped, Ndoro Guru Kakung sat me on the back of his bicycle, and with Pak Dukuh following we set off for Wanalawas. All the way, the teacher kept trying to lift up my spirits with consoling words sent over his shoulder: 'Lantip, you must earnestly try to let your mother go, to release her from your heart. We, all of us, including you and me, must ultimately die too. Such things lie in the will of God.'

But my eyes were filmed with tears. I blinked to look more clearly at the road that connected Wanagalih with Wanalawas, a ribbon of dirt so dry and so hot that out in the distance it seemed to rise and fall. I looked at the growths of vegetation and at the houses passing on each side; and everything was homely, unchanged, as if time had overlooked these scenes of my first childhood, these regions that I had traversed so often with my mother, as if time had forgotten them when it laid its hand on all else.

'And remember, too, Lantip, that she was only entrusted for a while to this world. Allah has called for her return. We must accept that. She is happy now.'

I kept silent because I did not know what to say. I wanted to get to Wanalawas as quickly as possible to look at my mother for the last time, and to have explained to me how she could have died the way she did. When we arrived at our house there was a crowd of people gathered there: her neighbours, other tempeh sellers, teak-leaf sellers and such. They pressed around me and led me into the house, and I saw her there, stretched out on a mat, her face ashen and tinged by a kind of bluish under-pallor. But she had a calm expression, and her lips, oddly, were set in a faint smile. The oldest neighbour there, Aunt Sumo, came to me and stroked my hair.

2. Lantip

'Oh Allah, dear boy . . . your Mbok has gone, dear. We are so sorry for you. It's unbelievable, this morning everything was the same, and now, suddenly, she's gone. She went out to the fields to look for mushrooms. Odd, that. Your mother hardly ever ate them. But, dear, it's the will of Allah. She had a bit of free time this morning and she went looking for mushrooms, said she felt like eating some. Be patient, it's God's will.'

My mother's body was washed by the women, and that afternoon she was buried in the village graveyard where her mother had been buried before. In the evening the neighbouring menfolk came to the house, some to recite the confession of faith, others to just sit around and talk. I was strangely impressed by the sight of Ndoro Guru Kakung joining the villagers in close conversation. It was an unexpected thing: a leading priyayi of the district appearing to involve himself with these people? There was no one approaching his rank in our hamlet, yet he was talking with those around him as if they were long known to him.

I heard one of them, Uncle Suto, the village head who had reported my mother's death, saying to him: 'Yes indeed, had the *gupermen* allowed the school your honour opened here back then to continue, Wanalawas might not now be as dead as it is.'

'Yes, that could well be so.'

I was startled. More signs that Ndoro Guru was acquainted with Wanalawas. Why had I never had any inkling of that? Not once had he revealed any interest whatever in the place or discussed it in my hearing with his wife. And my late mother, what had she known? Surely if there was some connection or other she must have been aware of it too; then why had she never said anything to me? I sat there with my questions in a dark corner of the house. Towards nine o'clock the teacher stood up and took his leave of the others, and I accompanied him to the front fence.

'You better stay here for the three days until they have the *selamatan* meal for your mother. I will send Kang Trimo to pick you up.

'*Inggih,* Ndoro.'

I saw Ndoro Guru pedal off into the night and disappear, leaving me perplexed in the darkness. I remained mulling over to myself the meaning of his exchange with Pak Suto, and of his other conversations with my mother's neighbours. Could Ndoro Guru have spent some time here once, in Wanalawas? When?

3. SASTRODARSONO: the bearer of destiny

The moment the buggy I had hired turned northwards, and the main road between Solo and Madiun disappeared behind me, my heart began to beat faster. In front of me now was a rural lane some five kilometres long and pointing straight towards Kedungsimo: my village, the village of my parents. At the end of those same kilometres my father would be standing waiting to meet me with his arms spread wide and a smile no less wide and embracing. I had no doubt of that welcome, nor of his pride and satisfaction. How else could it be? This day, I, Soedarsono—only child of Mas Atmokasan, peasant, native of the village of Kedungsimo—was returning from Madiun, in my pocket a letter of appointment as an assistant teacher at Ploso. That document meant I was the first among all of our kin—all our extended family to the outermost reaches of fading cousinship—to have won through to the status of a priyayi, had become a member of that class of salaried gentry which stretched by gradations of rank into the highest Javanese nobility! Granted, I was at the very bottom of that class, but that was unimportant for the time being; what mattered was having put my foot on that ladder. In a few years, with diligence and faithful service to the *gupermen*, I would become a full teacher at a village school, further securing me in my new station; and should I reach the level of Mantri Guru—headmaster!—why, that would be distinction indeed.

My father was a village peasant and nothing more, born and bred one; thus too were my uncles and my grandfather, peasants all. Everyone in our extended family, as in most other peasant families throughout the island, hoped that one day one of their number might be so elevated: that someone, dissatisfied with the never-changing fate endured by his like, would break out and become such a conduit of hope and welfare to the rest. Thus with that aim other families too had sent their children to the school in our village, in the way that my cousins and I had been, all without exception nurturing that vision and ambition for their progeny. But, alas, being village children we saw school only as an enclosure divided into stalls in which we were mustered under the subjection of a ferocious keeper called a teacher. The majority of my classmates, and I too for that matter, had no native endurance and we found little in this confinement to our liking. We missed the rice-fields and the dry-fields that were our playground, we missed the buffaloes and cows, the mangos to be knocked off branches with stones, the birds to be brought

3. Sastrodarsono

down with catapults and then roasted with great noise and excitement over a heap of burning leaves. And, too, most parents could not really afford to lose our labour for so long, we were sorely needed in the house and in the fields. It therefore would seem that my father and mother were of some exceptional mettle in being so determined that I should persist at school. Each time I gave any hint of rebellion, of letting my childish longing to roam and play imperil my studies, my father had no compunction about taking a whip to my back. I had no choice, my parents forced me to stay on at school; while my uncles, for example, soon joined the majority of those who found one reason or another to withdraw their children or tolerate their abscondings. My father in fact showed quite early that he had an unusual measure of willpower, which was perhaps why my grandfather, Embah Martodikromo, favoured him over my uncles. Embah was of course also a peasant, but there is evidence that he had higher aspirations, in that while he farmed as everyone else did he also doubled as an overseer in the sugar factory not far from our village. Although as overseer that was all he ever progressed to, his ambition for the family was made clear on at least one occasion when, so recounted my father, Embah made this pronouncement to his then still-young children: 'Attend to me now. You can take the easy way and do nothing—then you'll live and die in the mud. Or you can pull yourselves upwards. But for that—to become priyayi—you must go to school. There is no other way. Hear me and take note!'

As time showed, the old man's judgement was not successfully acceded to by even one of his children: none of them, including my father, finished the most basic schooling. But having failed to do so himself, my father, it seems, was determined that I at least should not fail.

The banyan tree, which I knew stood like a marker where the lane entered the village, was still invisible from the buggy, and that meant I must be a good three kilometres yet from my goal. Nothing, so far, had revealed any changes to the countryside in my absence. To the left and right the same tall *trembesi* trees spread their generous shade over the lane: umbrellas of foliage capable of shielding travellers from the heat of the fiercest noonday sun. Behind the lines of those trees stretched rice fields, rice fields everywhere. Moving to a gentle breeze, or warping and wavering in the light of a hot afternoon, the fields looked like a wide green sea in motion. These were the acres of Pak Lurah, the village head, Pak Carik, the village clerk, Pak Jagabaya, the village constable, of Ndoro Seten Kedungsimo, the assistant district head. Somewhere beyond them spread the fields of the smaller fry, the plots of peasants like my father; except that my father was fortunate in being able to extend his harvest by also cultivating a portion of the field owned by Ndoro Seten. As a consequence of that arrangement, his relations with the latter were good; although, naturally, those were relations between Ndoro Seten

Kedungsimo, priyayi, and Pak Atmokasan, very much a commoner. But it was due to these relations that I came at birth to receive the name Soedarsono, for otherwise it would have been unthinkable to nominate an infant of my social origins so resoundingly. My father told how one day Ndoro Seten happened to meet my mother when she was far gone in pregnancy, and out of the blue he said to her: 'When the child is born, Mbok, if it is a boy, call him Soedarsono.'

My mother was startled. She had actually been turning over in her mind some rather more prosaic Islamic names, this despite the fact that we were not at all assiduous in the faith: such names as Ngali or Ngusman. Did not my father himself have a compound name that included 'Kasan'? And was not that, in its original form, 'Hasan', the name of a grandson of the Prophet? She also doubted that a village child could be capable of supporting the weight of such a name as Soedarsono, and might succumb beneath it in infancy. But my father talked her into accepting the proposed name, arguing and inveigling until he got his way: 'How can a gift from a priyayi bring bad luck? No, no, it's a very safe name, stop worrying.'

The magnanimity of Ndoro Seten did not end with that 'gift' of the name, because later when I had completed my five years at the village school he smoothed the road onward for me. By his good offices with Ndoro Wedana the district chief, and a word to various other high personages in Madiun, he obtained an assistant-teacher candidacy for me in that town.

An inestimable sense of indebtedness on the part of my father towards Ndoro Seten followed that coup. When my father attempted to convey his gratitude to Ndoro Seten, that gentleman smiled and said that it was merely a return for my father's honesty and correctness when working on their adjacent crops. Ndoro Seten was pleased that my father was a worker who could be depended on to deliver his proper rental of harvested grain and stooks, was never short, and conveyed what was due without delay. Naturally, my father's gratitude, simple and big-hearted farmer that he was, only grew with such praise, and all kinds of additional produce periodically flowed across from his household to that of the priyayi. During the mango or the guava season, for instance, there would infallibly be at least a basketful of fruit delivered to the residence, and on the occasion of some ceremonial meal or other at the Atmokasan house a portion must go to Ndoro Seten's kitchen. In addition, whenever that personage held a banquet himself for some event such as a circumcision or the wedding of one of his children or he entertained visiting superiors, high officials of the district or of the kabupaten, my parents were never slow to contribute their labour. They set up the marquee and the seating in the grounds of the residence, slaughtered chickens and goats, cooked rice by the hundredweight, and so on.

The banyan came into view at last and grew taller, advancing, it seemed,

3. Sastrodarsono

towards me to meet the buggy. In a few moments more I had arrived at the yard of my home and distinguished my father's form among a crowd of uncles that included Pakdé, his older brother. So, the notification that I was coming, entrusted to a nephew of Ndoro Seten whom I had met by chance in Madiun, had arrived.

It was, as I expected, a warm and triumphant homecoming, although on the surface far more reserved compared to the effusions which subsequent times allowed. In my later days, when members of my own brood came home after completing their Dutch middle-schooling, my wife and I might well have tears of joy coursing down our cheeks, and we would be unceremoniously hugged by our returning children, even kissed in the European manner. That custom, I admit, never ceased to makes us both uncomfortable, as much as we had grown used to the other liberties. But such were the ways they had picked up in the course of their education and lives in the bigger centres, and from what they had seen in the Dutch homes they visited. Ah well, we told each other, times change and each epoch has its own ways of expressing the same emotions. On the occasion here, my smiling father advanced towards me with his arms indeed outstretched, but he dropped them at the last moment to merely grip my hand briefly and very tightly, and I responded by bending over his own for a filial kiss. As for my uncles, they simply patted my shoulders and escorted me into one of the cooler inner rooms of the house. We sat there and sipped sweet tea and ate rice cakes and squares of sticky rice with palm sugar. My father asked me again where I would soon be working.

'In Ploso, Pak.'

'Oh, Ploso, Lé? Which Ploso? Aren't there at least two: one north of Wanagalih and the other to the south of Jogorogo? Which one is yours?'

'The one south of Jogorogo, Pak.'

'*Wah*, a bit far from here, Lé. But that's all right, you can get there by buggy or cart.'

And the talk took a turn for some time to the subject of village names, particularly of those near the two called Ploso; and there was some dispute about where those other villages were and precisely what each was called. At that time, about 1910 by the Christian calendar, Javanese villages were still surrounded by considerable forests, and all sorts of animals roamed in their depths: striped tigers, for example—handsome, dangerous beasts—and native wild oxen as well. In fact, the name of our village, Kedungsimo, still retained its meaning as 'Place of the Tigers', so those must have been common in the vicinity. Similarly, Kedungbanteng, a village nor far from Wanagalih, meant 'Place of the Javanese Wild Ox': evidence for the former prevalence of *banteng* in that area. (Yes, and that reminds me that after I had become headmaster at Karangdompol and lived in Wanagalih I was sent as a gift from the

Gentry

Bosbesem office the stuffed head of such a *banteng*, and the skin of a striped tiger. . . .) Anyway, the talk went on and on, and I was virtually forgotten for a while.

Dusk was approaching, and that meant that the evening meal would be appearing at any moment. In the villages we always ate at about this time, unlike the local priyayi and government employees in the towns, who might have their dinners at seven or even eight at night. Peasants work all day, with a short midday rest and a quick meal in a field-hut, before resuming their labours until late afternoon. By day's end, they are tired and ready for that last meal and for bed. But this evening was clearly an exceptional one. There was fried chicken; there were side-dishes of vegetables cooked in coconut milk; there were portions of roasted meat garnished with shredded *sembukan* and wrapped in banana leaves—a special dainty that, also made with fish, and much-loved by my father—there were anchovies steamed with grated coconut, wrapped too in banana leaves; and of course there was a shrimp-and-chilli paste of the fiercest hotness.

(I must say here that in regard to food cooked with *sembukan*, otherwise known as *daun kentut* or stink vine, I never understood wherein lay its fame as a delicacy. The after-effects of eating it were undeniably known—to the sense of smell. Not for nothing did *kentut*, with its sulphurous odour emanating from the bruised leaf, also contribute the word for 'breaking wind'; and those who consumed it soon gave the nose full evidence of the fact—the smell, *masya Allah*, was always terrible! Almost anywhere one went, one was confronted by that concoction of *sembukan*-seasoned fish or meat roasted or steamed in envelopes of banana leaf, and by the consequent odours. Yet I must admit that the reeking vegetable and its suspected or actual consequences on the digestion of diners seemed in those times an inevitable part of good-natured—not to say hilarious—commensality, no doubt coarse and outlandish to outsiders, but apparently conveying to the peasants themselves a sense of their earthy sociability. Be that as it may, when I eventually set up my own household in Wanagalih, that particular culinary item disappeared from the very vocabulary of our kitchen staff. Whenever my father happened to visit us, we neither offered him anything with *sembukan* nor even alluded to such fare in case he should ask for it. Apart from my dislike of it and its effects, my wife and I held that it was food suitable only for the unique atmosphere of village dining. But perhaps I digress again.)

When we finished eating, and the leftovers had been cleared and taken to the back, my father and uncles remained sitting at the table with the big old kerosene lamp burning above us. Tobacco was passed around and rolled in dry corn-leaves, and while each man sucked noisily on his cigarette and sent billows of smoke into the air, my mother occupied herself in cutting up more squares of corn-leaf. When she saw that enough had been handily

3. Sastrodarsono

stacked beside the small wallet of tobacco, she reached for her betel container, made herself a quid, and began chewing. At that time I had not started to smoke, apart perhaps from the odd puff on a cigarette taken to the fields by my playmates.

Pakdé, my senior uncle, suddenly turned to me and asked: 'Not smoking yet?'

'No, not yet, Uncle.'

'*Wah*, you're a man now, boy. You'll be earning money soon. Go ahead and smoke. That's what a grown man does.'

Everyone laughed, including my father and mother. And so I too must without any show of reluctance reach for a corn-leaf, take a pinch of the home-grown, acrid tobacco, roll the stuff into a tube, and puff on it.

'Looks like he knew how to smoke all along,' someone said. And they all laughed again.

But a moment later, the mood around the table grew serious. Everyone turned to me, and my father began speaking.

'Lé, Pakdé and all your uncles aren't here by chance: I've asked them to come today. Of course we're also here to welcome you, welcome you back as an assistant-teacher, and naturally we're happy about that. But there are two other important matters your uncles have been called here to witnesses and to approve.'

My father paused and took a deep pull on his cigarette, then he began again: 'The first is, as of today we consider you an adult. You're an assistant-teacher. With an appointment. So that speaks for itself.'

Pakdé and my other uncles looked at me gravely and nodded in confirmation.

'Therefore, my boy, it's only right that you should now bear a proper adult name. Soedarsono is a good name as far as it goes and it suited you as a child. Now it no longer suits you. *Sastro*darsono will be your new name. We think it is more appropriate for a teacher. *Sastro* is all about books and writing and all those fine things. Isn't that right, lad?'

I could do no other than bow my head, accept, and agree: '*Inggih,* Pak.'

My father, though a villager, was very precise in his use of the language and ceremonials required of one when dealing with gentry, and his knowledge of the three levels of Javanese, and which of them were more or less appropriate on different occasions, could be said to be excellent. That might have been an effect of his frequent meetings with Ndoro Seten and the need to watch his tongue in the presence of a priyayi, or it may go back to my grandfather's ambitions. If the old man had never risen above farming and the rank of factory overseer, nevertheless he knew priyayi etiquette, and his children, despite failing to complete village schooling, had a good grasp of higher Javanese. My father, for example, always used a semi-formal middle level towards his own older brother: 'Will you condescend then, Kang, to witness? And you others can witness too. From today the lad's name will be Sastrodarsono.'

The older man condescended, and the 'others' responded with a respectful *'inggih,* Kang', acknowledging by that title their own subordinate-sibling relationship to my father.

I sat in somewhat dazed silence, not having foreseen this sudden development. Naturally I had expected that in time I would have been give an adult name by my parents, probably when the matter of marrying and establishing my own family came up, but that was a dim prospect and not something I had given much thought to. No, at the moment there was not the shadow of a candidate for the role of my life's partner. There had, at one point while I was still at school here at Kedungsimo, been a girl called Sayem, whose father was a rich peasant. We used to spend time together in the fields and in the village, and I suppose I had been friendly enough with her; but her father had married her off long ago.

'Now, my boy, to the second matter. Have you had any plans to marry yet?'

I sat stunned. Had he been reading my thoughts?

'No, not yet, father.'

'*Lho!* He says no, not yet! You've become a man now, with rank even. Oh, all right, it's only that of an assistant teacher; but next to no time you'll be up there as a full teacher.'

'But Pak, *wah!* . . . What's the wage of an assistant teacher? That's not enough to raise a family on!'

My uncles, old and young, broke out in a gale of laughter, and my father, smiling widely, said with an expression of incredulity: 'I've raised a dullard! Since when has anyone started a family on enough? It's never happened. Ask your Pakdé, here, and any of your uncles, how ready *they* were in that way for married life.'

I turned to Pakdé, and he said kindly: 'My dear fellow, ready? Miles from it. Your grandfather married me to your aunt without giving the matter a thought. He found us a hectare or two of paddy, and after that we were on our own.'

I had no reply and sat with bent head, desperately trying to see where all this was leading.

'Well, lad, it's like this. We, your mother and I, have found you a nice girl. The thing's been talked over with your Pakdé and everyone else. We've weighed up all the factors. We've taken into account your new position as a gentleman. The girl will be a perfect match for you.'

What response could I make to this sequence of announcements, drummed one after another? I said nothing, while in my mind I hurriedly ran

3. Sastrodarsono

through the possibilities available. Who on earth had they chosen for me?

'Now the bride does live a little far from here. She's called Ngaisah, hey? The daughter of a distant uncle of yours, Uncle Mukaram. He supervises the sale of opium in Jogorogo. Do you remember him?'

Suddenly, my mother cut in: 'How you go on, father—Ngaisah, Ngaisah! A good name ruined, conjured away with your Ngaisah!'

'Eh? What? Who would that be now, mother?'

'I'm talking about Aisah, A-isah. Isn't that one of the Prophet's wives? Well, then?'

'Oh, I see. Yes, Ngaisah . . . hem, yes . . . Well, isn't that how we say it in Javanese? It's our tongue, isn't it? Ngaisah?'

My uncles laughed at the interruption, but my mother went on brooding and muttering for some moments about how men always pleased themselves and thought whatever they liked.

'Now, my boy, you'll surely remember the lassie. Back when you were in second or third class at school your uncle Mukaram invited us to an outing in Jogorogo. You remember now, don't you, don't you?'

I could not say that I did remember much of it: how many years ago was it? In my mind rose a misty picture of a little girl in a floral dress. As for her face: nothing. I could only hope that she had been pretty.

'Anyway, the important thing is that the Jogorogo side has agreed that she'd be a suitable partner for you. Next week we'll get a good party of us together and go there to have you two meet again. It'll just be to look, just to take a peek at the possible bride. And to begin bonding the two families. And to decide on the wedding day.'

I sat overcome. What a procession of developments in one day! Only that morning I had left Madiun; at midday I was wobbling on a buggy past an ocean of rice fields; tonight, suddenly, I had been re-named by my parents and handed a wife.

'You should call in on Ndoro Seten in the next couple of days, and on Pak Lurah and Pak Carik as well, to tell them about your appointment. Don't you worry yourself about those other plans: your mother and I will go around and announce them properly.'

The following days were busy ones. I carried out my father's instructions and went dutifully visiting, reporting here and there on my advancement. At the residence, both husband and wife showed pleasure and satisfaction at the news of my success, and I listened to a little sermon from Ndoro Seten.

'You should be aware, dear boy, that this is an important step up in your life. You have entered another sphere now, you are no longer of the common people. Keep that always in mind. Your world will be very different. Learn how to carry yourself in this new world, what your attitude to others should be now. With care and honesty and obedience to your superiors and following the regulations of the *gupermen* you will certainly move on in rank. The road to the whole world of the priyayi is open to you now, my son.'

I listened with all possible attention: there was simple but ponderous and incontestable advice here. My life was going to change greatly and I must adapt myself to its new order. But I expected to be able to cope, because in Madiun while studying to become an assistant teacher I had had a modicum of opportunities to observe priyayi from a close distance. And, after all, Ndoro Seten was a priyayi too; although we were divided by so many things, little had escaped my observation of his world, and I knew many of his habits. In the morning he would either walk or ride on his horse around the local villages, come back and take his rest in the open-walled pendopo detached from his house, sitting there in a rocking chair, sipping coffee and snacking on fried bananas and market pastries. Then he would have his bath and return to eat breakfast, which consisted of rice and a goodly array of side-dishes. Then he would take his place in the office annexe of the pendopo to read reports brought to him by an attendant. Or else he might take a buggy-trip to the residence of the district chief at Bangsri, and not return until after midday. In the heat of the afternoon he, his wife beside him, would sit in the pendopo and enjoy the cooling breeze passing through it, gazing about his yard and out onto the lane, drinking tea and eating Dutch cakes from a stoppered glass jar. Came the holidays, those afternoons grew festive indeed with the arrival of grownup children and their offspring on vacation from school. Yes, I saw much of this close up, if obviously from another level, for all the time an awareness of the gap between us was never absent from my mind. Even when, in his goodness and at moments of relative informality, Ndoro invited me to come and play at the residence, I was reluctant to do so very often. My father repeatedly stressed to me that we villagers were on a different plane in the order of things. As I say, I found the world of our gentry engrossing but kept my proper distance from it. And now I was being eased into it by this kindly man who had become merely my senior in that shared condition.

The day we were to go to Jogorogo arrived, to 'take a peek at' but obviously in fact to formally meet my future wife and set the wedding date. We went in five gharries, and on the preceding day my family had sent ahead a cart filled to the top planks with all kinds of produce: sweet potatoes, cassava, corn, squashes, and whatnot. The gharries were jammed with uncles and aunts. As the preparations for the trip expanded and extended before my eyes, I had grown anxious.

'But Pak, don't you think we're going to a lot of trouble?'

'Trouble? We're out to win the hearts of our future in-laws! So how else

3. Sastrodarsono

do you think it's done? Remember that your Uncle Mukaram is a priyayi already. An official in charge of the opium trade is someone who has the trust of the *gupermen*, boy. We've got to look dashing, cut a figure, even if we *are* farmers. And don't forget that what we're offering for sale is you yourself, a priyayi too.'

It was a noisy and animated trip and very long. Throughout, there was a continuous jingling and tinkling of harness-gear, punctuated by shouted exchanges between vehicles. We had to stop a number of times to drink and refresh ourselves, stretch our legs and relieve our bladders behind the *trembesi* trees or in the monsoon ditches bordering the fields. We were dressed in our best clothes: the men, including myself, in sarongs, jackets and headcloths bound into the shape of the Javanese light turban; the women in sarongs and blouses. During the heat of the day, such full accoutrements meant that we poured with perspiration. Finally, after hours of negotiating numberless bends, stretches of forest, and seas of rice, the signal to stop came from the forward gharry. We were approaching Jogorogo and needed to descend and tidy our dishevelled clothing. When the convoy resumed moving, I can only remember that by then, at this final short distance to our goal, my apprehensions had worn me out past imagining what could possibly lie ahead.

Uncle Mukaram's house appeared before us. It was big, built of timber and topped by a roof in the shape of a pyramid, and in front it had a capacious veranda. Although he was of the gentry, there were signs in my uncle's yard and about the house that this was an establishment not far removed from the life of the surrounding village. Hens and ducks roamed freely, and on the thatched roof of a lean-to attached to the side of the house were winnowing trays in which rice leftovers from his table dried. But inside, it was clear that this was the home of a priyayi, for here stood good, carved furniture, large kerosene lamps hung from the ceilings, and glass-fronted buffets displayed dishes, crockery, and fashionable bric-a-brac. In the corner of a front room I saw a row of ceremonial spears standing ranked in a wooden rack.

After an extensive exchange of courtesies and salaams, we from Kedungsimo were invited to take our rest on the veranda and in the central room, refreshments of tea and cakes appeared; and now the heads of the two families commenced a trade in compliments of the most perplexing conventionality, and in a language which was almost incomprehensible to me. I have always been interested in broadening my knowledge of the formulas and idioms of our tongue, and at school I got good marks for Javanese, receiving praise for the little speeches I had to deliver before the class. Our teacher held that I had some aptitude in language and literature, and I always thought that polite Javanese sounded so well to the ear. Now, however, the two elders drew from truly archaic procedures, the intent of which I began only gradually to understand. For instance, my father—gracefully curving his hand to point his thumb in my direction—began introducing me to his host in what I felt was a rather excessively humble presentation, one which however also almost in passing managed to puff me up by more than an equivalent measure: 'Yes, yon stripling, our Master Soedarsono there—possibly you would deign to remember him: runny-nosed, a dunce at school—unaccountably, heaven be praised, got through his course and is now an assistant teacher. With tenure even. At the five-year school in Ploso . . .'

My father continued in this vein, pained one moment to acknowledge the parentage of such a dismal scion, then in the next rebuilding the apparently hopeless wretch. I had no doubt that Uncle Mukaram knew everything there was to know about me already: the first delegation from Kedungsimo to Jogorogo, sent to sound things out, would have said everything there was to say about me; and when my father had come himself to propose marriage on my behalf, he would have repeated every detail to the last syllable. So what were all these ritual iterations, what was this glorious redundancy for? Well, the answer is that it was always thus, in those times at least, it was something inherent in Javanese life. Without those circumlocutions, that verbal choreography, living would have been so much duller. And, after all, some of those were also staples of common, daily communication as well. Was it not through such forms and ceremony that a poor peasant approached a richer neighbour for a loan? Or how else could a father promote the nuptial interests of a marriageable daughter than by singing her praises in this generous and ready-to-hand lexicon? Its proper use required a refined sense of the verbal proprieties, of the niceties of gesture, but those were by no means a monopoly of the higher Javanese gentry.

However, at that point in our visit I was hardly in a condition to judge the excellence or otherwise of my father's exchanges with Uncle Mukaram. All my thoughts were on 'little sister' Ngaisah, *Dik* Ngaisah, my candidate wife. And where was she, anyway? Since our arrival I had been peering discreetly about, anxiously and fearfully trying to catch a glimpse of her. Would she have changed so much as to be remote even from the little of her that I could remember? I desperately wanted to see what she looked like. I had no real expectation that she would turn out to be some fabulous beauty, but I hoped earnestly that she would at least be pretty, be it with that somewhat dusky but sweet visage which girls in the backblocks of Java often have. I had to consider that in the years to come, as I, hopefully, stepped up the stages of promotions, my wife would need to be a capable partner fitted in every way to ascend by my side. If she was plain, especially if she was ugly, if she was awkward, if she was unintelligent . . . well, I would have a hard time of it. But then, *masya Allah*, I chided myself, was it not true that Dik Ngaisah had been a member of a priyayi family from her birth, and therefore knew more about

3. Sastrodarsono

that world than I did, who had only just entered it? I felt ashamed at my conceit. Nevertheless, I still had to see her.

Evening came and the meal was set on the table. Dik Ngaisah finally appeared, inviting the company to come and be seated.

'*Lha*, there we have my daughter Aisah, brother Atmokasan, *Siti* Aisah, if the chit's name must have its due. Regard her as your own in your kindness. Master Darsono, you met the lass once, I believe? Brother Atmokasan, I leave it to you, my good sir, deign to think of her as your daughter, unworthy thing, a little dull-witted too. She only managed five years at the village school. Oh, and a year with the wife of the *administrateur* of the sugar factory in Mbalong, living in, doing chores there. They treated her like their own family. Knows a little Dutch now: *een, twee, drie*, what? But still so inept, so backward . . .'

Uncle Mukaram was taking his turn at the game. But as for me, what a relief I felt with my prospective bride's arrival into the room! Dik Ngaisah turned out to be as I had hoped, with a pretty, suntanned, open and expressive face, a shy smile on it at that moment. Furthermore, she had received a very reasonable education, spoke her *een, twee, drie* of Dutch! What would happen next during that visit to Jogorogo no longer mattered to me, except to be told the date of our wedding.

It was decided the event would take place a little before my moving to Ploso. The festivities around my marriage to Siti Aisah—Dik Ngaisah, as my father stubbornly continued to call her, and therefore necessarily so must I— summoned forth an extravagant effort, such at least as was within the capabilities of the two families. It was to be expected that the two sides would do all in their power to put on a feast which would be remembered far and wide for a long time to come, a show befitting the union of Dik Ngaisah, only daughter of Mukaram, gentleman and local controller of the opium trade, with one lately known as Soedarsono, now Sastrodarsono, sole son of Atmokasan, yeoman-peasant in the village of Kedungsimo!

It took place in two acts. The first, at Jogorogo, was attended by numerous government officials, all of course priyayi of various levels, and by many Chinese retailers in the opium trade. It was a very lively affair, a grand flourish, featuring a wayang performance with leather puppets playing *Partokromo*, the marriage of Arjuna to Sembadra, obviously chosen as an example to us of a harmonious couple. A virtual avalanche of wedding gifts poured in with the guests. Then, the following week, in a celebration of the occasion when the girl removes to the bridegroom's home, the scene progressed to our village. My father, not to be bested by his new in-laws, mobilised all the means available to him to make his part a triumph. The structure that was set up in his front yard could accommodate a hundred guests. Labour and other contributions from numerous paternal and maternal relatives were employed unsparingly. A troupe of dancers was hired to sustain the gaiety: professionals of easy morals, with kisses and more within their gift. All the leading figures of Kedungsimo and the surrounding villages were invited, and most were at one time or another seen on the dance platform, clutching the waist of a dancer, to return sweating and be refreshed by the copious arak provided. Inside the house were card tables for male and female guests, where *pei* with its distinctive tiny *ceki* cards was played. It was all great fun; although, after all the noise and merriment and the expense incurred by my father and our relatives, this feast of welcoming the bride—or her abduction, as it used to be—was never other than an affair of the peasantry. Compared to the one held by my in-laws in Jogorogo, deemed for those parts and times luxurious and in high taste, ours, do what we would, ape a little the ways of the gentry, was all just homely village-revelry and no more.

There was one exception to that, though. Ndoro Seten, always generous, made his wedding gift a memorable one. He offered us a shadow-puppet play, to be held on the night following that of the festivities and meant to run the full length of that second night. Wayang, gamelan, the *dalang* who animated the puppets, the percussionists, the singers accompanying the gongs—he bore the full cost of all those, only asking us to let him choose the episode to be portrayed. Naturally, we bowed our heads in humble acceptance, conscious of the breathtaking munificence of such a gift. The story was *The Servitude of Sumantri*, carefully selected for its valuable insights into the kind of life I was setting out on; since, Ndoro Seten said with great seriousness, it held up a mirror to all young priyayi preparing to devote themselves to public service.

'I ask that you follow this tale carefully, my son, a beautiful tale and of value to all classes of people. It has things to say to the common folk as well, teaching them by an object lesson the virtues of modesty, self-awareness, and thence the self-control which accepts what fate apportions when that cannot be altered. And when fate does allow men the fulfilment of an opportunity to rise from the common lot to a higher level—and that is your case, Darsono—this story is especially important as a pointer to the limits of action. Sumantri is an example of someone who although low-born devotes himself to the service of his rajah and realm; but he becomes conceited, and through thoughtlessness kills his young brother, and then grown in arrogance he defies his rajah, flaunts his magical powers at him. The impropriety of his attitude and behaviour, and his resulting downfall, is a story with valuable implications even for the priyagung, those priyayi who occupy the very highest levels and move in circles of great power. Finally, it even speaks to the summit of power, it teaches how a rajah needs to be patient and wise, to know when to act to defeat his enemies, when to forgive them.'

My father and I nodded respectfully and gravely. When Ndoro Seten set

3. Sastrodarsono

out to instruct, he made his points meticulously and with authority. And once the wayang began on the second night of festivities, no one, myself, my father or anyone else, could turn away from the screen on which the shadow drama unfolded. The narrator was one Pak Gito, well-known in the residency of Madiun. The skill with which he manipulated the figures, his literary knowledge, the beauty of his language, all served to make the night's performance utterly convincing. Sumantri, as he was represented by Pak Dalang Gito, lived and touched the emotions: a man of the common people, who bravely and with determination achieved his goal of breaking into the sphere of the court nobility. There was a terrible price to pay for that success: the death of his brother by Sumantri's own hand was a necessary result of that ambition. I was stunned when Sumantri released the arrow which pierced Sukrasana's breast: Sukrasana who had assisted Sumantri, who had cried tearfully for compassion from his elder brother! What a truly heartrending episode: the hair stood on the nape of my neck! Could ambition for power, then, so pull and affect one as to make such destruction possible? Surely, an authority must stand supreme and unquestioned over ruthless individuals, to regulate and preserve our lives in common? And for the continuation of that social order, should not we, people and priyayi alike, be ready to sacrifice personal aspirations? During the scene in which Sumantri puts the sacred powers of his rajah, Prabu Arjuna Sasrabahu, to the test, I could feel my heart beat faster. Sumantri in his arrogance parades his magical skills by changing himself into the gigantic Triwikrama, infuriating Rajah Arjuna, who in turn changes himself into an even more colossal giant. Sumantri, subdued, weeps. Common man, however brilliant he may be and however godlike he imagines his powers, must remain subordinate to his ruler. Once again I felt an eerie sensation, something which I took away with me as I walked to the wedding chamber when dawn was lighting the sky, and the night-long play had finally concluded.

I found Dik Ngaisah fast asleep on a bed strewn with buds and open flowers of jasmine, and in that instant my weighty thoughts fell away from me and dispersed. There before me was my wife, God willing the future mother of my children. She slept and there was a faint smile on her face. I undressed, happily tired, lay down beside her and gently embraced her.

There is little to say about our journey to Ploso except that it was wearing. We were left relieved when our accompanying relatives finally departed and we two remained in our small house alone. It was not far to the school from there.

Dik Ngaisah, *alhamdulillah*, proved to be the wife of all my hopes, a woman well-prepared by her parents to become the companion of a priyayi.

Gentry

She was intelligent, capable, and knowledgeable in all aspects of that role. She turned out to be a skilled cook herself, but in addition managed the kitchen help competently. Her authority in the household was firm. She knew how to set the dinner table, arrange our bedroom and all the furniture, how the chairs should be placed in the front room where the guests sat, where others were positioned around the house; I had come to our married life ignorant that there was a proper order for such things. Everything she did left its mark that this was the house of a priyayi family. She trained the servants to always place the plates face-down on the table, fork and spoon on the left and right, and to remember the serviettes. (Ah, but how often they *did* forget them!) When visitors departed, any chairs and tables that were moved had to be put back. The servants were required to clean every item in the house daily so that everything shone. Coming from my background, I sometimes looked with a sense little short of awe on all this implementation by my wife. I was aware with gratitude of the indispensability of her domestic support, as I remembered the words of Ndoro Seten about how radically my world would be changed. My father, with all his wonder at the life of the gentler-bred, was never able to introduce anything substantial from it into his own home. The way my mother ran the house, cooked food, served it to us: all that was folk-like and nothing more. Things were unadorned, you knew that with my people you took potluck. Dik Ngaisah, however, clearly came from a finer upbringing, her demeanour and language attested to that. And I should also say that while her expression was pleasant and her face often bore a bashful smile in those early days of our marriage, yet I soon detected that this was a woman who might well at certain moments act with considerable resolve. I often reflected during that initial period on my good fortune in being blessed with such a partner, until in time I stopped feeling awkward and settled into my position as head of this household she had created around me. And Ploso, a village somewhat smaller than Kedungsimo, readily accepted our home as a priyayi one: indeed, because of its tasteful presentation, we actually came to be looked up to by the other teachers as something in the nature of social leaders!

But in the event, we lived in Ploso for only one year; Ndoro Seten Kedungsimo made representations to his superiors in Madiun, I was promoted to full teacher and transferred to the village of Karangdompol in the kabupaten of Wanagalih. I had no idea how it happened or even that anything was afoot, until one day I was summoned to Madiun by the *schoolopziener* and asked without preamble whether I would be prepared to move to Karangdompol: the school there had a vacancy. He said that it was an important school in that the village was near Wanagalih and there was a growing timber industry in that town, needing local labour and staff;

3. Sastrodarsono

and he also informed me rather stiffly that the offer was being made to me following a recommendation by the assistant district head in Kedungsimo. I expressed my readiness to take up the position, while wondering to myself in some astonishment how my benefactor could have managed the matter.

On the way back to Ploso I called at his residence in Kedungsimo to report to him on the result of his efforts and to find out for myself how he had done this extraordinary thing.

'Sastro—from today we can be less formal and I shall call you Sastro, agreed?'

Such were his first words when I arrived to hear his explanation. I bowed my head in a most humble and heartfelt sign of respectful assent.

He continued: 'And also, from now on don't address me as 'Ndoro' any more, all right?'

'Yes, Ndoro.'

'H'm. You can refer to me as *Romo* and to my wife as *Ibu*. As we will thus be on terms of a father and a mother towards you, so your father and mother will now be as a brother and sister to me and to my wife, and all your family will be as my own family. Most important in all this is yourself, Sastro. You will found an extended family of new priyayi. I have watched your progress over the years and felt confident in approaching the *schoolopziener* on your behalf.'

I bowed my head to each of these observations; however, I felt there was something more, something at the root of the matter which I did not understand. I was deeply grateful to the assistant head for such a bestowal of faith on me, but when I left him soon afterwards I knew little more than when I came.

My father and father-in-law were also astonished to hear how Romo Seten had nudged me up a step on the priyayi ladder, both marvelling at such a generous sign of his belief in my abilities.

Dik Ngaisah and I left Ploso, bound for Wanagalih, she well-advanced in her first pregnancy. We had resolved that if the child turned out to be a boy he would be called Noegroho.

Our decision to live in Wanagalih and not in Karangdompol itself, the village where I would be teaching, followed also the counsel of Romo Seten Kedungsimo (whom I continued to have difficulty in not addressing as 'Ndoro'), counsel endorsed by my father-in-law, Romo Mukaram. Karangdompol, despite its school, was a small village, smaller even than Ploso, and it contained few of the conditions which could promote advancement, either social or through the professional ranks. An important path to that advancement, so ran their advice, lay simply in meeting other priyayi whenever possible, and where in Karangdompol could one do much of that? With the exception of some teachers in my school, the village and the district around it was populated exclusively by farming peasantry. Anyway, I wanted to open for myself a life more diverse and colourful, more interesting than the tedious routines of the countryside. A town where all kinds of people gathered and lived together promised that varied life.

And in fact that decision proved to be the correct one. We bought a house built of butted boards in Setenan Road, and although small initially we later extended it and were fortunate in that the walls, the structural supports, and the frames of the doors and windows were all made of old and beautiful teak. Wanagalih was surrounded by teak forests, and with the help of Romo Seten Kedungsimo and Romo Mukaram, both of whom had connections with the Department of Forestry, add to that my own now substantial position as a teacher, obtaining such a house was comparatively easy. I must explain that it had been the home of a *Bosbesem* official who had left Wanagalih to go into retirement.

If the house was not large, it did have an extensive area of ground around it. It had a substantial backyard planted as a kitchen garden, while behind that stretched a field suited for unirrigated rice. We were very much dependent on the help of our parents to finance a large part of the purchase. Clearly, Romo Mukaram supported us more than my father could do, he still recovering from the dent to his finances occasioned by that royal outlay to celebrate my marriage. I must admit to having felt uncomfortable in accepting help from my father-in-law, there being a nagging doubt in my mind about the source of some of his money. But he pressed it on me cheerfully: how could he not offer a hand to his own children, he reasoned.

'You're one of my own now, too, aren't you? Blood and family are everything in this world; so you might say I'm only being prudent. And, actually, we were all related even before you married Aisah, weren't we?'

As soon as we moved into our new house, we set out with our servants to create the home of our dreams, an establishment fit for a genteel young family whose gaze was bent hopefully upwards at the ascending steps of future professional advancement. Yet, inside me, and even also in Ngaisah, the promptings of my own and her peasant blood still had their resonance. We decided we would not let out our land to a sharecropper, as Romo Seten had done in agreement with my father; we would instead hire labourers who would be reimbursed partly with money and partly with sheaves of rice at the time of the harvest. As seasons passed, I became more expert in working my land, helped along by my father and his older brother on their visits to us. They advised me that the area not actually under rice should be planted with various kinds of tubers, with bananas, and with common herbs needed in the kitchen; while as for the rice, because our crop would not be irrigated and must depend on rain, then only the variety known as *gogo* suited.

3. Sastrodarsono

And together with his practical guidance my father preached this little homily to me: 'You may be the great gentleman now, my boy, but keep in mind where you've come from: the bean-vine forgetting the pole it grew up on, what? Your house may be priyayi, but you won't run it on your wages alone. A priyayi is someone looked up to by people, not someone who grows rich. His learning is what makes him respected. If you want to be rich, be a merchant, a market-trader. But having said that, you've still got to stand on your own two feet. And to do that you've got to grow things, just like our peasants; to grow enough for the pot, for a full stomach, so that you won't have the worry of lack distracting you all the time.'

My father's words surprised me a little, because I had come to believe that he wanted to see me totally free of the trappings of his own world, wanted me in another setting altogether, as the founder of a clan in a class above his own. Now, he was talking about beans and bean-poles? Was he perhaps starting to feel old and growing uneasy that I, his only offspring, was moving away from him? And it was true that I was responding more actively all the time to the prospect of becoming the head of this new priyayi line, was increasingly realizing that the rural world of my origins was no longer my world. Since little, I had been repeatedly cautioned by my father not to get too involved in the life of rice-growing and rice-tending, was allowed to romp and soil my clothes while other children worked. The paddies were not totally foreign to me, of course, I knew them well enough, I knew about tending stock and getting into all the escapades that village children concoct. Yet my father and grandfather had nurtured in me the will to leave all of that one day and step into another life. I had accepted and absorbed their ambition and made it mine. I had chosen to become a priyayi and a salaried government official, and had understood that choice to mean that I would, God willing, found a family of some consequence, a new kinship of succeeding generations that would trace back their origins to me. But by leaving my past I was certainly not revoking ancestral continuities and duties. I wanted them eventually to be applied in my own family, after all. There could be no question but that I would therefore remain faithful to my obligations towards my own father: the roots of the bean-plant went too deep and were too fast in the Javanese soil for any other possibility. And this was also an issue involving my own feelings and not only what was formally expected of a son, involving the strength of my affection for my father as well as what was right: and on both those certainties he could rest easy.

We settled in and time passed quickly; we soon got to know our neighbours on Setenan Road and grew quite intimate with a number of them. They included the family of a pensioned seten, an assistant district head from whom Setenan Road had once received its name; another was the family of the public prosecutor, Raden Supangat, a person of good birth as indicated by his title; also with the family of Mansoer, an instructor in the Javanese martial arts. Others we were friendly enough with, such as the hardly exalted and perhaps less reputable family of Pak Martokebo, a broker in the water-buffalo trade, living at the end of the road. As a young priyayi couple, the youngest on the street, we visited each house in turn to introduce ourselves, and we were quickly accepted as part of the Setenan Road community. And through my father-in-law's connections we came to know the local supervisor of the opium trade and the official who managed the government pawnshop. In addition, we met and formed a good acquaintance-ship with the only doctor in Wanagalih, something which in time proved very convenient to our family. This was Doctor Soedradjat, a *Dokter Djawa* and graduate of *Setopia*, the title formed in the local vernacular from the Dutch acronym STOVIA, for *School tot Opleiding van Inlandse Artsen*, set up to train native doctors. Despite his Western education he dressed in the Javanese manner, complete with sarong, white jacket and head-cloth, and his whimsical and easy-going, bantering ways made him a known and well-liked figure in the town. He it was who attended the birth of our three children and circumcised the two boys; but possibly of even greater importance, he introduced my wife and me to the games of *pei* and *ceki*, which I subsequently often played in a *kesukan* group that included the opium controller and our lawyer neighbour. I say it was important because it was during those evenings of relaxation and sociability that we exchanged news and gossiped about all kinds of things occurring in Wanagalih and in the residency of Madiun generally. This was what Romo Seten had intended when he recommended keeping in with priyayi circles, and my small experience of priyayi affairs was considerably enlarged by the conversations I heard around our card tables. It was there that I began to hear of the adulteries and the heavy gambling occurring among priyayi high in the Indies administration. At first I had little to say, hardly understanding what was being referred to; then I too began to offer the odd opinion, and I was encouraged to do so by Pak Dokter Dradjat, as I soon came to call him familiarly.

'Dear chap, it's good that you should hear this stuff, what goes on in the odd dark corners of our oh-so-genteel world. A young teacher like yourself needs those human insights. It'll broaden you.'

I speedily became a regular and I think well-liked member of those groups, where I was accompanied also by Dik Ngaisah whenever the wives were invited. Pleasant as they were, it all got to become a drain on our energies when invitations came to us not only for Saturday nights and holidays but during the working week as well. When our card games ended at three or four in the morning, well, I really had to labour through the rest of that day. I needed to pedal some three kilometres to the Madiun River; there be

3. Sastrodarsono

ferried across; then pedal another kilometre or so to my school at Karangdompol. Throughout the course of that journey I sometimes felt like a kite gone adrift.

Our children were born in two-year intervals, Noegroho arriving two months after we had moved to Wanagalih. Because he was the first and a boy, both our parental families alternated in providing assistance to my wife while she nursed him. Naturally, Dik Ngaisah and I were very proud of him, so were all our relatives. This was the first-born male, who would carry our aspirations forward into a progressively widening family; this was the male child we had hoped for, had dreamed about; he was the one we saw in our imagination one day standing in my place as the strong pillar of the Sastrodarsono house, at the head of a young and ever more thriving and honoured priyayi family spreading around and below him in a growing pattern of brothers and sisters, children, nephews and nieces, grandchildren, and so on and on. As an expression of the importance of the occasion, we and our parents celebrated Noegroho's birth with a special *selamatan*, a grand ceremonial meal attended by a large number of Wanagalih dignitaries.

Then followed the births of Hardojo and Soemini. My wife and I felt relieved and grateful that all three of our children had come into the world intact and healthy, and as they began to grow older that none showed in their appearance any features which would too obviously mark them as being of peasant derivation. Their lips were not too thick, their cheekbones not too pronounced, their noses not too flat—why, they were even pointed if anything!—while their complexions were a creamy yellow, akin to *langsat* fruit, a tone then admired in distant courtiers and fashionable beauties. We two could make nothing of it, why our children should look like that; for our part, we were both as tanned-brown as ripe sapodilla plums, and, although by no means flat, our noses were not sharp, nor were our lips particularly thin either. We acknowledged that we ourselves had the clearly visible features of an undeniable peasant inheritance: so how had our children come by such—one might call them—noble lineaments, then? I attempted to explain it to my wife in this way: it was the result of our intense desire to create a Sastrodarsono line of priyayi. There! Very likely, as happened in many wayang stories, a wish and will to some end had been heard and answered by Allah; in our case the Deity granting us such fine, handsome offspring, who moreover came possessed of the visible features of the class they were destined to enter. *Lha!*

Naturally, we had no intention of sending them, our own progeny, to any common village school. Such schools had been created to fulfil very limited purposes: to educate and instruct village children to a level deemed sufficient that the odd one might rise to a positions of leadership in his community, a village *carik*, for example; others might become workers in the kind of employment where some literacy was needed; and, only very occasionally and by good fortune, as in my case, would allow yet others to snatch at an opportunity which might elevate them to something higher. No, we would send our children to an HIS, a *Hollandsch Inlandsche School*, a primary school set up by the colonial administration for the children of priyayi to maintain the continuance of indigenous upper-class families in government service. Priyayi children at an HIS were taught Dutch, extremely important for attaining a position in a government office or to further their education in a middle-secondary or higher-secondary schools. Those were designated MULO, from *Meer Uitgebreid Lager Onderwijs*, and AMS, from *Algemene Middelbare School*. With Dutch, one might train to become a secondary teacher, studying towards that role first at a *Normaalschool*, a *Kweekschool* or the like. Were any of my children to go later into teaching, there would be no mere assistant-teacher course for them—all that had been accessible to their father—no, they would progress immediately to higher teacher-training institutes, true teachers colleges.

And when the time came to start their schooling I was lucky in the following respects: I already had a position in education; I was the son-in-law of an inspector of the opium trade; I had relations with Romo Seten Kedungsimo; and I was closely acquainted with Doctor Soedradjat as well as a number of other substantial figures in Wanagalih. Considering that I was only a teacher at a village school, and that certain administrative strictures were beginning to be applied by the colonial government at that time, those factors significantly eased the process of enrolling all three of our children in Wanagalih's own HIS.

After I had taught for five years in Karangdompol I was given the fourth class to teach, regarded as an important responsibility, preparing candidates for the lofty final year of village schooling. At that time, education for most native children ended there in that fifth class, and those who managed to complete the full five years were viewed by the surrounding rural population as being little short of enlightened, as having 'mastered the sciences'. That is, they could count, read and write, knew their Javanese fairly well, and even had a smattering of the Malay lingua franca. At our school, in particular, we had a headmaster who urged and encouraged us to exert every effort in imparting a good knowledge of arithmetic, calligraphy and the Javanese language; and the product was visible in our graduating pupils, who generally had a good hand, knew their tables, and used the proper Javanese levels. I often had cause to ask youths who had graduated from

3. Sastrodarsono

an HIS why their handwriting was poorer than that of our village-school products: I could see the difference in my own children, whose lettering was not as fine as that of my pupils in Karangdompol. I finally had to suppose it was because acquiring Dutch and a fund of increasingly academic knowledge was coming to be considered more important. At any rate, in that fourth class I certainly continued to take great care in how I taught arithmetic, reading, good writing, and Javanese grammar; and that was both in response to the policies of our principal and because I felt personally that the village school at Karangdompol ought to be one we could all be proud of. Its graduates should leave it with some chance of getting work, perhaps within at least the lower ranks of some department, and they should be fit to take up a course of study at a modestly higher level if that opportunity ever presented itself.

Apparently the *schoolopziener* on one of his inspections must have given my methods some favourable attention. One day on his regular visit he called me into the headmaster's room, vacated by the head for the occasion. He praised my teaching and the way I kept order in my classroom, that second point seeming of particular concern to him, for he thought that our pupils at Karangdompol were in general insufficiently disciplined. But I was startled by the following question and remark about our school principal, Kamas Martoatmodjo: 'Dik Sastrodarsono, do you know that we've been concerned by the activities of Dik Martoatmodjo, and have been investigating him?'

'*Lho*, investigating? Investigating what, about Kamas Martoatmodjo?'

'There have been two matters. The first is his involvement with a certain movement. The second is his relations with a professional dancer in the village of Karangjambu.'

'*Wah*, I heard nothing about such things!'

'Well, now you know, and as a consequence we would like to warn you, Dik Sastro, to be careful and not become involved in those activities of Dik Marto. Moreover, we would hope that you might help us keep an eye on him if he oversteps things altogether. Were he to follow further those proclivities ... well, a pity. There would be consequences. But if he won't be advised, what can one do? You must be ready to take his place.'

That conversation disturbed me greatly. I had always been on a friendly and respectful footing with the school principal. He had been a good superior, understanding, intelligent, and ready to guide younger and less experienced colleagues such as myself. I had indeed heard something vague about his relations with a dancer in Karangjambu, but it had never become a matter of serious interest to me. For one thing, it was, as I thought, just an idle rumour; and, secondly, were not entertainments with hired dancers so common in Javanese life that little was ever made of some escapade involving one of them? Furthermore, how many priyayi were there—and socially well-established ones too—who had more than one wife, or kept a mistress somewhere? There were quite a few. So why had the issue attracted the attention of our *schoolopziener*? Was it perhaps because of the position occupied by Mas Martoatmodjo, a concern that as the head of a school he should be considered a special model to others? But why might a teacher not dally or even fall in love with a dancer, while others employed in government service were apparently free to do so in the eyes of their superiors? *Wah*, should a teacher need to be such an example of purity, compared to an assistant district chief, or an inspector of opium? Well, perhaps he should. But was the problem less a matter of comparative propriety, and more likely stemmed from something else? I returned to what Kamas *Opziener* had first said about Mas Martoatmodjo's connection with members of some movement. Could that really be what had caught the *gupermen's* notice? But what was that connection, and who in fact were those described as members of a movement? Such matters were outside my knowledge; but one thing was certain: Mas Martoatmodjo was in a grave situation, very grave.

The warning by the school inspector, to keep away from whatever Mas Marto was involved in, and to be ready if necessary to change places with the head, left me troubled and with a bad taste in my mouth. At home that afternoon I was too unsettled to take my nap, and so I strolled over to the field behind the house and there paced up and down, watching the workmen turning up the soil and planting seed; but that could not long engage me, and the morning's questions returned. Finally, I determined to call on Mas Martoatmodjo.

Despite being a school principal and above me in station, he had less to do with the priyayi of Wanagalih's civil service then did I. His relations with them was friendly enough but not close, as mine were; for example, he took no part in our card groups nor seemed to belong to any other *kesukan* circle at his own level, preferring to play *ceki* with the lesser priyayi of the kabupaten or with the village elders in Karangdompol and Karangjambu. His house also appeared rather plain and was located in Wanagalih's outskirts.

'Hello Dik Sastro, what a nice surprise! You've come to visit us at this time of the afternoon? . . .'

I felt rather sheepish for a moment, unsure how I should begin talking about something so queer; and felt uncomfortable, too, because his greeting reminded me that I had neglected to visit him and socialise with him as regularly as perhaps I should have done.

'Well . . . yes.'

'And how are things with your good lady and the children? Everything fine, I hope?'

'Well . . . yes, thank you.'

3. Sastrodarsono

Overcoming my hesitation, I began carefully repeating to him what had been said during that morning's interview in his room at the school. If I felt relieved after having disburdened myself, I still remained unsure of what his reaction would be.

A moment passed while he pushed a glass of tea and a plate of sweets closer towards me; then he looked up, smiling, and began quite serenely to reply: 'I'm very grateful to you for this report of yours; for coming here to tell me these things.'

'No, Mas, that's no matter; but tell me, is all this something really out of the ordinary?'

He smiled again.

'Dik, you're still young. You probably don't know all the ins and outs of the games superiors play.'

'Oh, I don't, Mas?'

'Well, for example, you probably aren't even aware of the risk you've taken just coming here.'

I returned to feeling uncomfortable.

Then Mas Martoatmodjo explained his situation. Apparently, he had known for some time that his activities had been under surveillance, not only by the *opziener* but by the police as well. What he told me troubled me exceedingly and made me aware of how little I really knew about what went on in Wanagalih. And what precisely was the crime that had brought him to the attention of the authorities? He showed me a few pages of some newspapers or journals which I had not seen before. One that took its title, *Sarotomo*, from the sacred bow of Arjuna, was in Javanese; another, in Malay, was the *Medan Priyayi*, the Priyayi Forum. I turned over a number of those pages, pausing to read from the *Medan Priyayi*. It appeared to be a weekly, declaring itself to be 'The Voice of Rajahs, Native-born Aristocrats, Gentry and Merchants.'

'Interested in the *Medan Priyayi*? Take it home and read it. But it's no longer published. Its editor has been arrested and jailed.'

'But if it's not being published any longer, what harm is there in you keeping copies of it?'

'Well, there is. Keeping it and reading it.'

'Just that?'

'Practically, Dik. They consider it to have been a militant paper. The authorities are saying that it was trying to stir up the people. And almost all of those in the *Serikat Dagang*, that new union of traders in the Lawean batik-making quarter in Solo, were reading these papers.

'But you don't have anything to do with people in Solo, do you, Mas?'

'That's just it, my wife's first cousin in fact comes from that quarter and has been bringing us these papers when visiting us. And another thing is that

I've been offering them around to friends, discussing articles printed in the *Medan Priyayi* and so on. Just to broaden a little their understanding of what goes on in this country of ours.'

I asked myself why he had never invited me to take a look at and discuss those papers. As if reading my thoughts, he said: 'I have to apologise, Dik, for not asking you to those sessions, but, you know . . . Look, I'm sorry, but the problem was your friends, our local priyayi. There's been nothing really wrong or important in what I was doing, but I thought they might misunderstand.'

'Oh? Misunderstand?'

'Look, it's like this. Your friends are fairly high-ranking officials. They're frightened by this sort of writing. They worry about losing their positions. See how I'm under surveillance by the police and the inspector? Can you imagine *them* being under surveillance, being reported to their superiors? Threatened by a drop in rank?'

He began again.

'But the *opziener* is correct in his conclusion, and I agree with him.'

'Oh, what conclusion?'

'When he said that you should replace me, Dik.'

'*Wah*, don't say that, Mas!'

A little later, as I prepared to go, taking with me a page of the *Medan Priyayi*, I mentioned the second matter to him: 'As to that other thing: I suppose that's just talk, Mas?'

'What thing? Oh, Karangjambu you mean? Shush, not a word about that here! My wife's not too happy about that.'

His face broke into a boyish grin as he said that. So it was true.

I pedalled back to Setenan Road in the dark.

Dik Ngalsah grew worried and then alarmed as I described to her my conversation with the inspector and subsequently with Mas Marto; but that was nothing compared to her panic after she quickly scrutinised the page of newsprint I had brought back.

'*Wah*, have nothing to do with Mas Marto! What on earth are you doing, looking for trouble there! If something happens, think about me, think about the children! . . .'

My wife's reaction gave me a moment's pause, although I had to some extent been expecting it. I hardly knew what to think, and while I gathered myself I went more carefully through the columns on the page. They were written on a variety of subjects and were interesting. I read a Malay translation of a letter that had been sent to King Wilhelm III by someone signing himself 'Multatuli'. It was a passionate plea for reform and movingly written. An article deplored what it called the '*regenten bond*' of bupati: a collection of regents, it said, who acted like petty rajahs and were partial to brandies-

3. Sastrodarsono

and-soda and pea-and-ham soup. That same article praised in contrast His Majesty the Soesoehoenan of Solo, who had lately opened a religious school and saw to it that mosques were repaired, wherein he himself prayed and recited the Koran. I remained puzzled as to why the *gupermen* should be worried about such writing, although I had never read this kind of criticism before. I admit that up to then my reading had been more or less confined to texts on teaching and to the odd tome of Javanese literature, and that my thoughts and concerns were limited to whatever happened in our immediate neighbourhood. I decided that I would broach things to Doctor Soedradjat and the others, the prosecutor, the opium inspector, and whoever else met at that night's *kesukan*. I would see what they thought.

'My dear chap, playing with fire? Don't do it. Dangerous, you know.'

And uttering the word 'dangerous' Doctor Soedradjat slapped down a card on the table.

He continued: 'Yes, I do recall the *Medan Priyayi* used to make some fascinating comments; but now it's closed down and Mas Tirto the publisher is in the calaboose; so that's that. Don't go looking for trouble, dear boy. You're young, you've a long and good life ahead of you. Don't ruin your prospects by being found reading that stuff. It's done for.'

The others of our group took the same position and urged me to get rid of the newspaper and especially never to get into any discussions about its contents with Mas Marto. These were my seniors and I had to take this expression of their point of view as virtually a command: I must return that page immediately to the headmaster.

The lawyer offered a placating argument: 'Come now, there are many ways to advance this country. What you do as a teacher: doesn't that move things forward? Instructing peasant kids about things: what's wrong with that? And if you work conscientiously in your new role as headmaster, after replacing Mas Marto, well, there you are, you can do even more to lift up your people. And I might also tell you, my young friend, that we in the attorney's office have been raising our level of vigilance lately; we've been looking carefully at certain troublemakers, certain elements that seem intent on causing a disturbance in these here Indies.'

So Mas Martoatmodjo was right. My friends, these partners of mine around the nightly card table, this array of salaried gentlemen, were fearful, were in fact cowards. Cowards? But was there not truth in what they said, that quietly bringing education to the children of our villages was work which moved things forward? And that, on the other hand, being found reading a defunct newspaper could destroy my future? And yet, there was this other aspect, of the headmaster living under that threatening scrutiny, which left me unhappy and I found distasteful and saddening. Was he not, as the principal of a school, already proved to be an exemplary worker; and if beyond that he chose to further society in his own way, by taking note of what was in progressive newspapers, was that so wrong? What I heard from my card-playing colleagues, older than I and in their own way reasonable, left me troubled and unconvinced.

Although the night was well-advanced I found my wife awake. The children were asleep in their room, all in one bed. They were growing to be healthy and strong, and Dik Ngaisah had spoken to me already about our having to think of how to set up another room for them, at least for Soemini, who would soon be needing her own.

I remember how my mother laughed when she heard us talking about extending: 'A proper *Londo* mansion you'll soon have, a warren of rooms!' she said, using the village form of *Belanda*: Hollander.

Standing there, looking at my three children fast asleep in a tangle of limbs and bodies, I thought again of my intent to launch a family of priyayi, which would, God willing, be extensive in the traditional way, and characterised by the many proved virtues of our race, but should be modern too, moving with these new times. I must therefore create a home with adequate facilities to sustain the first generation of such a family and show an example that would not shame our posterity.

'Not sleeping yet?'

'No. I've been troubled. I keep worrying about our future, after hearing you talk about the *opziener* and what he said about Mas Martoatmodjo.'

'Well then stop worrying, I'll look after that side of things. You just think about the best way to raise our children.'

'Raise our children, you say! All very well, but how can I think about that when all of a sudden our future looks so frightening?'

'How, frightening? Nothing's happened yet, and you're panicking? If anything were to happen, won't I be there to think about it and decide what's best? Leave it to me, I'll work it out.'

'Yes, but you know how stubborn you get when . . .'

'Now, Dik, that's enough. It's late and I've got work tomorrow. We both have to get up early.'

I spoke abruptly, and from the corner of my eye I saw Dik Ngaisah stiffen, and when I looked again a moment later a tear trickled down her cheek. Eh, women! I made no sign of having noticed anything, changed for bed, and lay down. But before I finally went to sleep I made a decision: during the coming vacation, due to start in a week, I would take my family for a visit to Kedungsimo and Jogorogo. It had been some time since our parents had seen their grandchildren, and I wanted to hear what my father and father-in-law, and Ndoro Seten as well, thought about these odd developments and new prospects surfacing in Karangdompol.

3. Sastrodarsono

The decision to take my family for a holiday in the villages was, as I expected, met joyously by them, and the journey though tiring was full of excitement and happy anticipations. Jogorogo was our first stop, where my father-in-law welcomed us with his vast good will. The old man's face always beamed whenever he set eyes on his grandchildren, as if he had 'come upon a cache of jewels', as the expression goes; and they in turn were lively and noisy around him. After a due interval of relaxing and enjoying village life, I carefully broke the issue of Karangdompol to him. His response was, as in fact I had expect it to be, that of a government inspector of the opium trade.

'Well of course your doctor and lawyer and those others in Wanagalih are absolutely right. Agree with what they tell you, that's my advice. And this school head of yours—what's his name, Marto-something?—he's treading his own path, following his own fate, so you leave him to it. Seems he's found a role for himself in some drama or tragedy. Well, leave him to act it out. And don't think twice about stepping into his place either—take it, boy!'

As he talked, Dik Ngaisah sat nearby with Soemini drowsy in her lap, and as she stroked the child's hair I could see a vindicated look on her face, and she nodded in full agreement with her father.

In Kedungsimo, my father also saw the question simply and plainly.

'Look, I'm just a village man, I plant rice, I see this thing the way we look at all those outside matters, as farming folk here do, little people, *wong cilik*, because that's all we really are. If the *gupermen* sends you down a regulation, well, you obey it. If you don't, then that's it, you're in the wrong. If that school head has done something that's gone against a regulation, and the *gupermen* says he's wrong, then you don't give it a second thought, he's wrong. If they tell you to take his place, you've got to take his place. Goodness me, are you going to refuse, or even stand up against them? But anyway, as I say, that's the thinking of a peasant, pure and simple. Why don't you go and visit Ndoro Seten? You know, I still can't call him *Kamas*. Ask him what he thinks. And what did your father-in-law say?'

I told him, and my father nodded several times.

'Yes, he thinks the same. He's a *gupermen* priyayi, so naturally that would be his advice to you.'

On this occasion it was my mother with Dik Ngaisah who listened to our conversation. My wife once again nodded her firm satisfaction with my father's words, and her face showed she was now quite cheered at the inevitable end to the matter.

I was startled at Romo Seten's appearance. Had it been so long since we met last? He seemed to have aged: his face was more deeply lined than I remembered, there was added white in his hair, and his eyes had lost their former gleam. Something had evidently struck at his spirit. Had he met some problem with his family, or with work? What else could it be? He was relatively young, some distance yet from pension age; in fact I had heard that he was about to be promoted to wedana. But he brightened a little on my arrival and the melancholy look was replaced by something more forceful.

'What news, Sastro? All the family well, I hope?'

'They are, owing to your kindness, Romo; as I hope your own are well. But Romo, may I say, you seem a little unwell. Or have you been, recently?'

He did not reply but led me to chairs inside the pendopo, and when we had sat down his gaze was directed thoughtfully into the distance. While I waited for him to speak, the silence in the building grew heavy; somewhere nearby there was a cage of jungle fowl, and their occasional clucking made the stillness more palpable. At last I saw him draw a deep breath.

'I've heard a few things about your affairs in Wanagalih. About what's been happening at your school in Karangdompol.'

'Oh? You know about that matter at our school, Romo?'

He smiled unhappily.

'Well, I *am* the assistant district chief here, Sastro. I get to read all kinds of reports in the Madiun residency. And now that we have Governor-General Idenburg in charge, things in these Indies are becoming more regulated, more closely supervised . . . tighter.'

I tried to fathom what had caused the displeasure audible in that last word. He drew another long breath.

'I know that *schoolopziener*, the one who talked to you. What a waste. I mean what's happening with Martoatmodjo. A good educator. And a patriot.'

He stopped again, mused for a moment and then began again: 'Did you know that I too subscribed to the *Medan Priyayi* and our other native newspapers?'

'*Wah*, no, I did not know, Romo. Could high-ranking priyayi such as yourself subscribe to that newspaper?'

'It was possible. A good number of bupati even assisted in its circulation and sale. But things are different now since Idenburg. Control over what gets published has grown stricter. That kind of journalism is dead now.'

He stopped again, this time longer, before continuing: 'Damned spies and boot-lickers like that *schoolopziener* have caused everything to fall apart!'

I was stunned. I had never heard Romo Seten use such language before.

'You're surprised I let myself go like that? It's because I'm revolted by people like him. Why? Because he's dangerous, stupid, and evil. His activities are negating all the efforts of our progressive priyayi. Carefully, prudently, we've worked towards extending the number of such priyayi; and now a tramp like that comes along—a puppy, tail-wagging and begging at the hand of *Londo!*'

3. Sastrodarsono

Evening was falling and the servants were beginning to bring out the kerosene lamps. The fowl in their cage had quietened some time ago, their final calls succeeded by the chirping of crickets and the croak of frogs responding to one another in the paddies.

'Why do you think I exerted myself to get you into that teaching course, Sastro? And others like you from the villages under my jurisdiction, whom I managed to get schooled in one way or another? It's all been in a cause which I and thinking priyayi with some position have long worked for: that of creating a class of modern Javanese functionaries—not little rajahs, content to lord it over the *wong cilik*! And apes like our school inspectors, police superintendents, and who knows what other grubby spies—bought by a handful of guilders and without any compunction about informing on their countrymen—undermine everything we've been trying to build!'

Well, Romo Seten was in a truly extraordinary temper! I could see he was totally gripped by anger. And there was evidently more to come: it seemed as if he had been waiting a long time to meet someone into whose ear he might pour all this animosity. But after a pause he took control of himself, his face returned to its usual composed expression, and his eyes to their previous melancholy.

'And now, Sastro, I find that my work here—what I felt was my duty—is coming to an end. No, no, don't say anything, let me finish. Some months ago, I provoked the displeasure of the district chief, and it seems of the bupati as well. I've been accused of recklessness in encouraging ambitions among the peasantry. Accused also of irresponsibility in having connections with individuals belonging to the modernist movement. It's part of the pattern which you've already met with your friend Martoatmodjo. Although my superiors have told me that their comments are merely meant as a warning to me, as a solemn warning, still I know that my future in this officialdom of ours ends here. There was talk of my moving to the rank of district chief—well, that way is now closed. But all that means nothing to me personally, Sastro. I don't regret anything. When the time for taking my pension comes, I will move to Surabaya and spend the rest of my days quietly tending to my children and grandchildren.'

So that was what had brought about this transformation of Romo Seten into an old man. Ah, what a pity, how saddening that it should happen to a gentleman of so much goodness and intelligence, while advancing such worthy aspirations!

'The important thing is yourself now, Sastro. Be resolute and take Martoatmodjo's place if you are offered it. I know you won't be happy to succeed someone who has been demoted in that way, but you have to see it as a means of continuing Martoatmodjo's work. However, you will have to be very careful. The Indies administration is becoming a far more efficient machine than it used to be, so be prudent. But I press upon you this—be one of the new priyayi!'

That ended my talk with Romo Seten. As I returned through the darkness towards my parents' home, I contrasted him with my father-in-law, my friends in Wanagalih, the doctor, the lawyer, others. Obviously, the subdistrict head was one of a noble caste with a lofty sense of duty, a dynamic conception of that duty, whilst the others could reconcile their high status with a role of submission and steady service. I recalled the drama chosen by him at the time of my wedding, *Sumantri's Servitude*. It appeared to me now that there were more aspects in the testing of that hero's loyalty than those which Romo Seten had asked me to consider at that time.

At my parent's house I chided my father for not sending me word about those unfortunate developments that had taken place with Romo Seten; but my father replied that it had been so willed by Romo Seten himself, who had stressed that he wanted to pass on personally an important instruction to me. It seems it was the one that ended our conversation at the residence. Riding past it in the gharry that was taking us home to Wanagalih, I felt close to crying. I bowed my head in the direction of the building, bowed in deepest respect, in infinite gratitude, for all that he who brooded within those walls had done for us all.

On arrival at Setenan Road after that long break at Jogorogo and Kedungsimo, I received a letter of appointment. I had been promoted to head the school in place of Mas Martoatmodjo: he was being sent to teach in the village of Gesing. Gesing! An arid region, with hard, broken, lumpy soil; isolated in the foothills of the Kendeng Range. What a heartbreaking, devilish outcome!

One afternoon, the day before we at the school were to hold a farewell *selamatan* for him, Mas Martoatmodjo brought his wife and children to visit us. We welcomed him with all our sympathy and with barely suppressed emotion. Dik Ngaisah, who could now direct the questions uppermost in her woman's mind to the person she would consider the most affected by all this, took Mbak Marto and her children aside, while I listened to her husband's calming response to my expressions of pity.

'No-o, it's nothing, Dik Sastro. We accept it all in the spirit of a challenge. A test, if you like, by the Deity. Perhaps He wants to see how long I can endure the life of an anchorite in Gesing, mm? But we go fortified by the good wishes of your family and of so many other friends. I expect, *insya Allah*, to just carry on quietly working away in my new school.'

I thought to myself, O noble spirit! and wondered what manner of substance was it from which the Creator fashioned such people: so upright, so strong.

3. Sastrodarsono

'Next thing, Dik Sastro: I ask that tomorrow's event at the school be a quiet affair, nothing out of the ordinary. And I ought also to advise you, Dik, not to seem over-friendly towards me, nor should you look too regretful, or whatever. As I told you once, there are those around who might misunderstand; and you'll be living on here among them.'

The parting meal was indeed low-key; we merely surrounded the ceremonial dish of yellow rice, took a few grains, and then the whole school bad Mas Martoatmodjo good-bye. When it came to shaking his hand I barely restrained my tears and almost embraced him. He gave me a cheerful wink, turned and left, holding his children's hands and followed by his wife.

At the Wanagalih HIS, the teachers were addressed as *'Meneer'*. Naturally, as one who had only done five years at a village school and merely trained as an assistant teacher, anything in Dutch was a trap to me, and after the best help from our neighbouring priyayi and Dik Ngaisah's *een-twee-drie* pennyworth, the closest I could get to pronounce that word was *'Menir'*. Well, no matter, *Meneer* Soetardjo, the school principal, and *Meneer* Soerojo, who taught Dutch, geography, and history, accepted my effort. They were friendly towards my family, and as conscientious and interested teachers they often visited us to chat about how our children were coming along. Of course nothing swells the heart of a parent more than hearing from teachers how his children are advancing in their studies and how bright they are: then all the burdens and hardships of raising them vanish in a moment. The Javanese have an expression: 'To look at a potsherd and see a gold nugget.' In other words, ugly as a child may be, it will seem ever so handsome to its Javanese parents. Badly behaved? Not at all, the little dear is very quiet and attentive at home. An ignoramus? Why, its parents will detect a pretty fair intelligence there! And so when a teacher comes to sing the praises of your offspring: well, no question but he is confirming gold! *Meneer* Soetardjo and *Meneer* Soerojo gave our children excellent grades in general, and all three showed specific aptitudes: Noegroho in his history and geography; Hardojo in Dutch especially, and also in composition, and he did well enough in arithmetic too; while Soemini was particularly fluent in Dutch: understandably so, I reasoned, she being a female. With her, it went well beyond any *een-twee-drie*, for according to both teachers her grasp of the language was nothing short of impeccable. Their visits gave Soemini frequent opportunities to exhibit her fluency, with *'Goedenavond, Meneer'* and *'Dag, Meneer, tot ziens'*, at their coming and going, and many other politenesses which lost me completely and left me marvelling. My own best attempts at such phrases always resulted in something like *'Goeie napen, Menir'* and *'Dah, Menir, tot sien'*.

My wife may well have praised Soemini's Dutch as quite equal to that of a *nyonya Belanda*, and naturally I bowed to this estimate by one who after all had once stayed with the lady-wife of the administrator of Mbalong's sugar factory; but now, suddenly as it were, I realised that Soemini was already in her fifth class, and in two years more there would be an end to her accomplishments. What were we to do with her then? She was intelligent, certainly, but she would also soon be a grown woman. Without doubt my wife and I were in agreement with the emancipationist ideals of the noble-born Kartini, daughter of the progressive regent of Japara. We were proving that well enough by giving Soemini an education at an HIS. And we had not kept her in seclusion or shackled her inside the house: we had bought her a bicycle, let her learn dancing in the kabupaten's pendopo, allowed her to go wherever she wanted, as long as she asked us first and never stayed out after dark. Yet, a daughter was a daughter: she would have to marry, start a family, raise children, work for the wellbeing of her husband and her own home. Further schooling? Seven years in an HIS was more than enough for a girl. Soemini's ability to express herself in Dutch was excellent, as it was in Javanese also, her grasp of the latter's levels was confident and sensitive; so what need was there for additional schooling? What she would have when she graduated ought to be more than enough to serve her as the wife of the choosiest priyayi. With her good sense and intelligence, what husband could not but deem himself fortunate to have acquired such a partner? I turned to my wife one night to discuss the matter. She smiled.

'Allah, father, fa-ther . . . the child is barely in her fifth class, and you're planning her wedding-day! A chit of twelve years—for goodness' sake!'

I was surprised at her attitude. Javanese mothers were usually happy to forsee their daughters paired off and smoothly moving towards a wedded state.

'Well, yes, of course, she's twelve and in her fifth class at the moment. In another two years she'll be in the seventh class and fourteen. When she finishes school, she'll be nearly fifteen.'

'Well?'

'Well! Don't we have to start looking now, dear woman? With our own family background, finding someone for a girl like Soemini is not going to be an easy matter. Do you think when our parents organised our marriage they put the whole thing together in a moment? If I'm not mistaken it took some considerable time.'

It seems my words must have had an effect, because after this exchange we began to consider together the names of various prospects, both within the network of our own relatives and some outside it. We preferred that it should be a candidate from within the wider kinship, as long as the connection was suitably distant, as had been the case when we ourselves had been paired. In the end, we sought the opinion of our respective fathers, and they

3. Sastrodarsono

proposed sounding out one Soemodiwongso, a retired headmaster living with his family in Soemoroto. He was a first cousin of my mother-in-law, and thus sufficiently far in consanguinity. The Soemodiwongsos had a young man who was a graduate of the Probolingo OSVIA, the *Opleidingsschool voor Inlandse Ambtenaren*, which trained native-born civil servants, and he presently served as a police inspector in the district of Karangelo. With some energy and luck he should in two or three years be elevated to assistant district head. My wife and I decided to investigate this possibility: he seemed right for Mini.

We sent a letter by hand of an envoy, who as a matter of course also transported with him a variety of our choicest produce: black potatoes, famous in our parts for their texture when boiled and the way they peeled easily, sweet potatoes and cassava, two kinds of sticky rice, and various other things. Following etiquette, these were offered merely as provender for the family's servants. In the letter we begged to introduce ourselves as distant kin in a lineage whose elements had regrettably drifted apart, and which the Soemodiwongsos out of natural sentiment might like to see draw closer together once more. The usual folk-metaphors concerning the relationship of flesh to bones, limbs to body, and in short labouring the virtues of organic unity, illustrated that simple and reasonable objective on our own part. They replied with warmth, embracing our admirable desire to strengthen the ties of kinship, and with their best wishes towards that end came a basketful of Magetan mangoes, various delicacies made from sweet rice, and a quantity of jackfruit taffy.

We next made ready to receive a visit from them; not by any means the kind I had made to Dik Ngaisah's home, virtually to settle the last details of an inevitable wedding: this occasion would indeed be simply a first, investigative step, and whatever happened afterwards would depend on the impressions everyone derived from it. The day came, my wife had been busy for hours seeing to the tidiness of the house and yard, and by the time the guests arrived she and the servants had set out a wide array of light fare, while a grand meal intended to thoroughly smite them continued being prepared out at the back. Soemini, also mobilised to help, had no inkling that all the bustle and fret concerned her in any way. The boys at that time had finished HIS and were away at the *Kweekschool* in Yogya, on their way to becoming teachers. We had weighed up the costs and what best to do for their future, and had decided we should send them there. If they did well, they might go on to a *Hogere Kweekschool*, an advance which would qualify them to teach immediately in any HIS. For the head of a village school, could there be anything to swell the heart more than seeing his sons obtaining a higher teaching appointment than his own! Should they pass HKS, their starting salary, so I heard and could hardly believe, would be about 110 guilders—a fortune!

Gentry

Our guests were older than we, and their son, Harjono, bearing the title *Raden*, was an only child. Dik Ngaisah and I were well-impressed by Police Superintendent Raden Harjono: we found him courteous, handsome, intelligent, and as far as we could there tell he seemed a generally good person. Whether Soemini understood what was happening or not, the Soemodiwongso parents were quite taken by her, and the two young people made friends immediately. They were quickly chatting in a mixture of Javanese and Dutch with such casual panache as had us all drawing our breaths in admiration. They made a good show together, and Mas Soemodiwongso went so far as to declare that the couple exemplified the best of our modern young gentry, and were just what Princess Kartini had in mind when she wrote her enlightened letters. The principal result of this first visit was an agreement that the two sides should meet again to further enjoy each other's company. All in all, as their gharry left our house and we stood waving after them, we were well-contented.

In advancing the fortunes of our family, we did not limit to our own three children those towards whom we felt a duty of welfare and education. As other Javanese priyayi did, and indeed Javanese peasants as well, we could not be indifferent to our wider kin nor enjoy alone those means which fortune had given us. A sense of obligation to help other relatives was impressed on me by my father, and on Dik Ngaisah by hers. Thus, although I was an only child, as was my wife, neither of us felt lonely in our paternal homes, as there was always the latest of a turnover of relatives living with us. And so it was with our house in Wanagalih. We had Ngadiman, the son of a first cousin of mine, committed to me by his father to be schooled at the Wanagalih HIS; another nephew from my side of the family; plus two more children of relatives from Dik Ngaisah's. Those were Soenandar, and Sri and Soedarmin. Altogether with our own three it was a lively crowd. Parents tended to drop their offspring into our hands with a 'See if you can knock something into this one's head: a little schooling might make the wretch worth feeding . . .' and that, as some child was surrendered to us for perhaps years, tended to be the extent of its parents' hope-for-the-best and naive view of the matter. And my wife and I accepted our charges happily and with all our hearts, while knowing, too, the burden and the responsibility involved.

Despite the fact that the children had been given over to us unconditionally and we had a fully parental relationship with them, still the reality was that they were not our own: kin-related, yes, but undeniably stemming from other elements than those which had produced our three. And they came to us already formed to some extent. Ngadiman was an extremely shy boy, timid, not particularly bright, but he was honest, a good

3. Sastrodarsono

worker, and reliable. Soenander, on the contrary, was quite quick, but he proved a schemer, was untrustworthy, and a liar. Soedarmin and Sri were the son and daughter of a cousin of my wife and came from a village of *santri* peasants, devout adherents to Islam. They were an unexceptional pair, prayed a lot, were obedient, studious enough, but inclined to keep to themselves. Given that my wife and I came from a tradition that was *abangan*, whose Islam accommodated a dash of Javanised Hinduism as well as elements of immemorial native lore, we hoped that the arrival of those two would rebalance our children's religious outlook: for the three were more inclined to delight in wayang stories than in the scriptures, either Koranic or of the Sacred Book revealed to the prophet Jesus. Who could tell, we thought, perhaps the good influence of Sri and Darmin might open our children to a more precise understanding of Islam? I have to admit in all honesty that my own hardly impressive religious upbringing in Kedungsimo had over time faded even further from my consciousness. Naturally, I would always declare to all and sundry that ours was a Muslim family, but that amounted to little more than an assertion of its official status. I was actually more taken by what my neighbours the doctor and the lawyer had to say, one on the subject of theosophy and the other about Javanese spiritualism; so my occasional resolve to send our children to learn Koranic verses tended in my variable state of mind to quickly languish. There was a standing opportunity for them to practice with our well-known catechist, Pak Mansoer, who lived near us and who incidentally also taught the art of Javanese self-defence. But when Sri and Darmin arrived, we thought this would be an opportunity for our children to receive a living view of Islam presented to them by their own kin rather than any outsider. It would be good for them to learn of other heroic figures besides the Pendawas and Kurawas of the wayang epics.

But as it turned out the result was far different: Sri and Darmin, on the contrary, began to neglect their prayers and joined the company of those who came to listen to me relating the deeds of the great wayang characters: something which I often did for the benefit and entertainment of the other children during my free evenings. There were also frequent performances of shadow plays in Wanagalih and the surrounding villages, and those too they attended with the rest of our family; thus they were the ones who became more exposed to fresh ideas. Moreover, what must have been even more subversive than my evening-storytelling, and the generally less-than-pious atmosphere of our home, was their time at HIS. There, they were taught Dutch, history, geography, to sing Dutch songs, and were generally confronted by all kinds of fare very different to that previously offered them by their village school and village catechist.

What a contrast with those two was my nephew Soenandar, whose bad behaviour was unending, and who caused more disturbances in our house than could be believed! He would wait until Sri was in the middle of her evening prayers, muffle himself in his sarong, and appear a terrifying figure looming in the darkness outside her window. She would let out a shriek, while he laughed like a maniac out there. On one occasion, I found both Sri and Darmin in tears because they had been tricked by one of Soenandar's ruses into eating fried chicken-blood, and when I came upon the scene he was prancing around them, chanting: 'Who's been eating chicken-blood, chicken-blood, chicken blood! . . .' It should have come as no surprise then when one day, at the stage Sri and Darmin were respectively in fifth and sixth class, their father and mother arrived and asked to take their children back.

Distressed, respectful, and humble, the two villagers were nevertheless determined. 'Oh, a thousand, thousand apologies, Mas . . . we are heartbroken to have to ask for our children . . . it's just that, you see, we built a new mosque in our village, our family gave the land and we all built it; and now we feel our children should come back to look after it and to help teach the verses. With all that schooling they had here, we think they should go back now to lead their brothers and sisters in the village. . . .'

And there was more apologising and more explaining; and although I accepted that the facts were as they described them, we could not fail but feel that we had mishandled things and were being reproved; my wife in particular felt that, since these were kin on her side. We interpreted their action as implying dissatisfaction in our ways of teaching, or mistrust of our home as a suitable environment for their children. The way Sri and Darmin were changing must have been clearly evident to these cousins of my wife whenever the two children returned to their village on vacations: those were intervals when the parents might make some understandably worrying observations. Whatever the cause, we felt sad and a little ashamed: sad at their going, because we had come to feel the two to be part of our life and our home, and sad also because of their terminated education.

'But we can still come to visit you and Bapak sometimes, Bu?'

'Certainly, dear; both of you have a second home here, isn't that so?'

Sri was crying as she hugged my wife for the last time; Soedarmin, departing, bowed low to us.

I heard Soenandar behind me mutter: '*Wah*, no *santri* gospellers left to twit . . .'

'*Hus!*' I snapped at him, scandalised.

I never stopped wondering why this nephew of mine had been such a bully to his cousins. It seemed that persecuting them, or any other child for that matter, gave him some special satisfaction known only to himself. From his teachers we received constant reports about his misbehaviour in school. They admitted that he was intelligent enough, but said he was lazy, often left his homework undone, and that it seemed his special pleasure was to pester

3. Sastrodarsono

the girls and provoke fights with other boys. And then, finally, he was brought one day to our house by *Meneer* Soerojo, at a time when I happened to be at home feeling off-colour and had not gone to work. My wife and I were startled to see *Meneer* Soerojo pedalling towards us on his bicycle, doubling Soenandar on the rear rack.

With his usual affable good nature the teacher told us what had happened: 'I do beg your pardon, Mas and Mbak, calling on you like this, bringing your boy, Soenandar.'

'It is rather a surprise, *Menir*. Nandar? What's he done now?'

Meneer Soerojo smiled, gave the boy standing with his head bowed a sharp glance, and began.

'It's like this, Mas and Mbak, forgive me, but this time Soenandar has just gone too far. He was detected stealing the pocket money of one of his classmates; and, furthermore, we have a report from the woman who runs the stall in the school garden that it seems Soenandar likes taking snacks from her but doesn't pay.'

I was shocked. Such shameful news was enough in my state of health that day to make me feel quite dizzy.

'My God, *Menir* Soerojo, it's we who must beg your pardon, and that of *Menir* Soetardjo too! This is a disgrace, and the boy has indeed gone past all patience now! But look, I can promise you I'm going to give him a thrashing that will straighten him out! Just don't expel him, we beg you!'

'I have already spoken to *Meneer* Soetardjo about that. It would be a pity to expel him when he's already in fifth class; *Meneer* Soetardjo and I are of one mind on the impossibility of doing that, Mas. We will leave the boy in your hands now, to do something about these troubles he gets himself into.'

I was embarrassed to an extreme by this visit of *Meneer* Soerojo. We were humiliated by having to face the fact that there was in our family one whose wickedness had lowered him to the point of stealing. And the generosity of the two HIS teachers only compounded our discomfiture.

'Nandar!' In my fury and shame my own voice sounded unnatural to my ears. 'Nandar! Here! Move yourself!' I was holding a length of rattan in my hands.

'Yes, Pak.'

'So, you cover yourself in ignominy, scoundrel! Stealing from your friends! Can't be bothered to pay! A disgrace to your family! What sort of priyayi are you going to become? Follow me!'

Everyone, family and servants, stood silent; no one was about to intervene on behalf of Soenandar in my state and while I was gripping that cane. They knew that when it came to the cane it had to be an offense beyond the ordinary, for I seldom brought it out. I can remember only once or twice having to use it on my own children. The last time, I think, had been to chastise

Gentry

Noegroho and Hardojo when they were in fifth and fourth class respectively, after they disobeyed me and had gone into the Madiun at a time when the fishermen were stupefying fish with pulped *tuba* plants. With all the excitement of the catch, they too had waded into the drugged water. And as to Ngadiman and Soedarmin, I never had cause to use the rattan on either of that quiet pair. But Soenandar! Countless were the times I had had to thrash him.

We walked to the storeroom at the back of the house, and I saw, or could feel, that everyone's eyes were on us. Just as we were about to enter, Soemini suddenly took my hand from behind and whispered: 'Don't hit him too hard, Pak, please; you won't go on too long, will you?'

'*Hee-ish!* Keep back, you silly female! Following us about . . .'

Soemini was then in fifth class. She recoiled and returned to her mother, while I slammed shut the door of the storeroom. When I turned to Soenandar, he had already taken off his shirt and was standing with his bare back to me, ready for the cane.

'So, you evil monkey, ready then, are you?' Down hissed the cane, punctuating each of my infuriated utterances: 'Dis-*grace* to your parents! Don't know your *luck!* Been sent to *H-IS!* If you fail *school*, what's to be-*come* of you? If you *stop*, like Sri and *Dar*-min, that's not too *bad*, they're of some *use*, in their *vil*-lage! They can grow *rice*, teach the Ko-*ran*, tend to their *mosque*. You? You'll have *naught* ahead, but *steal*-ing, *swind*-ling, scratching for a *liv*-ing!'

Swish and swish and swish the cane came down, until Soenandar's back was black and blue. If my anger lessened, I don't remember it. I do know I noted that the lines left by previous beatings stood out clearly, even as the new blows fell among them. When I left the storeroom I forbade him to step outside for a day and a night. He remained in there for that time without food or water.

But as it turned out, it appears this ferocious punishment taught Soenandar nothing, did not impress him for long, he remained the same person. He was caught stealing again just a couple of months before he was to go into sixth class, and we were forced to decide that we must remove him from the school, to end the cycle of the good teachers bringing him to me for another round of chastisement, one more chance to behave, and so on. We were mortified before them, at a loss, our sense of what it meant to be of the priyayi order deeply affronted.

And there was another sad side to the matter. We felt that we had been inadequate to Soenandar's mother, a cousin of mine this time, a widow living in wretched circumstances in her village. My wife and I agreed that while Soenandar must be withdrawn we would not send him back there, that it would be just too bad if he were to continue his escapades at home and cause

3. Sastrodarsono

additional distress to his mother. We sent her a letter explaining the situation and our plan to keep her son in Wanagalih. The woman arrived hurriedly, bringing with her a present of some few musty and hard rice-cakes, probably ones she had kept a long time for a special occasion. The moment she saw us standing with her son in a group waiting to greet her, she burst into tears.

'Oh, Allah, Kang and Mbak, a thousand, thousand pardons that we've been such trouble to you both. It was the right thing to punish the boy and to take him from the school. He should be sent back to the village, but then what would become of him there?'

She was a pathetic sight: her sarong and blouse were tattered and faded, and I guessed that she had nothing else to wear. We made an effort to eat a little of her cakes, nibbling where the green of the mould was palest, showing our polite appreciation.

'Oh dear, Kang, Mbak. The cakes are very ordinary, I'm afraid.'

'Why, no, they're delicious.'

That night we tried to ease her and to reassure her by putting our plans for Soenandar in the best possible light, explaining that she had no need to worry about him and that we would surely manage to find him some suitable work. And when a few days later she left, we saw her off provisioned with new clothes, a little money and some rice. During her stay with us, Soenandar made an effort to be good and well-behaved, and we were grateful for that.

When Soemini was in seventh class, the proposal of marriage arrived. In the letter, the young man, already distinguished by the title *Raden*, had had the flowery 'Cokrokoesoemo' added to his name, and now we learned that Raden Harjono Cokrokoesoemo had been raised to assistant district chief at Karangelo. It hardly needed saying that I and my wife were very ready to accept the proposal. Since that first meeting, the families had visited each other on a number of occasions, and on our side we had noted how Soemini and Raden Harjono got along increasingly well together; so we wasted no time in calling our daughter and her brothers to a family conference. As it happened, the two boys were at that moment vacationing with us from their teaching courses.

It felt strange, speaking with my children about the proposal, and I was nervous and initially had difficulty finding the right words to start with. It had dawned on me that this gathering had to do with the future of our family's only daughter, and perhaps for the first time I was really aware that she had passed childhood, was ready to be married, and therefore to fly away from us to a new nest of her own. That sense of impending loss must have been the cause why I began rather awkwardly. And yet, was it not true, I quickly reasoned with myself, that a Javanese marriage united two families, and that

Soemini's betrothal would mean not her departure from us but rather that the prospective in-laws would become an adjoining part of our immediate family and we of theirs? And I also admitted to myself that I was not well-practiced in these new consultative ways; things were easier in my father's day.

'Now, children, it's like this. Today we received a letter of proposal from your uncle Soemodiwongso in Soemoroto, requesting that Soemini should become his daughter-in-law. As you see, because you have before you a father who is not an old conservative priyayi, I have asked you, and especially Mini, to come together so that you three might also express your views about this very important matter.'

Having laid it before them, I waited gravely for their response. I waited. None of them gave a sign of wanting to express any view whatever: they sat silently in their chairs.

'How about you, Noegroho? You're the oldest boy. As a father, I would like to hear your thoughts about this.'

There was more silence. The young man probably felt overwhelmed, I thought; being asked to contribute to such a momentous decision might be a bit too novel even for a modern youth. Then he spoke up: 'Father, as far as my opinion goes, it's this. You should ask Mini. She's the one they're proposing to.'

I was taken aback at hearing such an unvarnished offering. I would never have answered my father so casually and bluntly. Ah well, I supposed, the times were changing: being brief and to the point was probably another effect of their Dutch schooling which we older ones would have to grow used to.

'I see. All right then. And what about you, Hardojo?'

Hardojo smiled at me, and also said rather blandly: 'Yes, I'm with Mas Noegroho. It's Mini's marriage, isn't it? Let's hear what she wants.'

Again I was left speechless for a moment. A serious matter like this, to take such a careless attitude to it? . . . I was beginning to grow annoyed, looking at them sitting there, their blank expressions unhelpful. But one had to be patient. These were new times.

'Well, mother? Seems your boys just want to drop it all in Mini's lap.'

She now smiled. 'That's enough of that now. Let's just ask Mini.'

I drew a long breath and turned to Soemini. 'Right, my girl. It looks like your brothers are not going to be much help. We await your opinion.'

Soemini did not answer immediately; in fact there seemed to be a very long pause. Evidence of understandable shyness, probably. I would have to prompt her to some reply.

'Now then, Mini. You appear to have got along pretty well with Raden Harjono, isn't that right? As your mother and I have come to see it, you two

3. Sastrodarsono

would make a very good pair together. You're a girl of the gentry, well-educated, about to finish HIS, and your Dutch is excellent. The young man is a graduate of OSVIA, has just been promoted. Well, yes, there *is* a bit of difference in your ages, but that's no matter, is it, child?'

I thought I saw the expression on the faces of the boys grow a little tense. Maybe they disapproved of the fatherly manner I was using to help Soemini along towards her decision. But she on her part seemed quite calm. Only, she had still not said anything.

Finally, she spoke as well: 'Since you have asked me, very well. Bapak, Ibu, Mas-Mas, I accept the proposal . . .'

'*Now* then, *that's* the spirit, girl! That's my daughter! I was beginning to think that you were going to refuse or sulk or something.'

'Yes, but wait, Pak. I accept. However, there is a condition.'

'A *what?*'

'I would like to ask a thing from all of you here, but especially from Mas Harjono.'

'Allah spare us, child! Do you think you're Wara Sembadra—lacks nothing but won't wed Arjuna unless she gets a gamelan band sent down from the heavens?'

My wife intervened: 'Paaak, let her finish. Let's just hear what this daughter of yours wants.'

Soemini had a strange smile on her face, and her eyes were particularly bright as she said: 'I want to go to the van Deventer School. As soon as I graduate, I'll be Mas Harjono's wife.'

Oh, my God—*Pan Depenter!* Another two to three years more of schooling. What on earth would the bridegroom do during that time? Could he reasonably be expected to wait so long? If he wouldn't, he would drop the girl, and all our work towards the match was lost, done in vain! . . . I would never get over my shame before the Soemodiwongsos, who had been so good. And to try again to find such a catch as Raden Harjono—how easy would that be? Education, family background, rank, appearance—every condition met! Could such a fortunate find be stumbled on a second time in any conceivable future?

'Dear girl . . . Come now, you mustn't just think about yourself, only about what you want. More time at school: it means that your young man would have to wait for so long. All very well if he's got the patience—if not? You should give it some thought, you know.'

'Yes of course, Pak. But I *have* given it quite a bit of thought.'

At that moment I remembered with a wince that Soemini had always had a stubborn streak in her since childhood, and if she took a fancy to something it had to be hers immediately. Thankfully, it was a characteristic which was infrequently displayed, but it was there. I turned to her mother and brothers for their thoughts on this outrageous development.

'Well, mother? She's your daughter.'

'This idea of further schooling, dear, what brought that about? Haven't you done enough studying already?'

'My view, Bu, and Pak, is that I have not. And I don't feel ready for marriage. When I graduate from HIS I'll just be nearing fifteen, that's all. Aren't we gentry, and don't we agree with Raden Kartini that girls shouldn't marry too young? And I want to learn more about the world, to spend some time at a good school in a bigger place than Wanagalih. A school in Solo or somewhere like that.'

I lost my patience. The girl was going past all limits! 'A school in Solo or somewhere, she says! Well now, do you think your father's made of money, one of those millionaire merchants in Batavia? We've strained enough to put your brothers through school in Solo and Magelang—no, my girl, I won't agree!'

Soemini's face flushed and then turned pale. The room fell silent. No one spoke and the silence lengthened until the chirp of a gecko and the ticking of the wall-clock became distinct. I saw that Soemini was trying to control her tears, but they started to trickle anyway, and she had to lift her handkerchief to her eyes and nose. Her subdued sobs could hardly go unnoticed in the quiet. Hardojo looked up at me.

'If I may, father, could I say something?'

'Say away!'

'Don't be annoyed, please, father, but I also think that Mini is too young to be married just now. And van Deventer is a good boarding school and not too expensive. I'll be staying nearby myself, as you know. Don't forget that Aunt Soeminah lives in Solo. We could have Mini visit her every Saturday, to stay with her and keep her company. Two or three years is not very long.'

I glanced at Soemini, and saw that she was brightening up a little. She nodded in agreement with Hardojo's words and smiled gratefully at him. Noegroho seemed to be still weighing up some considerations of his own. I was not very pleased to find myself being asked to be reasonable by the younger boy.

'And you, Noegroho? We haven't heard anything from you yet. What about it, do you agree with your brother?'

Reluctantly, he replied: 'Well, yes, van Deventer would be a good school for a girl like Mini, but I keep thinking about the other side of this, what the Soemodiwongso family will say when we ask them to put off the wedding.'

'But in principle you're with Mini and Hardojo?'

'In principle, yes. But telling them in Soemoroto will be a delicate matter.'

No one added anything to that, and I felt cornered by my own children. For a moment or two I nursed a feeling of resentment, even anger towards them. The ingrates only thought about themselves! Where had all duty to parents gone? Had they no consideration for the work we had done towards this match? Then with an effort I calmed myself, and I began to see some merit in what they had said. I found myself being swayed towards agreeing that my Soemini was indeed rather young to be leaving our care so soon. Her mother had been older when we married.

'Very well, very well. If that's what you all think. But I can tell you that if the Soemodiwongso side starts objecting, I'll probably be just too mortified to go on with it. I don't know what I'll do. Noegroho, you're right. We will have to be very, very careful how we communicate this to them.'

After another pause while everyone reflected again, Soemini spoke: 'If you, Bapak and Ibu, think it would help, I could write a letter to Mas Harjono in Karangelo. I would ask for his understanding. We know each other pretty well now, and if I can make my thoughts sound reasonable to him, he might agree and turn his parents to agreeing as well.'

We decided to do that. Soemini wrote the letter and I sent her brothers to deliver it in Karangelo. Two days later they returned, bearing a very cordial reply: the young man was not only willing to be patient and wait until Soemini finished more schooling, he also praised her as a modern young woman whom he would be proud to have as his wife when the time came. All in all, I found myself totally at a loss to understand the attitudes of this new generation. So self-assured and bold in their thinking. Was this where Dutch education was taking our youth, then? But, thankfully, with this new-fangled readiness to present their own opinions to their parents, they still on the whole kept to the polite forms, the respect for elders, used acceptable language. At least, I comforted myself, the domestic part of their upbringing had left its mark; and surely my story-telling from the wayang epics must have done something to shape their characters as well, their views on life and on what was right and what was wrong? I could only hope so.

It seems Raden Harjono was able to convince his parents, because when we sent a formal and full answer to their proposal, they returned: 'Understand, appreciate, and accept your conditions, Mas Sastrodarsono.' And so, when Soemini finished HIS in Wanagalih we accompanied her to Solo to enrol her at the van Deventer School and to meet Mbak Soeminah, a cousin of ours of actually rather distant consanguinity. Separating from our third child, and in a fluster of mixed feelings, we delayed our good-byes as long as we could by all kinds of unnecessary instructions and iterations: stressing to Soemini that she must visit the old lady punctually every Saturday, bidding her to study well; and to Hardojo we once again itemized his responsibilities towards his sister. Then we left.

Gentry

My wife and I returned home on the SS, as it was known: the *Staatsspoorwegen*, a State Railways train servicing that division of the island's rail network. We actually got off at Paliyan, Wanagalih itself having no railway connection. Perhaps it had never had one as a result of its disobliging soil, or else because the town was deemed to be an unprofitable destination; thus if one took a train from Solo or Surabaya, Paliyan was the nearest station to our town. The rest of the journey might be taken by buggy or gharry, a matter of six or seven kilometres through rice fields on a typical *trembesi*-shaded lane. Rocking drowsily in the vehicle on our way back, the realisation suddenly came to me that when we arrived at our home on Setenan Road we would be met only by Ngadiman and Soenandar, and that it would be very quiet there, and sad for a while.

Each afternoon, my wife and I habitually sat on the front veranda opening onto our yard, cooling ourselves by the light airs which arrived at that time of day. Wanagalih is a hot town, located in the limestone foothills of the Kendeng Range, and it knows only two periods of pleasant temperature in the day: just after dawn, and towards dusk. Most of the time the weather is hot, sticky and fairly oppressive. For as long as anyone remembered, those two cool periods were always set aside for certain very specific needs and agreeable activities. Following dawn was a time when our elderly folk, both pensioned priyayi and those still in employment, emerged in the streets and open spaces to stroll in the fresh, clean air, usually with much early-morning coughing and clearing of throats, to gather at last in the square for the inevitable gossiping and good-natured arguments. The wives of Wanagalih, rising as early as their husbands, or earlier, never took part in that routine. It was as if an unwritten rule had once and for all time declared that their concerns lay elsewhere, nor was it fitting for them to be abroad among the males. No, they dealt instead with their own important dawn duties: preparing the hot coffee, the fried bananas and boiled yams, the bucket or two of warm water for the morning sluice, and with overseeing the morning's climax: breakfast itself. We husbands long saw this situation as falling into a natural division of labour, and we had no reason to believe other than that the women accepted their role and that it brought them satisfaction. And, after all, men and wives did meet over the light repast and then again at breakfast. In our house, that first snack never varied or wearied us: always fried bananas, boiled yams, and a small portion of rice and blanched vegetables topped with peanut sauce: that last appetizer done in an especially spicy Wanagalih way by Mbok Soero, who brought it to us on her invariable rounds, packaged in teak leaves. Such a dish could only be made further agreeable by a sprinkling of Chinese *petai*

3. Sastrodarsono

beans, or perhaps were it to be accompanied by fried tempeh, firm and pleasurably salty, also a local delicacy. Actually, I always considered this first morning fare to be on its own as good as any breakfast.

The other end of the day was a time to rest and inhale the mix of evening fragrances, when husband and wife sat at peace together, although they might also be joined at will by others of the family. However, with our children away in another town and only Ngadiman and Soenandar at home, and those two never a part of that atmosphere, we were the only ones who sat out there now on the veranda in our rocking chairs. Spreading before us was our front yard, a corner of which was occupied by a large jackfruit tree, growing in that spot since before we had begun to live on Setenan Road. It was a robust tree, with a good extent of branches and amazingly large fruit which it reproduced seemingly endlessly. That fruit was known throughout the neighbourhood and had probably been enjoyed at the furthest reaches of our road, had certainly delectated many at our card parties, either fresh or as taffy. Looking at the tree on this particular evening I became suddenly aware that twenty years had without our detecting their passage somehow passed since we first came to live here.

'How, *suddenly*, father? Haven't we seen enough going on here to count the years by; and you find them gone so suddenly?'

I smiled. 'Mother, all I meant was, I was looking at that jackfruit tree and suddenly I thought to myself, how come it's gotten so big? Look at all those leaves, and that fruit! So then I thought, yes indeed, suddenly twenty years have passed.'

'There he goes again with his *suddenly*. Here in this house we brought three souls into the world; we took in another four from relatives; we've had our share of problems; we sent off our children out of town for their schooling; we married off your daughter Soemini in grand style. What else? Soemini is pregnant and our sons are making their way, and before we know it we'll see them married too. So you never noticed anything then, among this whole crowd of events? Really, father—*suddenly*!'

I laughed. Dik Ngaisah, little sister: how long was it now since I had called her that? She had been a wise wife, she had always worked hard, had been a support to all of us each time we stumbled on some difficulty, had always managed to recover well herself from her own problems. Even the time of that calamity with her father, Romo Mukaram: sacked by the *gupermen* after finally being caught trafficking in opium with Chinese smugglers. She had accepted that blow staunchly. And so too, when a little later he had fallen ill, a sad, shamed man, had then died. She had still maintained a resolute heart. I knew how, beyond her sorrow for her father, she felt also mortified, humbled by the scandal. I knew the way she felt because I had to listen to the unsubtle remarks of our own controller of the opium trade here in Wanagalih. He often joined us for our Setenan Road *kesukan* nights.

'That's what happens when you start smoking it yourself. What did he want to do that for? Makes you sick, that stuff.'

What could I say? I was deeply embarrassed but had to remain silent. It was all in all a bad business. Whatever his faults, he had been my father-in-law, my wife's father, and I did all I could to keep the matter low-key and vague; but that became impossible once our opium inspector—a hard-boiled veteran of the trade himself, but talkative—leaked details of it. When gossip spread beyond our circle, there was little in my power to limit it. There is a saying: 'However long the village lane, malicious tongues are longer.' So after a while all I could do was to stand by my wife and share the humiliation. A wayang episode called 'A Pandawa Plays Dice' was brought to mind by our experience: wherein the whole Pandawa family are disgraced by the action of one of its members, Yudistira, who dices with the rival Kurawas and by losing causes the expulsion of the Pandawas from their lands. At that time I thought of Romo Seten Kedungsimo, who would often talk of the knightly qualities of a true priyayi. Had he been still alive, I felt sure he would have at that time urged me to gird myself in the qualities of acceptance and courageous endurance.

He had often counselled: 'A true priyayi, Sastro, is known not only by his valour in victory but also by the manner in which he accepts defeat.'

My wife resigned herself and bore bravely the burden of shame for her father's transgressions, once she became fully aware of them. She tried to cheer him up, to lighten the old man's pathetic contemplation of his folly; she attempted to convince him that Allah was testing him and the whole family for steadfastness and patience. But when in his last days he tearfully begged her and his own wife to pardon him for infecting the body of the family with his disgrace, she, his daughter, acknowledged defeat; but she remained calm and brave in that.

'You've been looking a long time at that jackfruit tree, father. Is there something out there?'

'No, no, mother, it's just that the tree is getting very old, and that's been reminding me of all sorts of people. Our parents, who have all gone now; Romo Seten Kedungsimo, gone too. They were folk who helped us get to where we are today.'

My wife said nothing and remained silent for some time, probably also thinking about those old ones who had passed on and left us; and I thought I should say something comforting, having begun this mood of retrospection: 'They made their journey as decently as they could, for the sake of their families, and as widely as was allowed them they helped others in their journeys too.'

3. Sastrodarsono

'Yes. I just felt sorry, remembering the way father came to his own last days.'

'There, now; it was something of a disaster, but we should think of his good services to our family and to others, shouldn't we? You can't deny that he brought you up well and gave you a good education, and that he kept an open house to all sorts of relatives, helped them along in life. And there was the building of the village mosque that he gave money to.'

'Yes, that's just it. He'd done so much, and then his life just crumbled at the end, just as he was about to get his pension.'

'That's the nature of the world, human life's like that, mother. There's that true saying of ours that too much craving for all kinds of things leads to forgetting that some of those things are good and some are bad.'

'But just think: what more did my father need, what else could he have thought he needed?'

'Well, that's part of human nature too: we're always wanting something more.'

Then I began to think about all those exchanges and arguments we had in our card group, playing *ceki*. The doctor, the opium controller, the lawyer were all now retired, but they remained fervid players and there was no question of breaking up our routine: what else would have been left to them for their amusement? So we often mulled over various matters at the table, such as the question of the origin and goals of life; the limits, if any, to our human desires; whether we ought to pursue them to those limits, and beyond, or restrain ourselves and practice *sakmadya*: temperance and moderation. Doctor Soedrajat was of the opinion that mankind should be satisfied with whatever was sufficient to it. Why struggle for more? It made one greedy and fixated on never-achievable final satisfactions; and the prosecutor and opium controller agreed. But was it because none now needed to support children, and their government pension was enough to live on, and even left a few rupiahs to bet with at *ceki*? While as far as the discussion on origins and ends went, Doctor Soedrajat held that life was merely a momentary stop on a long journey, comparable to calling in at a roadside tea-stall, and we should give it no more than the casual attention that such a stop warranted, and not fall into excited indulging in such pathetic gratifications as were offered there: carousing to the extent of losing sight of the continuing journey. And as usual the good doctor contributed his views on such matters while carefully studying the cards in his hand, forcefully slapping a card down on the table, sipping a little of the Wanalawas peasant-brewed arak, a glass of which habitually stood beside his coffee. Just look at how our young teacher here got to be principal of his school, he would address his cards. Did he have to scheme and machinate and fuss? But then, the doctor qualified, *sakmadya* did not mean that one need became a hermit, starve and be without a place to sleep in.

Gentry

Our lad the teacher there still needs to have his nights of relaxation, such as here, where he might sip a little arak from time to time, mm? And when there's a party, and dancing girls, why shouldn't he take a round with them occasionally? That would be my view. But everything with *sakmadya, sak-madya!* And he would slap down another card on the table.

'Father. Hallo, father! . . . Since Mas Martoatmodjo moved to Gesing, did we have any more news about him, after that one letter from him when his daughter was married and we couldn't come to the wedding?'

I sat in silence for a moment longer after this question from my wife, because I had in fact only a little while ago heard from the prosecutor that Mas Martoatmodjo had been in more trouble. He had been sent to the Besuki area in the eastern tip of the island, under suspicion of having renewed his contacts with activists. Additionally, he had opened a 'wild' school for illiterate farmers in Gesing. It was thought that he had not only been teaching them to read and write and learn a little arithmetic, but was also inciting dissatisfaction with the colonial government. The old lawyer usually kept a stiff composure when speaking about my former superior; however, on this occasion I saw with some interest that he passed on his news with a semblance of compassion. The instruction deemed subversive to the *gupermen*, and partly the reason why the teacher had been sent into deeper exile, had not been the 'usual political nonsense', as the prosecutor put it, but related to the chronicles of Java's gone greatness. The might of Majapahit, the power of Sultan Agung, ruler of Mataram, his victories, his ultimate defeat by the invading Dutch, those had been the burden of Mas Marto's lessons. We two, the prosecutor and I, discussed the new banishment with an unusually-shared sadness; and now, telling my wife what I had learned, I found I had to choose my words to break to her dispassionately this latest news about the teacher.

'But goodness, Pak, what about his wife and children?'

'Oh, well, according to what I heard they've gone to Besuki with him.'

My wife murmured about the distance, shaking her head, and then said: 'She's a true Sembadra. Loyal, following him like that without question.'

'Hah, was Sembadra all that loyal? Aren't there episodes where she attacks Arjuna?'

'If there are, they happen at times that show her defending their marriage. But as to Mbakyu Marto's marriage, well, do you suppose she didn't know about her husband's fling with that dancer in Karangjambu?'

I felt uncomfortable and said nothing. So the wives had got wind of that and talked together.

'Mbakyu Marto let that matter pass, didn't make an issue of it, did she? She just kept what she knew to herself; but I know she would have patiently gone on doing what she could to improve things in her family. And meanwhile, he gets moved to Gesing, among strangers, she follows him; then next

3. Sastrodarsono

he's sent to the ends of Java, and she follows him again.'

I listened to my wife talking and imagined the vexation and sadness of those exiles as they removed further and further from their home. Nobility in adversity, Romo Seten had said. I felt there was a strength in the teacher, and in his wife, which would ensure they would survive and overcome their misfortunes.

'As a mother, I can just imagine the difficulties and worries of raising a family in one of those horrible areas. What a distant, unheard of country is that Besuki! They're not really Javanese, are they, Pak, those people out there? What will happen to the children when they grow up, what are they going to become, later on?'

'That, no one can predict; but when we remember how strong-willed Mas Marto is, with what courage he has always met life, we must hope that it will all come out well in the end.'

My wife sighed and concluded: 'Yes, everyone's lot is different, a unique destiny as they say.'

I wondered if she included the fate of her father in that observation and in that sigh. Just then the twilight was falling, but since our house faced north we could not see the sun setting below the horizon. It quickly became dark, and Paerah came to tell us that the evening meal was on the table. The odour of stir-fried beans and chilli peppers had indeed been wafting to us for some time.

Dinner had almost finished, when we were abruptly startled by voices from the back of the house: a babble punctuated a moment later by shrieks! We recognised Paerah in those: she had a little earlier left attending us at the table and returned to her quarters. We rose hurriedly and went to see what on earth was happening. Outside the room of the female servants, which was by the kitchen and the storeroom, Ngadiman and others seemed to be witnessing some commotion. We arrived, and those crowding by the door of the room stood aside for us. Within I saw Paerah sprawled on her bed, her clothing dishevelled and revealing a bare thigh, her eyes agape and darting in all directions. Under strands of loosened hair her face was pale and perspiring, and she was breathing in and out and squealing between breaths, one of her arms held out stiffly from her body. Soenandar was standing beside her bed, had a grip on her outstretched hand, and was pinching her fingers, evidently with vice-like force.

The moment we arrived, Paerah reduced her noise to a whimper and Soenandar began bellowing into her face: 'You, in there! Speak your name! And where your kip! D'you live in yon jackfruit tree? Or in the bamboo grove in the back field? Or in this house? You, in there—speak!'

Barked at like that, Paerah began a terrified wail again, which seemed to rouse Soenandar further: 'Frightened, eh? Speak up in there—say who I am!'

'You're R-raden . . . Soenandar; Ra-den, Ra-den . . . aw, you're hurting me!'

While I kept looking from one to the other of them, and tried to understand what was happening, Soenandar kneaded Paerah's hand and went on taunting some invisible object: 'Scared of me, ha? Then depart! Leave her body! Leave her, evil one, ghost, bookless banshee!' And he started to mutter something unclear but sounding vaguely scriptural.

Paerah appeared to calm down, but I could see terror in her eyes. I advanced into the room to put an end to this madness.

'Soenandar, move away! Now!'

'Paerah's got a devil in her, Pakdé.'

'Oh yes? And how did you come to work that out?'

'She was standing behind the door in the dark and then suddenly she started screaming. She was stiff and trembled.'

'And what did you do?'

'I opened the door, Pakdé, and then she started thrashing about to get free, so then I squeezed her thumb and she cried out again. It's a sign that she's got a spirit in her, Pakdé.'

'Well no wonder she cried out, with you crushing her thumb!'

I ordered a *kendi* of cold water be brought to us, and we made compresses, while my wife rubbed and stroked Paerah's hand and soothed her: 'It's all over now, dear. There, now, settle down. Who's that out there? Bring that bottle of fragrant oil from my room! Quickly now!'

One of the servants ran to get it and returned, and my wife sprinkled some drops on a handkerchief moistened in cool water; and whether it was those ministrations or the reassuring voice, Paerah grew calmer, her breathing became more even, and while she remained tense her eyes had lost that look of dread. Just then Ngadiman arrived leading someone into the room, an old man.

'Here's Mbah Kromo, Pakdé. The healer from behind the cattle market.'

Before I could react, Mbah Kromo with a show of professional efficiency directed himself straight to Paerah's bed. At the arrival before her of this withered ancient with a white beard, Paerah let out another shriek, at which the shaman turned confidently to me:

'*Wah*, no doubt about it, Ndoro Guru. The girl is possessed all right.'

Both Soenandar and Ngadiman nodded with satisfaction at that and spoke together: 'It's true, Pakdé.'

'It's possession, Pakdé, Budé. I saw the signs, just like I told you.'

'Possession my foot, Nandar. If she was possessed, the three of us here couldn't hold her down!'

I recalled a gharry driver in Karangdompol some time back. He had had a fit of that kind, had demanded to be brought a bunch of flowers to eat, and then could not be held down by three bystanders. But Mbah Kromo, unheeding, went into action. He produced a small bundle, extracting from it and reverently unfolding a handkerchief to reveal a sprig of flowers and a stub of incense derived from gum benzoin.

'Now just a moment, Mbah, what are you up to there with those?'

'These, Ndoro Guru, these flowers and this incense, are the food of airy spirits. I'll offer them to the one that's possessing the girl, if you'll just stand aside for a moment, and then I'll talk it into departing back to the local abode where it lives.'

'That's enough, thank you, Mbah, don't put yourself out any further. Off you go home. We'll look after Paerah. And here's for your trouble.'

The offended shaman's expression of displeasure quickly altered to one of happy satisfaction at the sight of the five-cent piece I had pressed into his hand.

'A thousand thanks, Ndoro Guru, a thousand thanks! And if the lass has a relapse, do call me again! A thousand thanks!'

As soon as the famous healer left, Paerah became visibly calmer. I sent Ngadiman and Soenandar to their room and bade the servants disperse to their own quarters, then I questioned Paerah. I wanted to hear from her what had started this commotion. Haltingly, she told how Soenandar had entered her room without knocking and began to embrace her. At the time, she was undressing and had screamed in shock and fright.

H'm, I thought to myself. Soenandar . . . Soenandar. . . .

In two areas, art and religion, I was conscious of being sadly inadequate; or actually I might even say that I felt a serious lack when it came to those two. In gloomy moments I accused myself of failure where the education of my own children in those subjects was concerned. Many would consider this strange: how could a priyayi, a schoolmaster furthermore, someone with a wide social acquaintanceship and knowing the expectations of our society, fail in that manner? But the fact was that in our family, and who knows in how many other gentrifying families, those lapses did occur. The simple explanation, and one which could be applied widely to my peers, stemmed from our parentage. My parents were peasants, and their views on life and its conduct were those of their situation. Although they had the aforementioned ambitions for their son, and admired everything that appertained to the higher class, in particular its vocabulary and etiquette, they neither could live nor probably themselves in their own hearts really wanted to live above the station they had been born in and were accustomed to. Now, with regards to the various artistic disciplines, a knowledge of which should have been early instilled in any Javanese who was to be considered educated, well, on occasion, my father might join the hired dancers at some celebration; but of the courtly, classical steps he knew nothing. He could not play the gamelan or operate the wayang puppets, much as he enjoyed a wayang performance. In short, where the arts were concerned he was, as in so much else, a simple man; and, living with him, I grew to adulthood with an aesthetic sense no more trained than his.

As far as religion went, he was of course a Muslim: his birth-name, Kasan, as I said, having an Islamic derivation. 'Atmo', its prefix and meaning 'of the soul', with a nod to Hinduism and its doctrine of transmigration, was tacked on at the time he was deemed to have reached adulthood. But as to praying, my memory is that I never saw anyone in my parents' family do much of that. We all, of course, celebrated Idul Fitri, the end of the fasting month, as an important family-day during which the children and grandchildren gathered; but as for the fasting itself, we never took Islam's Ramadan seriously. My parents did fast on Mondays and Thursdays, often having plain rice without side-dishes or salt, and that occasionally for weeks at a time. Or they limited themselves to eating just yams or corn or various tubers, also simply boiled and served without garnish. They considered fasting done during Ramadan according to Islamic convention to be trivial and unhelpful in inducing the necessary light, spiritual condition in which one might approach the Deity. Fasting is more than ritual, my father used to say, and should not be done by halves, as in 'that Arab fashion'. It is only an affair of the spirit when it entails true bodily self-denial. The body doesn't like to be set aside, it registers discomfort then, and that tells you you're on the right track. Yes, they go some way—again, 'those Arabs'—but not to the extent of our real, Javanese, fasting. From time to time he would prompt me to fast in that tradition, and for a while I would follow him.

But in actual fact my father was rather more concerned with educating me practically: to lead a good, secure, pleasant life here in this present world, or at least attain those states to whatever degree events made possible. That meant mixing with others in social activities; dealing with them as one would be done by; measuring one's coat to one's needs indeed, but cutting it to the going fashion. Become a priyayi, he would say, but learn humility too; remember the less fortunate multitude remaining below you. And such thoughts and folk maxims and commonplaces, which my father would have first heard from his father, and he from his, I received in my turn, absorbed in their considerable number, and subsequently found occasion to plant again in my own children. All in all, as I said, it was hardly a deeply religious inheritance for any of us.

In our *kesukan* group we, as already noted, often exchanged views on life, lamented worldly impermanence, and so on, agreed there was comfort in the

3. Sastrodarsono

belief that life had a spiritual aspect, and that believing such a thing allowed hope of an eventual everlasting existence in union with the Godhead, the source of that spirituality. The more we discussed such issues, the more firmly we decided that prayers and rituals, mandated by all kinds of religions, were virtually pointless physical acts, repetitive exercises that had nothing to do with the soul and its inherent intent to meld into God's essence. That too I conveyed to my children. And that too was an excuse for effective non-observance.

Thus, given my uneven commitment to things religious, when the boys asked to be allowed to learn traditional self-defence from one of our neighbours, Kamas Haji Mansoer, and as a consequence soon decided that they also wanted to recite Koranic verses with him, I readily let them. I repeat that I had no objection to my children becoming more familiar with the concepts, and if necessary the rituals, of our religion, thinking that added to such scraps of Sufic Javanese spiritualism as I had on occasion imparted to them, their appreciation of Islam would at last be broadened. It was in this spirit that we had welcomed Sri and Darmin into our home; but there, of course, the reverse of what we had hoped occurred, when those two were drawn more into our own *abangan* and rather relaxed observance. Well, my hope that our boys would now take to religion more seriously than I had done in my youth was soon disappointed: following an initial show of piety, they grew bored. And that was after we had bought them sarongs and a *peci* each, and heard how they intended to follow the five daily prayers with their full complement of bending and bowing, and that they would be attending the calls to prayer at Haji Mansoer's house. For some dawns my wife and I kept our ears pricked to hear how the boys would continue this regime; but it seems that they suddenly found various reasons to break it: football practice, choir attendance at school, the end-of-year celebrations which were being staged then, the excuses were many. I felt awkward and embarrassed before the good haji, and tried to encourage the recalcitrants back to their religious studies, but eventually to no avail. I could hardly blame Soenandar for his lapses during this period, when my own boys were being thus shamelessly wilful. And so at last the only way left was for me to go to Kamas Haji Mansoer and apologise.

'No, no, don't concern yourself, Dimas Sastro, it's nothing. We old ones have to be patient. I'm sure the moment will come when they'll want to return here. Or if not here, then at some point in their lives they will find prayer again. And then I feel certain too that in your own home, Dimas, you show them the best possible example, provide them with useful instruction.'

'Well, yes. We do our best, Kamas.'

'If I may ask, Dimas, just what sort of instruction do you provide them?'

'H'm. I must say, Kamas, as a teacher I should perhaps be more active in that respect than I am. I just tell them stories.'

'Stories? What stories, for instance?'

'Well they're mainly from the wayang. I have this hope that they'll follow some of the best models from the various plays.'

At that point I saw Kamas Haji Mansoer smiling broadly.

'Do you know, Dimas, that all the stories of the wayang are in the Koran?'

I was startled. 'The wayang stories are in the Koran?'

'Certainly, Dimas. And not just the wayang stories either. Everything, all manner of things are there. The Koran is Allah's book after all, is it not? Therefore, if we read it with diligence, with devotion, why, we can find anything whatever in it, anything we may be looking for.'

I understood that he hoped my children, and perhaps I too, would at some point take seriously to reciting the Koranic verses, possibly with him, and I promised to speak to the boys about it. I could make that promise, knowing that the two would soon be going away to another town to begin their secondary studies. But as I was returning home from my meeting with the catechist, I suddenly bristled at the memory of what he had said—about the Koran containing the wayang! I was not at all pleased to be told that.

Hardojo—we called him Yok—our second-born, developed into the brightest of our children, and while he was with us the easiest to get along with. He was Soemini's favourite, although Noegroho, most shrewd and practical of our children, also remained close to his ingenuous brother. We parents were very easily swayed to go along with almost any of Hardojo's boyhood plans: he had such an attractive personality, was so amusing, persistent and adroit an arguer. But why, then, when it came to picking a bride did he have to cause such an uproar in the family? Noegroho, in due turn following his sister Soemini, had the year previously married without any complications whatever and now was in the initial stages of raising his own family in Yogya, where he had been posted to teach. Thus he and Soemini were well and truly launched. But Hardojo! The first we heard about the matter of a wife, was when he wrote to us asking whether we would object to him marrying a teacher, a *Kweekschool* graduate who happened to be Catholic! Her family were well-established people, he said, the father taught at the HIS *Katolik* in Solo, and all her side fitted eminently as in-laws. He went on in the letter to describe the girl: sweet, affable, a bit of a coquette, deft, quick-witted, a veritable goddess in looks, Wara Srikandi no less. He was certain that we would both love her.

We put down Hardojo's letter and just looked at each other. A boy who had never troubled anybody or caused difficulties, a boon to his parents—what a thing to drop on us!

3. Sastrodarsono

There was no misunderstanding the letter: the lass seemed decidedly a good choice in all respects as far as our family was concerned; in all respects but one—her religion. Why, oh why could he not have found someone who was just like her but a Muslim, as each and every last member on both sides of his parental family was? Yes, we readily admitted that neither of us, his mother or I, was ever strongly religious, but Muslims we remained. We came from a community bound to that faith: by birth, circumcision, marriage, and the liturgies of burial. Did we not make the great profession of our faith: that there is no god but God, and Muhammad is his prophet? Did we not proclaim our conviction? While this girl, Nunuk, was of a Catholic family, therefore of a religion which, so one heard, was as firmly adhered to by its congregation as ours was by us. Or was this Nunuk prepared to marry according to Islamic rite; or, God grant the hope, would she convert to Islam? But no, if her family had brought her up a strict Catholic, surely they would not permit that. More than likely they would try to convince Hardojo to convert. We were perplexed, could see no way to a solution, and so decided to call a family conference. Hardojo himself, Noegroho, Soemini and her husband were all summoned to Wanagalih to discuss the situation.

The meeting began agreeably: nothing is more pleasant to a Javanese couple of advancing years than being visited by their children and grandchildren, to see them gathered for the ceremony of a family meal, to witness around the table the evidence of replenishing generations. At that time, we were grandparents to only one youngster, Soemini's, who was then nearly two years old. Noegroho's wife, Sus, was seven months pregnant, and with that weight to carry insisted on accompanying her husband. Fortunately, the Yogya-Solo SS was quick and comfortable, so she was not excessively tired when she descended at Paliyan to take a gharry to Wanagalih. My wife was of course greatly troubled to see Sus arriving in her condition, and Noegroho had to reassure her by explaining that they had broken their journey at Solo in Aunt Suminah's house.

'Yes, but have you held a *selamatan* for her seventh month yet? Have you or not? If not, then you absolutely must have the meal here or you'll be struck down with something frightful. Ogre Betoro Kolo will devour the child!'

We laughed.

'Look at you all, laughing! Don't you know about the wife of the salt controller in Sokolilo who gave birth to a deformed baby? She didn't have the ceremony either, didn't observe the seventh month. And there are other examples...'

And examples aplenty there seemed to be, ready to be circumstantiated in all their horror; until Noegroho pacified the noisy contributors by saying that the observance had been carefully followed earlier at the home of his wife's parents in Yogya.

Gentry

We had dinner in a lively and very genial atmosphere, one almost forgotten in our home, now that more often than not the number at our table had declined to just the two of us. Soemini's child was paraded around after its afternoon nap, and stole everybody's heart with its bright ways and chatter. Then we gathered in the middle room and sat at the round table, where so many nights had passed at *kesukan* in the company of our neighbours.

Hardojo initiated things by producing a photo of Nunuk; at which Soemini smiled and said mischievously: 'Aha—look how cunning he is! Aren't you now, Mas? Brings out his girl's photo, and we're won over. And she *is* as sweet as honey. Who could object after seeing that face, don't you all agree?'

We began the discussion in a good humour.

Step by step, in a firm voice and with convincing warmth, Hardojo introduced his Nunuk to us. Her full name was Maria Magdalena Sri Moerniati; she was a primary teacher at a selective school for girls in the Beskalan district of Solo; her father was a teacher at the HIS in Solo's Margoyudan district. Hardojo had met Nunuk at a wedding, and following that they had become friends, then increasingly close. He was on the best of terms with everyone in Nunuk's family.

'They've been treating me like one of them, have for some time. I ask you all, Bapak, Ibu, Mas Noeg, Mini, Mbak Sus and Dimas Harjono for your blessing. I want to marry Nunuk.'

No one spoke for some moments after hearing that one sentence we had all been tensely waiting for. I knew that the others were expecting me to begin and so I asked: 'Tell me, Yok, have you declared your feelings to Nunuk?'

'I have, by implication. And in the same way, she has agreed.'

'H'm,' I muttered. And I thought to myself: They follow some fine new ways, these young ones today. They go looking for their wives, get to know girls before they marry them. Very agreeable, no doubt. I met my wife-to-be the day my father set our wedding date, and now these youngsters practically force their parents to accept any girl they take it into their mind to marry. But I roused myself.

'What do you think, Yok, will her father agree to such a marriage? Give his blessing to it?'

Hardojo did not reply immediately. I glanced at my wife, at Noegroho and his wife, Mini and her husband, all were looking attentively at Hardojo. When I turned back to him I saw he was about to answer.

'Bapak, Ibu, Mas Noeg, Mbak Sus, Mini and Dimas Harjono, what is of first importance to me is your own blessing and agreement. Will you all accept Nunuk as a member of this family? That's the most important thing, Pak.'

Ah, the youth of today! They go and fall in love, head over heels, jostling and impatient, forcing things. And this polite and modest boy has been drawn

3. Sastrodarsono

into that turmoil, has been no exception.

'Whoa, there, boy! Let's be sensible. Our accepting Nunuk as a member of the family is not the important question; in fact when we heard you describing her, when we saw her picture, I think that we were all drawn to her. No, Yok, that's not the problem.'

'Then what is it?'

'Now look, I've always taken you to be a smart kid; and you won't see it?'

Hardojo bowed his head, and I thought that perhaps I should be less brusque; but the issue had to be faced: 'Look, it's like this, Yok. The girl is a Catholic, yes or no?'

'She is.'

'There! And is she prepared to become a member of an Islamic family like ours?'

'You mean, Pak, and all of you, that she must become a Muslim?'

'That's it.'

Biting his lip, he looked around the table and one by one into our faces.

'But do you all believe that this family of ours is really and truly Islamic?'

Noegroho now reacted, startled: 'Hey, what does that mean?'

'I mean, Mas Noeg, have we ever really persisted in following all the requirements of Islam?'

'If you mean praying five times a day and all that, the answer may well be no; but we are Muslims, Yok, Islam is in our soul, and there can be no other religion for us to choose.'

'But I ask you, Mas, can't an Islamic family, one such as ours at that, find room in it for someone who is a Catholic?'

'When it comes to marrying, it gets difficult, Yok. If Nunuk passes into our side of the family, she will need to convert; and if you go to theirs, you'll probably need to convert. Hard, isn't it?'

The talking stopped again. Hardojo looked unhappy and very thoughtful. I tried another way towards an outcome: 'Do you know if Nunuk has approached her parents about this; the way you are doing with us now, Yok?'

'I believe she hasn't yet.'

'Ah, well, then I think we should wait until we see what sort of result she has from them.'

He said nothing, then drew a long breath and sighed: 'God, why do religions put us into compartments like this? Fancy dividing people so that they can't do something as natural as joining in marriage?'

Soemini had been following the conversation with an expression of pity for her favourite brother, and now she broke in to add her opinion to mine: 'Mas Yok, do be patient. I think father's point makes sense, and there's not much good in labouring our way towards some solution here while we don't know how things stand over there.'

'Can we at least decide on one thing now? To accept Nunuk if she converts to Islam?'

Soemini countered: 'There's a more likely possibility that Nunuk's parents will allow her to marry on condition she remains a Catholic and turn the question of converting on you. That's something we would have to come back to discuss, wouldn't we?'

I sat considering how we would deal with first the one possibility, then the other. Harjono, Mini's husband, had remained silent, to the extent that I thought he would merely second whatever Mini contributed. Now he spoke: 'It seems to me, *Mas Yok*, that if it came to you both retaining your religion, then a way out would be to be married not by a priest or imam but at the *burgerlijke stand*. A civil marriage could be the solution.'

Wah, another notion outside our small-town ken here; an option though. But, no. No priest, no imam? Utter hell. What sort of a solution was that? Who would offer the necessary prayers, the blessing? I was about to voice my rejection of such a thing, but stopped myself when I saw poor Hardojo's expression of misery and bewilderment.

My wife entered our deliberations at this point: 'We ought to stop here tonight. It's getting late, and tomorrow we want to cross over to Karangdompol and then go down the river to take a look at the old fort. I've told Mbok Soero that we'll need an early order of her peanut salad. I too think that we should wait until Nunuk has talked to her parents.'

To that there was no more to be said. It was indeed late, the town watch had passed by our house twice, reminding all honest-living dwellers to be vigilant for robbers, and we were all tired. Hardojo alone may have been still anxious to continue.

Then, about a month after this, he visited us again. His expression told us that he was bringing unhappy news.

'Bapak, Ibu—I've lost Dik Nunuk. They will only agree to a church marriage, and I would have to be baptised a Catholic.'

My wife went to our son and hugged him: it was like the spontaneous action of a mother-bird, spreading her wings over a distressed nestling. And I thought of Hardojo's complaint during that first meeting. About how religions so often separate instead of unite.

When I look back on my experience in bringing up our quota of nephews and nieces, I have to conclude that my rate of success was pretty poor. Our own children received a very satisfactory education and went on to good jobs and positions in society; but the results were quite different when it came to their cousins. As I have described, Sri and Soedarmin were removed early from us by their parents, we suspected because they thought us incapable of giving

3. Sastrodarsono

their children a suitably devout upbringing. With Ngadiman, things went slightly better: he obtained a position as a basic clerk in the office of our kabupaten, his parents married him off to one of his cousins, and now they were occupying the little pavilion in our back yard in which all our charges once lived. Yet I did not consider him a real success either. Yes, people treated him as someone better than a commoner, but barely so. His father, my cousin, had hoped his son might become a true priyayi, with the status of my own children; but, sadly, the boy simply was not very clever. He was slow and backward in his lessons, so much so that he failed classes twice, and it was only by my influence with friends in the kabupaten administration and by relying on the help of our lawyer neighbour, that we obtained for the boy his modest situation. It must be said that he did have some few accomplishments, a good, clear writing hand for instance, and he was honest and conscientious; and I had after all to concede that in possessing those alone one was reasonably provisioned for life in such a place as Wanagalih.

My most evident failure and source of continuous anxiety was Soenandar. Some evil spirit must have possessed him in his youngest days. What wicked qualities did he not have? He was cruel, devious, and if not stupid then unteachable; and we found as he grew older that he was a menace to women. Paerah was plagued by such devilry that it almost resulted in her asking to be released back to her village. The rattan appeared to have no effect on him, his behaviour after each beating only worsening. My promise to his mother to keep him in Wanagalih and make something useful out of him, continued in its second part to be unfulfilled. We put him in charge of the men who tended the crops growing behind our house, but his relations with them turned quickly bad: he developed a high-handed, brutal manner. When it came to taking our produce to market, the money he brought back never seemed to tally, and my wife and I tried without success to discover where the missing amounts went, whether they disappeared in gambling or on prostitutes.

The worry with Soenandar often had me mulling more generally over what precisely it was that had caused those disappointments with him and the other children given into my charge. Had I not attended to them enough, was my concern for them not warm enough, so that they felt themselves to be outsiders? It seemed to me, during those moments of reflection, that I definitely *had* cared for them. I had sent them all to HIS, just as I had my own children; we had been forced by consideration of space to put them in that back pavilion, but there was nothing poor or overly-cramped about it; and their food, also, was surely sufficient: usually taken in their own quarters, but often enough eaten with us in the house as well? Or did we make them feel ill at ease and embarrassed to be beholden to us? God forbid that they should have felt constricted in our home, and their development been curbed!

Gentry

Granted that Javanese upbringing tended to instil a habit of diffidence in the presence of one's elders and superiors, and sometimes when exaggerated that led from deference to awe to dread; but I often reminded myself of the solemn advice once imparted to me by my benefactor, the late Romo Seten Kedungsimo:

'A good priyayi, my son, accepts the respect of subordinates and in turn respects those above him. Could our hierarchies and our society exist without that respect? An unimaginable situation. Sensitive giving and receiving of respect practices us in awareness of the true circumstances of others, including their feelings, and on occasion their distress and suffering. Those without the ability to respect, and are covetous for honours only to themselves, will not be respected. However, no one should be immobilised by excessive respect. A priyayi must after all still know when and how to act.'

Had those youngsters from the villages, put into my charge by their families, had, despite my heeding such advice to the best of my ability, been overawed and shrunk into themselves? But what about Soenandar then? 'Respect' and 'awe' were words foreign to him.

One day, without our expecting it, a letter came from Mas Martoatmodjo. It appeared he now lived on his teacher's pension in Surabaya and was running a private *schakel particulier*, an informal 'gap' school located in the Plampitan district there. It seems he had found retirement boring, and the teaching he was doing, he wrote, although falling outside that approved by the colonial inspectorate did represent modest social work serving to advance the community. My wife and I were very pleased to receive such news from this admirable man. We replied immediately to express our happiness and relief at learning that he and his family had apparently survived well their exile in the eastern wilds of the island. When I added an invitation to visit us in Wanagalih, my wife said that she doubted it would be taken up: that old Karangjambu affair would remain too much of an issue with them, she predicted. I smiled, and thought to myself that women often have such queer ideas; but a reply came soon after, in which Mas Martoatmodjo apologised for not being able to accept our invitation at present.

'There, Pak, wasn't I right? You just twisted your mouth when I said they wouldn't come.'

I smiled again. But there was another interesting part to the letter. The village head at Wanalawas, Pak Soetoredjo, who was a cousin of Mas Marto's wife, lamented that there had never been a village school in his community, not even a three-year one, so that many children had missed any chance of getting the most basic education, and the current younger ones were about to miss out too. A few had been released by their parents to attend school in such villages in the neighbourhood of Wanagalih as had one, but was Wanalawas as a whole doomed forever to turn out nothing more than peddlers of

3. Sastrodarsono

tempeh and teak leaves, brewers of arak? Was there no hope that an educated individual, a pioneer priyayi, would someday emerge from there? Mas Marto wondered if I might not be able to help raise at least a three-year school in Wanalawas. I had good relations with many officials in the kabupaten: could I not do something for Pak Dukuh Soeto and his people?

I immediately set about canvassing that possibility among my contacts, going so far as to make inquiries with one or two of the assistant district chiefs; but somehow I could get no settled answer from anybody. Perhaps it was felt that Wanalawas was sufficiently provided for, being considered relatively near Wanagalih and to several other villages with schools in the Madiun River zone. If that was the reason, I found it unsatisfactory, and during further exchanges with Mas Marto he finally asked me whether I would like to try on my own initiative to open a '*sekolah partikelir*' in Wanalawas, such a school as he presently taught in and had described to us. I was affected by the concern which Mas Marto showed for the little village, and became quite aroused by the thought of such a project; and so one Sunday I took Ngadiman and Soenandar with me, and riding bicycles we went to Wanalawas to have a talk with Pak Dukuh Soetoredjo. A crowd of villagers soon gathered outside his house, among them many children ranging from about three years to those who, I could see, should at their age have been sitting regularly on school benches. The children's clothing was tattered and unkempt, they were runny-nosed, their eyes were inflamed, and I could tell from the russet tinge of their dry and tangled hair that they spent little time indoors. Nor was it a healthy freedom, for their legs were covered in scabs, while other bare areas of their bodies showed the white blotches of skin fungus. Yet, I detected no particular expressions of wretchedness in the younger children, for they jostled happily, chased each other; and it was only among those of both sexes who were approaching young adulthood that I noted what I thought was a sort of quiet dejection or resignation, a torpor in their movements. It was from the older group of adults, the parents and elders surrounding Pak Dukuh, that I caught better signs of spirit and questioning looks. As I considered this crowd of villagers pressing about me, I suddenly felt as with a sharp pang the sensation of standing in a foreign place, populated by a backward race arrested in common misery. And yet, these who were responsible for that strange sadness dwelled quite close to us, only a few kilometres from the Wanagalih where we conducted our daily life!

'*Wah*, Ndoro Mantri Guru, all this is just our people eager to look at a real headmaster. It's been a long time since such a high priyayi, a priyagung from Wanagalih, visited us. May we hope Ndoro Mantri is well, lacks nothing?'

'Yes, yes, Pak Dukuh, I'm fine, thank you. And very grateful to you all for your welcome. I too hope that you who have come here and all in the village are well.'

Gentry

Such sanguine concern for each other's wellbeing was elaborated for some time, as one by one all the worthies assembled there were introduced to me. Our *wong cilik* are admirable in the way poverty and a wretched life never seem to eliminate their love of long-winded salutations and retarding etiquette. We eventually got to the questions of education and livelihood. Pak Soetoredjo repeated to me what he had written to Mas Martoatmodjo, that the villagers of Wanalawas had been long pained to see their children approaching adulthood without ever having gone to school. When I asked why there should be such an interest here in schooling, while in Karangdompol it was a difficult thing persuading many parents to release their children, Pak Dukuh began a rambling explanation:

'In Karangdompol, Ndoro, they have good rice land and don't like to lose the labour of their children. They need them in the paddies, both the small ones and the older ones. Here, farming is harder, it's always been dryland crops relying on the rain. We only have a little stream, and the well is often dry. So people here live by making tempeh, they gather teak leaf and *ploso* leaf for wrapping food, and then some also brew arak, and that's about all. The situation of the young ones here, Ndoro, is desperate, and all they see ahead is hard work from an early age, and that they will end up like their parents. It's sad to think that Wanalawas should go on like this forever. I turn to you all, you fathers and mothers, do we want this to go on?'

'No-o, Pak Dukuh, we don't wa-ant, Pak Dukuh!'

The reply, given in ragged unison by the villagers crowding near the house, sounded hardly enthusiastic, and it reminded me of sheep being driven on Tuesdays to the animal market behind Setenan Road. I thought to sound them out further to see just how aware and determined they actually were regarding the difficulties of setting up a school.

'Now look, Pak Dukuh, I ask you, is everyone here really firm about this?'

'*Inggi-ih!*'

'So you people truly want a school then?'

'Tru-uly . . . Wa-ant . . .'

There was that herd-noise again.

'But when you have the school, what then, what's it all for?'

This time there was no reply and most of them looked blankly at each other. Finally, here and there individual voices rose from the crowd:

'For to learn to read, Ndoro.'

'For to count.'

'All right. And when you've learned to read and write and to count, what will you do then?'

Again, they looked at one another; until someone at the back spoke up: 'Work in the kabupaten office then, Ndoro.'

3. Sastrodarsono

I glanced at Ngadiman and Soenandar, who had both been silently following the conversation. Ngadiman appeared to smile thinly, probably remembering his own difficulties in class and at the office, while Soenandar's face was expressionless. I turned to the village head and suggested that the time had come to discuss a few details in his house, and he, some elders, my two nephews and I went inside. But as we were filing in I happened to look back at the departing villagers, dismissed a moment ago by Pak Dukuh, and once again their dreary, colourless throng reminded me of beasts driven to market. I asked myself why I should see them in that light now, while formerly, in Kedungsimo, I had been just such a one as they were, and I drew my breath in astonishment and shook my head at this revelation of the distance I had travelled since those years.

At that meeting in the dukuh's house I proposed to set up as a trial a small class in reading and writing for children of seven years and some few others above that age who had never been to school. In addition, we considered how we might find time for instructing any adults who wanted to learn to read and write. I decided to leave Soenandar behind in the village, to act as a permanent teacher and administrator, while I with Ngadiman would come from Wanagalih twice a week: each Thursday afternoon and all day Sunday. Soenandar was visibly taken aback by this verdict, but I endeavoured to impress on him that in helping the *wong cilik* he was engaging in honourable employment, and that it would be for his own eventual good to undertake some active work among people.

'Don't forget, my dear lad, that you too came from such a village and was a child of people like these!'

Soenandar in response to my tone could hardly dare say more than '*Inggih*', but I saw that his acceptance of this new role was less than wholehearted. His thieving had awakened some dissolute tastes in him which could scarcely be satisfied in a poverty-stricken hamlet. But, who could tell? This might prove precisely the thing to direct him into a life of duty and devotion to the interests of others less fortunate than himself. I must say, though, that I was somewhat surprised at my own decision.

And I have also to admit that I had not foreseen what a burden the whole project was going to be. As a minimum, I had to find slates, slate-pencils, chalk, and a blackboard. As for benches and tables, I had no idea where those would come from. Obviously, it all would involve expense: who could I ask for help? But what I had not expected was my own pleasure and the enthusiasm which gripped me with the opening of that little school. Something of the spirit of Mas Marto moved me perhaps, and a sense of satisfaction I am sure he would have recognised. My wife's help was invaluable, and its wholeheartedness was more than I had expected, considering the disapproval she had previously shown towards Mas Marto's views and activities. She may have joined me in admiring the bravery and resolve of that family, but I knew that she retained an element of concern that we should not seem too closely associated with it. Also, I sent word about the project to all our children, and Hardojo was the first to respond with money, and even with an offer of his own services whenever needed. What touched me most was the pride he wrote he felt when he learned about this initiative of mine. Noegroho as usual wanted to consider carefully how the thing might best succeed and not be just lightly launched on the urge of some philanthropic ideal. Cold rationality was needed for it to prosper, he said. But he too sent money, together with not a few suggestions about how best to spend it: he the most 'Dutch' of my children.

Soemini, as the wife now of a high official, an assistant district chief and climbing, sent the expected cautions: 'Father, you need to be attentive that your good work is not seen to be connected in any way with Pakdé Marto. Even if he is now outside the *gupermen* school system, they still have him under surveillance. He is presently suspected of being involved with the *Partai Nasional Indonesia*.'

She too, loyal daughter, sent money. Ah, my excellent children!

Finally, everything was ready and teaching could begin. All the materials, humble as they were, had been gathered. Rude but serviceable benches and a table were fashioned from local timbers by a co-operative of the villagers. The class was set up in the front room of Pak Dukuh's house, the most spacious place in the hamlet for such a purpose.

As to Soenandar, he lodged with Mbok Soemo, an elderly widow with a daughter, Ngadiyem. Both women lived by making and selling tempeh. I must say that I was somewhat uneasy placing Soenandar there, partly in view of the proprieties, but mainly because of my all-too-precise knowledge of that young man's character. I conferred with the village head: was there no alternative place for Soenandar? But that worthy's view was that Mbok Soemo's house was the best, being uncrowded, clean, and, unusually in such a poor settlement, possessed a partitioned room. Pak Dukuh's own quarters were crammed with children, evacuated from the designated classroom, and other houses in the village were no better in that respect. There was nothing for it then, and the Soemo house was at least close to the school, and therefore to Pak's oversight; and so with some remnant of concern I gave in. But that last uneasiness was quickly overtaken by the happiness of witnessing the successful beginnings of our venture; nevertheless, I made sure that Ngadiman kept an eye on that often-straying cousin of his; while I repeatedly lectured Soenandar about the credit he would bring to the family, the fine, worthwhile results for others that his best efforts might achieve; adding, just in case, a threat to throw him out into the street if he caused anything untoward to happen. Each time, as usual, whether to my encouragement or commands,

3. Sastrodarsono

he bowed his head submissively. He could display the powerlessness of a sheep when it suited him.

In any event, in a few months the school was a reality and things seemed to be progressing well: the children attended their reading, writing, and arithmetic lessons regularly; and between times, to enliven matters, we taught them various part-songs in the nature of nursery rhymes. These were just ditties commonly sung by children gathering in impromptu choirs during moonlit nights in Wanagalih and Karangdompol, but I was astonished to learn that here they had never been heard before. Was Wanalawas then so remote that its children should gaze at us in amazement when they heard such trifles for the first time? And this Wanalawas, according to legend, was the original seed-bed of Wanagalih, now the capital of an important kabupaten in the regency of Madiun!

Yet, what amazed us more, and touched my heart profoundly, was the sight of parents also trooping in to be taught, and the pleasure and zeal *they* showed. It was something to see those hands, stiff and awkward and rough from heavy work in fields and kitchens, taking up a slate-pencil and a slate, moving wrists and fingers to a totally unfamiliar rhythm, their owners laughing at failures, undiscouraged, persisting; and then to hear the surrounding applause as one by one each adult learned to grasp and manoeuvre the pencil effectively!

My two nephews seemed now to demonstrate their true worth for the first time, carrying out their work faithfully as I had apportioned it to them. Ngadiman could finally display his superiority as a calligraphist before creatures infinitely less talented than himself, and his interest never flagged. Soenandar, with quite unsuspected new energy, fulfilled his duties diligently, perhaps braced by his responsibility and by seeing himself as the one on whom the wellbeing of the project depended; or perhaps because the sense of authority gratified him; or, finally, because he found himself living in increasingly good relations with the girl Ngadiyem, who was pleasant-looking and for an inhabitant of a deprived village kept herself spotless.

However, somewhat less than a year after the school's opening, and all its courses progressing healthily—the blow fell! Everything must cease. The whole endeavour, the pride of our family, must needs shut down. Totally. Allah so wished it, I had to suppose.

I was distressed, shattered. And how ashamed I felt towards the people of Wanalawas, towards Pak Dukuh, Mbok Soemo, her daughter Ngadiyem, and towards all those who could now to some useful extent write, who were beginning to read those elementary story-books I had begged from all sorts of places, who had even been proceeding to relatively difficult calculations! How sorry I felt for the children, choiring now those simple lyrics of farming life, raising *standens*, turning somersaults during intervals between lessons!

There were two reasons for this sudden reversal.

Unannounced, Ndoro *Schoolopziener* arrived at my school in Karangdompol and without any preliminary formalities confronted me thus: 'Mantri, I've received a report that you and others have opened a school in Wanalawas. Is it true?'

'Why yes, it is true, Ndoro *Opziener*.'

This was an inspector younger than the one who had caused the removal of Mas Martoatmodjo, and one even more arrogant, who considered himself of the *Raden* level in the official nobility and thus required that he be addressed as *Ndoro*.

'But don't you people know that that's contrary to regulations?'

'Why no, Ndoro. I mean, when all's said and done what we have there could hardly be called a school at all. It's just a small class helping the villagers and their children to read and write. And it's carried on outside my working hours here, Ndoro.'

'That's quite irrelevant, Mantri. It's a wild school, you can't do it, and that's the end of it.'

I said nothing for a moment and bowed my head. Then I spoke again, carefully offering a desperate rationalisation which I hoped might just save matters: 'Ndoro, might I say that this so-called school has been a project conducted by my family as admirers of Raden Ajeng Kartini? By opening it, we have simply been responding to the modernising encouragements of that great lady.'

'Oh, come now! What would you say if I submitted a report indicating that it was all started on an initiative of that Martoatmodjo?'

'Well, yes, Ndoro. I've known Kamas Martoatmodjo well, being the one who replaced him as headmaster here. And he did tell me about the sad situation in Wanalawas, so . . .'

'So don't waste time trying to wriggle out of it! Look, I just want to help you, Mantri. Martoatmodjo is an activist, he's being held in Surabaya, and there's no more to be said about this matter. Close down the school and I won't take any action. And anyway, Mantri, if you had continued, tell me, what would your villagers and their children have expected to do with their new knowledge of reading, writing and counting? What's the point? They would have gone on with their miserable lives just as before.'

I bowed my head again. Angry, affronted, and sad as I was, I had to admit to myself that such a cruel perception did have its truth. I had hoped that perhaps I might have eventually steered at least some of those children towards work in the towns, and they could have gradually pulled more of their relatives into promising spheres. But how that would have turned out in fact was now beyond knowing, I was powerless before the disapproval of a *schoolopziener*. Disobedience was impossible; there were many things to consider if I attempted to persist with the school: my name would be blighted, my friends and acquaintances would point me out as someone, the headmaster of a government school, who had dared to defy the government. I had to consider the position of my own children if my repute were to be blackened in this way, how they would fare if I stubbornly continued with a project which had received its death sentence from my superiors. They, my children, would be drawn into my own misfortune, would be condemned by their own circles, by their colleagues and perhaps by their relatives-in-law. And suddenly it occurred to me that there was a question here too of my advancing age, and, as my wife and I grew older and would expect to depend more on our children and grandchildren, their lives and welfare had become of pragmatic concern to us. I reflected on the history of such people as Mas Martoatmodjo. I could not stop thinking with wonder about their determination in adhering to what they thought was important, adhering to the outmost, while taking into account the plight of their families: knowing that not only they themselves would almost certainly fall into wretchedness by defying the *gupermen*, but accepting that their children's future would also be blocked in that event. I was awestruck by their fortitude and their integrity, yet it remained incomprehensible to me that they were prepared to gamble in this way with the fortunes of their loved ones. Once again, I looked back to Romo Seten Kedungsimo, a priyayi, a knightly, noble figure, who loved the people he was set above, yet someone who acted without rashness, with due consideration and measured steps. He had known defeat too, but had kept his name unsullied by the taint of rebellion, nor had he sacrificed his wife and children to his cause. He had given way, so that his children might seek and pursue their own path in life.

But the second matter confirming the demise of the school in Wanalawas was an event occurring in that place itself, an event which I felt heaped even more shame on me and on my family. One afternoon Pak Dukuh Wanalawas arrived breathless at my home in Setenan Road.

'A disaster, Ndoro Mantri, a disaster! . . . I have some terrible news, Ndoro Mantri!'

'*Lho*! What on earth is it, Pak Dukuh?'

Pak Dukuh collected himself, bowed his head, and when he raised it again his expression was pained and anxious.

'A thousand pardons, Ndoro Mantri, a thousand pardons—Gus Soenandar has gone!'

'Gone? Gone where?'

Pak Dukuh bowed respectfully again—and not for the first time it occurred to me with some irritation that there were occasions when all this obeisance by the lower orders might well be curtailed! Renewing his pleas for pardon, he finally exclaimed: 'He's run off!'

'Eh? Run off? Are you certain? He hasn't just gone for a stroll to Wanagalih?'

'No, Ndoro . . .'

And the whole story came out. It seems that Soenandar having lived for some time in Mbak Soemo's house had won Ngadiyem's affections. The mother—long considered a widow, ever since her husband had disappeared on a *rantau* somewhere and never returned—was quite flushed with happiness and pride to see the developing relations between the youngsters, happy that life was returning to her humble and always silent home. To the old woman, life up to the time of Soenandar's arrival had been nothing other than a constant round of preparing and peddling tempeh, each long day bound by the same two events: the rising of the sun in the east, to the crowing of roosters, and its setting in the west, to the chirp of crickets. And the joy and new excitement was also felt and displayed by her daughter, whose cheerful laughter was heard frequently now, and her face brightened with smiles; even the work of making and selling tempeh seemed to have grown lighter.

The relationship between the young pair burgeoned, until one day Ngadiyem found that something had happened to her menstruation and she felt that a change was occurring to her body. When she told her mother, the overjoyed woman threw her arms around her daughter, told her excitedly that this was the happiest news possible, that she, her dear girl—imagine—was carrying the seed of a priyayi! But when Soenandar was told, he said nothing, and in the days following his face took on a dismal cast and he began to grow fretful and angry towards Embok Soemo and her daughter. He now claimed that the house was too hot or too small, the side-dishes to the rice were inedible and peasant-fare; and, finally, he snapped at Ngadiyem that she stank of old tempeh! Then one night he disappeared. Mbok Soemo and Ngadiyem only discovered that he had gone when next morning they found Soenandar's room empty, his clothes gone from the rack where they had hung, and—the final, awful stroke—there had been a money-box, a poor clay thing in the shape of a hen, kept on a bamboo shelf and containing all that the women possessed—it too had gone. Bewildered, distraught, the two had run to tell Pak Dukuh, who thus became acquainted with how things had developed between Soenandar and Ngadiyem up to this calamity.

'And that is how it has turned out, Ndoro Mantri. A thousand pardons, Ndoro Mantri. It's God's punishment on all of us in Wanalawas for being so careless, Ndoro Mantri.'

I could barely control my fury or my tongue. I felt shame, shame, and more shame towards the people of that little community. I could only hiss: 'Oh that devil Soenandar! Oh that sneak thief!' Then: 'Enough, Pak Dukuh.

3. Sastrodarsono

This is not your fault or anybody's fault in Wanalawas. It's that rotten scoundrel Soenandar, one of my boys. I'm going to look for him until I get hold of him, and then I'll drag him by the collar to Wanalawas and make him marry Ngadiyem! Leave it to me, Pak Dukuh, go back now. Tell Mbok Soemo and Ngadiyem to be patient and trust in God. I'll get Soenandar back for them, I assure you all!'

For many days after this I tried with Ngadiman to track Soenandar down, looked for news of him in every shop and stall, every wayside booth where vehicles stopped to pick up passengers, every cheap restaurant, gambling den, and riverside brothel. Having given people Soenandar's full description, one or two thought they may have seen him, but no one could tell us with any certainty where he had gone. We finally put the matter in the hands of the police; I even made a plea personally to Wanagalih's mantri polisi for his help in tracing this crazy nephew of mine. For weeks I and my wife waited, filling the time with questioning ourselves and self-reproaches: how had we erred? We mulled endlessly on that, trying to discover our fault, and, having failed to find it, we sought once again to plumb the nature of this boy. It seemed as if no manner of instruction, no correction of any severity had the slightest effect on him. He was clearly bent on doing precisely what he pleased. But what was that? Merely to be destructive? My wife could only say that it was a relief that Soenandar's mother had died: the poor woman's heart would have finally broken, hearing of this latest escapade.

Kamas Mantri Polisi at last sent a messenger to our house: my presence was requested at the station. When I arrived in his office he pointed to a photograph. It had been taken of a band of criminals led by one Samin Genjik, 'the Boar': a reckless gamecock of a man, who despite having a deformed leg and a limp was considered by the populace to possess uncanny powers. In the photo, Samin stood between two policemen with slung carbines and drawn sabres, while behind this trio could be made out a row of his crew, captives likewise guarded by police. I found myself looking, within that row, at the face of none other than Soenandar! . . . Allah spares us! Soenandar, a nephew of mine, son of one of my nearest cousins, the boy she had put into my hands to be made a priyayi—a member of Samin Genjik's robber band!

'Where can I meet my nephew, Kamas?'

The mantri looked at me for a moment, and then made his reply in a measured tone:

'I'm sorry to have to tell you this, Dimas. This photo was taken some weeks ago, following the arrest of these men after a robbery in the Gorang-Gareng area. After the photo had been taken, while they were being escorted to Madiun, they managed to break free and to beat off the police. How that was done is being investigated. They fled to an empty house in a kampong and were surrounded. A local shaman who was aware of Samin's reputation for magical powers advised that the house should be set alight. The police and the villagers did that. The house was burned to the ground.'

'And the robbers, Kamas?'

'I'm afraid, Dimas, they were all killed, totally consumed in the fire. Including, I'm sorry to say, your boy.'

I returned home utterly despondent. What a terrible fate, what a contemptible end! What unimaginable sin could Soenandar's parents have committed to produce such a doomed child? Next day I went to Wanalawas on an even direr and saddening errand, to confront Mbok Soemo and Ngadiyem. For the length of the road to the village I racked my brains for the best way to tell them what had happened. The village head accompanied me to their house. I noticed for the first time that it seemed to be sagging somewhat and needed repairs, had an abandoned look, and the yard around it was filled with tall, coarse grass. Inside we found Ngadiyem and her mother sitting lost in a muse, their eyes expressionless when they turned them towards us. The girl was now visibly pregnant.

'Come now, Mbok Soemo, Genduk Ngadiyem. It's the will of Allah. The Almighty has prepared for each of us our part in life. We can do no more than follow dutifully what He has granted us. Patience and resigned trust—isn't that the best way now, Mbok Soemo, Genduk Ngadiyem?'

The two bent their heads low in apparent agreement, but I could now see tears on their cheeks.

'And as for the child later, don't worry. It will be like one of my own grandchildren after all. I'll see to it that you won't be short. Pak Dukuh and I will be talking about that side of things. So don't worry, all right? If you need anything, ask Pak Dukuh. He'll deal with it. So there won't be any need for you two to go to Wanagalih, understand? We'll look after each other, pray for each other. *Insya Allah*, everything will turn out well.'

The village head too wanted to contribute something cheering: 'So, it's all clear now, Mbok Soemo? Ngadiyem? Any problems you have for Ndoro Mantri, you just tell me, right? You'll have nothing to worry about now.'

After I had stopped at the head's house to discuss how I was to help the pair with money when they should need it, I prepared to leave. Passing through the front room I saw that the benches and blackboard of our class were still there. The room was dusty and there were already spiderwebs: the head apparently out of some forlorn hope had still not repossessed it. I drew a deep breath as the memory of those first days returned to me. Outside in the yard, and then on the paths through the village, those now muddy in the early days of the wet season, I slowly rode on my bicycle past children playing unconcernedly. Excited groups leaped about on grids marked for catch-me-if-you-can in the soft ground; and in my gloomy state of mind I hoped it was

3. Sastrodarsono

the passion of the game and not some deliberate indifference that was the reason they did not stop to salute an old teacher.

I never returned to visit the two women in Wanalawas again.

4. LANTIP: the hero resolves

That night, after I had seen Ndoro Guru Kakung leave on his way back to Wanagalih, I left the fence and returned thoughtfully to my mother's house. One by one, the people of the village said their good-byes to Pakdé Soeto and to me, until at last only he and I remained. I approached him uncertainly and asked if he would take a seat, and he, apparently aware that the night had not yet ended for him, good-naturedly went to one of the crude chairs in the house. He took out tobacco and a leaf of corn from his purse, rolled himself a cigarette, lit it and drew deeply on it. He continued smoking like that for some moments, patiently watching me.

'Pakdé, I want to ask you some questions.'

'Oh, questions, boy?'

I gathered myself to ask things that had been building up in me for a long time now.

'Pakdé . . .'

I took another breath and began again: 'Pakdé, who are my parents?'

Pakdé Soeto smiled.

'Clearly now, Lé, you're Ngadiyem's boy. Ngadiyem, whom we together buried this afternoon.'

'Yes, I know that she was my mother, but who was actually my father then?'

Once again Pakdé Soeto drew deeply on his cigarette.

'Well, who did your mother say he was? Did she talk to you about your father?'

'She did speak of him sometimes, when I asked her.'

'And what did she tell you?'

'She said he was someone from these parts. That he was away on a *rantau* now, to earn money.'

'Well then, what else do you want to know, if that was what your mother said?'

'Yes, I know that's what she said, Pakdé. I suppose I should be happy with that. It's just that when you, Pakdé, were talking with Ndoro Guru Kakung, I got to feel that he knew Wanalawas well, and knew people here well too. And I heard you saying that there had been a school here set up by Ndoro Guru. I never heard of that before. And as far as I know, Ndoro Guru Kakung and Putri only met my mother when she came to bring them tempeh.'

4. Lantip

Pakdé Soeto said nothing, only smoked on.

'And also, Pakdé, I remember there were times when Ndoro Guru lost at cards and called me all sorts of names if I didn't bring him more money quickly: things like "offspring of a thief", and he shouted something about a robber band. I didn't know what to think then, Pakdé. And now I wonder whether my mother and Ndoro Guru Kakung have known some secret about my father. And also when I think about how kindly I was taken into their house in Setenan Road . . .'

Pakdé Soeto said nothing for such a long time that I finally burst out accusingly: 'Pakdé, are you keeping some secret from me too . . . about my father?'

At last he stubbed out his cigarette, and after fixing a long, appraising look on me began: 'Wagé, my boy . . . now don't mind if I call you Wagé and not Lantip tonight: if I'm to answer your question the name seems to go better with the whole tale of your father. Very well then, I'll tell you the secret which has been buried in this village many years. I just want you to do two things.'

'Yes, Pakdé.'

'First, don't interrupt me and just listen on bravely, calmly. Secondly, you must promise that after you've heard this thing that I'm about to tell you, you won't repeat it to anyone or reproach anyone, and especially not Ndoro Mantri Guru Kakung or Putri. Agreed?'

I felt my heart beat faster as I listened to these conditions. This secret must certainly concern some terrible matter.

'Yes, Pakdé.'

Pakdé said nothing further until he had rolled and lit another cigarette and then drawn on it.

'Your father, Lé, was Den Bagus Soenandar, the nephew of Ndoro Mantri Guru Kakung . . .'

And the tale continued in this way, as I recall it and reproduce it more or less in Pakdé's words:

'Your father was the son of a first female cousin of Ndoro Mantri Guru Kakung; therefore, he was second cousin to the teacher's own children. They say that your father came from a remote area fairly distant from Kedungsimo, which was the native village of Ndoro Mantri's family. That remote area was somewhere in the foothills of Mount Lawu and not very fertile. Den Bagus Soenandar's father and uncles were all peasants. However, it seems that unlike the other brothers, your father's father descended into really dire impoverishment. Your father's mother appears to have been kept at some disadvantage by her brothers—there were no other sisters—and when she was married off to your grandfather, the couple had less than one hectare of land. Now compare that with the three to four hectares of paddy that each of your uncles owned, not to mention the area of land Ndoro Guru has now! So you see the contrast there in your father's beginnings with those of others; and even more so with what he met later in Setenan Road. Ndoro Mantri Guru was fortunate in having a father who despite being a peasant was forward-looking, who let his son be educated and become a teacher and is now Mantri Guru, and so obviously far more highly regarded than any of his family who remained villagers. Such are the things that can distance people from one another: means, or lack of them; opportunity, or lack of it. Now your father, if I am not mistaken, had no brothers or sisters, was a sole child as far as I know; but despite that advantage he was still the child of a poor family, compared to his relatively comfortably-off cousins. From his earliest days, he had to work hard to help his parents make a living. It's possible to imagine the grudge he might have felt towards his friends and cousins, who would have appeared privileged and spoiled. Whenever he had time to join the other children's groups and games he would have felt belittled and ignored—mind, Wagé lad, these are my own thoughts, but I've had a long time to think on the matter. Now perhaps the boy, this boy who was to become your father, felt left out of things and unjustly done by. He grew quarrelsome, aggressive towards others. The low point of the family's fortunes happened when his father suddenly died from some kind of stomach ache which developed into a fever. The mother and son were left in utter bewilderment, hopeless. By good fortune, Ndoro Guru, just a young teacher then, stretched out his hand to them, touched by the plight of this woman who had been excluded and ignored by her own brothers. And that's how the boy Soenandar arrived at Setenan Road in Wanagalih, where he was taken in with other nephews and a niece, was well-received and brought up well, just as they were. But it would appear that the damage had been done, your father's outlook on things was by then set.'

The story continued with Pakdé's generous excusing of my father's descent into recalcitrance and then petty crime: as products of young pride, as self-esteem unsettled by generosity as much as it had been in the past by perceived rejection. He described the boy's removal from school, the new hope placed in him as a young man by the opportunity to teach in Wanalawas, the joy and subsequent anguish when the promise of mutual affection between him and Ngadiyem, my mother, was dashed by his abandoning her, pregnant. It was at this point in the tragedy that Pakdé had begun his efforts to bury its details, urging the people of Wanalawas and anyone else with whom his influence counted to maintain a kindly, discreet silence. It was done out of compassion for that wretched family which had already once endured the departure and disappearance of Mbok Soemo's husband, only to see something similar repeated in her daughter's turn. The account of my father's death after joining a gang of robbers ended the story, and Pakdé summed up:

4. Lantip

'Yes, such is the tale. I heard some of it from Ndoro Mantri Guru, some from your mother herself, and of course I was there too. I haven't added or left out anything of the facts known to me, haven't made your father a better person than he was, nor, as you heard, did I make him out to be altogether bad. We all have our faults, and that was how it was with him; so accept it, Lé, and when you go to bed at night pray for the loosening of his sins, the forgiveness of the dark things he did, so that his journey in the hereafter may grow lighter. Be strong and resolute, and don't forget your promise. What I've said is for you only, not to be spread around. Don't ask anything else from Ndoro Mantri Kakung or Putri nor claim anything from them. Your mother never did.'

It was almost dawn by the time Pakdé Soeto had ended the story and tirelessly added to it further advice and encouragements. Finally, as the cocks answered each other, and the eastern sky lightened, we stopped talking. Before the kind old man left for his home and whatever rest remained in the next hour or so, I thanked him with all sincerity for having revealed to me so much that had been unknown and kept hidden.

So that was how things stood. It seems that I was an illegitimate child, born in sin; my father had not wanted to marry my mother; and on top of that he had been a criminal, one of a gang of robbers. Everything I had heard flung at me in moments of impatience by Ndoro Guru Kakung had been facts: I *was* the child of a thief and so on. I sat for some time thinking, trying to better understand and settle in my mind all that I had heard. Certain things were now clearer: why my grandmother had acted so queerly, brooded, muttered to herself, seemed unhappy with herself as much as with anyone else. I understood what my mother meant when she said that Embah Wedok had become like that because she had been deserted by those she had loved or placed hopes in. And I could see why my mother tried so hard to keep the secret of my father's identity hidden: it was done for my sake, that I should not feel ashamed, rather than for her own, to hide a transgression. She wanted me to keep the possibility of imagining a wonderful father. And it was clear why she had persisted in her self-denying efforts to bring me into the circle of the family on Setenan Road: she had wanted me, even at the cost of surrendering me, to sample something of the better life of a priyayi, to partake in it at least, since I had been deprived of it in full.

O how sorry I felt for the two women, my mother and grandmother, for their unfortunate lives! I felt such sorrow and regret now, thinking of that time when I lived as a young boy in my mother's house. Now that I knew how she had suffered, I was astonished and felt even greater respect for the firmness with which she met the problems of her life. I remembered how she made time to teach me those children's songs which we would sing together during moonlit nights; and it was a pathetic thought that most of those were songs which my father would have brought to our village when that class of his was still in being. From that tiny income which she earned selling tempeh, my mother still could spend one cent or two cents for some little dainty or market-toy to bring home for me. And under the burdens of her existence, she still smiled, still laughed: for I remembered the ring of her laughter during those happy times when we lived together. An exceptional woman she had been, a noble one. And as I recreated to myself all her aspects, more clear now in the light of my new knowledge, I grew better able to free her from my mind and to farewell her. I was now able to see her death as a merciful release from the pain she had known in this world; and except that I made this act of relinquishment towards her shade, that pain would only have been prolonged in any forlorn memory I kept of her.

And as for my father? Another sad existence had ended there as well. In his early days luck and opportunity had passed him by, he had known only poverty, and inherited little from a father incapable of helping him to compete with others in life's race. My father's slyness and cruelty were at least no longer inexplicable if they resulted from hopelessness and a sort of mad fury in someone impatient and unacquainted from birth with the possibilities of acquired skills and an educated intelligence. So let his shade also pass on. Whatever else, infamous criminal that he was, he had done one good thing that I could bless him for: he had caused me to be born from the body of such a loving if unlucky woman as my mother.

And what of that noble, gracious couple, Ndoro Guru Kakung and Putri? What else could I feel towards them but gratitude and an inestimable indebtedness, unrepayable as long as I lived? I would go back to their home, to return to their protection, but live to serve them and their family. I would no longer be hurt by those old allusions, but would on the contrary heighten my esteem for those who despite their truth had taken me in. I would uphold the name of Sastrodarsono and strive to inter any dishonour to it.

After the third-day's *selamatan* meal at Wanalawas, Kang Trimo arrived to take me back. As I passed through the village I detected nothing unusual in the placid expression of people: the secret remained safe with them.

As with other places in Java, the Japanese army entered and took possession of Wanagalih without difficulty. The Jamus Bridge across the Madiun River, the only iron bridge linking the town with areas east of the river, was blown up by the Dutch, but that did little to slow the Japanese advance. My feeling at the time was that suddenly, virtually overnight, the Japanese were everywhere. They quickly took over all government offices, and the wheels of the previous administration ground rapidly to a halt. Announcements were put up all over town threatening instant shooting of anyone caught stealing, and

4. Lantip

those warnings were taken very seriously by the populace. All kinds of stories and rumours about the extraordinary might of Dai Nippon circulated everywhere and understandably enough took on the character of myths. A horde of gnomes, bald-headed, bow-legged, eyes aslant, had easily defeated the tall, bearded *Longo* who had dominated the land of Java for centuries. Obviously, these were no ordinary pygmies. A race of people who could overthrow the descendants of *Marjangkung*—that Jan Peterszoon Coen who had defeated Sultan Agung in the 1600s—must certainly have invincible dark powers and might not be taken lightly or provoked. Thus their arrival was met by the ordinary Javanese with total awe, and their commands were obeyed without question. And then, the Japanese also said that they had come to free us from the fetters of Dutch colonialism, and we believed them. In the early period of their occupation we were allowed to sing 'Indonesia Raya', which I discovered had been composed by someone called Wagé Rudolf Soepratman. It might be imagined how proud I felt, having once been called Wagé too. Surely the other bearer of that name must be some great-souled individual, to have endowed us with such a stirring hymn! In actual fact, the song we then heard on the radio was accompanied by a humble trio of viola, guitar and ukulele; yet, how that simple tune moved us! *Indoneesch, Indoneesch, mulia, mulia*—Indonesia, our noble Indonesia! Even that new name was still rendered in the Dutch way. But be that as it may, the honeymoon with 'Indonesia Raya' sadly lasted only a short time, as it did with other patriotic enthusiasms, soon proscribed by the army of Dai Nippon, arrived to liberate us from Dutch chains.

All the schools around Wanagalih, including that of Ndoro Guru Kakung in Karangdompol, were closed for some considerable time while the incoming administration converted the educational system from one à la *Hindia Belanda* to something complying better with the immediate practical requirements of the new state. Basically, the result seemed to be an unceremonious simplifying of the old regime. Primary schools had until then been compartmentalised into vernacular schools of the 'second rank', such as the regular three-year village schools and irregular five-year *scholen schakel*, of the sort run by teachers like Ndoro Guru Martoadmodjo; secondly, the official *schakel* schools such as the one I attended, and HIS; and finally, those designated ELS, from *Europese Lagere Scholen*, that is, schools for Dutch children and the children of high-ranking native officials. All were thrown together to become one school.

At that time I had finished my fifth year at Karangdompol, and while we all waited for the new system's birth I helped out at home. It seemed to be a period of reversion: I returned to cleaning rooms, sweeping the yard, carrying water from the well to the bathroom, and generally assisting in the back. Both

Gentry

Ndoro Kakung and Ndoro Putri filled those days with attending more to what was happening with the garden crops and the rice field. This period of uncertainty appeared to have the effect of rekindling in them some primal instinct that had remained dormant: something from the long line of their progenitors whispered that this was a time for putting aside stores and preparing for dearth. If people had imagined that with the arrival of the Japanese all prices would fall, that expectation soon evaporated; prices did not fall, rather all kinds of products began to disappear from the markets and the shops.

One morning, a sudden demand arrived at the house for Ndoro Guru Kakung to present himself at the kabupaten and join there all the other teachers: an announcement would be made about new regulations concerning schools. I was excited to hear that, and hoped it meant that classes would soon be starting again; but when Ndoro Guru Kakung returned in the afternoon, looking depressed and tired, I grew worried. I immediately thought it might mean that classes were *never* going to start, and that any timid expectation on my part of advancing my education beyond the village school at Karangdompol was about to be dashed. Ndoro Guru Kakung propped his bicycle in the covered passageway under the eaves and went into the veranda to sit down on a rocking chair. As usual the Wanagalih day was scorching, and he left untouched the warm tea his wife brought him, asking me instead to get him a glass of coconut milk with a pinch of palm sugar in it. I knew by such an unusual demand at this time of the day that he was greatly troubled; and in fact he not only finished the drink in one draught but asked for a second glass. I hurried to bring it to him, and only after that one was consumed did his thirst seem satisfied. His batik headdress was on the table beside him, several buttons of his jacket had been undone, and I brought him a fan that he might cool his perspiring chest and neck. His wife waited patiently in another rocking chair to hear what had happened at the kabupaten. I sat on the outside stairs, ears cocked, while the teacher continued for some time fanning and mopping himself.

Finally, he cleared his throat: 'Hem . . . Difficult times are ahead.'

'Oh, difficult? How, Pakné?'

'*Nippong* has ordered the schools to open from next week.'

'But, why, that's good, Pakné! The children have been idle too long, they'll be getting into mischief soon.'

'But wait till I tell you what happened. I've never seen a meeting like the one this morning, or so many people from every rank and office and department in one crowd like that. Three Japanese—we were told very carefully to address them as *Tuan* . . . shades of our Dutch masters, what? Three of them, I say, were there, and a couple of Javanese tuans as well, dressed exactly like the Japanese. Even the way those two carried themselves would make you think they were Japanese. It certainly hasn't taken long for this nation of ours

4. Lantip

to adapt itself! The Tuan *Nippong* who must have been in command gave a speech in his language—which of course none of us understood. It was followed by a translation from a second Japanese, given in some hilarious kind of Malay: the way it came out at us sounding like a lot of snapping and barking. Then, *that* was followed by a *third* version, supposedly Indonesian, from one of those two countrymen of ours: *it* sounded like a lot of snapping and barking. Anyway, the point of those speeches was to inform us that we will be following a new order in our schools. Every morning, both pupils and teachers will face northwards and bow deeply to *Tenno Heika*, the king of Japan; who, they say, is the descendant of a god. After that, we will have a session of *taiso*, which is some kind of group calisthenics. Only then do we start lessons. Every day, there will be lessons in Japanese: for which a number of selected teachers will have to take an intensive language course. In short, Buné—trouble!'

Ndoro Guru Putri remained silent and seemed to be turning over in her mind what she had just heard; and from my position on the steps I too tried to imagine what the carrying out of those new mandates might entail.

'Think about it, Buné, someone of my age scraping and bowing towards the north every morning, giving my reverential greetings to a god—can you see it? What a business! Offensive? Why, we've dodged complying with our own rites as often as not, and here one is being ordered to make obeisance to somebody else's god! And studying a new language—I never picked up Dutch, and that was here for centuries; now they expect me to learn in quick-time their *Bahasa Nippong*! Unbelievable! No, Bune, I want my pension now! But, no, another thing they expect is that those of pension-age will keep on working—I must still go to Karangdompol! Hah! But we'll see about that!'

Ndoro Putri continued to remain silent; while to me the tone of Ndoro Kakung's rumblings and complaints gave rise to troubled thoughts: was he truly aware of how much the old ways had changed under the Japanese administration? Could he not see that simply attempting to retire from teaching might now seem like defiance? Possibly considering something of the sort, Ndoro Putri tried to distract and calm her husband: 'All right now. That's enough for the time being, Pak. We'll think about it all later. Have something to eat and then go in for your afternoon nap.'

'And another madness, Buné. From next week, all schoolchildren have to be shorn down to the scalp, must go around bald! Can you imagine it? The children of gentry looking like shorn sheep!'

'Yes, yes, Pakné. Let's go and have something to eat.'

I ran inside to get everything ready on the table. But when he came in, Ndoro Guru Kakung seemed to have little appetite, barely touching his favourite sour-vegetable salad.

Gentry

It became evident that Ndoro Guru Kakung was serious in his determination to retire. On returning from Karangdompol, he informed Ndoro Putri that he had just announced that intention there. I had gone to the school with him and had in fact witnessed him doing so to his colleagues, who showed alarm and tried to induce him to stay on a little longer while he reconsidered. But no, he would retire. Ndoro Putri accepted his decision tranquilly, once she saw that it would be useless to argue against it. And as for myself, it had been clear to me by the way he marched away from the school, and the grimness of his expression, that I had witnessed the end of the teacher's career. But his countenance changed when we were on the ferry and crossing the river. I saw him looking out at the usual small craft being paddled down towards the junction of the Madiun and Solo Rivers—canoes and rafts loaded with the usual vegetables, teak leaves, chickens, baskets of rice, marketing villagers—and I noted that he had grown peaceful, as if disburdened and now free of all tension and tiredness.

He pointed to the river traffic and said: 'Those are fortunate people over there, Lé. They work hard, are industrious and happy. They're left alone, no one forces them to kowtow to the north every morning.'

Looking back on it, I suppose in that crossing of the river he saw his own transition to some simpler state, believing himself relieved now of the rigours and enigmas being visited by the new times on the old.

But one morning, about a week after that, a group of men arrived at the house in Setenan Road, among them a Japanese officer wearing a uniform with a white band marked with something unintelligible around one sleeve. The others were Indonesians, and among those was *Meneer* Soetardjo. Both Ndoro Guru Kakung and Ndoro Putri hurried to welcome the visitors, and Ndoro Guru Kakung, in some confusion at the unexpected arrival of such a party, begged them to be seated. I noticed that *Meneer* Soetardjo was no less flustered.

He began to explain the invasion: 'I . . . I beg your pardon, Kamas Darsono . . . for arriving so suddenly . . .'

'Why, er, not at all, *Menir* . . .'

Before these awkward politenesses could be prolonged, Tuan *Nippong* broke in with some words of astonishing Malay addressed at *Meneer* Soetardjo: '*Ano*, him? Tuan Sasturodarusono—is so?'

'Ah . . . yes, Tuan, yes.'

Ndoro Guru Kakung's incomprehension visibly deepened. *Meneer* Soetardjo attempted to reassure him by explaining that the Japanese officer was Tuan Sato from the local administrative area, and he, Tuan Sato, just wished to have a talk about the school in Karangdompol.

'Tuan Darusono, guru Karangdomoporu—is so?'

Ndoro Guru Kakung could barely do more than nod his head.

4. Lantip

'*Hai*—yes?'

Meneer Soetardjo glanced quickly at Ndoro Guru Kakung and hissed: 'Say *hai*, Kamas, *hai!*'

'*Hai, hai*, Tuan Sato!'

I saw the yellowish pallor of Tuan Sato's complexion suddenly redden.

'Darusono, *warui desu ne*! Bad! Stink!'

A fearful silence followed this.

'Darusono don't rike *saikere kita ni muke?*'

Ndoro Guru Kakung seemed on the point of losing his wits totally. Turning to *Meneer* Soetardjo he stammered a question that was half a plea for help: 'Wh-what's he saying, Dimas *Menir* Tardjo?'

'Oh dear, Kamas. Tuan Sato is angry because he had a report that you would not perform the obeisance to the north.'

Suddenly, one of the Indonesians who had come with the officer said briskly: 'That's enough now, Pak! Admit it! Give in and be done with it!'

Meneer Soetardjo reacted with a scandalised expression: 'Hush! You mustn't speak to a colleague of mine like that! Let's all be calm now. Kamas Darsono, let me try to explain matters to Tuan Sato.'

And with great care he made the case to the Japanese that Ndoro Guru Kakung was old, was a pensioner who had only been asked to help out in Karangdompol but was not now a teacher. *Meneer* Soetardjo begged for Tuan Sato's understanding that at the time Ndoro Guru Kakung had been engaged to teach he would have been unclear about all the new regulations at the school.

The Indonesian attendant burst in again: 'Kamas Darsono, I must ask you to beg Tuan Sato's pardon!'

'Beg his pardon?'

'Come now, Kamas, get on with it! I'm telling you this to save you and your family.'

Now Ndoro Guru Putri added her own distressed urging: 'For God's sake, Pakné, tell them you did wrong, tell them you're sorry!'

Ndoro Guru Kakung, stammering and manifestly reluctant and resentful, delivered his apology: 'I-I b-beg your pardon, Tuan Sato.'

Sato took two rapid steps towards the teacher, grasped him by the back of the neck and began to force his upper body forward and down.

'*Ayo!* Bend, Darusono, bend, bend!'

Creakily, Ndoro Guru Kakung managed to perform an ungainly curve with his body. Sato was evidently dissatisfied with the result. Without a word of warning his hand flashed down to give the back of the declined head two clouts: *Plack! Plack!* Ndoro Guru Kakung staggered forward and *Meneer* Soetardjo and I just managed to catch him. Together we helped him to a chair.

'Darusono, bad! Stink! *Genjimin bagero*, stupid native!'

Gentry

With that, Tuan Sato turned on his heel and departed, his retinue packed closely around him. The veranda was left silent.

Gradually the tension dissipated; but when I glanced at Ndoro Guru Kakung, his face had gone deathly pale, become that of a tired old man, and he was crying like a child: 'Oh, Allah, Bu-u. I've never been so humiliated. He hit me on the head, Buné. On the head!' And he sobbed bitterly, distracted, with a childish grief. 'On the head!'

Ndoro Guru Putri quickly tried to soothe her husband, and she signed to me that I should come to them.

'Now, now there, Pakné, don't worry about it now. Don't mind it, don't think about it anymore. Let's go inside now, and you'll have your rest on the divan. And Lantip is going to bring you your coffee. So we'll go in now, Pak, all right?'

I helped Ndoro Guru Putri support his arms and we led him slowly into the inner room, muttering, dazed: 'My head! Barbarian *Nippong*. He hit me on the head!'

I ran to the back for some hot, strong coffee.

Next morning Ndoro Guru Putri gave me letters to post to each of their children. They were all being asked to gather at Wanagalih.

Their arrival proved an effective tonic to the teacher. He had since his experience with the Japanese officer been sluggish, had lost his appetite, and spoke little; but now he brightened up. His youngest son, Ndoro Kakung Hardojo, brought his wife and his son Gus Hari, who was some years my junior; while Ndoro Noegroho and Ndoro Den Ajeng Soemini arrived with their spouses only.

Oh, how affectionate is the connection between a father and his children! If only I too could have felt that warmth, that spiritual bond with my own father! For many days, the house in Setenan Road was alive with conversations and laughter. In the first part of the morning, while the water was being prepared for the morning wash, everyone sat at the round dinner-table inside, eating a pre-breakfast snack of rice, blanched vegetables and peanut sauce: Mbok Soero's speciality, wrapped in teak leaves and purchased with a hail as she passed outside. Later, all went in a happy group to look at the crops in the garden at the back, to admire the growing rice, and sit in the field-hut, looking out at the parakeets flying and chattering with that busy *tet-tet-tet* of theirs. On some days they sent me to bring them lunch in the hut, and then it was a merry feast in there. I would bring from the kitchen red rice, steamed whitebait in banana leaves, shrimp paste, hot fried tempeh, pickled vegetables; and then the whole hut, by no means overlarge for that company, creaked and swayed from the happy jostling of the hungry diners. On other occasions, the family might take an outing in sampans, and we joined the river traffic of local boats carrying produce to and from market landings. At night,

4. Lantip

everyone gathered in the inner room around the dinner table for the usual noisy banter and jokes and for serious talking as well. The teacher might at those times while almost drowsing listen to the voices around him, lying on the divan while I kneaded and rubbed his feet. Many times over the years I witnessed such scenes in that house, and it was something I could enjoy endlessly, like watching an old favourite film which one never tires of seeing again. And for Ndoro Guru Kakung Sastrodarsono, those meetings seemed to act like a powerful elixir that returned energy and spirit to his soul.

On one such night, some days before the visitors were to go back to their cities, we came together once again in the inner room. Ndoro Guru Kakung told me to bring his rocking chair in there, and when he was quite comfortable he beckoned me to sit on the floor close to him. All this was unusual, and I thought that he would now want me to massage his feet. But no, he had something else in mind.

'Tip, sing for us the first verse in 'Pocung', from the epic of *Wedhatama*; and after that the first verse of 'Kinanti', from *Wulangreh*.'

I was surprised to be asked that. It was a long time since I had recited those verses in school or sung them quietly with Kang Trimo behind the house. 'Pocung', 'The Sheaf of Truths', is a song from *High Wisdom*, a theosophical tract which teaches ascetic attitudes and self-control; while 'Kinanti', 'Guidance', from *Lore and Disciplines*, introduces the convert to the practical techniques by which passion and egoism may be overcome.

'*Wah*, Ndoro! A thousand pardons—I do beg to be excused! It's long since I last did that. All Ndoro here will surely be displeased at my mistakes.'

No one believed me, and they insisted I should begin forthwith, Gus Hari, who had never heard me recite-sing a *macapat* before, adding his voice to those of the elders. I gathered my courage and breath, said a mental prayer that I might still remember all the words, and launched into the old lines from 'Pocung'.

'Such calming knowledge comes
With bravely learned self-rule!
O cleverness indeed
That salves regret and hurt,
Heart's fervours pacifies . . .'

And having apparently concluded that stanza successfully, I continued with the excerpt from 'Kinanti':

'Strengthen thy spirit with wisdom;
Heed all, be sentient ever;
Let mind and soul grow quick;

Gentry

The body's cravings shunning:
Whose hungers and fatigues
Perturb thy steps to bliss . . .'

This stanza too, *alhamdulillah*, I completed safely. I turned my head up to look about at the family, and was relieved to see them nodding their approval. The silent satisfaction of the adults was suddenly broken by Gus Hari's noisy clapping, followed by him throwing an arm around my shoulders.

'Very, very nice, Tip! What a singer you are—wow!'

Ndoro Guru Kakung and the others laughed at Gus Hari's spontaneous actions, and now they followed with their own praise: 'Yes, Tip, Hari's right. You *are* very good. Thank you very much.'

Then Den Ajeng Soemini asked: 'But father, why did you ask Lantip to sing those? Did you have something in mind?'

'There was a reason, Mini. Or there were two. Firstly, I felt we should listen to something soothing and agreeable tonight. The second has to do with my choice of those verses. I hope that you all took notice of what they were about.'

We all kept silent in expectation that the teacher was on the point of conveying something important and grave to us.

'Actually, there is one other text I would have liked all of you to hear, the *Tripama, The Three Patterns*, which like the *Wedhatama* was composed by His Lordship Prince Mangkunegara IV in the last century; but I'll leave that for another time. I chose the two pieces, one from the *Wedhatama* and the other from the *Wulangreh*, by His Highness Paku Buwana IV, because they relate very much to the troubling period we are enduring now. It took some slaps from that silly uneducated Japanese to awaken me to the gravity of what we are experiencing in these times and in this country.'

Ndoro Guru Kakung paused at the sound of Pak To, the *wedang cemoe* seller, passing outside and calling his wares. Normally there would have been a scramble to go out to him; but tonight no one dared do so, and we sat unmoving in our chairs or on the floor while the teacher continued: 'The two sets of verses we have just heard, complement each other. That from 'Pocung' tells us that serene wisdom can be achieved by persistent striving, striving to calm the passions clouding the heart. The poem tells us to resist those evil coils of anger and excitement trammelling understanding, resist by assuaging them.'

Ndoro Guru Kakung took a sip of his coffee, then he looked around his attending family until his eyes rested on Gus Hari.

'This is something you should take note of, Hari; and you too, Lantip. Both of you have a long education yet ahead of you, a long road. If you are to get the best from what will be taught to you soon, calm self-discipline must play

4. Lantip

a part. But even for you others, my adult children, those are significant verses you heard. The pursuit of wisdom after all is a lifelong effort, is it not? You've become noted as priyayi. People will continue to respect you and accord you wisdom by the efforts you make in that pursuit.'

His two sons and his daughter bowed their heads in acknowledgement of the words, as did their spouses. I had to ask myself to what extent that gesture of theirs might be meaningful, for they would have had opportunities to become familiar with those old songs, and must have accepted or not accepted their purport by now. Or had his children in fact ever heard them at all in their time at HIS and during their Dutch secondary schooling?

'Now *Wulangreh* fills in with the methods by which we train the spirit to heighten its sensitivity and understanding. And that's certainly not by eating and sleeping our way through life. Controlling the desires of the body promotes that necessary fortitude, that calm resistance just spoken of.'

I noticed that Gus Hari appeared to grow uneasy at this last advice by his grandfather, who now smiled at the boy.

'Hari, this concerns you too, you know.'

'*Wah*. It sounds very hard, Mbah.'

Everyone laughed. His father, also laughing, said: 'Hari's heard he's got to cut down on the fried rice and snoring in bed till midday. Impossible, isn't it, Hari?'

They all laughed again, and Ndoro Guru Kakung continued speaking, but reassuringly: 'Well now, Hari. In your case, since you're still little you may eat well enough and as much as you need, and sleep as long as you need to. Just remember the point of what we are saying: awareness, awareness unobstructed by too-worldly considerations is everything.'

All the adults nodded again at those words.

'My children, a mad epoch has begun, I see the signs everywhere. But the seers who long ago predicted our subjection to a white-skinned race have also said that the period of time we are to be ruled by a supplanting dwarf-like yellow one, one come from the north, will only last as long as the life of a maze plant.'

Ndoro Den Ajeng Soemini, who showed signs of never having heard the old Kediri prophecy, exclaimed: 'But that's not long at all!'

'Yes, the time may well not be long, Nduk, but we could find it a hard time. It was not so long ago that your father was cuffed for his pains, resisting the rule of those dwarfs.'

As Ndoro Guru Kakung said that, I saw he was smiling, and I was relieved. It meant that he himself had taken a philosophical view of the matter. All the other adults smiled with him, and they too appeared thankful he had found comfort in that attitude.

'So let us all meet this difficult time in the spirit of the old teachings. All of you now have important positions and duties: be vigilant in your behaviour, thoughtful and careful.'

This time, judging by the moment of deliberation which delayed one or two of the bowed responses, the teacher's children and children-in-law could well have been reflecting on their own daily difficulties, working under the Japanese.

'Hardojo, I have a request to you.'

'Yes, Pak?'

'If you and your wife will agree to it, take Lantip with you when you go. It's time he should be moving on to the next stage of his schooling, and you have only one child, Hari. If, Noegroho, you had had only one child, I would have sent him with you to Yogya; or with you, Nakmas Harjono, from the same consideration to Madiun. So what do you think, Hardojo, would you like to do that?'

'Certainly, Pak. Of course. We're up to it. We actually thought about the possibility before this. Hari, you're happy about that, aren't you, to have Lantip as a friend?'

Instead of speaking, Gus Hari again clapped an arm around my shoulders, and grinning broadly into my face rocked me back and forth a couple of times. I was speechless at this unexpected proposal by the teacher, and could only submit to the boy and bow my head.

Next morning, I asked permission to make a parting visit to the graves of my mother and grandmother in Wanalawas and to say good-bye to the village head. I invited Gus Hari to come with me, and we set off on bicycles, not forgetting to take slingshots for the birds in the rice-fields on the way. For the sake of town-bred Gus Hari, I chose a route along the shaded side of the fields where it was cooler, and also because we were most likely to pass turtle-doves and pigeons there, or at least finches and sparrows, when they settled on the rice from the trees. It was long since I had hunted birds like that and I wanted to show Gus Hari one of the country pleasures of children in these parts. But in my heart I knew that I was also saying good-bye that day to all such things: the birds, the hunting, the countryside itself. I imagined that in such a great city as Solo I would have few further opportunities to ramble with a slingshot or see much of rice fields. So we travelled slowly, stopping often to take out our weapons. Gus Hari had never used a slingshot before but soon learned, and by the time we arrived at Wanalawas we had quite a bag: five doves and six pigeons. It was approaching midday and we gave the birds to Bu Dukuh to roast for our lunch, and the subsequent meal in her house was very pleasant. This was the first time Gus Hari had eaten with a real village family, and he liked the food and the people and felt comfortable with them; indeed he seemed to have a ready sympathy for everyone he met, of whatever rank they might be. The rice, had we not contributed our birds, would have been only supplemented by some watercress and flavoured with a little paste of chillies pounded with salt.

Afterwards I took Gus Hari to see my mother's house. Oddly, no one in the village seemed to have been interested in doing anything with it, and it was empty and unmaintained. Was it thought to be an unlucky place? The front door sagged and was half open; inside, spiderwebs hung from the dusty chairs and the table and from the cupboard and shelves. As we walked through, a lizard and then a rat scurried away into cracks, and it was evident that the rats had made themselves at home. Gus Hari appeared troubled and astonished at the state of this house which had been my home.

'You lived here, Tip? Really?'

'That's it, Gus. I was born in this house and grew up in it for some years. That was our room; my mother, my grandmother and I slept in it. That one was my father's.'

'Oh, your father slept alone in his room, and you three were crowded together in that one?'

'Yes, that seems how it was, I don't know why.'

'And now they're all dead, Tip?'

'My mother and grandmother are dead. My father went a long way away, somewhere on a *rantau* and never came back.'

I don't know why I did not simply say that my father was dead, why I should not want to admit it finally. My promise to the village head was there of course, but surely he would have allowed such a confidence to someone as intelligent and sensitive as Gus Hari, particularly since we were both leaving the area? But was it also because I had not witnessed my father's death, and there remained some lingering comfort in imagining that he might still be alive, although far away somewhere, God knows where?

'If you like, Gus, we'll go now to the cemetery.'

'Yes, let's. I'm just surprised that this house is going to be left empty for the lizards and rats and spiders, Tip.'

'Yes, I know, but look at it now. Who's going to want to live here?'

We went to the village cemetery and found it surrounded by untended frangipani trees: by the profusion of flowers and intertwined twigs and branches no one it seemed had given any thought to the trees for a long time, and in the gloom under them we had difficulty finding the two graves. I felt that I should have visited sooner than this. I said my prayer silently, and then Gus Hari and I squatted by the side of the two mounds.

'When your mother died, did you cry, Tip?'

'Oh, yes, Gus. It was my mother after all.'

'And when your grandmother died?'

'Then I did not. But my mother cried, as I recall.'

Gus Hari gazed at the graves, seeming to reflect on something. Then he said to me: 'I'm very sorry for you, Tip. No grandmother, your mother dead, your father gone. And look at how your house is falling to bits. But you'll be happy when you start living with us in Solo, Tip.'

I was touched by this simple effort to comfort me. He resembled his father a lot, the way he could feel for others. We left the cemetery, and on the way back we stopped at the house of the village head to say good-bye.

'And good luck to you, lad. Be good and obey those you go to live with. Work hard and honestly at school and everywhere else. Don't forget our little agreement. And whatever you do, you know the motto: Lift high! Dig deep!'

We pedalled slowly through the middle of the village, and just as in that now-distant time when I was departing after having buried my mother, I saw girls playing hopscotch and boys marbles. They barely glanced at us as we went past, although many of them should have recognised me. Hari, on the other hand, looked at them with curiosity; then he turned to glance again at the village after we had passed its boundary.

'Your village is very pretty, Tip.'

'Oh, is it, Gus?'

'But it's a bit sad, too.'

We pedalled on, and I asked myself where Gus Hari, coming from the well-to-do of a city and never known the mud of our villages, could find the notion to speak like that.

Next morning, we all boarded a gharry to go to the station at Paliyan, where we would catch the SS to Solo. In the moment before I was to step into the cart, Ndoro Guru Kakung bent over me and blew down a puff of air at the crown my head; then Ndoro Putri stretched out her hand and stroked that spot for a moment, smoothing my hair back where her husband's gesture of good-luck must have displaced it.

I would miss both those good people.

5. HARDOJO: new lives, first variation: reach and withdrawal

After I had failed with Dik Nunuk, a lot of life's excitement drained out of me. When I was still expecting to marry her, and after those early days—those heady days—when I began to sense that my feeling for her was not one-sided, not one hand clapping as they say, I felt inflamed with life, fired with passion, energy. I taught at the HIS in Wonogiri, and from that town to Solo where her school was located was about thirty kilometres; but I never really noticed the distance, although the trip meant taking the train or a bus, or even at times hiring a taxi. For one thing, I could afford those: I was a bachelor earning 110 guilders; and I could stay at Budé Suminah's house, near the Penumping market. But it was Dik Nunuk herself who made the distance and the journey bearable, made them seem a very slight inconvenience in the scheme of things, hardly to be noticed. Each Saturday afternoon, after my school had closed for the weekend, I would take a seat in a carriage of the small train linking Wonogiri to Solo; or if some duty delayed me and I missed the train and then also the bus, I had no qualms, as I said, about taking a taxi. The important thing was to be in Solo before nightfall.

Budé Suminah, an aunt widowed long ago, put up with the animation and impatience of a young person head over heels in love. Came Saturday, I arrived at her place, in a rush to wash, change my shirt and call a local buggy: for there were no pedicabs then. Laughing, she would try to deflate me, and she could be a great tease.

'Jeng Nunuk's not likely to have a fit of absentmindedness and dash off without you, Har, is she? Where's the rush, Lé? It's early.'

'Ha, you don't know the modern girl, Aunty. They're not as meek and patient as they were back in your time. If I don't get there smartly, she'll be gone.'

Budé would persist, smiling and well aware that she was holding me up: 'Gone, you say, gone off without you where? With whom?'

'*Wah*, Budé, a girl like Nunuk? Lots have an eye on her, especially among the Catholics. I've got heavy competition there. If I dawdle I'll be left a mile behind.'

But I did not let this go on for long, because I was quite truly in a fever to go; I wanted to get to kampong Madiotaman where Nunuk's parents had their house. But even as I boarded the buggy I would still hear Budé laughing from her veranda: 'Take care, Har. Don't trip now. Those shawls the Solo girls wear, they're the devil to get tangled up in.'

In the vehicle at last, I would smile to myself: Budé Suminah, a heart of gold. And along the way I stopped to buy something Chinese for dinner, perhaps noodles or stir-fried vegetables, skewers of chicken, maybe a crepe omelette folded over spicy pieces of meat. Nunuk's family waited for me to eat with them, and the meal always included what I brought.

It was a sociable and lively table: a circle of parents, younger siblings, a changing collection of cousins; and I had felt quite relaxed there for some time now, not even awkward when they preceded the meal by grace in the Catholic manner. I felt that to be something totally natural, and when in the course of their prayer I sometimes almost uttered a *bismillah*, I imagined they would have accepted it in the same spirit. After the meal, people had their usual places where they sat: those of Bapak and Ibu being in the inner room. Dik Nunuk and I talked with them for a while, and then we left them there listening to the radio or chatting together and drinking tea. Accompanied by some of the younger folk, we would go out strolling about the town or to see a film or do whatever else came to mind. If we two did not feel like going out and the weather suited we simply sat outside on their veranda and talked quietly into the late hours. On Sunday mornings the whole family of course attended mass. I generally met them afterwards outside the church, then we would all go together to their house, where I remained for lunch, leaving in the afternoon for Sangkrah station and my train to Wonogiri. So that was my weekend routine for a long time, and however ordinary and repetitive it might seem I never tired of it. I used to talk to Budé Suminah about that, and she had her reply ready: 'That's the way of it, Har. You're just plain lovesick and that explains everything. A bad dose of *perlip*, the Dutch call it.'

'*Perlip*? Oh, *verliefd*. Yes, I admit that, Budé. And yet, you'd think, back and forth to Madiotaman that way . . .'

'It's what I say, you innocent lamb. Lovesick.'

'And don't we ever tire of all that then, when we're in love?'

'Oh, that will come soon enough. But not now. You're at the happy stage.'

I said nothing, wondering to myself what it was about Dik Nunuk that had this power over me. Or was I just taken in by the spell of a wholly unimagined and unprecedented situation, by the amiable yet strange ambience of her circle: the family of polite, modest Gregorius Dwidjosumarto the Catholic? As I said, it was a time of rapture, but also of much incomprehension.

I must have had a musing expression, because Budé, long aware of the conundrums of youth, made to comfort me in her usual mildly ironic way. Laughing, she patted me and said: 'Now Allah be with you. I suppose, my dear, you'd like to hear your old aunt say that you'll never be bored with going to Madiotaman where one there called Nunuk awaits, and she with all the beauty of the goddess Sembadra about her?'

5. Hardojo

I could only mutter something sheepish in response.

But among Dik Nunuk's cousins, I have to admit, was one who when I first met him at her house I thought behaved fairly coolly towards me, and whose expression subsequently never shifted to any degree of approval, retaining something rather sour there in fact. At first I took little notice of certain allusions he made, remarks about how well Chinese noodles go with pork, that sort of thing. I think I replied offhandedly that that was probably true. However, when questions touching on pork seemed to crop up so often with him, I began to conclude that Pran—from Franciscus: his full name was Franciscus Xaverius Suharsono—had some definite intent by them. What he had on his mind surfaced one night after we had finished dinner and were all sitting in the inner room as usual. Without preamble, Pran began addressing himself to me: 'I'm always astonished, Mas Har, with the way Islam forbids its adherents the eating of pork. Everyone knows that pork is flavoursome and pigs are fine animals; and if the problem used to be tapeworms, then it is so no longer. Slaughter is conducted in abattoirs under the strictest hygienic conditions.'

My heart began to beat faster. I was never a particularly staunch Muslim, but I bristled to hear someone from another religion remarking on mine. Nevertheless, aware that I was a guest there, among people I respected, one of whom moreover I loved, I controlled myself. Glancing at Dik Nunuk and her parents I saw signs of restlessness among them, and I made my reply as neutral as possible: 'Well now, Dik Pran, the fact is that pork is not only forbidden to Muslims but to Jews as well, to those of a religion which preceded both Islam and Christianity. Therefore, it seems that the proscription came to us from a very old Middle Eastern tradition with its own justifications. Pork may well be nice to eat, and that could be precisely why it became proscribed, as a form of discipline, a training in warding off temptations, sensual ones in particular, Dik Pran.'

I had spoken as calmly as I could, and I saw that Dik Nunuk and her father and mother were relieved that I had not adopted a tone of indignation or given any sign that I had been provoked, and that with what I had said the matter seemed now closed. But Pran appeared more obstinate than anyone had expected.

'Very well, Mas Har, I accept your explanation. Now we come to the question of the four wives you people are allowed to take. Could you clarify that for us, please?'

Devil of a boy. I was preparing myself to serve him another little lecture, as patiently and explicitly as I knew how, but then Dik Nunuk's father cut in: 'That will do now, Pran. I'll ask you to say no more. We'll have no more talk about how other people regulate their religion. Each religion has its own rules, and grew to fulfil the needs of its own people. We must therefore take the view that every religion is good. Now we should talk about something else.'

'But Pakdé, the question of four wives is important! Especially important for Mbak Nunuk...'

'Pran! What did I just say? That's enough, stop! Whatever lies in your Mbak Nunuk's future will be dealt with by her mother and me. Nak Har, I must beg your pardon for this persistence by your Adik Pran. I'm sure there's no mean intention in it. You're not offended, are you?'

'Of course not Bapak. I don't see any problem.'

But I remember that the conversation during the rest of that evening was unusually careful and formal. Dik Nunuk too looked dejected: the reason, more than any irritation with Pran, why that night remained in my memory as an unhappy one. And the lingering effects of that spat showed up next week, when Dik Nunuk and I were walking in the Sriwedari amusement park. We had been looking at the animals, throwing peanuts into a cage, talking about nothing in particular. Dik Nunuk was exceptionally pretty, but also thoughtful.

'Will you get tired of me one day, Mas?'

I was astonished at the question. We were following the antics of the monkeys inside that large cage; some visitors were throwing peanuts, others fruit: Sunday was evidently banqueting day for the animals. One of the female monkeys, with a small infant in her arms, had attracted the favour of a male monkey, which from time to time sniffed the mother and infant in a most friendly manner; at other times it collected nuts which had been thrown into the cage and brought them to those two. This went on until the male for no detectable reason ceased his attentions there and departed to another part of the cage, and could now be seen unconcernedly frolicking with a different group of monkeys.

'You've been asked a question, Mas, and I hear no reply? Daydreaming?'

I smiled. I had indeed been held by the activities of the animals.

'Oh, I heard your question. Tired? Now if you were as ugly as these monkeys... But really, Dik, what a thought! And you know what my Budé Suminah says? That you're as beautiful as Sembadra, Arjuna's wife.'

'Allah!—as if your Budé Suminah had ever been personally introduced to Sembadra! I'll bet her Sembadra's like one of those actresses in a country troupe: all sugary dialogue, billing and cooing. Would that be how you'd want me?'

'I would, I would!'

And we both laughed.

'But I asked you seriously, Mas. I don't like the idea of me following you to the death, and you being free to drop me and go elsewhere.'

'But why this sudden concern?'

5. Hardojo

'Come now, I haven't forgotten that your religion grants you a quota of four wives.'

Aha! So that conversation had been on her mind since then.

'Dik Nunuk, have you been worrying about that nonsense with Pran all this time?'

'I know, it shouldn't worry me. But clearly it does. It's something that won't leave me, maybe because the matter is so alien to us: to Catholics, Protestants.'

'Oh, but look, it's a question that never arises for the majority of Muslims either. I mean, although the fact of polygamy is there, most of us know that very, very few men are capable of taking it up with all the conditions set by their religion.'

'What are the conditions?'

'A man has to be just and even-handed towards each wife. Absolutely. Now, who could be that to four wives? See what I mean? So the majority of Muslims very early on put aside any thought of having those four wives. It's impracticable.'

'And I suppose you think the proof of that is the number of Muslims who have even *more* than four wives?'

'Oh, there you're touching on something which doesn't just involve Islam. There are men in every faith who have mistresses and goods laid away in addition to whomever they once married officially. There, ultimately, the question comes back to the individual concerned.'

'Very well. And now, Mas Har, what is *your* attitude to the question?'

'Dik Nunuk, I'm stunned! How can you ask that? Here I've a wife of unsurpassed, indeed celestial beauty, and I should go looking for another? No but actually that's not very original. My father used to say that to my mother whenever she bothered him with this kind of thing. But let it remain a sort of family parable.'

Dik Nunuk pinched me, smiling. She seemed happier now, perhaps relieved, perhaps in anticipating the pleasure of those ever-renewed qualms and reassurances my mother had known.

And in this way, our feelings for each other grew continually stronger and closer; the house in Madiotaman with every visit seemed more like my own. Nunuk's parents accepted me as one of the family and I even spent the night there at times, sleeping in the room of the younger Dwidjosumarto children. I still heard occasional remarks concerning Islam and my being a Muslim from Pran; but I, and even the others, now paid little attention to that. In fact, things appeared to go on so trouble-free and so cordially, that Nunuk and I, and it would seem her family as well, never gave thought to any possible difficulties which might arise in the path of our inevitable marriage. I was so happy, so unthinkingly content with the state of things, that I never even got around to fixing a day for the formal proposal, which of course in the Javanese fashion had to be made to the girl's family. No, Nunuk and I were intoxicated by our love and our intimacy; until at last her parents decided the time had come to take a more sober look at what was happening.

Dik Nunuk broached their thoughts to me: 'Mas Har, some days ago, father and mother asked me to come and have a talk with them.'

'Oh, yes?'

'They wanted to know how matters stood between us two, whether it was a serious relationship. Silly, of course: everybody knows. But they have to ask.'

'Yes, well of course, they would want to be certain. I can understand that. Go on.'

'They suggested you might like to sound out your own people.'

It occurred to me now that her parents must have been patiently watching me for a sign that I would act, and I should have quite a while ago taken that initiative with my own parents, not waited for my prospective in-laws to send a delicate reminder via their daughter.

I wasted no more time and prepared what I thought would be the best approach to my father and mother. In advance of an eventual visit to Wanagalih, I sent them a long letter detailing in the most careful language the story of my relationship with Dik Nunuk, our blossoming love, the description of her family, who they were, what they did, the fact of their religion of course, and so on. My concern in sending this forewarning, intended to diminish any untoward surprise, proved more than justified, when in my father's reply he not only summoned me immediately to make my report personally, but I learned that my brother and sister and their spouses were also being called to Wanagalih to hear it. I was further made uneasy by my brother's attitude when on the next Saturday, and I was as usual in Solo, he arrived from Yogya, he and his wife having broken their journey to stay the night at Budé Suminah's house on the way to our family conference.

'You're a fine one for warning people, Yok! Not a word from you about this great passion, this *verliefd* over some girl, and then, bang!—you declare you want to marry her! A Catholic! Bapak-Ibu must have gone into a proper daze when they got that news.'

'Oh, really now, Mas, you know our parents. They haven't had our education but they're broadminded. No, I'm optimistic, Mas. And they've never been exactly fanatical when it comes to their own religion.'

'Well, let's hope you're right, Yok.'

'You'll be behind me on this, won't you, Mas?'

'Yeah, well, we'll talk about it when the family's together at Wanagalih.'

'What about you, Mbakyu, you'll support me, wont you?'

5. Hardojo

'Oh, look, I'd better listen to what comes out of this meeting. I wouldn't dare to say a thing at the moment.'

'Can I ask *you* to back me up, then, Budé?'

'Dear, I'm not going to Wanagalih. But I can tell you that I'll pray for you. I'll pray that the conference with your family ends well and with the best result for everybody. There!'

For heaven's sake, I thought to myself, why have they all become so cautious, talking like a bunch of diplomats? I became aware that there could be things going on which had not entered into my calculations. I may, after all, have misjudged my whole family's attitude by assuming that marriage outside our religion would be inconsequential to them, that any doubt about it would be easily smoothed over. Had I been in total error, then, in estimating their tolerance towards other faiths? They might endure Muslims belonging to sects in conflict with their own, but not folk of another religion? I had been thinking that since my family were such a syncretic lot, *abangan* Javanese whose Islam could uncomplicatedly house features of Hinduism and even animism, it should not be too difficult for them to accept the existence of mixed marriages. However, now, after the reaction of my brother Noegroho and his wife, and even that of Bude Suminah, who up to this had joked and teased about my relations with Dik Nunuk and had never appeared disapproving or rigid, I felt my spirits start to droop somewhat. Could all of my family now go against me, would every relative far and wide reject me? It was all beyond imagining.

Sadly, at the family meeting in Wanagalih my new fears turned out to be warranted. The position of all without exception was that Dik Nunuk must convert to Islam, or, as a second and extreme option, the marriage might take place at a registry office, a *burgerlijke stand*. I was in a turmoil throughout the meeting and felt totally drained by the end of it. I was encouraged to talk with the girl's parents to see whether they perhaps could arrive at some solution; but that possibility promised little comfort. I racked myself with the thought that had we earlier—Dik Nunuk and I—carefully, slowly, by stages, worked through this difficulty, we could somehow have resolved it. Or if I had done this or done that, Dik Nunuk by now might have been ready to consider converting. But then, what of her parents? Yes, polite, kind and sympathetic they were, but also staunch Catholics, very staunch. Me, they would have accepted as the convert, certainly; and as for a civil marriage, that was out of the question: the sanctity of a church-wedding was paramount to them.

I did indeed give thought to converting and being baptised; a momentary thought. But no, it would have been impossible; how could I bring myself to do that? As a nominal adherent of Islam I had paid scant attention to its teachings; yet, still, I felt myself to be under an obligation to this religion of mine, felt contracted to it, however poorly I understood that bond. No, Islam, half-known to me, had so much in it yet to comprehend and admire, and was I to turn my back on all its possibilities, all its unexplored expanses, and transfer to some other and even less understood religion? I would have felt myself a reprobate, even a traitor, taking such a desperate step; and dishonest and hypocritical towards the other religion as well.

Despite this impossible situation there was nothing for it but I must confront Dik Nunuk's parents and myself make my hopes for her hand explicit. Some days before meeting them I found an opportunity to go to Solo and tell Dik Nunuk about the conference in Wanagalih and its results. To be sure that we would not be disturbed I invited her to Budé Suminah's house. My aunt already had some idea of how events were tending and she found something to do in the back, leaving us to talk alone. It was one of those fine, cool nights, and from a divan on the veranda we could see the sky slowly reddening and growing dark, swept by the weakening rays of a departing sun. A half moon had already arrived to take its place.

As I began to speak I well remember her face, turned up to me with an expression a little startled, a little questioning, faintly smiling in agreement when I asked her to be calm while I gave her my news; and I remember that my heart felt like breaking at the sight of her. I kept my tone and manner as passionless as possible, but Dik Nunuk looked increasingly pale and tense, and finally she had to draw out a handkerchief to dry the tears in her eyes. My own feelings were chaotic, yet I had to remain quiet and patient while waiting for her initial shock to lessen enough to let her respond.

'What can I say, Mas? I always knew this was possible, but I suppose I thought it could be overcome. Or maybe I just drove the thing from my mind. We were so good together, what we had was so strong and sincere. You've been very good at creating that. And so, when what we had *was* so strong, there didn't seem to be any threat that we couldn't deal with. And I thought it included this religion matter. But I see now that we haven't judged our position all that well. Or judged our families. Or judged how inflexible religious ties really are.'

And she went on talking like that, pouring out her bitterness in a monotone; and I, now when it was her turn, after I had told my luckless tale, I had not the heart to stop her: I listened patiently to her, word by word, sentence by sentence, patiently but despairing. She spoke again of religion. A barrier indeed: one prays to the Almighty in one way, another in another, and that difference can tear apart two loving, committed, sincere people. As if those prayers were not directed to the same end, or as if they went to a god jealous of any love between human creatures. I listened and continued to sigh silently and to protest inside myself: Why, when in Allah's infinite wisdom He set a condition that only those might love each other who pray alike, why then, in this instance, had He allowed such unsanctified love as ours to happen?

5. Hardojo

Nunuk ceased. She had stopped crying and now fixed her eyes on me with a look that caused me to draw my breath in, startled. Then, suddenly, I was in the grip of another sensation: desire for her overwhelmed me, I wanted to embrace her and possess her body utterly, to unite with it and savour it to satiety! And we fell into each other's arms, passionately, unrestrained, kissed desperately and long; until at the height of these mad minutes I was prepared to pull her to my room. But, equally suddenly, the moment passed, and from some reservoir of self-control we found the strength to slowly part. It was as if an invisible hand had disengaged that fierce embrace of ours. We fell back to rest against the rear of the divan and sat like that until Dik Nunuk spoke. And she looked calm, her face pure and untroubled: 'Thank you, Mas Har.'

'Oh God. For what?'

'For everything. Please take me home now.'

On the way to Madiotaman I told her that next Sunday I would talk to her father after the family had come back from church. She nodded. We both realised that it would be the day when our hopes would come to an end.

I found my aunt still up and waiting for me. In the turmoil of my thoughts and feelings she appeared quite composed, and she surprised me by inviting me to join her in the evening prayer. She knew I never prayed.

'At least do the ablutions and sit behind me. Ask God for guidance.'

I did as she said. She was an understanding woman and knew that there was really nothing else I could do now. And indeed when she raised her palms in the ritual opening gesture, I followed suit, and although at first I could only murmur '*Allahu Akbar*' over and over again, when she had finished and left me I remained sitting cross-legged on the mat, begging Allah's compassion.

The next Sunday was a strange day. We, everyone—myself, Dik Nunuk, her parents, siblings, various cousins who happened to be there, even Pran— affected a most odd calmness. The report on where my family stood was accepted gravely; to its objections to the marriage, the Dwidjosumarto side now put forward corresponding objections, and all progressed politely and with frankness. Dik Nunuk listened attentively but quietly as I did when her family made its conclusions. There was nothing else we two could do. Everyone had known before the meeting started what the finale to this 'great love' of ours would be. Dik Nunuk had already told her people everything, and they were prepared to meet me with their conditions. In other words, all of us assembled there were confronted by a dead end and accepted that fact civilly with resignation. The event closed and we even had lunch together; and that afternoon I sat dazed in the train going to Wonogiri, looking out of the window of the carriage at the rice fields. Rice fields, rice fields everywhere. . . .

I only taught at the HIS in Wonogiri for two years, most of that time spent in getting over my disastrous failure. I had found out for myself how deep and slow-healing is the wound left by unfulfilled love. As a curative process I immersed myself in my work. In Wanagalih, *Meneer* Soetardjo, my old teacher, was wont to visit his pupils' homes regularly; I had done so too, but now increased the frequency of my visits and grew closer to the children. I organised football games, softball competitions, took them camping to Mount Gandul and the Ketu Forest and sometimes to the south coast. My excellent parents came to stay with me from time to time, worried about my isolation in Wonogiri and me living in an empty house. They had never had my experience and tended to exaggerate the significance of its superficial aspects. Their marriage had been arranged soundly and neatly by effort of parents and relatives on both sides; the result had been flawless; and so the collapse of my independent attempt was understandably shocking to them, a tragedy as far as they were concerned, although one in a somewhat different sense to that which I felt.

'Dear boy, what you've just gone through proves that not every modern way suits these people of ours.'

'H'm.'

'Yes, take this business of finding your own wife, Yok. Our ways of going about that kind of thing very seldom failed to the extent of a total breakdown. We always looked far ahead and weighed things up, compared this with that, and talked it over among all the parties. By the time everything had been discussed and the young people been paired off, only the ceremonies of the proposal were left to do.'

'Weren't there failures too, Pak?'

'There were, my boy, there were, but not many. I believe that if you had consulted with us from the start, it all would have come to something better than this.'

'Yes, but Pak, even if I had done that, how would you and our relatives have solved the problem of the different faiths?'

'Why, there wouldn't have been a problem! Because we would have carped at you from the earliest moment not to go ferreting outside your own religion, and we would have plucked at your tail, and you would have been surrounded, for your own good, by such a circle of disapproval and nagging that it would have distracted you and kept you from ever drawing too close to the girl. That's how!'

In point of fact, whenever the subject came up I would have liked to have debated it with my father, because I felt that I had done no wrong, the love which Dik Nunuk and I had for each other was good; but I abandoned the hope of coming to any understanding with either of my parents. They felt they should have been involved in my relationship with Dik Nunuk, and so it was also a matter of wounded pride and regret for them that they had been

5. Hardojo

left out of the matter. And I took the view, too, that sad as my experience had been, I cherished it. I considered that I had done what was needed and needed to be done by me and no one else: I had struck out alone and won the heart of a young woman, unassisted by the vast circle of a family. I savoured, was inspired by, the beauty, the joyousness and poignancy of that relationship. My life had become a richer, broader thing since I had known Dik Nunuk and her world. Failing to wed her I considered a misfortune, a matter of fate. My father's era was receding quickly, a new approach to many things was needed, and if the approach failed in its results, that was not necessarily because it was new. My father talked confidently of his way being best and most successful: his wife had been chosen during a family conference, the girl herself was a distant relative. And it had to be admitted that their marriage worked: the two had passed through the whole process without first meeting or having had time to consider braiding any sort of affection before being wed, and yet their marriage had worked sincerely and strongly to their present old age. But was that their good fortune, I asked myself, disgruntled, and was that the only difference with my experience? Naturally, my father would reject that it was just fate—while as a good Javanese he believed well enough in fate and the need to submit to it, or to Lord Allah, anyway—and, on the other hand, he held that human beings should not merely suffer and endure but should work, strive, and seek out better, more apt ways of doing things, ways of living. And that ought surely to encompass new ways of finding one's life-partner. Well, perhaps the best compromise this age could offer, or at least appeared to have offered my sister Soemini anyway, was the manner in which she had married: involving the satisfaction of both families and yet giving the couple a reasonably long opportunity to get to know each other and partake in the decision.

With many such equivocal thoughts, I set myself to confront my future.

One afternoon, I was supervising a game of softball, and as usual the children were excited and there was lot of banter and noise. It came to the turn of one of the girls, Sumarti, to take the bat. I had noticed before that she was rather slow and not very good at games, and on this occasion she missed the ball several times. Finally connecting, she flung the bat away and commenced a shuffling run towards first base. Our playground was an uneven field which had been planted with crops in the past and was now grassed-over. Slow as she was, yet prodded on by the general shouting and the sound of someone behind her pursuing her with the retrieved ball, Sumarti tripped and measured her length on the ground, just short of the base. Without pity, the pursuer whacked the ball into Sumarti's back. Sumarti gasped, but it was not from the sting of the ball but because something had happened to one of her ankles, which she now grasped with obvious pain. I stopped the game and went to her, and it appeared that she had a sprain, winced and was unable to stand when I tried to help her up. I had a buggy called and took her to the local doctor, then returned with her to her home, she with one ankle bandaged from the heel up. We surprised Sumarti's parents, arriving like that, and as they helped her to hobble into the house I was asked in with the usual ceremonies and courtesies. I explained what had happened, assured them that it was just a light sprain and recommended that Sumarti should rest the foot for a few days.

The accident meant that I had to visit the house for some time daily to see how my injured pupil progressed. Her father was a retired subdistrict head, had acted as an assistant wedana in Selogiri, and now lived a pensioner in Wonogiri together with his wife and this his only child. It occurred to me then that Sumarti must have been an offspring of the couple's later years, to be at HIS in the seventh class when her father had passed retirement-age.

Her performance at school was average, not brilliant but even; she was certainly by no means a bad pupil: in fact, achieving her levels was quite laudable, especially when those were in Dutch, history and geography, subjects beyond the usual bounds of a girl from an outlying kabupaten such as Wonogiri. A Wonogiri lass who could extend her interests beyond the domestic, could master a sufficiency of those modern disciplines, and manage to finish HIS, would be deemed *algemeen ontwikkeld*, 'generally well-educated', and so fitted for entry into the world of the Javanese gentry-professionals. Why, I began to consider further, such a one, were she to marry a rising priyayi, should be well able to cope with the social demands of the class, be capable of meeting the wives of her husband's superiors and the *nyonya kontrolir*, the European wife of the local Dutch district officer. Soemini was just such an example, although she had known certain advantages in her case, had gone to van Deventer and so on. Now the wife of an assistant district head, my sister was smooth in company, fluent in Dutch, infallible in matters of etiquette: in short, an ideal wife for that role. Sumarti was no Soemini, was far more humble a case, could not be called particularly beautiful either. Not that she should be termed ugly by any means. She had a rather sweet face when one considered it. Hardly to be compared with Dik Nunuk's, of course. But then . . . well, one best did away with that kind of thinking.

I became an increasingly familiar visitor at the Brotodinomo house, located behind the Wonogiri jail. At first it was partly formal calls: a teacher's interest in the family background of one of his pupils, chatting about any problems which might affect school-work, that sort of thing. There was the additional motive of checking on Sumarti's injury. But my visits in time grew to become those of a familiar and welcomed acquaintance: I would often be found there having tea and fried bananas or potato chips, the usual afternoon snacks of the region. In time, their hospitality extended to dinners: not overly-

5. Hardojo

sumptuous but far less dismal than those of a lone bachelor. I did have a servant who cooked for me, but his talents were wretched, and anyway what mattered most was the appeal of being among people; although, alas, the anticipation of those visits tended to bring to mind other evenings at Madiotaman. But enough of that, I kept telling myself; and in time and with an effort I learned to forestall those intruding scenes by playing a sort of trick on them: I would interpose memories of equally agreeable warmth and laughter at past family dinners, in Wanagalih!

Sumarti herself was not much seen during my visits, and when she did emerge to greet me it was with the retiring manner of one for whom I was as much *Meneer* Hardojo there as at school. To display her school-Dutch to her parents, I would coax a few phrases from her, more or less as *Meneer* Soetardjo had done with Soemini in past days: and, yes, it was with an awe so reminiscent of my parents' that the Brotodinomo couple listened to their daughter speaking Dutch. At dinner, Sumarti did not eat with us but waited at the table, sitting beside it and encouraging the guest, the honoured *Meneer*, to take more of this or that, all in the soft tone and modest demeanour of a Javanese girl being brought up to the world of priyayi manners.

One morning, I was summoned to the office of the school head. As I entered I saw someone there who by his long jacket and batik headdress I recognised as a court official, and Wonogiri being within one of the Mangkunegaran-administered kabupaten I surmised he came from the Prince in Solo. *Meneer* Soedirdjo, the school head, introduced the visitor as a gentleman of the palace who had been instructed by His Highness to oversee the recruitment of a teacher to head a new centre in the principality devoted to adult instruction and the promotion of certain extracurricular youth activities.

'In my opinion, sir, Dimas Hardojo here would be very suitable for your purposes. That is, if you were to be interested, Dimas.'

I was unable to answer, the offer coming so suddenly. I needed to sound it out.

'I'm very gratified to have been considered for such work, but somewhat astonished. Are there no others better qualified?'

Meneer Soedirdjo understood well that I was hedging my response while I awaited more information; and in any case it would not have done to reply at once too categorically: that would have been a sin against the rules of Javanese negotiating.

He answered: 'My dear Dimas Hardojo, we, those of us with an interest in an indigenous education system, have kept an eye on you and been impressed by your talent for organisation as well as teaching. You like sports, excursions, you go camping with the children, and in addition you have artistic interests which appear to us to rub off on those you teach.'

Here the visitor joined in: 'If I may be straightforward with you, *Meneer* Hardojo, *Meneer* Soedirdjo and I have been considering you for some time, and we have decided that you are precisely the sort of person the palace would like to employ.'

'Well, I'm overwhelmed. I can only express my unbounded thanks to you both.'

'Yes, but what is your opinion, *Meneer* Hardojo? Is this an attractive proposition, do you think? Although I must tell you immediately that the pay would be a little below what you presently get from the *gupermen*. The jurisdiction of Mangkunegaran is not quite as wealthy.'

I considered the offer. The matter of a drop in wages did not bother me greatly, I was unmarried; and, anyhow, whatever the palace paid would certainly be enough for the normal needs of its employees. For an instant, the thought of living in Solo, a place that held so many poignant memories for me, made me almost dizzy, but I mentally waved it aside: nearly two years had passed, long enough to erase that particular smart if I was ever to make a go of life as a professional person and a man. The offer was attractive and challenging. Although I was happy enough to do anything involved with teaching, doing it in a dull little place like Wonogiri did diminish that satisfaction.

'Why don't you come with me to Solo, *Meneer* Hardojo, and I'll introduce you to a few of my superiors? There's the deputy bupati, and His Excellency the Chief Minister, and perhaps His Highness himself will tell you in his own words what we have to offer.'

'Yes, and if Dimas Hardojo here would like to do that, sir, I'll be happy to give him a few days' leave. What do you say, Dimas?'

Good, generous *Meneer* Soedirdjo, prepared to lose one of his own teachers for this cause! I agreed to the suggestion and made preparations to leave for Solo on the morrow. Also, before departing, I wrote and posted detailed letters to my parents and to my brother and sister, informing them among other things that I would visit Wanagalih after my interviews at the court. I was becoming more careful now about keeping everyone abreast of any significant intentions of mine. On the train to Solo, a curious thing happened. Perhaps it was some lingering idea of my parents and how they had been betrothed and lived so well together, a thought I now associated with the endless landscape of growing and ever-reproductive rice, so characteristically Javanese, but I became aware that I had been looking out of the window and thinking of Sumarti. By the time the train reached Sangkrah station the fields had long faded and been replaced by the image of her face.

What the palace functionary had kindly represented to me in Wonogiri, did in fact occur: I was fully briefed by various court officials on the scope of

5. Hardojo

my proposed duties, and on the last day of my visit was brought into the presence of His Highness himself. When the Prince's invitation came, I was thrown into some disorder. Yes, I was the son of a priyayi, yet my father was one of the lowest of that order, merely the head of a village school; and my family were no natives of Solo but of the Madiun area. Madiun had once been a tributary of Mataram, and continued its connection long after the time when Solo had broken away from Mataram and, more in favour with the Dutch, had developed as a rival to Mataram's capital, Yogya. And my passing through HIS, *Kweekschool*, and then a higher *Kweekschool* for Javanese, was all very well, but hardly enough to have fashioned me into any particularly confident, sophisticated, 'Europeanised' adult. Suddenly, I was aware that I would be coming into the presence of a descendant of one of Java's royal lines; a minor rajah, admittedly, who shared Solo with a sultan senior to him and was thus only one of the two titular heads of a fragment from that old Mataram; yet, minor or not, this was a Javanese rajah, and I must needs owe him respect, however reduced his pomp and power.

I had been told to present myself in the Prangwedana pendopo, the gathering place of military staff in former years. It was a smaller building on the east side of the central palace, and I was escorted to it by the same official I had met in Wonogiri. He acted as both my guide within the grounds and as an instructor in palace etiquette, and as we entered the pendopo he mentioned that this small but impressive structure had come to serve as the court of the princely heir next in line of succession. A group of boys and girls, van Deventer pupils I thought, and possibly some from the girls' school Siswo Rini, were just finishing their dancing lessons. We sat down to wait in a southern corner of the pendopo. Soon His Highness appeared striding towards us, and as we rose the first thing I noted was his clothing: ivory-white long jacket, sarong, batik headdress. We greeted him reverentially with a *sembah*: palms together, fingertips upwards and touching the forehead. He asked us to be seated, and as we assumed deferential attitudes in our places I had the opportunity to quickly note that His Highness, Prince and Supreme Bupati, The Most Noble Mangkunegara VII, seemed actually quite a dashing person, with a handsome face sporting a small, thick moustache. That rather secular detail, and a first impression of cheerful vigour that by no means detracted from an aura of authority, I found effectively calming.

Unexpectedly, his first words were addressed directly to me and were in Dutch: '*Hoe gaat 't met U, Meneer* Hardojo?'

I replied to the greeting by the most refined Javanese I was capable of: implying by doing so that my own Dutch could not possibly attain to the perfection acquired by His Highness. What followed next was a monologue of the kind one hears in a shadow play, where a rajah unfolds to his subordinates the high plans and visions of a noble, ambitious mind. The monologue was conducted in a mixture of high and medium Javanese interspersed with Dutch, never descending to the unadorned and ritually demeaning informality available to those of his rank. I could only respect him the more for this generous, essentially democratic gesture: by it we were all being elevated to the one level, his.

And the subject matter was appealing as well: in lively language it invited me and my esteemed guide to imagine the realm of Mangkunegaran, minute though it might be, as a flourishing, bountiful land preparing to meet the challenges of the modern era. Two reasonably large sugar factories were already operating in Tasikmadu and Tjolomadu; rice harvests and the production of other crops were going well; the district surrounding the Mangkunegaran palace in Solo was complimented for its cleanliness; schools were going up and teaching was very satisfactory, with the Solo HIS Siswo in particular staffed by graduates from HIK, HKS and van Deventer, some even holding the *hoofdakte* higher diploma. The arts were thriving, with various gamelan and dance groups active and presentations of dance and wayang drama staged on a regular basis in the Mangkunegaran pendopo; so too with seminars on Javanese culture, philosophy, and art, conducted in this very pendopo we were in now; all with the aim, His Highness said, of making his little principality into one that would be progressive and welcoming to modern ways. But promoting this goal still further required raising the general literacy of adult villagers; and as for the youth of the principality, he was concerned that they should be involved in physically and socially developmental activities in addition to their schooling, His Highness repeating several times his conviction that the foundation of even such a small, perhaps powerless but advancing Javanese princedom as this, must be its people, young and old alike. Therefore, he desired that a plan of attack on adult illiteracy should be implemented forthwith, which in addition would also contain programmes of health-education, the furthering of handicrafts and home industries, and in the schools a campaign should begin to popularise scouting and youth sports.

When he fell silent I could sense his gaze on me.

'How do you see this plan, *Meneer* Hardojo? Do you find it interesting, perhaps appealing to your instincts as a teacher?'

'I find it very interesting, Your Highness.'

'Would you be prepared to leave your employment with the *gupermen* and move to Mangkunegaran?'

'Ready and willing, Your Highness.'

'There is one matter, which I think Minister Sarwoko here has already broached. Our wages aren't as high.'

'I was told, Your Highness. I am prepared to accept, nonetheless.'

'Good. I hope you'll be happy with us. Whatever else, here you'll be working with your own Javanese administration, not that of the *gupermen*.'

5. Hardojo

And thus I made my decision. I would move to Mangkunegaran at the end of the school year, leaving me one last term of teaching in Wonogiri. On my way to Wanagalih aboard the SS to Paliyan, I silently pondered the course of my career up to now: an unlikely-seeming progression. Who would have thought that after enjoying a secure position in a *gupermen* HIS I would consider returning to the villages to teach or to oversee the teaching of grown peasants and their children?

Gazing out of the window, the thought of Sumarti returned to me, and dwelling on her face I suddenly wondered: Now look, what *is* this? Calf love at your age? Could it be possible? Such an ordinary girl, distant from you by some eight years? I had to admit to having grown fond of her gradually, by unnoticed stages which began that day I brought the poor inept child home with her injury, and then subsequently over many visits; so slowly compared to the radiant blaze of that time with Dik Nunuk. My feeling towards Sumarti, I saw now, had developed much more quietly and unseen; there were never those hours of walking out together, movable settings for love's explorations and discoveries; yet by those accumulated moments in Sumarti's home something serene but similar had burgeoned. At least in my feelings towards her. But had she responded? I now hoped and imagined that she had. Or was I deluding myself? Whatever the case, I must speak to her. Or should I go straight to her father first? And how old was Sumarti, actually? Probably no more than fourteen, or if she had started school late or failed a class, then fifteen. I recalled the time in my parent's house when we discussed Soemini's marriage and I had supported my sister's plea that she be allowed to continue her studies at the van Deventer school so that she should become better-educated and a little older before marrying. Could I now seek to marry Sumarti at *her* age? I decided to put aside these astonishing new revelations while I saw how other things developed.

My father welcomed me in Wanagalih with every sign of gratification. The letter I had sent him explaining my move to Mangkunegaran had indeed amazed him, but pleased him too.

'A good choice, my boy. Your mother and I are proud of you. Not a small matter, exchanging one hundred and ten guilders of *gupermen* pay for service at Mangkunegaran. I value that decision.'

'Yes, Pak, well there is the other matter that what they offered was far more interesting.'

'And that's to be expected. They say this Highness Mangkunegara Number Seven is something special; might amount to someone fit to follow his grandfather, Mangkunegara Number Four.'

'What else was the grandfather known for, Pak, besides writing the *Wedhatama* and the *Tripama*?'

Gentry

'What else? He started the sugar factories in Tjolomadu and Tasikmadu, that's what he did. He wasn't only a great scholar, he was a practical rajah as well, knew how to turn a coin. He was far-sighted, wanted to see his domain do well and his progeny have solid finances after him. This Number Seven, going by the plans he's outlined to you, is following in the other's footsteps.'

Before leaving my parents, I told them about my intentions towards Sumarti.

'Well, we can only consent, my boy, knowing that you've made an unfortunate choice once and must have learned by it. So, good. Write to us when you're ready, and we'll come to Wonogiri to make the proposal.'

My father in his usual parting homily urged me to be a careful, industrious worker in the Prince's cause.

'He may be a small rajah, nevertheless he's of your country's royalty, Yok. Don't trifle in those surroundings. That rajah has powers. You'll be close to luck and magic there.'

The way I chose to probe Sumarti's feelings towards me was to write her a letter. I gave it to her one day at the end of classes, asking her to read it carefully and not reveal it to her parents. In it I wrote that I hoped for a reply in the not too distant future; and in fact I did not have to wait long for that. Her short note did not respond directly to the sentiments I had declared to her, but consisted merely of an invitation relayed from her parents to come to dinner next Saturday evening. *Wah*! I thought, don't tell me she showed them the letter! And on Saturday I arrived at the house behind the Wonogiri jail in a disordered state of mind, with a sense of trepidation, youthful shyness, and a beating heart.

But the evening flowed along smoothly enough, the meal was the usual simple and good one: a spicy chicken-stew, fried tempeh, spiced vegetables, stir-fried spinach sprinkled with dry whitebait. The conversation meandered over various subjects, until we finally moved to the veranda for coffee and nuts; whereupon Sumarti's father leant forward on his chair, and seeming to fix his eyes on me for rather a long moment said: '*Meneer* Hardojo, if you would care to guide and educate Genduk Sumarti until she attains to some further maturity, my wife and I have no objections. And our daughter has likewise told us that she would be happy to receive your help and guidance in furthering her education.'

Well, I thought to myself, so that's the way of it! And as Sumarti's father was speaking I caught a glimpse of the girl herself standing on the threshold of the doorway to the inner room. She was looking at me and smiling. Sumarti, then, evidently no less successfully than my shrewd sister years ago, had found the art of inveigling parents to yield to a daughter's will!

Shortly thereafter, we—Sumarti's parents, mine, Sumarti and I—agreed

5. Hardojo

to hold the marriage one year after I had become established in Solo.

Almost without our being aware of the passage of time, suddenly it was 1940: which meant that we had been husband and wife six years and I had worked in Mangkunegaran seven years. We had a boy, Harimurti, who also had grown astonishingly quickly and attained the age of five. We had given him a name that translated from the Sanskrit as 'Touched by the Light of the Sun', because at birth his body was quite red, and wisdom had it that this was a sign he would grow up to be swarthy. With such a name we hoped the boy would be favoured by Lord Krishna, who also in his popular incarnation was dark, and indeed whose name literally means 'Black'. Krishna, characterised as Harimurti in the Javanese pantheon, was the avatar of Vishnu. Now, there was no question of involving our son in some claim of descent from the latter, but we did hope he might at least become wise in the manner of Vishnu incarnate, Krishna, he of the exemplary kingdom of Dwarawati; we hoped that he would be as wise and as heedful, sharply intuitive, capable of reading the signs of a changing era. That was something I truly wished, for the times were undergoing very great changes. Hitler and Germany had begun to move, and it might not be long before Holland was attacked, then what would happen to the Netherlands East Indies and to the jurisdiction of Mangkunegaran embedded therein?

Those six years of marriage, and seven in the service of the Prince, working practically directly under him, were happy, highly satisfying ones. As far as my domestic situation went, it hardly varied from that of my parents; a continuity which I had hardly expected, being someone who considered himself of the new, worldly generation. In the past my father and mother had advised and urged me more or less explicitly to follow in their steps, and I had nodded and duly replied with a dutiful *inggih*; but I had retained my reservations, I wanted to find my own way. Yet, surprisingly, the course of my life had taken me to Sumarti, and with the minimum of modern romantics we had succeeded in creating a mutually satisfying and happy marriage. Sumarti, my junior by quite a few years, matured quickly into a woman, a wife, and my counterpart in our social life. She rapidly took charge of our home, and followed appropriately and intelligently my position and duties as an official and employee of the Mangkunegaran court. If we knew essentially little about each other before marriage, there was ample time afterwards to warm into sweethearts and lovers; until occasionally I could imagine my father observing us from somewhere on the other side of our mosquito net, nodding at the way my wedded life had developed, smiling and murmuring: Didn't we tell you?

Gentry

My work, as I had anticipated, also turned out to be gratifying and full of interesting challenges. I frequently travelled to the districts and sub-districts of the principality, inspecting developments in outlying villages, eventually becoming familiar with all the divisions of its two kabupaten, Wonogiri and Karanganyar. Those divisions were Wuryantoro, Jumapolo, Ngadirojo, Jatisrono, Eromoko, Mojogedang, Matesih and Tawangmangu; and our attacks on illiteracy in them did indeed go well beyond just instructing the children, for I went from school to school encouraging the teachers to set up adult classes, and I stressed that the subject matter in those must be of interest and relevant to the daily life of grown-ups: the language should conform to the pronunciation and vocabulary they heard at home, in the fields, the markets, and about in their villages. And it was a gladdening thing and very moving to watch the attentive faces of those rugged peasants following their lessons in such classes, the men often come straight from the paddies, having leant their mattocks and other implements against the school wall, the women perhaps arrived earlier than their husbands, frequently bringing their infants with them to class. Yes, their seriousness, the enthusiasm shining from those plain, country faces, could almost bring tears to the eyes. Was I so stirred because I could always visualise in the back of my mind the lives of these people: hard, invariant, often miserable? Or because—and it frequently worried me—I knew that what they were studying, were reading and writing with such effort, represented knowledge and skills of uncertain value to them? There was an occasion when I said as much to my father, knowing that he had attempted to do similar things in Wanalawas once and had sadly failed in that initiative.

'Yes, Lé, I know what you mean, and I too questioned the use of what I was doing.'

'And?'

'Well, you see, I said to myself, I'll supply them with this knowledge, these provisions for life if you like, and we'll see. It's in the nature of even our *wong cilik* to hunger for greater knowledge and awareness about things; and if it doesn't go further than satisfying that for most of them, yet a few may get some practical value too.'

'And, Bapak, you didn't regret it when you had to stop mid-way?'

'What I regretted was stopping because of the sins of Soenandar, your younger cousin, that poor, unfortunate, misbegotten boy. But I don't regret starting the project. For the spirit in which I ventured on it, I am indebted to your Pakdé Martoatmodjo. *There* was a brave person, and he opened your father's eyes. And if there's anything else that I'm troubled about, it's the fact that I didn't have the courage to confront that damned *schoolopziener* and risk being fired.'

He drew a long breath and remained silent for a moment.

5. Hardojo

'But I have to tell you, my boy, that I and your mother had to be careful at the time, and to consider that you and your brother and sister had not set yourselves up in life then; and so if I had lost my position I would have been in the wrong in not being able then to do a father's duty by you all. That's how I see it.'

I was touched to hear this explanation, half-defensive, from my father, and felt sorry for him; and felt also as if I had been prying into something which should have been left alone.

'And there, Bapak, as regards your bringing us up, you and Ibu will never have any reason to blame yourselves. We three have been fortunate in having you as parents. You'll both be our heroes, always.'

There was a moment when my father's eyes seemed to glisten and grow moist, and as usual my mother chose the right moment to change the subject.

'Time to eat. We've got some nice beef stew to go with the rice tonight, and it'll get cold if we don't go now.'

I left them soon after, knowing that I was taking with me one unspoken instruction from my father: to do what he had been unable to complete in Wanalawas, to continue to a conclusion the work I was doing under His Highness in Mangkunegaran.

Hari, as we commonly called our son, proved to be our only child. Sumarti was a rather small woman for the size of the baby, and the delivery was a hard one and had everybody worried. Fortunately, the birth was successful if painful; however something must have happened internally with Sumarti, because we had no more children after that. After two or three years, we saw that Allah had decided it so. And after all Sumarti also came from a small family, and we were happy enough to have produced a son. And our sense of satisfaction was not misplaced, for Hari grew into a strong boy, rather dark-complexioned as we had guessed, and as intelligent and considerate as we could hope. By the age of six he could read well and calculate: obviously having a teacher-father employed in anti-illiteracy work must have been no handicap there. He delighted in animals, little and large, and our house when he was young resembled a small zoo, with two dogs—reproductive and difficult to keep to that number—a cat, an indeterminate horde of rabbits in a cage, and several birds: a dove, a bulbul, and a golden oriole. Caring for those kept Hari and the house-servant busy.

But what particularly drew our attention as parents was Hari's choice of friends. When he began to go to school, those friends were of course other schoolchildren, and since he went to the Mangkunegaran HIS Siswo, a school for the children of priyayi, his companions were of that social level. But at home, Hari mixed with the kampong children living behind our house. Ours was one of a row of houses in Punggawan, so-called mansions built in masonry and with relatively large front and side yards. This row was occupied mainly by officials of the court and those employed by the *gupermen*. Behind it was the Punggawan kampong, the majority of whose residents were labourers working in the sugar factories and various businesses, and there were as well sundry repairers of bicycles, batik-dyers, handymen, food hawkers, and such like. Those households were crammed together, often a number of families occupying the space intended for one: subletting of free rooms and other space by those who had been first to dwell there being a common practice. The kampong children played wherever they could, in the gaps between houses, on roads and pathways, some as young as or even younger than four, following their supposedly attending older brothers and sisters about. Hari's acquaintance with those ragamuffins began at a time when two trees growing in our front yard, an ambarella plum and a rose apple, came into luxuriant fruiting. He was just five then, and as a child of our status the only time he had been allowed past the fence was when an invitation came to join friends deemed suitable, and that was only in their homes and if he was accompanied there. On this occasion, an afternoon, he was playing under the plum tree with Sadimin, our servant who acted as the boy's caretaker and general assistant in his games. A group of the kampong children collected on the other side of the fence and stood there.

One of them called quietly to Hari: 'Gus, hey Gus, can we have some plums, please?'

Hari looked at them in surprise, as if he was seeing their like for the first time; then he gave them a cheerful wave and grin.

They waved back happily, and the same one repeated the appeal: 'Yeah, Gus, just a little bunch, Gus, please.'

'Just a little bunch? Come in. Pick all you want.'

Sadimin was shocked, and immediately protested: '*Wah*, Gus, your father and mother will be cross—inviting a lot of scruffy kampong children in here!'

'Oh, let them in. I bet they don't have any fruit trees where they are. It makes you sad. Let them in. Come in, come in.'

Without further ado, the children entered and began climbing all over the tree, and Sadimin soon afterwards came to report this strange transgression to me. Sumarti and I were both taken aback, imagining our clean, well-dressed boy among a tribe of ragged kampong children, who probably seldom got a bath and might have scabies and those white blotches of fungus all over their bodies. Such seemed to be their typical state of health.

'Now, Sum, what is it with this boy of yours? You're letting him play with the kampong children now? Call him in here!'

'Yes, I know, but he does need friends after all. He's growing quickly; only five, but the way he thinks and acts, he's far more mature. Like a seven-year-old, I would say.'

'But they're not fit companions for someone like Hari, Sum, don't you see? They use all kinds of improper and bad language. We're Mangkunegaran people. How would it sound if our child suddenly broke out with something frightful in company?'

I saw that Sum was smiling, and that stopped me, surprised.

'Come now, Mas, come. What kind of people are we, did you say? We're from Wanagalih and from Wonogiri, two little towns, hardly more than villages.'

'Er . . . so?'

'So we, including Hari, don't differ all that much from those children out there.'

'Well there, Sum, I have to disagree. Our back-country children may be poor, but they do use polite language, and I'm more concerned with that than with fungus and scabies.'

Sum smiled again.

'You're too quick to see trouble, Mas. Hari's with us most of the time. If we hear that his language is being—contaminated—won't we be here to bring him back to order?'

I gave up. Ultimately, I respected my wife's untroubled tolerance in the matter, and her willingness to be a good example to both Hari and the kampong children, and so we let him have his way. As a result, we now frequently saw in our yard grids marked out for team games, groups of children intent on marbles, and so on. What was painful to look at was the state of our two trees: the fruit was never given a chance to ripen but was pulled down mercilessly when still green.

Hari was among the youngest there, yet it was noticeable that even the older of the street children deferred to him. Whether this was because of the status of our family or the fact that he was then in the first year of HIS, whereas they attended some version of a village school, or indeed had no school to go to at all, I cannot say. I have to acknowledge that my worries about his language deteriorating, and the perils of skin disease, eventually faded. Hari's vocabulary did broaden—and sometimes to our dismay—but we controlled that aspect reasonably successfully; and, interestingly, at least inasmuch as I could judge, the behaviour and language of Hari's kampong friends improved. Sumarti often talked to them and now and then treated them to banana custard of an afternoon, and that might have had something to do with it.

I was particularly happy to notice in this open-hearted behaviour towards the local children that Hari gave all the signs of developing into what we had hoped at his birth: a person capable of feeling sympathy towards his fellows. I have increasingly been of the opinion that all children contain in their bodies, hearts and brains those qualities which naturally tend towards each child's best flourishing, given the right conditions. Perhaps in that respect, and in view of later developments, I might have allowed Hari more liberty to mix with those friends in a less controlled way, and then his generous view of them might eventually have become qualified by reality: for he was never allowed to leave the boundaries of our property, to follow the kampong children into their world, their own streets, to wander with them among the drains, looking for tadpoles and minnows. Even that can sound like he was denied an idyllic freedom, whereas my intention is to say that his association with them, his knowledge of these children of 'the masses', was ultimately somewhat coloured and distant. Unfortunately, those superficial impressions on a tender-hearted child seemed eventually to have had some unhappy consequences.

I was invited one evening to come to a conference on developments in the Javanese language, featuring as speakers a number of Solo scholars prominent in cultural areas and language teaching. The conference took place in the Prangwedanan pendopo, where His Highness was also to attend. In fact he spoke as well, after having listened attentively to the guests. One of those, Raden Mas Pringgokusumo, made the point that knowledge of Javanese was becoming erratic among the new youth, and younger Javanese were increasingly confusing the levels; tending nowadays to employ a middle level or an informal one, irrespective of the person being addressed. Following this observation by Denmas Pringgo, a debate went on for some time around the question of who should be responsible for correcting such a situation; concluding that it could be none other than teachers and parents. His Highness closed the night by delivering a positive instruction: the beauty and richness of the Javanese language, an inheritance from our forefathers and integral to our culture, must be preserved from misuse or, God forbid, demise. Towards that goal of safeguarding Javanese, he wished that children should be guided to use it in its entirety, and be urged to employ the correct levels even when speaking to their friends and siblings. Children should become practiced in the fine social distinctions that the language levels implied and conveyed, and, with that, acquire the necessary etiquette of social interactions. Correct speech and good manners are the mirror of a cultured people, His Highness said.

As I pedalled home on my bicycle, I considered the thought-provoking points that had been made at the pendopo, and then the two Mangkunegaran kabupaten I frequently inspected came to mind. I knew that good Javanese was used there, even in villages furthest from the court. I often asked myself how those ordinary peasants managed to know so well our complicated, confusing language. On the other hand, I remembered that in the villages around Wanagalih the levels were not quite as well adhered to; and that made me wonder if it had to do with the distance of our Wanagalih people from the direct influence of a Javanese rajah, and the fact that they came more under the control of the *gupermen*. Or was it that those living around Wanagalih had never felt the levels of the language to be so important? Yet in my parents' house and among my father's friends they certainly *were* considered important. Had that to do with it upholding their own position: did my father and his card-playing colleagues, debating around the *kesukan* table, believe that a full mastery of Javanese was a significant quality in a priyayi, perhaps in their view the most significant? So what was a priyayi? Was he not, after all, just a Javanese on an administrative ladder, unconcerned by the question of who employed him, the *gupermen* or others? And then I remembered the sharp and interesting three-way dispute among Soetan Takdir Alisjahbana, a modernist and emancipationist; Sanoesi Pane, who focused on the glories of the Hindu-Javanese past; and Ki Hadjar Dewantara, whose concern was with creating a practical national education. How brilliant and daring they were, and what a far-sighted view they had of our culture, our civilization! Could the culture and language of Java be safeguarded during the coming times of change, wished for by Tuan Alisjahbana, feared by Sanoesi Pane, expected as inevitable by Ki Hadjar Dewantara? I wondered how much, ultimately, even such a wise and careful authority as my own rajah, here in Solo, could influence this issue. I understood well why he needed to be prudent and self-restrained. Mangkunegaran, small and weak as it was, remained a fragment of the once-mighty kingdom of Mataram, and even his instruction to us tonight to confirm Javanese youth in the language and culture of their forebears might be the cause of some careful deliberation in the residence of the chief Tuan near Purbayan. That gentleman observed very closely indeed every movement of the prince; and, for that matter, of the sultan of Solo, the other, if less obtrusively active, local potential successor to Mataram.

There was still time to get some fried noodles for Sumarti from Pak Kromo in Keprabon; she should be up yet when I got home. But who should I see leaving Pak Kromo's handcart, in a gharry with her husband? Dik Nunuk. I had thought they had gone to Semarang.

That night the noodles seemed strangely tasteless, and it was only after I had been staring at the ceiling for a long time that I finally fell asleep.

Eyang Kusumo Lakubroto was a very distant granduncle to me. When the Javanese say that a member of their extended family, some uncle, be he pakdé or paklik, is distant, or a nephew or niece or any other such relative is distant, they mean that the connection is almost invisible, barely traceable. Eyang Kusumo Lakubroto's until-then unsuspected existence in the thickets of our family tree was suddenly revealed by the gentleman himself arriving to reside with us on Setenan Road, one day when I was still studying at HIS. My father, caught unprepared, recovered quickly enough and introduced him to us carefully by the title *Eyang*, 'Grandfather', although in point of fact he was no more than something of the order of an elder uncle to us, an almost undetectably-remote pakdé. Part of the explanation for the honorific emerged while my father with some effort located the place our visitor occupied in a complicated and to us incomprehensible family genealogy. Part required that form of address because it seems we had just welcomed into our home a person of some considerable spiritual proficiency and eminence, who had arrived specifically to bathe in our holy river Ketangga. Now, it may be known but worth explaining again that the Ketangga, although a small stream compared to our Solo and Madiun Rivers, is believed by many of the older folk living thereabouts to possess an inordinate and eerie magic. Thus, as one who travelled about the island to meditate while immersed in such transcendental waters, and who had furthermore seen fit to adopt the name Kusumo Lakubroto—rendered in common language as 'Blossom of Austerity'—the old man considered the appellation *Eyang* to correspond best with what he himself regarded as his status.

We in my parent's family were never allowed to forget our fortune in having among us someone so illustrious, and while he remained with us in Wanagalih Eyang Kusumo was the centre of respectful attention, our parents treating him cautiously as a wise old sage deserving deference of the highest order. They never dared speak to him other than on the royal level of Javanese, and they totally accepted that he was an incomparable mystic; at least I think they believed such a thing, I was never quite sure. Typically, he would get out of bed well after ten o'clock; by which time my mother and the servants had long been up and my father gone to his school. Yawning, he would enquire disinterestedly of my mother: 'That spouse of yours . . . gone off already, mm?'

'Gone, Eyang. What would Eyang like to drink this morning?'

'Coffee as usual, do I need tell you? Nice and strong, Nduk, thick and sweet.'

My mother would smile at being addressed like a servant girl.

'Oh, Eyang, how could I presume? You might like something else one day.'

Yawning again, the old man would dismiss that and go on to another tack: 'Strange, how every morning I want to get up early to go with your husband and always seem to miss him. I could help him if he waited. He doesn't know that a morning walk is a kind of spiritual exercise too.'

'Oh, he'd be happy enough just to get a breath of fresh air, Eyang.'

5. Hardojo

'Fresh air? Foo to that, Nduk! You don't know much either. That first stroll in the morning, what you see as just that, is an act replete with spiritual profit if you and your spouse only knew. And that's why I really must take him in hand. But I seem always to miss him. I should at least join him for breakfast before he goes.'

'*Wah*, Eyang, and you up to the neck in the Ketangga almost every night, practically till dawn. Don't think of it. We don't mind. Get up as late as you want, Eyang. This is your home too.'

'Yes, well, all right. Is that coffee coming yet?'

'Coming, coming. And your morning savouries, Eyang.'

'*Wah*, save those for the children. I have fried rice in the morning, is that clear? I'm getting bored with this peanut sauce and boiled rice and vegetables that get served up all the time.'

'Fried rice? Immediately!'

And mother would rush off to fulfil Eyang's demands.

But in time she, and father too, would grow fatigued in this service. Eyang's residence, sometimes lasting for weeks, would finally produce a tremor of restlessness throughout our whole household; and when the time came one day when he would declare that he must go roving to some other holy spot—to Mount Lawu, Mount Merapi, Mount Kedul, or heaven knows what other Mount—well, what a surge of relief was felt! My father would press some money into Eyang's hand, almost as if to speed him on his way, money which would initially be resisted and then accepted with ill grace. Nevertheless, when he returned, months later or whenever, I recall with what excitement and noise we received him again. Particularly mother, who would eventually be the most exercised of us all; and she would lay duties on Soemini too, who as another female must leave nothing undone in the service of Eyang Kusumo.

After we had grown up and left Wanagalih, we tended to adopt a far less awed attitude towards the old man whenever we returned to Setenan Road, even daring to annoy him. This was at about the time, as I recall, when Lantip had just come to live with us in Solo. That was how our own nephews and nieces too were beginning to respond to this 'grandfather' of theirs. But when we were still young we would gather around him in the evenings, before he left on his nightly expeditions to the kali or to some other local site of wonders, and we looked forward then to his stories as much as he enjoyed telling them. Eyang had little money to spend on the likes of us, but he made up for that by the exciting fund of mysterious and frightening experiences which he recounted serially.

'Eyang, have you really been troubled by ghosts and genies when you go to bathe in the Ketangga, and met many celestial beauties?'

'Ah, often, lad, many a time.'

'Really? Often? Well, what do they look like?'

'*Wah*, horrible. Unless they come to you like damsels to tempt you. But that beauty of theirs only lasts for a moment, and then you see they've got fangs. To get at your blood, see. Heeeee, but it gives you a fright.'

'But, Eyang, you wouldn't be really scared, would you?'

'I would, just for a moment. But your grandfather knows some mantras to cope with those demons. They clear off when I begin.'

We clicked our tongues in astonishment; and someone like Mas Noeg might ask Eyang if he would teach him one of his mantras.

'Heh-heh-heh . . . not at your age, my boy. One day when you finish middle school you might be ready, and then Eyang will come and instruct you properly.'

But, alas, such a promise never led to anything; and it might very well have been given the last time we 'grandchildren' surrounded Eyang for one of his nightly performances, because about then he seemed to disappear for good one morning, and we never saw him again in Wanagalih. A considerable time afterwards, when I had completed HIK, the upper-secondary teacher-training school of the Dutch period, we heard that Eyang Kusumo Lakubroto had become the boss of a travelling troupe and garnered two of its best ladies for himself.

Then, one afternoon years later, when I had become the head of a family and was in the Mangkunegaran service, and Lantip had been with us for some time, a gharry rolled into our yard in Solo, and who should be sitting in the back? None other than Eyang Kusumo! Yes, it was inescapably his shape beneath the canopy. Except that when the vehicle came to a stop in front of our veranda we were startled again: for Eyang inside it, who might have been expected to have grown older since we had last seen him, appeared now positively withered. His erstwhile rather handsomely-mature countenance was furrowed and frowning; and if we had imagined him, in his role as a troupe manager, surrounded by his harem and looking like nothing if not Prabu Anglingdarma, the incarnation of Vishnu . . . well, we were thoroughly shocked by the picture of affliction he presented. We, all of us, my wife and I, Hari and Lantip, hurried down to proffer a chorus of welcome to our descending guest.

'Pay the driver, dear boy, will you.'

I quickly changed course to the front of the gharry, paid, and just as quickly returned to join my wife in supporting Eyang up the stairs into the house. His luggage consisted of one much worn suitcase, and the boys took that up. The moment we entered the inner room, and before we could offer him a seat, he suddenly threw his arms around me and in a heartbroken tone keened: 'Oh, Allah. Oh, heaven. My dear young ones, your Eyang is finished, his old carcass is done in. It's the end, children, the end.'

5. Hardojo

'Take a seat, take a seat, Eyang! Leave everything to us. Sumarti, get some hot tea!'

'Coffee, Nduk, black. Make it strong, plenty of sugar.'

'Oh, certainly, Eyang, certainly.'

I had once described the old man to Marti, and she was smiling as she left the room to carry out his command.

'That would be your wife then, boy?'

'Yes, Eyang.'

'Seems alert enough. And this one, who's he?'

'This is my son Hari, Eyang.'

'Reasonable-looking chap. And who's this? Oh wait, isn't he the peasant boy from Wanalawas, who worked as a servant for your father? The sprig's grown. Could take him for priyayi stock.'

Lantip gave an embarrassed smile and acknowledged the unintended compliment: 'A thousand thanks, Eyang.'

'Hush your mouth—you! Don't you dare refer to me as your eyang! When you were the height of a monkey from Randublantung Forest you knew enough manners to call me Ndoro Sepuh—Honourable Ancient—and now that you're grown a bit, you dare forget yourself?'

I hurriedly explained things to our prickly visitor: 'Pardon, Eyang, I beg your pardon, but you must understand that we took Lantip here into our family and now he's like our own child. We see him as a kakak to Hari, as Hari's older brother.'

'We-e-el now, that's fine for you and it may be your view of it, but to me he's that village boy from Wanalawas. Your Eyang stands by his title of Raden Mas, expects that level of courtesies—and it and they, I might tell you, are not far lower than a regent's.'

I lacked the courage to further defend Lantip's situation. It looked very much as though Eyang Kusumo had actually changed very little. When he had drained his coffee, he told us the sorry tale of what had happened to him. In brief, his travelling troupe had disintegrated after Eyang had piled up debts everywhere. One day the troupe had to dissolve, and his ladies were acquired by another company of players.

'They all, all of them, left me. All those I had taught the most sacred lore, taught the art and techniques of acting. They forgot me and departed. Oh, Allah, if only you could conceive the bitterness of it.'

'Don't take it too hard, Eyang, be easy. You're with us and safe now.'

He seemed to pick up at this, his face glowed a little, a hint of the old Prabu Anglingdarma returned to it.

'Really, my boy? I could rest a little while here? Nduk?'

Sumarti and I looked at each other with some dismay. Then we both smiled. We nodded to him. Eyang rose quickly to his feet and kissed us both vehemently on the cheeks, then he ruffled Hari's hair, and even Lantip's.

'Where's my room?'

Sumarti and I smiled again at each other. Yes, Eyang Kusumo was the old Eyang Kusumo, and we rapidly needed to adjust ourselves to being at his service for who knew how long. And, as expected, living with him was sometimes messy and his demands difficult to meet; yet there were many moments of entertainment too. Hari and Lantip were regaled endlessly with stories from Eyang's days of touring and presenting stage works: stories about royal Anglingdarma and his miraculous powers; about Prince Ronggo, the valorous son of glorious Senapati who founded the Mataram dynasty, the lad Ronggo begotten by Senapati from Ratu Kidul, the Empress of the South Sea; about the horrible spider Siluman, defeated by Prince Ronggo: all told with ardour and spellbinding histrionics. Hari's eyes in particular shone during those performances; but Eyang did not neglect to address his words to Lantip as well, who apparently humbled himself to the old man's satisfaction, calling him Ndoro Sepuh and always adopting a punctilious manner towards him. Until one day, some three months after Eyang Kusumo had come to live with us, Sumarti arrived breathless at my office, with concern and incomprehension written on her face.

'Mas, it's Pak . . . I mean Eyang Kusumo!'

'Oh, what's happened to him?'

'He's gone, left us!'

'What? Has he died?'

'No, no, he's gone away. He left a piece of paper.'

Sumarti gave it to me; and in brief it explained to 'his children' that the time had come for him to move on. We shouldn't try to look for him or to go after him. Surely, we would all meet again one day.

We returned home and found Hari in tears and Lantip sitting in contemplation. Then I hurried to Wanagalih: who knew, perhaps he had gone to Setenan Road. But no, they had had not seen him.

My father spoke calmly to me: 'Let him go, Hardojo. Don't look for him. That Eyang of ours has always been a person out of the ordinary. A free spirit, like a bird, like a bird that stops in a tree for a moment and then flies on, who knows where or why. It's a way of life that seems to satisfy him.'

I could only nod reluctantly. And on the buggy to Paliyan station the thought of Prabu Anglingdarma would not leave me. The king of so many mysteries.

6. NOEGROHO: second variation: reach to new limits

As soon as I returned from visiting father in Wanagalih, to help soothe him after he had been thumped by that wretched Japanese officer, I resumed teaching at the HIS Jetis in Yogya. Or, to be precise, that had been its name in the time of the *Nederlandsch Indie* administration; the Japanese had redesignated it a Comprehensive Public School, or a 'People-Perfecting' School, in their curious style. I have to say that I was never as foolhardy as father in the matter of carrying out that business of bending to the north, the *saikere kita ni muke*. I did it and my colleagues did it and we complied entirely with all their other queer requirements: getting out in the school-grounds with our classes to do the *taiso* exercises in groups of eight, accompanied by a piano on a radio loudspeaker. Well, what could you do? It was a performance going on Java-wide at that time of the morning. Poor father, imagining that he had nothing to worry about from the new authorities, being practically retired and getting on in years; but as for me, I had three young children to bring up—see me taking risks over trifles! Even less likely after my father's experience. If they treated old men like that, I had a fair idea of what they would have done to me. Their *Kenpetai*, had eyes and ears everywhere, and there was always talk going around about their particularly inventive barbarities. And, anyway, you could always see an amusing side to those things; and were *Nippong's* demands so excessive after all? Why, all that bending and *taiso* choreography in the morning was positively healthy! And what exactly was the problem if we paid our so-called respects to some sun-god when none of us took it seriously? We still went home and did our five prayers as usual, those who did; and as far as we were concerned, Allah was our God, Muhammad was his Messenger, and all that bobbing on the one hand and our own on the other: well, you drew the distinction and that was that, period.

But as for the other changes that happened in our schools with the occupation—what a shambles! Almost overnight we had to teach everything in Malay, which now became our new Bahasa Indonesia, and every Dutch textbook had to be replaced by one in Indonesian. We teachers knew Malay well enough, although it was not used commonly, certainly never as a language of instruction; but now, suddenly transformed into the national language, we were seriously pressed to master it, and to use it itself as a medium by which to do that. We became learners alongside our own pupils. But looking back, well, there was some stiffness and bother at first, but soon enough both teachers and children were using this novel language that had been handed down to us pretty well. And bearing in mind that it was what had been called high Malay and not market Malay, the speed with which Indonesian was adopted was in fact surprising. And another surprising thing was how quickly we learned Bahasa Nippon, and then how we adapted to their *kyoren*, the Japanese military training. I was one of those picked to undergo instruction in Japanese and *kyoren*, and I was not totally displeased after I had given it some thought. Such things opened up prospects well beyond teaching. I was young and prepared to take a chance, to step outside a lifetime's security in teaching, my father's trade; to take a chance, yes, but a reasonably calculated one. Such were the times: difficult, but suddenly offering unexpected developments, useful possibilities.

Those were new prospects, meanwhile however life was grim. In the matter of a year the pinch of a war economy could be felt everywhere. Goods of all kinds, not just luxuries but of daily importance, began to disappear from the markets, even rice was hard to get at times. Those working for the Japanese, and as a public servant I was one such of course, had an allotment of rice and other staples, but the quantities were never enough. We understood now how well we had lived before the invasion: a *gupermen* teacher on a salary of 110 guilders had been more than well-off. My wife, Sus—Susanti, or Suzie as her mother called her—was in a perpetual daze and almost hopeless in this time of decline. As a young girl she had picked up a taste for Dutch dainties that her mother brought home from the Elizabeth Hospital where she was a nurse. The old lady had still managed to have access to the hospital kitchen even after she retired. Now Sus was baffled at every turn, trying to run the life of a house where everything had grown scarce. In better times she had happily spoiled us—what were we not fed! Rump steak, fillets, tenderloin, potatoes cooked in every way, glasses of juice on the table, mixed salads with mayonnaise, nothing of that was foreign to us. In the morning with our fried rice we might have wedges of cheese or an omelette; and the children took to school sandwiches of good bread and Dutch butter, with Betuwe jam and God knows what else. We all had excellent clothing, well-maintained, wore quality coats of stylish colours and cut, things incomparably better than any seen on the backs of ordinary Javanese. Once or twice a month the family ate at the Restaurant Oen, following that with ice-cream at the Tip-Top. So our descent into this misery of the new era came as an unimagined shock. Sus never stopped wailing about the impossible conditions; and there was little I could do beyond explaining to her, from my elevated perspective in the paramilitary, that this was war and everything was being sucked away by the necessities of war. Of course that did nothing to calm her.

Then in the early part of 1944 I was suddenly summoned to join the new national defence force *Peta*, the *Pembela Tanah Air*: I must depart forthwith

6. Noegroho

to Bogor for training, and then there would be a posting to a *daidan*, one of the Japanese-patterned battalions being raised for stationing in various parts of Java. The order came as a rude surprise to me: while accepting the benefits, such as they were, of being one of the *kyoren*-drilled assistants to the new tuans, I had more or less hoped to be overlooked when it came to anything more active than a walk-on role in that sort of nonsense. But it especially horrified Sus: I could just imagine her dealing alone with the problems and scarcities of the time! In the past she had developed a healthy, well-rounded figure, but since the war much of her glow was lost and she had become thinner. We commonly now had to alternate meals of rice with some sort of poor-quality porridge. Nevertheless, there was nothing that could be done, she would have to cope and I to go. I sent a letter to my parents in Wanagalih to tell them the news, and other letters went to my younger brother and sister. Hardojo in Solo was only sixty-two kilometres from Yogya: I relied on him to keep an eye on my family and help them as needed. I told everyone that as soon as the training in Bogor had ended I hoped to call at Wanagalih before being posted to my *daidan*.

On the way to Bogor I sat in the carriage and gave a good deal of thought to the changes which were taking place in my life, above all by this new occupation I was embarking on. I—was to become a soldier? There was no such tradition in the Sastrodarsono family, nothing like it. At school, one occasionally heard someone boasting of descending from warriors who had fought with Diponegoro against the Dutch; or another one might claim distant relatives who had gone with the Mangkunegaran Legion to Aceh in 1873, this time as auxiliaries of the Dutch; or somebody else had an uncle or cousin in the *Koninklijk Nederlandsch-Indisch Leger*, the KNIL, the colonial army; but even trifling connections of that sort were unknown among my people: we all looked back to a typical farming-peasant paternity and nothing more. Now, I would be the first among us to 'bear arms'? Was I particularly proud of that? I had to suppose that I should be. Were not priyayi in essence knights, the second in the classic social order, aristocratic warriors, thus soldiers? Yes, but then, who would we be actually fighting? That was a confusing question. Bapak Gatot Mangkoepradja, a pre-war nationalist and admirer of the Japanese, had been the first to dream of an Indonesian defence force and was said to have lately sent a letter written in his own blood to Bung Soekarno, urging him to approve such a force. In my understanding, this *Peta* of ours was being raised as an auxiliary arm of the Japanese for the internal defence of Indonesia, were the archipelago to be attacked, but would not act beyond our borders, the way the *Heiho* labour units recruited earlier in the war were doing. Thus it could not be denied that the Japanese were only raising *Peta* for their own purposes. Well, let that be as it may, first things first, some kind of Indonesian army was being created from scratch. And so, with a nod to my new prospects, and with the vague consideration that if it came to battle I would be fighting for my country, whoever in the end was our enemy, I began my training in Bogor.

Those who started with me were by no means all teachers: the intake included a variety of younger leading figures in their communities, including a number who had been educated in various previously unrecognised religious institutions of the *pesantren* type, and had therefore been deemed unqualified for the purposes of the Indies administration; there were juveniles of all kinds; but the majority was broadly of a priyayi background. Some were pressed to join up; others, mainly from lowlier families, could see a livelihood in the ranks. Those on my social level and above expected less of that immediate gain in most cases, but were willing to put up with what was to come, motivated either by the new spirit of patriotism or by a perception that there would be high opportunities, careers, new kinds of status made possible by this scheme of the Japanese. Not that ambition necessarily excluded a sense of duty, but the nation was awakening and much was in the offing. By the time we had undergone the last manoeuvres in our training, I had attained the rank of *chudancho*, company commander, and soon afterwards was posted to a *daidan* in Jebukan, Bantul, south of Yogyakarta.

As I had hoped, at the end of training and before joining my unit I was given leave to go to Wanagalih, so I took my family and arrived there just after my brother and sister, who also had brought their families. And what a relief it was: a time to wind down, return to basics as it were after Bogor, and to meet everyone again. It was growing to be the usual thing for us to come to Wanagalih in this way at important moments, sometimes at critical ones; and of course my father and mother were still the centre of those gatherings. We were growing up, forming ourselves, setting up families, finding our places in the world; but we let our parents, and especially my father, be again at those times the sun we turned around. Yes, dazzling us I suppose, and in a kind of warm and sedative way reducing us to children again. Looking back, what my father said at those gatherings we took like the exalted, weighty, authoritative words of an old sage, accepted them as little less than fatwas and unarguable. But then what? When we left to return to our problems and our own lives, we reconsidered or forgot what we had heard and went our own ways. No different to the common people, with their *Inggih! Inggih!* to your face, and who then make no effort to carry out what they are agreeing to. Yes indeed, we Javanese have unending respect for our elders and betters, but how easy it has always been to reduce the voice of authority to some barely audible echo! As, for example, in our response to father, with his heroic standards plucked from the wayang tales, and lecturing us on 'Pocung' and 'Kinanti', no doubt trying to stiffen our backs in our dealings with the Japanese; which I thought was an admirable appeal but never to be put into practice. And now

6. Noegroho

here was I, an officer, a *chudancho* in the occupiers' language, supposedly filled since Bogor with the spirit of *bushido*, their knightly code: how was I to act towards my father, what had I done to his authority by donning a Japanese uniform, a son who had 'adapted' as he could well say, to those new aggressors who had insulted his own father? But, after all, should not what really matters be the love and respect we give our parents? Beyond that obligation . . . well, the world is very large.

I was making my way actively enough in that world, discovering its possibilities outside Wanagalih, but I have to say that the old town drew me back just as much as it did the others. I felt mellow, grew sentimental returning there. The things that never changed around our parents' home and beyond were always good to see again: the rice fields and the fields of secondary crops starting at and spreading out from the town limits; the never quite flourishing, ever hot little town itself; the Madiun and Solo Rivers: all were very ordinary yet restorative sights after periods of stress and hurry outside. For people born and raised somewhere else, Wanagalih had little in it to notice, but to us it was a shelter when we were harassed, and then everything about the place brought back other times with our parents, innocent childhood events, special and exciting. And our own three young ones were much livelier than at home in Yogya whenever they were brought here.

But I anticipate; most of that was especially true later. That day, we got out of the gharry that had brought me, Sus, and the children to Setenan Road, and a row of faces on the front veranda turned as one towards us. They were all there: Bapak, Ibu and the full collection of my siblings and their families, sitting there waiting to catch the first glimpse of the family's *chudancho*. As it happened, regulations required that I went about fully dressed in my green *Peta* uniform: forage cap, boots and puttees, the whole outfit, complete with one of those short samurai swords that look like a toy, compared to the full version the Japanese carried. They stood up to better gaze at me, to stare pop-eyed and open-mouthed.

After a moment, Hardojo let out a whoop and shouted: 'I say—here's General Tojo! General Tojo's arrived!'

I groaned. Idiots—they should know better than to shout such things! The Japanese are not Dutchmen. They are not just more arrogant, they are still establishing themselves. Disrespect is a threat to their power, and they have ways to deal with threats. I had learned that well in Bogor, where almost every punishment meted out to us by our Japanese instructors was related to this question of perceived disrespect. We should remember what had happened to our own father. General Tojo—good grief!

'Sh! If the *Kenpetai* arrive you'll catch it!'

They quietened down at that. Then we all sat on the veranda talking, all those relatives of mine, and Lantip too: he had been with Hardojo for some time now. They crowded around me, some standing and others sitting on the floor near my chair, everyone keen to hear how I had become an officer in *Peta*. They handled my sword, my cap; but what most astonished them apparently was my head, barbered almost bald. Hari, as usual the least backward of any of our children in pestering people with questions, came out with: 'Pakdé, you know you look just like a Japanese, with your bald head!'

I managed a smile, what else could I do? But his father scolded him immediately: 'That's enough now, Hari. One doesn't joke about adult people's heads.'

'But, Bapak, I only wanted to say that Pakdé looks fierce like a Japanese officer.'

'Yes, yes, Hari. I'm sure Pakdé here is very grateful to hear you say that.'

Everyone laughed, while Hari looked puzzled.

'The kids in the Punggawan kampong say that the Japanese are really great fighters. Is that true, Pakdé?'

'Yes, Lé. They're fearless and never retreat.'

'*Wah*. And you've been getting lessons in fighting from the Japanese?'

'Yes, that's right, Lé.'

'*Wah*. Then if you've had lessons you must be a terrific fighter too now, Pakdé?'

'Well, yes, let's hope so.'

Hari's mother now moved in to stop the boy's questions: 'Don't pester Pakdé, Hari. He's only just arrived and wants to rest. And anyway we grownups haven't had a chance to get a word in, a tadpole like you taking over. Go and play with your cousins over there.'

I was grateful to Sumarti, and I was in fact tired: suddenly I felt the effects of the exertions and stiff discipline in Bogor. We had lunch and then dispersed for an afternoon nap; although resting in the heat of a Wanagalih afternoon was never particularly profitable, and it really only acted as an interval before the time we met to talk around the *kesukan* table in the inner room. On this night a swarm of grandchildren competed with each other to knead Bapak's feet and earn the cents to buy snacks from passing vendors. At some point, they began demanding stories from the wayang: bapak was always a riveting story-teller.

'No children, not tonight. For a change your grandfather wants to hear Uncle Noegroho tell *his* story.'

All the children left to scatter on the front veranda, to wait for the *wedang cemoe* seller to come past.

'So then, tell me, Lé. Did you really have your heart set on becoming an officer?'

'Now, Pak, what would have happened if I refused? Did I have any choice?'

6. Noegroho

My brother and sister smiled at father's question.

'Yes, no, what I meant was are you satisfied with the way things worked out? Did things work out the way you hoped?'

'Yes, Pak.'

'Then, God be praised.'

I saw my father's expression as he sipped his coffee was thoughtful and serious.

'Lantip! Lantip! Come in here for a moment, Lé.'

'*Inggih!*'

And Lantip, who had been watching over the younger children on the veranda, left them and entered. My father gestured to him to sit down on the floor beside his chair.

'If Hari wants to come in and listen, let him. Now, Tip, remember I said I would be checking, after you left for Solo, to see if you could still recite. Do you recall?'

I saw that Lantip was puzzled.

'*Wah*, I have to recite something now, Embah?'

I have to say that it sounded odd when Lantip called my father *Embah*, or called me *Pakdé* and my wife *Budé*; but there was little that could be done about it now: Lantip had been adopted by Hardojo, and Hardojo had asked us to treat the boy as his natural son, and my father and mother had blessed the arrangement.

'Do you still know the *Tripama*, or have you forgotten it? It's a tract which was composed in the very place where your Bapak works now.'

'I think I still know it, Embah. But if I miss something, perhaps somebody could correct me.'

'Yes, of course. Begin then, please.'

And Lantip again lifted up his voice as he had done a year or two before, after my father had been humiliated by the Japanese officer, and we heard more of those old verses.

'Warriors, gain ye virtue from exemplars past . . .'

The sound rose and fell. It was a quiet night, apart from the crickets outside. This time the stanzas told of Sumantri's loyalty to his sovereign Arjuna, that of Karna to Suyudana, and Kumbakarna to the kingdom of Alengka.

When Lantip stopped, there was silence. Then Hari burst into applause, clapping noisily, and we all looked at each other. I thought I caught a faraway expression on some faces. Like people waking after having dreamt something nice.

'Now, my children, you will remember that time we met here and I asked Lantip to recite from the *Wedhatama* and the *Wulangreh*, from those moral and spiritual textbooks? And at the time I said we would come in turn to the *Tripama*? This was the moment.'

We nodded. We were ready for the inevitable homily which must follow tonight's narration. I assumed my father would say something relevant to my situation as an officer in *Peta*.

'My choosing the *Tripama* at this moment is, I feel, very apt, with Noegroho having entered the army; but appropriate also for you, Hardojo, to consider as an official of the Mangkunegaran court; and you, Nakmas Harjono, who have been promoted to serve in the high administration of the Madiun residency. The *Tripama*, *The Three Paragons*, describes to us how to conduct ourselves with dignity in challenging times'

All at once our attention was cut through by shouts from the veranda: the children had sighted the *cemoe* seller! Bapak was forced to delay any further speech while the young ones scurried from the veranda and in and out of rooms, including ours. Such a crisis could only be dealt with by the mothers, who soon penned the children in the dining room at the back with their glasses of *cemoe*, while we adults gathered ourselves to listen once more, sipping from our own glasses. Lantip and Hari remained with us.

'While the *Tripama* seems to concern only those who go to war, it in fact is relevant to all who belong to the class of priyayi, because the essence of its instruction relates to the constancy of that class, its loyalty to ruler and nation. The three figures from the wayang, Sumantri, Karna and Kumbakarna, exemplify that loyalty and sense of duty, each in his own way.'

I saw Hardojo's face show puzzlement, and he said: 'But Bapak, someone like Sumantri seems hardly a gallant example of his class. He's more someone to point to as an ignoble priyayi.'

'Now Mas Hardojo, don't be impertinent, let father speak.'

'No, Mini, I just wanted to understand that particular figure. In pursuing his ambition to become a priyagung, to rise into the court nobility in the kingdom of Maespati, well, he's so devoured with desire for that position that he can bring himself to sacrifice his younger brother. And then there's the occurrence where to become King Arjuna's first minister, Sumantri defeats a thousand kingdoms and captures their rulers, but then he challenges his own king. What martial dedication is this, to be testing the might of his own king thus? Sumarti ultimately dies in battle protecting Arjuna, but this is a soiled loyalty, surely?'

I saw my father smiling and nodding. This young brother of mine was always a talker, a nimble and convincing one sometimes.

'Yes, very good, Yok. I probably haven't told you how at the time your mother and I were being married we were given a wayang performance as a wedding present by your Eyang Seten Kedungsimo. The drama was *The Servitude of Sumantri*. Romo Seten had chosen it to as it were provision me for

6. Noegroho

the life of a Javanese gentry-official. And that's how praiseworthy Sumantri appeared to him. And if His Highness Mangkunegara IV also chose him as an example, and the first of the three at that, it was probably for Sumantri's heroic, hopeless fight against the giant Rahwana to fulfil his ultimate service to his king. And then to set beside Sumantri's late-found notion of noble responsibility, next His Highness selected Karna, for his resolve to side with the evil Kaurawa brothers.'

'Oh, Pak? How does that story go?'

'It's like this, Mini. Karna is in fact the oldest of the Pandawa brothers. Born illegitimately to the deity Surya, from Kunti, the mother of the Pandawa clan, he was cast out of it in childhood and raised by a stable-hand in the kingdom of Ngastina, ruled by the Kaurawa brothers. From youth, then, Karna served the latter, and because of his great sanctity he was their mainstay. When the Baratayuda war was imminent, his mother approached him to return to the Pandawa side. He would not, because according to the knightly code he followed, due must be given to those from whom one receives rank and livelihood.'

'Even when that means going to war against your own brothers?'

'Yes, even so. And even though he would be killed by an arrow launched by Pasopati Arjuna, his younger brother and rival.'

'A soldier's honour can have a high price, then, Bapak. Can entail some sad inner conflicts.'

I had to smile at this. My innocent, grave young brother! I thought I might be expected to answer this, and spoke for my father: 'A hard path indeed, the martial one, Yok. I can add to what Bapak says. In Bogor the training also stressed duty to ruler and nation. In the spirit of *bushido* in our case: the code of the Japanese knights, their *samurai*. A *samurai* incapable of doing his duty to defend his country is required to kill himself by committing *harakiri*.'

'And, Mas Noeg, you're in agreement with such values? With such a spirit?'

'Yok, I think the question of agreeing or disagreeing is irrelevant. The point father was making was that one does one's duty.'

The room fell quiet. The children, who had been happily noisy in the back of the house and intent on their *cemoe*, now were asleep in their room. Hari and Lantip still remained with us, and I had noted as we talked that Hari's eyes were swivelling around attentively from face to face; and so it was with Lantip, who despite been brought into our family as a full member still sat to one side, inconspicuously cross-legged on the floor.

'And then we come to the third case, my children, that of Kumbakarna, also interesting. Kumbakarna is a tender-hearted giant, younger brother to the evil Rahwana, the slayer of Sumantri. Kumbakarna opposes his brutal and egoistical brother, but dies in battle defending their common territory when the god Rama arrives to invade it. Here we see the priority given to one's nation. However hateful its government may be, our duty must be to defend the nation.'

'But an unjust leadership will make for an unjust nation: fighting for the latter supports the former, doesn't it?'

'Yok, I repeat that a soldier's duty is to his nation. He must dismiss that consideration. Leaders are transient, the continuance of the nation is paramount.'

There Hardojo turned to me: 'What about others in the service of the government, and who are not in the military, Mas Noeg? Should they fight as well?'

'I think they should, or indeed must, defend the nation in their own way. Not merely because it has given them their position and livelihood: in a certain sense they *are* the nation.'

Harjono, Mini's husband, as usual the quietest among us, now spoke:

'I agree with Mas Noeg. We all here, as priyayi, are instruments of the nation; only, some are military and some are civil. If the nation is at war we are all at war and are subject to the same code of duty. All these examples finally come to a question of duty.'

At this point, Ibu brought to our attention that the night was growing late and it was high time we should retire.

'Yes, Buné, we'll go to bed in a moment. Just let me summarise for the young ones here, for Noegroho and everyone else. Remember the prediction that *Nippong* will only be here for the life of a maze plant. If I calculate it right, that won't be much longer. We are now free of the Dutch, and who knows but we'll be free soon from *Nippong* too. The duty to a nation we were talking about tonight was of course duty to our own nation. What this nation of ours will turn out to be like, we don't know. The important thing, all of you, is to be faithful and dutiful to it. And as for Sumantri or Karna or Kumbakarna: the paths of duty are many and I leave it to you to choose which one to take.'

We stayed only a few days in Wanagalih, because I had to report to my *daidan* at Bantul.

As it turned out, life in the *daidan* passed reasonably well. The officers were not required to live with the men in their barracks: a pre-war sugar factory. We had our own quarters in large and quite luxurious housing that had belonged to the European staff. And as officers in *Peta* we found ourselves far better off than our civil counterparts, such as my previous colleagues who had remained teachers; if there were some discomforts, at least our rations could be said to be adequate; actually, more than adequate. Hardojo, for instance, as an official of the Mangkunegaran court, sighed over the difficulties of his life and had to be helped out by supplies of food from Wanagalih. Soemini's family was better situated, in as much as Harjono, her husband, could fall back on a rice field in his paternal village.

Sus had a return of spirits. Even if my position in *Peta* could not hope to satisfy her taste for things Dutch, still whatever delicacies could be had were now available to her. Nor were the children particularly affected by our life in Jebukan, since for their schooling and recreation Bantul was only a short train-ride to Yogya. I found my duties as a commander of a *chudan*, or company, not particularly arduous: *shodancho* and *bundancho*, the commanders of platoons and sections, did all the tiresome work. They were after all supposed to be infantrymen, whereas with my rank I verged more towards staff, even if in theory I was ultimately responsible for an infantry company. Of the *shodan* officers in the battalion, many were ex-MULO people, graduates of *Meer Uitgebreid Lager Onderwijs*, the Dutch-language secondary school, and others of HIS. They tended to be younger than the *chudan* commanders, who like myself were often former teachers and had gone through HKS and HIK. *Bundan* commanders were a mix of village school and secondary school graduates, while the average private had some village schooling. Many of both those latter, the section commanders and privates, had come to *Peta* straight from villages; unlike the platoon, company, and battalion officers, who were in the majority priyayi, with here and there a *santri*, whose former civilian advancement would have occurred through an Islamic education. I was very conscious that if at some future moment Indonesia were to gain its independence, we officers would become the nucleus of a national army. We were all very aware of that, and aware of our prospects in such an event.

And then—it seemed overnight—Japan was defeated; but *Peta* itself was in short order disarmed and disbanded. We who had been picturing a different consequence from the arrival of peace were left empty-handed and stunned. Would that be the end of the story for our envisaged national army and careers?

I took my family back to Yogya, to live temporarily in the house of my wife's mother, who had moved there since retiring in Semarang. The house was not very big, situated in the Jetis district, and actually not far from a primary school where I had taught, and where I might possibly find work again if all else failed. The old lady was very welcoming to Sus and the children, but after our recent officers' quarters we found the house cramped. At any rate, I had had the opportunity to bring away a good quantity of provisions with me before departing Jebukan, so at least we had enough of those to see us through this uncertain period. And in fact it was not too long before independence was proclaimed, and talk began again about setting up a people's defence force. I joined a group of ex-*Peta* colleagues, disbanded *Heiho* veterans, police, and assorted young men with military ambitions, and we determined in anticipation to form a paramilitary unit in Yogya. Our first need was to arm ourselves, and that meant taking weapons from the Japanese.

Gentry

If we had expected to put into practice the training we had received from them at Bogor, well, the event proved more like a riot. Nevertheless, the fighting in the streets around well-to-do Kotabaru was sharp enough to constitute a baptism of fire as far as I was concerned. Things might have gone more by the book if our so-called forces had consisted only of those trained in *Peta* and *Heiho*, but many joined in from the population of Yogya, all crowding into the attack, in a frenzy to be seen at grips with the Japanese. Bullets whizzed, wounded and dying were groaning all over the place; and by the time the Japanese surrendered, about twenty of those irregulars had been killed, mostly mere boys from the various kampongs of the city. Those who got through to the Japanese barracks near the Kridosono stadium, turned everything in the buildings upside down and carried off all kinds of weaponry, which they then shared among their friends. And what a show they made, afterwards! All manner of ragamuffins and beggars, strutting through the streets of the city and the kampongs, rifles slung over shoulders, pistol butts poking out of waistbands, heroes all! But for those of us who were trying to create an embryo army of a free Indonesia, the thought of all those weapons scattered about in the hands of God knows what rabble was a worry. But in the end, by gradual stages, we began to form proper units, and the arms were gathered in, together in many cases with those who carried them.

With the arrival of British troops to support the Dutch, I saw rather more serious action, commanding a force blocking the southward British push from Magelang. We succeeded in halting them with minimal armaments and with whatever tactics served: attacking with maneuvers learned in *Peta*, exploiting unconventional opportunities, and always relying on the determination and passion that had been ignited by the revolution. We forced them back to Ambarawa, and eventually they returned to their positions in Semarang.

By the time I came back to Yogya from that operation, I had acquired a motor car for myself, decided to take some leave, and took Sus and the children on a tour to Magelang and Ambarawa. Considering our actual military situation, and what happened later, I wondered afterwards at my own confidence in transporting my whole family around the countryside like that. But at the time one felt quite carried away by that early success and the control our forces seemed to have achieved over a part of Java's hinterland. I suppose it seemed safe enough to show off a bit. As we travelled on the Semarang road, I pointed out places where there had been clashes. We passed houses that had been destroyed or damaged, either through our own scorched-earth policy or by shell fire, and we saw many large and very nice houses that had recently been occupied by the Japanese and before that were the homes of Dutch families and now stood empty. We stopped to look into some of them and found them in disorder, with contents strewn everywhere, although

6. Noegroho

there were also still all sorts of belongings that were intact and valuable. We saw complete sets of European dinnerware which looked as if they had hardly been used by the owners, and Sus said without a moment's hesitation that we should take such things, since no one owned them now, and if we left them they would just be grabbed by the first group of riffraff that went past. That made sense to me, and I gave orders to our escort to load the car with whatever Sus pointed out. By the time we returned to Yogya we had a full load of things souvenired from houses around Ambarawa. Well, were they not the spoils of war? We were the victors after all, were we not?

The miseries of the revolutionary period turned out to be just more of what we had experienced under the Japanese. The exasperations and shortages endured under foreign occupation in a time of war were simply prolonged in the revolutionary phase, one felt; if in the latter period they were suffered by a nation seeking to reclaim its own land. Cities continued to be blacked-out due to limited electricity, daily necessities were hard to obtain, all just as before. Nevertheless, we the *kiblik*, as the word 'republicans' was domesticated, were not altogether deprived of consolations and even entertainment in those difficult times. Life had to go on, despite certain scarcities and general poverty. Malioboro Road, the centre of Yogya's world, was even in the dark of night always full of strollers, among them all kinds of ruffianly soldiery, lascars overgrown with whiskers and sideburns, pistol dangling at the hip, happy in their infamy as 'rebels' and' fanatics', so they were branded by the Dutch. Bicycles, gharries and pedicabs floated back and forth like fireflies in a rice-field, their source of illumination a twist of coconut fibre flickering in a jam-tin of oil.

Once again, thankfully, we found ourselves better off than most of those in civilian occupations. I thought I had given proof enough of my valour, and could justifiably transfer to some less glorious, more useful administrative activity. I was made responsible for the provisioning and welfare of my regiment, and in that role one could always take home food or other necessities that were deemed beyond requirements. One could so deem them. Sus ran a tranquil kitchen in our house, and we were even able to send something to the neediest of our relations. What was most trying were the uncertainties of the political situation, for just as the Dutch became increasingly lively, we in the military felt confused and were chagrined by the incomprehensible diplomacy of our government. Cabinet after cabinet fell, and with them our belief in the wisdom of our political leaders, for whatever accord they signed with the enemy seemed to leave us worse off. Whether it was the Linggardjati agreement or the Renville agreement, the outcome was a shrinking of the zone controlled by our forces, our units having to withdraw yet again into a diminishing area, and refugees from the occupied surrounds crowding into the remaining Republican towns.

Another exasperating aspect was the increasingly strident clash of policies among a rash of new parties. Those of us who were focused on a military outcome, and saw our future in a conventional military establishment, were alarmed when all kinds of ideologies began to unsettle our troops, and when units were infiltrated by activists of one faction or another. At that point came a climax to the army's troubles: then-president Hatta decided to reduce and rationalise the armed forces, sending a tremor of restlessness throughout its motley elements. I was anxious as much as anyone: who could tell where the axe would fall? It would be bearable if I, now a lieutenant-colonel, were to be reduced to, say, major; but if dismissed, what then? How would I support my family in those pinched times? But when the blow came it turned out that I was safe, only reduced to the rank of major: quite a relief, considering that our commander-in-chief had himself had to take a demotion.

The next worry was the growth of the *Partai Komunis Indonesia* and its influence within the body of the army, especially in Solo. I had been widening my contacts in the military, and from them and the accounts I received from Hardojo in that town I pictured a situation on the point of chaos: with kidnappings and assassinations, barricades and confrontations between units, some of which were refusing to disband as demanded by Hata's fiat. The climax of this was the September 1948 revolt in Madiun.

Madiun—good God! My thoughts went immediately to Wanagalih, a centre in the Madiun region and bound to become involved if the conflict spread. How would it go with my parents? According to reports, local priyayi of the higher ranks were being seized. What might happen to Soemini and Harjono and their children? I got in touch with Hardojo to discuss ways of going to Wanagalih and Madiun, perhaps using some tactical matter to do with the war against the Dutch as a pretext that might allow me and him passage through the insurgent lines. But he thought it would be better to wait until things had settled down and we understood better what was happening in the troubled area. Lantip was by chance in Wanagalih, called there by Bapak to help repair the rice barn, and Hardojo convinced me that we should leave the boy to look after Bapak and Ibu. We agreed to postpone our departure, while I followed developments with the help of colleagues in Intelligence. Their information continued to confirm that kidnappings and murders were occurring, even Governor Surjo falling victim, killed not far from Wanagalih. Hardojo and I grew increasingly concerned that Wanagalih would become a flashpoint. Finally, the Siliwangi division moved to the Madiun, Solo and Pati areas and succeeded in clearing them of PKI units. I quickly got leave from Army Headquarters, my posting at that time: three days to travel to Wanagalih, check on my parents, and then if possible visit Madiun. Hardojo, who was not under military restrictions, had no difficulty in getting leave from his new employer, our Ministry of Education, which at that time was located in Solo.

6. Noegroho

On arrival at Wanagalih we were met with tears and embraces by our parents, and we joined there Soemini and her family who had preceded us from Madiun. Thankfully, the tears were those of relief that everyone had come through safely. But my own relief and Hardojo's were soon overtaken by horror and amazement as the tale of our parent's ordeal was unfolded to us. I could barely control my anger when my father and mother, Soemini and her husband, and Lantip described the savagery of the PKI troops and the actions of the Party's local followers. Government officials had been murdered, so too religious leaders, followers of mystical movements, and members of Masyumi, the Muslim party. But above all I was furious to hear how my father, a retired headmaster, never involved in any of the revolution's politics, had also been proscribed in those bloody lists as one to be led out for execution in Wanagalih's own square!

From what I learned of this terrible rebellion, through the tales of my own relatives, as well as subsequently in the reports of those in the military who investigated it, the picture emerged of a countryside rife with angry murmurs and rumours right up to the time of the outbreak. What went about was that our revolution had lost its way from the moment the people had surrendered its guidance to bourgeois and feudalist elements and *santri* landowners. The people must now reclaim the revolution, and its true leaders were the Popular Democratic Front headed by the PKI. Following Muso's return from Russia and his assumption of the Party's leadership, large gatherings were mobilised to agitate for this demand. Units of troops in Wanagalih, containing more or less irregular lascar components supporting *Pesindo*, a socialist youth faction, were involved in fomenting the uprising in the surrounding region. It broke out widely when Sumarsono, the leader of *Pesindo* on the Republican eastern front, entered Madiun with local *Pesindo* troops from Dachlan's brigade and declared a National Front independent of the Republic. In Madiun and its neighbouring towns, such as Wanagalih and Magetan, the insurgents rapidly began to conduct purges involving arrests and detentions, then death sentences, and finally horrifying executions publicly carried out in the squares of those towns.

Harjono, as an official in the administrative system, quickly caught wind of the danger to himself and his family and packed them off to his parent's village, where, Allah be praised, he and they miraculously remained undetected throughout the purges. My father and many on Setenan Road were less fortunate. Pak Martokebo, dealer in water-buffalo meat and long a neighbour, himself also far gone in years, turned out to be a communist and one who took a prominent part in the liquidations conducted throughout Wanagalih. He suddenly appeared on father's veranda, at the head of a group of soldiers, shepherding before them others of our neighbours. Among the unfortunates were the religious teacher Pak Haji Mansoer, Romo Seten

Sunoko and Romo Jaksa: those last two, the old assistant district chief and the prosecutor, long ago retired and on their pensions. When the crowd of them arrived at father's house, Pak Martokebo was behind them, bawling and barking, brandishing a machete above the grey heads of his prisoners. For some reason, as it was described to us, the sight of the old trader waving his machete around like a windmill appeared so incredible and so ludicrous to my father that he could not restrain himself, he laughed.

Martokebo's eyes bulged, he levelled the point of the machete at father's chest and, usually so polite to father, he snarled at him in low Javanese: 'What now, Darsono? Laughing, you bastard? Laughing, hey?'

Father was stunned speechless, probably more by the language than the bite of the machete point.

'Have another laugh, you! Try! A village lordling, sucking the blood of the worker-peasants! Thought I hadn't spotted you, hey, priyayi? Or your blood-sucking ways? Crept out of the mud yourself and been lording it ever since over the people, what?'

My father fell silent. I could just imagine the cold sweat that must have dampened him from head to foot at that moment. Martokebo would have seemed in my father's eyes a total madman, or someone possessed. What other explanation could there be? A man who had all those years been faultlessly respectful, cheerful and friendly—to so suddenly turn into a vicious, murderous brute? And those others driven there by Martokebo and his soldier-cronies were also terrified and in a daze. Pak Haji Mansoer began a tremulous soft chant of *astagfirullah, astagfirullah,* God be merciful! God be merciful! . . . until he was cut off by a snarl from Martokebo: 'And there's another! Praying now! Babbling Arab gibberish! Wanna drop in on hell for a visit? Say so and I'll help you!'

And then—in the middle of Martokebo's deranged pacing, he still wielding his machete, in an interval of silence when the scrape of his sandals was the only sound—my mother appeared! She seemed to stray into the scene by accident. She approached the group on the veranda and walked calmly up to Martokebo. Surprised, father tried to catch her arm and draw her back, but he was too late, and she proceeded to address her visitor in formal Javanese and in a steady voice: 'Pak Martokebo. Come now. Let us be reasonable. We are all your neighbours. We've always lived well together. None of us are bad. Now, what is all this for? Be reasonable, Pak Marto, be patient. Why don't you take a seat, rest yourself and tell us what you have come for. Lantip, bring out more chairs for our guests.'

Incredibly, Martokebo—who had probably been fired up to meet only fear and hate, and must have been completely nonplussed by my mother's attitude—melted now into silence and obediently sat down in a chair, the machete still bare in his hand and resting on his knees.

6. Noegroho

When he found his voice to speak again, it was much more controlled: 'It's like this, brothers and sisters. This is what it's about. The *Pron Nasional* is the government now, here and around Madiun. That's the true government. That's because it's the government of the people. Them and their revolution. That one in Yogya isn't the true government. Because it's led by Soekarno and Hatta who are lackeys of the capitalist-boorjees of America and the Dutch.'

My father listened to Martokebo with the greatest attention, wondering where this new tack would lead.

'And so we, the people, have to clean out the country, sweep out all those against the revolution. Like you lot! *Santri*, fat bu-buricrats, teachers, priyayi, aristicrats! All of you!'

Martokebo had stoked himself into a passion again, and those present watched him palely as he stood up and began once again to wave his weapon.

'Pak Haji Mansoer, Pak Seten, Pak Jaksa, get moving! You're coming with me!'

'In a trembling old-man's voice Romo Seten asked: 'Wh-where are we going, Pak Marto?'

'With me!—that's all you need to know—with me!'

Pointing with the machete to those three and to the other neighbours there, Martokebo ordered his band of soldiers to drive the captives away.

But my mother! Once again she advanced towards Martokebo, intercepting him.

'Pak Marto, Pak Marto. I beg you to think back, Pak Marto. All these elderly gentlemen are good people, all of them, don't you remember, Pak?'

'Be quiet, Bu! Go back and don't interfere—you . . . you . . . *Bu Guru*! D'you want me to herd that husband of yours away with the rest?'

The last of my mother's strength gave way before that threat, and she said nothing more. The group of neighbours moved off, surrounded by their captors; and Lantip, who had been sitting all that time near the veranda stairs, quietly followed them. They were taken to a stockade on the edge of the square.

Lantip went to the square each day and unnoticed as just one of the boys who pastured buffaloes there he observed the death sentences carried out on the prisoners in the stockade. Groups of them were taken out to the centre of the square and some were beheaded and some were shot. One day he saw Pak Haji Mansoer with other Islamic teachers and one further individual, a shaman of famed spirituality, all taken to the place of execution. Lantip was particularly saddened by the arrival of Pak Haji Mansoer whom he knew as a teacher of martial arts and the Koran to the children of Setenan Road. The old man had always been a devout and gentle person, never known to have had the slightest disagreement with anyone in the area, and Lantip felt so sorry for him. When the catechist took his position in a line with those to be shot, Lantip could not go on looking, he turned away. He only heard the uncoordinated voices of the victims chanting *Allahu Akbar!* up to the time when the firing began. When Lantip turned again he saw an uneven row of sprawled figures on the ground.

Yet, so he told us, one person was still standing upright and smiling! This was Denmas Kusumo, the shaman renowned all over the Wanagalih district as a particular specialist in the mystical arts. He added to his numerous talents an expertise in martial arts, his version involving the application of unseen influences as adjuncts to the physical movements. He was also a marriage-broker and could cure any sickness caused by the incursion of evil spirits.

What followed in Lantip's tale may be accepted as fact by those inclined to do so, or it may join other famous and hard-to-disprove legends, such as for instance those that surround the doings of figures like Wanagalih's Kiai Jogosimo. Lantip told us that he and the other boys who were there that day, witnessing the executions, gasped to see Denmas Kusumo yet on his feet and calmly looking back at the PKI firing squad. The troops were quickly reformed, the order 'Fire!' was given again, and—Denmas Kusumo remained upright, smiling! In fact, as if showing his contempt for the squad, he even waived a hand across the front of his shirt in a show of brushing away the smoke from the second volley!

The commander of the firing squad, annoyed and impatient, sauntered up to Denmas Kusumo and shouted into his face: 'What's your game here? You got ghosts working for you? A familiar spirit?'

Denmas Kusumo smiled more broadly still and enquired: 'Bapak would like me to die?'

'Yes, dammit! I'm telling you—die!'

'Nothing easier, Pak. I'll do that. But there's a condition.'

'Eh? What condition?'

'First, Bapak must ask the Lord Allah for forgiveness; then me; then all the people here.'

'*Wah*, that's unreasonable. It's you should be asking the people for forgiveness. You who's been finagling them too long with your superstitions.'

'If that's your attitude, then I won't die.'

The commander fumed and cursed, then gave in.

'Dammit, you crazy old fraud. All right, I'll do it. But no tricks, you've got to die.'

The commander asked forgiveness from the Lord Allah, from Denmas Kusumo, and from all those witnessing the execution; then Denmas Kusumo asked him to have the barrels of the rifles lowered and the muzzles wiped clean on the ground; finally, he declared himself ready to die and took up the ascetic pose called *ngapurancang*: that is, standing with his arms crossed over his crotch. The commander gave his orders once more, there was a fusillade, and Denmas Kusumo collapsed on the ground.

I must say that neither I nor Hardojo could bring ourselves to give *total* credence to this tale of Lantip's, evidencing the sanctity of Denmas Kusumo. After listening to it and exchanging looks with my brother I remarked to him that I thought we had the makings here of something to take around the villages by a travelling troupe. But Lantip was ready to take an oath on the truth of every word, and he told us that we could ask people who had been there and they would confirm everything. . . .

Then in their turn the Siliwangi troops assaulted into Wanagalih, and having in short order freed it from the PKI the latter were now lined up on the square before firing squads. Lantip had continued to spend his days there, and finally he saw Pak Martokebo himself being led out and stood in line with other Party members. And, as with Haji Mansoer earlier, Lantip could not bring himself to watch Martokebo's body slump to the ground. He only wanted to remember the old man as he once was: taking the children of Setenan Road with him to the market behind our house, to the sellers of simples and salves, to the pens of the animals; remember him as the kindly person who treated everyone to *wedang cemoe* when he did well from a commission. And so Lantip looked away, and after the rattle of the rifles had battered his ears and he looked back again, Martokebo's body too lay sprawled on the square, the story of his life ending there as that of Pak Haji Mansoer had ended at the same spot.

But at least there was a better outcome for Romo Jaksa and Romo Seten Sunoko, because they were still waiting to be condemned when the Siliwangi troops entered Wanagalih. The ecstatic families lost no time in preparing a great united *selamatan* of thanksgiving.

On the evening of the day before departing to our respective homes, we sat talking in our usual last post-dinner gathering in the inner room, and our minds were on the recent turmoil and the rebellion. Hardojo spoke for all of us: 'I still can't comprehend how Pak Martokebo could have been one of them, Bapak. And then to turn so brutal.'

'Yes, Lé. He was a good neighbour.'

'He hadn't been ill-treated by the Dutch, sent to Digul or somewhere like that, had he?'

'Not that I know of. He might have been influenced by that son-in-law of his who went into what they called the Social Section, the one which was supposed to grow into a rival national army. The boy's family are from Solo. He was on the left, like all those lascars in that unit. They called it the People's *Tentara Nasional Indonesia*, the *TNI Masyarakat*.'

'Yes I can understand being influenced politically; but, Pakné, to change his *character* like that was awful. I can't stop thinking that he was willing to murder his neighbours.'

'Buné, Satan's got the ear of every sort of fanatic.'

Hardojo, who always relished a conversation of this sort, now asked: 'What was Pak Martokebo like, as a middleman in livestock, Bapak? Did he make money?'

'Not at all, he was always losing money at it. I heard he owed money, got into debt wherever he went. And his sons did no better, they went into the same business in Kedunggalar and Paliyan but got nowhere. And they liked to gamble too, I heard. When you think about all those troubles, you have to feel sorry for him.'

We fell silent. Probably the memory of former days with Pak Martokebo passed through the thoughts of most of us there. Hardojo went on towards the point he was leading to. He suggested: 'Maybe that sense of being dogged by bad luck, of failure in life, made him go like that? He became envious, and then embittered towards people nearby he saw were living more successfully?'

'Come now, Yok, envious of us? We live a life that's just so-so. Hardly more than that.'

'Yes, I know, Pak, that's how you and Bu would look at it. But perhaps from the point of view of someone who's only known failure, well, you two and Pak Haji Mansoer, Romo Seten and Romo Jaksa had all done well. Pak Martokebo would have seen steady lives, with certainty, money coming in from your pensions, a nice plot of rice land, children in some position, and so on.'

'Yes, Yok, but you've been told how he ranted about the bourgeois and the capitalists, people being sucked dry and all that. Someone must have given him an earful, to the point that it made sense to him, and then he went and acted on it.'

'Oh yes, it'll have been his son-in-law in the *TNI Masyarakat,* Mas. They were convinced enough to go and occupy Madiun, to set up their Front there, their *Pron Nasional.*'

While the others nodded, I made a point which it seemed to me they had all missed: 'It's lucky we have the army, that's all I can say. Who knows what would have happened without it in this Republic of ours.'

Harjono had said nothing, and Soemini entered the conversation on his behalf:

'There's Mas Noeg straining to get at the PKI with his bare hands. But you know, we in the civil service were in this too, Mas. They even killed Governor Surjo, and who knows how many others.'

'Yes, all right, Mini. But what's the ultimate weapon, the finale of Rama's epic, if you like? It's fighting and the army, isn't it?'

'Yes and no, Mas.'

6. Noegroho

We laughed at Mini's persistence.

'I mean, those who rebelled were army too, weren't they, Mas?'

'That was elements of the PKI which had infiltrated the army.'

'But they constituted whole units, surely they were army too?'

'Yes and no, Mini.'

We laughed again.

I have yet to tell the story of my children. In that same year, 1948, my firstborn, Suhartono—we called him Toni—was 16 years old and a second-year pupil in the B stream at the newly-constituted upper secondary school, the *Sekolah Menengah Atas*, serving Yogya's Kotabaru district. Our second was Sri Sumaryati—Marie. She was of the same age as Harimurti, Hardojo's boy. The last-born was another boy, Sutomo, eleven years old at that time—him we called Tommi. Toni and Marie, although having received some of their education at the HIS Jetis when I was still teaching at that school, should both really be called children of the Japanese and revolutionary periods. Toni could still remember some Dutch, because at the time of the invasion he was in fifth class, in the B stream there as well, and had the texts *Voor Jong Indie* and *Kembang Setaman*; while Marie, whose reading was only at *Din en Roes* and *Pim en Mien* level, with the elementary *Tataran*, had really very little Dutch. Sus, their mother, although ready enough to speak Dutch with me—and particularly so when gossiping scandal that she did not want the children to hear—was never very interested in raising their level in that language. Tommi was born after the start of the war and had no exposure to Dutch at all.

While Toni had been brought up to be obedient and polite and had attended to his studies, not brilliantly but well enough, he was just as affected by the revolutionary mood of that time as anyone else. It was a period of passion, spirit, confusion; and moreover the schools then operated on very irregular schedules. Many of his school-friends divided their time between classes and some involvement or other in what was happening at the front. We kept him from the front, but found ourselves compelled to let him take some part at least in less dangerous activities, such as guarding the offices of the civil administration, joining patrols in the city, and in the popular sport of that time: raiding the houses of the Chinese. Sus was worried for her oldest and favourite, but I tried to explain to her that a growing boy needs to find some channel for his energies. Other youngsters, Toni's fellows, boys who until recently had been his playmates around the house, were going out and doing all kinds of exciting things. A bit of guarding, patrolling, the odd Chinaman's house ransacked, would, I said, bring out the gamecock in the lad; and it was safe enough at that time in Yogya.

As for the two younger ones, we never had problems with them at this stage: they were good house-children, especially Marie, who was beginning to bloom and whose most immediate concern was with getting all the fashionable clothes she wanted. We humoured her as much as we could, engaging various people who had access through the lines to bring us back little luxuries from the Dutch sector. Once again, as in Jebukan days, I was well-placed to survive as reasonably as might be expected in the conditions; for at that time I had senior rank in our service corps, and so was able to organise such imports. It was very satisfying to know that despite living in the midst of a revolution we could enjoy those little extras, things that the privations of our struggle made more valued. When a courier arrived from the occupied areas, bringing us *brood*, *boter*, cheese, jam, and lengths of dress-material, I had to smile to see the eruption of excitement and delight in my family. The individual packets of Dutch food were opened as one unwraps ancient objects of great price, and Sus and the children ate carefully and slowly to extend as long as possible the enjoyment of those things. As an officer, I never felt any need to defend the sincerity of my republican credentials when engaging in those smuggling 'stunts', since I always made sure to share such importations with my army and civilian colleagues, and they in their turn made no bones about accepting whatever I passed on to them. The important thing, surely, was that we were all loyal to our cause. I did once receive an anonymous letter which threatened that if I continued eating bread and cheese I would be 'picked up' before much longer. The letter seemed to claim that I was somehow diminishing the seriousness of our struggle. But I gave the warning little attention—those left-wing lascars at their games, I thought! Still, I took greater care afterwards. To be accused of un-republican activities in a time of revolution, or, worse yet, of being rewarded for spying, was then no joke.

The Dutch attacked Yogya, finally. Waiting for their thrust had felt like the gnawing period before the bursting of a boil; yet we were still unprepared for the awesome roar of their aircraft above the city, nor the appalling bombing and strafing of Maguwo airport. But at least our troops had withdrawn in time and dispersed to various parts of the hinterland that remained in our hands. On the day of the attack I too left with a group heading to an area north-west of Yogya, on the way out taking a quick opportunity to visit my family. I was leaving them reasonably well-provided with food, and had come to tell them to stay together and take care. But—what did I find? It was just at this vital moment that we discovered Toni had disappeared! Our servant brought us a scrap of paper on which Toni had scrawled a message saying that he was going to join some friends in a *Peta* unit on the southern front—what a nuisance, in fact what a blow! I had hoped to rely on him to look after his mother and the other two children, and here he had wandered off, without any by-your-leave.

6. Noegroho

Sus was in shock: 'My son, oh dear, my boy! Oh God, oh God! If he's killed, if he's shot, what then, Pa-ak?'

'Heaven knows. But that's enough of that, he's gone now, we can't go running after him. Pull yourself together, Bu. Take charge of things and look after the others. Marie and Tommi take care of each other and your mother. I can't stay, I've got to go. *Belanda's* already at the airport.'

And without any further leave-taking, just a quick kiss and a hug each, I left them. I had to reconstitute the elements of our support system which had been scattered by the advance of the enemy.

And then, about noon one day, came the news. I had just returned to our camp from a trip around the villages, requisitioning from the *lurahs* supplies of food and materials for our troops, when a courier arrived from the city, bringing it. Toni had been shot dead by the Dutch while returning home to visit his mother and siblings. *Masya Allah! Inna lillahi wa inna illaihi rojiun*, the graveside formula—we are Allah's and to Him we return—sprang unbidden into my mind. And then the full import of what I had just said really sank in—the eldest of my children, dead! The first-born male, gone! So young . . . and I broke into tears, into sobbing, wailing grief. And a moment later I saw how poor Sus would be hit by this calamity, how inconsolable, distraught she must be even now, and the two children with her. My friends surrounded me immediately and said what they could to comfort me, to share the blow; but almost all of them urged me not to try to go back to the city at this critical time. According to the courier's account, the area of Trimargo, where my house was, had been cordoned off and the Dutch were conducting a search-and-clear operation there. In fact Toni had chosen that unlucky moment to arrive, had apparently been spotted, panicked, tried to run, and was shot without further ado. The report did not specify who the troops were: Dutch, Eurasian, or levies from other parts of the archipelago.

I was then with my unit in the area around Godean and knew that the advice of the others was indeed sensible: if I attempted to return I would probably be spotted and caught. I was broken-hearted, and maddened by my helplessness. I was a father, I must attend to the corpse of my son, wash it as ritual demanded; my son lay dead somewhere not twenty kilometres from here, and I was powerless. It was infuriating, a whoredom of a situation! I went alone into my billet, threw myself down on the bamboo sleeping-platform and lay there all night looking up at the ceiling.

Next morning, and unable to control myself any longer, I went to our executive officer and asked leave to return to Yogya for a short time: I pleaded the need to relieve my own distress and that of my family. He was a Manado man, understood my situation, and since he was only a major himself he could hardly stop me. I was asked to limit myself to one day, and cautioned that I could endanger the whole unit if the Dutch picked me up. I assured him that I knew how to look after myself, and if it came to capture guaranteed that I would not reveal our position. I left at about midday with one escort, a man who had been through the lines several times and knew the intricacies of the Dutch roadblocks around Yogya. At that time there was considerable traffic in and out of the city, and I thought that we should pass readily enough for civilians in our sarongs, short-sleeved shirts and *peci*. We carried nothing with us, not even money.

From the street, my home seemed to have a marked stillness about it, and at first it looked empty of life; but as I came closer I spotted my wife and two children sitting motionless and silent on the front veranda. They looked like manikins in a shop window, spiritless and without life. They stood up slowly, afraid to attract attention, and we only embraced and kissed when everyone had gone inside, and even in there our sobbing was muted.

'*Jouw zoon*, Pak, your son! What happened, what happened to your child, Pa-ak?'

'Yes, yes, I know, Bu. Be patient, Bu. Accept it. We must accept that our child is gone. There now, Bu. And Marie and Tommi, you two as well. We must all accept it, isn't that so?'

They all nodded and bowed their heads. And then we all resumed sobbing.

'Oh, Allah, Pa-ak. How could it happen? Such a good, good boy, and there, he's gone, so quickly. The Lord Allah wanted him back, so soon . . .'

'Enough now, Bu, enough. Just trust in God and remember that our children are only put in our charge for a time. When He wants them back, He will take them. And it will be for a good reason, of that we must be certain. And it will be for Toni's own eternal happiness, one has to suppose.'

Sus finally seemed to grow calmer after much more such soothing; but oh, if only she knew what was in my own heart! I was trapped in a confusion of feelings, confronted by the sight of my heartbroken family, miserable myself, denied even the last sight of my poor son's body. But as evening approached, our despair seemed to lessen enough for me to notice the details of things around me. Since I had left them, my wife and two children had grown noticeably thinner, their faces had an unhealthy pallor and sunken eyes, while every room showed evidence that little attention was being given to housekeeping. It seemed, too, that it was the neighbours who had taken over the arrangements for transporting Toni's body and interring it in the cemetery at Blunyah. They had dealt with the matter smoothly enough and inconspicuously, to avoid the attention of the Dutch or their spies. The funeral had not been announced in any way and was got through as quickly as possible.

I had to explain to my family that it was not feasible for me to stay longer than one night with them, and that I would visit Toni's grave alone on my way

6. Noegroho

out next morning. They saw the pressure I was under to return quickly; but anyway that night we slept as a united family, comforted sadly by our common sense of loss. In the morning, while my escort was checking that the way to Blunyah was clear, I made my farewell to Sus and the children. It was done in the house, and as I dropped down from the veranda and looked back I saw them still waving to me from inside. At the freshly-dug grave, which was nothing more than a flowerless red mound of dirt, I recited the *Al-Fatihah*, the short first chapter of the Koran, and the *Al-Ikhlas*, the renunciation.

The sentence came out unadorned, for there was really nothing else I could do or say: 'Bapak bids you good-bye, Lé.'

After I had reported back, my duties left me little time for dwelling on personal matters. I was instructed to redouble my efforts to gather supplies, and there was a general feeling that something significant and decisive was on the way; and indeed at a briefing some days later we were told that D-day for an all-out attack in *Wehrkeise III*—the Yogya sector—had been fixed for 1 March 1949.

I took no part in the attack on Yogya, launched on that historic day, but from my place in Headquarters I could follow the movement of our troops. I knew they would descend from the north and pass Trimargo and Cemara Jajar. There would be major clashes. I could only pray that no strays from the gunfire would hit our home.

7. THE WIVES: marriage in transition

It's three by our hosts' clock, three in the morning, and Marman, Ngadiman's boy, has come for me in the gharry. Bapak Tolé is still playing cards with those friends he hadn't seen for a while, and so he didn't want to come back with me. And then there's more wayang as well, with a *dalang* from Solo they say is famous. Can't think what he's called now. The story anyway is *Parto Kromo*: Parto taking a wife. We were invited to a wedding by the village head here at Ngale. The man used to be a pupil of Bapaké Tolé in Karangdompol-days, and now, imagine, he just married off his oldest daughter tonight!

   Ngale is quiet, as you might expect at this hour; except for the houses where the celebrations are still going on. On the main road, though, we join a stream of people going to town, five kilometres away. It's market-day in Wanagalih, and the hawkers are carrying their wares there, and the villagers their produce. They're lighting their way with those smoky torches you don't want to be behind. There are bullock carts as well: them you can hear in the dark by the bells on the necks of the beasts. It's cold. Luckily I thought to bring that shawl Soemini brought me from Jakarta last time she visited us. A good thing to wrap around the neck; covers the chest too. No joke catching a chill at seventy. Actually, it's hard to believe that: seventy. But there it is, it's 1962 after all. The truth of the matter is, I shouldn't be going out such a long way to those parties at my age. But try telling him. Bapak Tolé himself is close to 80, but he doesn't feel it, he says. He takes on just about all those invitations. And of course as a wife I have to go with him. Half a soul, we wives are, that's the saying: and so where the other half goes go I. Even to the *kesukan* nights; although lately Bapaké Tolé has been leaving the cards before dawn. Even to their oh-so-jolly parties with the dancing girls I have to be there. And there too he's just started to see at last that he can't keep up with the young men any longer, prancing on the floor. But then the way his eyes shine, the way he claps his hands and urges on the dancers and shouts 'Ha-e! Ha-e! Ha-e!' at them, he's there in spirit all right, right among those floozies. Actually, it only amuses me to see him in that mood, it doesn't hurt me in any way at all; it's a sight that only confirms again that men are just grown-up boys. Games of one sort or another are the centre of their lives. Card games, dancing, fooling around with women who should know better. All games. But Bapaké Tolé and women? H'm. No, that's going too far, that's pasture he's never strayed into. Or has he, though? Does anyone ever know? I certainly never caught him at

7. The Wives

it or heard anything about him being mixed up with someone. Perhaps in that regard Bapaké Tolé could be given a 'Satisfactory' mark.

'Hey, wake up!'

I had to speak pretty sharply then to the driver. The gharry seemed to be hardly moving. Maybe the horse has gone to sleep too.

'Why, Ndoro, I'm awake,' the man comes back, offended. Anyway, Marman—the boy's a grandchild to us, virtually, as these things go in our Javanese way—Marman who's sitting with the driver, he's definitely asleep. From behind I've seen his head nodding with the movement of the cart. I haven't the heart to scold him, poor thing. It's Saturday night and they haven't let him watch the wayang show to the end. Well at least he got to where the *dalang* raised the level of fun a bit when he brought out the three clowns. Gets a bit ribald there at times, the way those three, Semar, Gareng and Petruk, are sometimes played.

With that I wander back to Bapak Tolé and the possibility that he might at some point have been involved with a woman. But no, again I have to conclude that in that respect he's unblemished. And yet, and yet . . . the moment I come to that view, I also have to recall Mas Martoatmodjo, now gone from this world. There you had someone as good, as honest, as strong as ever you might want, someone who was always thinking of others, thinking about how to better the lives of the little people and so on and so forth—caught playing around with a dancer in Karangjambu! Can you explain that? Obviously Mas Marto, hero that he looked, like so many other husbands could fall to the temptations of that particular game. But then, if it is after all only a game, just a passing fancy, shouldn't wives be less concerned, be patient, and assume that in time most husbands will tire of that nonsense and come back to them? And an impatient wife mostly loses her husband. And what a dreadful division of the family takes place then, as dreadful a thing as can happen in this society of ours, a division that the children will oppose, will rebel against! It's why *Parto Kromo* is so often picked for weddings. The Javanese say that Parto, or Arjuna, is perfectly matched with Lara Ireng, or Sembadra. Despite the fact that in the process of wandering about the world, defending it from monsters and evil men and the like, Arjuna takes to himself from royal courts and from desolate mountains dozens of beautiful women, falls in love with them. But it all works out because he always returns to his own palace of Madukara, where Sembadra waits faithfully with her co-queens Srikandi and Larasati for him to arrive. H'm. Some of that morality isn't very easy to follow at this time of the morning.

But here we are at last, the wretched carriage has stopped in front of our house to let me struggle out. Coming back like this, for the hundredth time from some invitation like tonight's, lately I've had to stand leaning against something, looking for a moment at this house in front of me, this house that has been my home. Even in the first light of dawn it's easy to see how old it's got. We never neglected it, we always kept it in order, repaired it and painted it; but, yes, you can't mistake the signs. The two rocking chairs are on the veranda, and above them I can just see the stuffed deer's head poking its nose forward. It must have hung there for half a century now. Maybe more.

Marman helps me up the veranda-stairs and into the inner room; and as has been happening now, as soon as I sit down a feeling of great tiredness comes all over me, and a sleepiness which I can barely fight off. While I sit there, yawning, good old Paerah brings me the strong, sweet coffee she always has ready at the end of a *kesukan* night or after we've been to a wayang somewhere. She knows that I won't be going to bed now. It's coming on to five o'clock, and that means I have to be up anyway to see to the morning coffee and the savouries, attend to heating the water and preparing breakfast. That's what I do while Bapaké Tolé goes for his usual walk to the square. It's been our routine for so many years, and something which amazingly has never bored either of us. But then habits, things which you don't actually think much about, can never really become boring. Nor is my share in it particularly heavy, anyway. Paerah does most of the actual work, I just oversee things a bit, just to assure myself that everything is in order. It's been something I've always enjoyed, and on the other hand I tend to feel a little edgy if I can't keep an eye on it. There could never be any question of lying in bed while there's the possibility that Paerah might have missed something. Where's the pleasure if you're worried that there may be too many coffee grounds in the glass? Or if the coffee's too weak? And the sugar: what we take has come to be measured to a grain over the years. Paerah needs to go out to the stalls for the minor items. Sticky-rice balls rolled in grated coconut or soybean flour. Rice cubes steamed in banana leaf. We like them dabbed in syrup, just coconut water thickened with palm sugar, and then sprinkled-over with grated coconut. But the fried yams and bananas we do ourselves. Oh, and then there's Mbok Suro's rice and blanched vegetables with peanut sauce. Although we really shouldn't be calling it 'Mbok Suro's' any more since the old lady passed away, we should call it by her daughter's name now, who goes by our fence with her tray in the morning these days. And then there's the morning bath to consider as well. No, no, all that's impossible to imagine happening smoothly while I lie abed. No, I've always needed to keep an eye on it all. And, in the end, it's to please my husband, isn't it? And I join him too, in his pleasure, don't I?

'What are you up to, Rah? Dozing off? Ndoro Kakung will be back presently.'

'The coffee's ready, Ndoro Putri. It can be poured as soon as Ndoro Kakung comes. I'll go out for the snacks presently.'

'All right then.'

7. The Wives

My children and children-in-law are always bothering me with their comments about how I spoil their father, even telling me that I'm too devoted to him. I'm truly astonished at the way young people think nowadays. What a thing to say: spoiling; too devoted! All that's happening is a division of labour between their father and myself. Bapak wears himself to the bone to bring home an income, and I am the rear echelon which sees to it that everything goes smoothly. If it doesn't, Bapaké Tolé is thrown off his stride, goes into a rage, and that then could affect his work. Well all right, we're retired now, but the division of labour sort of goes on. Isn't a proper division of labour what makes a stable, harmonious life? Naturally that's the ideal. I know there's no guarantee that there will always be a proper balance, one that will guarantee peace in a family. In fact not a few of our own relatives and other people we know have marriages that are anything but harmonious. Even when the wives do a fair enough job in that rear echelon. That's because some husbands can never be satisfied, whatever you do. But then, on the other side, there are wives who could do more to keep up their looks and keep in shape. And a drop of scent wouldn't do any harm in some cases. Yes, beyond trying to keep active and on their toes they could acquire a bit more grace and charm as well, a bit more elegance. Something more properly feminine in their attitude and behavior. A husband will stay happy and less inclined to wander when his wife makes an effort to keep her femininity. Or am I a bit naïve there? Some domineering husbands are beyond satisfying, whatever you do; from looks to ways you present yourself, they'll still be at you, lecturing you. Now, would Bapaké Tolé be one of those? H'm, yes and no. On the question of feminine attractiveness, I seem to remember that he's never been particularly fussy, nor exceptionally demanding; but as regards my behaviour and the way I present myself to others, how I should weigh up people and act towards them, our relatives, our acquaintances, there Bapaké Tolé I must admit has had a fair influence in forming me, you might say. He's had more education after all. Of course, that doesn't mean I followed him in everything; I *have* stuck up for my own opinions too. I've even done it for no particular reason, or to relieve a conversation that was growing a bit heavy, or to probe more deeply what he was getting at. However, I've always conformed in the end, have let him win with his opinions; or else how could you preserve that important balance between you? And I'm a great believer in the maintenance of balance and harmony. You could say it's my philosophy.

I can hear the noise of the neighbours' roosters, and the sky overhead has taken on a pink tinge; and now there's the buggy with Bapaké Tolé arriving. Five o'clock on the dot, as I expected. *He* doesn't need anyone to help him down. I watch him from one of the rocking chairs, striding firmly across the yard and up the veranda stairs. He sits in the other chair, takes off his headdress and undoes one or two buttons on his jacket. Paerah's there with his glass of coffee.

'I don't think I'll walk this morning, Bu. Just as it was getting light, I started to feel tired and sleepy.'

'Well, yes, of course. That's not a young body, Pak, that you're forcing to stay up to all hours at *kesukan*.'

'Actually, I stopped playing cards just after you left, Buné. What kept me was the performance of that *dalang* from Solo.'

'What's so special about that story, Pakné? Arjuna wants to marry Sembadra. She asks for a gamelan from the abode of the gods, and after that a procession of heavenly buffaloes.'

'Yes, that's the story in essence, but the way it was presented in that wayang made *Parto Kromo* something different.'

'Oh, how?'

'Sembadra appeared bold, not spoiled and frivolous as she's often made out. While Arjuna was patient and firm, someone confronted by a testing challenge which he goes to meet confidently.'

'That's interesting. Mostly Sembadra is a pampered young lady, all pouting and sulking. And Arjuna is too much of a fighting cock.'

'Well, I must say I'm not sure I'm fond of Sembadra as a bold woman. I like her more gentle and refined.'

'Now, Pak, why can't she be a little of both those sides? She knows her own mind and here she's probably determined to give Arjuna the chance to prove himself worthy of her love. And he does prove it, whereupon they marry. And after that, she follows him meekly enough wherever he goes.'

I see Bapaké Tolé is smiling at me.

'You're talkative this morning, Buné. I don't know what to say.'

And I smile back. Men. Always startled whenever their wives say something that makes sense. I watch him return to his eating. A ball of sticky rice goes down; more rice in a banana leaf; a fried banana. For someone as old as that, he's got an extraordinary appetite. And he's never tired of this market stuff. Been wolfing it down all these years and still likes it. Amazing.

'Rah, is that hot water ready yet, or no?'

'Ready, Ndoro Kakung. The bucket is in the bathroom.'

'I'm off, Bu. I'll have my splash and another bite when Mbok Suro comes past and then I'll go to bed.'

'And I will too. The small of my back is all stiff and tired.'

And so, after our bath and Mbok Suro's breakfast we go and lie down. From the rear of the house comes the twittering of a pet dove owned by Ngadiman's children, and Ngadiman's fighting rooster wakes up to give a

7. The Wives

late crow. Another morning passes for me and Bapaké Tolé.

One day, about noon, we were surprised by Soemini arriving on our doorstep by herself, just like that, carrying a suitcase, and no husband or children in sight!

'Eh? You're here, alone? We didn't expect you.'

'Oh Bu, I hardly expected it myself until I decided to do it.'

And as she finished saying that, Soemini burst into tears and threw her arms around me.

'There now, there now, Nduk. Here, come inside, come and take a seat. Calm down, come in, dear.'

I could see Bapaké Tolé was bewildered. We quickly sat Soemini in a chair and brought her a glass of water. She went on sobbing, and we could do nothing until she quietened down at last. Bapaké Tolé then asked her where she had come from, to arrive in such a state. As if knowing her itinerary explained anything.

'From Madiun, Pak. And last night from Jakarta, by train.'

'Well, I never. So where is your husband then, and the children?'

Soemini began crying again. I gave Bapaké Tolé a sign that he should let me handle this, and he moved back a bit and nodded. I'm surprised at how I've had to step into situations where it should be he who is calming and reassuring. He's been capable enough most times at tricky moments, but at others, like the time the Japanese officer banged him, and when that crazy Martokebo was waving his machete over our heads, well those were clearly beyond him. And now, *lho*, a tearful daughter drops in on us and he's helpless. I think we must have sat there a good quarter of an hour before Soemini stopped wailing, took control of herself and told us, with a good deal of embarrassment, what had gone on in Jakarta.

To use more or less her own words and views on the matter, what she had discovered was 'a disgraceful situation, fit only to occur among uneducated, low-class, socially-inept vulgarians, an indecency which might have once been allowed to pass in smaller towns of the period when we, her parents, were still young, when Bapak was teaching in Karangdompol, but no longer in these modern times!' In a nutshell, Mas Harjono, her husband, had set himself up a mistress in Rawamangun. It seems that Mini had heard about it from a colleague of hers in one of those organisations she had got involved with, the colleague being in fact related to the mistress. Mas Harjono had met the woman at a party farewelling some people he worked with who were retiring. Soemini had excused herself from this minor get-together in her husband's office, saying she didn't feel well. The woman turned out to be a singer in one of those *keroncong* pop bands that government departments were raising. A vehicle was supposed to take the band away but was full, so Mas Harjono offered her a lift, and then things developed from there. He started coming home late, sometimes in the early hours of the morning: there were important meetings, he said, and overtime, and matters to do with the trouble in Irian Barat, 'incidents of a security nature', 'subversive activities' and so on, needing his attention. Mini took it all as normal, the times were edgy, and Mas Harjono, now a senior man in the Ministry of Internal Affairs, could be expected to work late pretty often. And she herself was busy with some women's organisation, and could be excused, she said, for carelessness and not keeping an eye on what her husband was doing. Then one of the other women came up to her at the end of a meeting.

'Yes, Mbak?'

'Well, Bu, it's like this. There's something I should talk to you about.'

'Oh? What, Mbak?'

'I'm sorry to have to report it, Bu, but the matter is important.'

'Well then, go ahead, Mbak. If it's important.'

'I don't like to talk bad about anyone, Bu, you understand, but the thing is a fact, and it's important that you should know.'

Mini told us that her heart began to beat faster. Then it occurred to her that this was probably about some squabble to do with rank or work-loads, or else someone or other shirking her duties in the organisation.

'My cousin, Sri Asih, who works in Internal Affairs as a *keroncong* singer, a member of that Ministry's employees union . . .'

And then she told Mini the story of Mas Harjono's relation with Sri Asih.

'I'm sorry, Bu, to have to tell you about it, but it has to do with the good name of my family and my relatives. And that of your own people too.'

Mini said thank you; and it appears, from what we put together of her story, that she departed the meeting looking much as usual; but on the way home she said she suddenly felt dizzy and her eyes could not seem to focus. She went straight into her bedroom and lay down on her bed to think about what she had heard. Might it all be a lie? No, there couldn't be any purpose in telling her those things if they were untrue. Then she tried to understand why Mas Harjono would have done such a thing: an involvement with a *keroncong* singer, after they had been living together married so long without any trouble of that kind. Why now, when they were getting on in years, were grandparents, with the oldest already married some time back and the others also ready to set up their own families? What did Mas Harjono need with a mistress? Was this some 'archaic instinct' of the higher priyayi rising to the surface in these times, the nobility reclaiming an old privilege? She remembered hearing stories told by her father and mother

7. The Wives

about Pakdé Martoatmodjo, a committed educator with high ideals, who also apparently had to find himself some dancer to keep somewhere. At least Pakdé Marto was a man of his circle, his era, when such things were common, if not indeed customary. Not to mention that he was relatively young then; unlike Mas Harjono, a senior ministry official in a modern republic, fifty-one years of age and four or five years away from his pension. No. This was all highly, highly improper.

Or was she the one at fault? There had been times when her husband was unhappy or had even protested when he came home to find her away dealing with this or that matter in some women's group, finding himself eating alone. Yes, but that didn't happen every night, and anyway she had everything prepared for him beforehand. The house was well-kept, the servants knew their duties, and there were no children now to create chaos. So what else, in fact, was Mas Harjono looking for? Finally, she asked him herself.

'Mas Har. Do you know someone called Sri Asih?'

His surprise was unmistakeable.

'I do. How did you know?'

'I've been told. What's your relationship with her?'

'Relationship? Well, she's a friend of mine.'

'Rot. There's more to that relationship than friendship.'

Her husband said nothing, while it was evident in his expression that he was seeking the right words to explain things, or perhaps to turn the accusation against her.

'All right. I admit that my relations with Sri are not just friendly.'

'Would you like to be more specific?'

'To be specific, I need a girlfriend with whom I can have an intimate relationship.'

Mini now felt the one checked and wordless. She was hit hard by the direct admission of her husband, and by what it implied regarding herself.

'So, then, I, your wife, don't function in that respect any longer?'

'It's like this. You are my wife, and you've been a good wife. However, now, perhaps because we've each been so busy with our affairs, perhaps because of the pressure of my work, or something to do with the age I'm at, I find that I need some other kind of woman. Even a completely different kind. And Sri answers that need.'

She could say nothing for a moment. Barbarian! A woman's just a thing that fulfils a need for him.

'From what you say, Mas Har, it's clear that I have no further use for you then.'

'Hey, now, wait a minute! You're still my wife and I love you. I didn't marry you to drop you just like that.'

And they carried on sparring: each trying to establish some stable moral position, he to defend, hers to attack from: until it suddenly all became tiresome to her and she decided what she should do.

'All right, that's enough, if that's how things stand. I feel sick. I'm going to Wanagalih tomorrow. I need somewhere quiet to consider this. I'll go alone, you don't need to come. If we require you there for some reason, I'll call you. There's no need to bother the children, their grown and have their own concerns.'

'There's Sumi. Her child might ask where grandma's gone.'

'That's up to you to answer. I'm off.'

If Soemini's story of what happened gave us a sense of herself being in charge and cool, here with us she was in tears throughout the telling of it and it was an effort to calm her. To me what we were dealing with was clear, and hopefully Bapaké Tolé could see it in the same way: a surfeited marriage could be the way to put it. When you thought about how well they had done, it was just astonishing. The husband with a position in Jakarta; the highest possible rank practically achieved; salary and whatever else coming with the job, more than enough to live on; the children all doing well and a cute grandchild newly arrived. So why not be satisfied? You're never satisfied and then suddenly there's too much, it all pales. What a difference to us here on Setenan Road, plodding along from day to day without an inkling of what the word 'surfeit' means. Maybe it's because we grew up happy to accept a humbler lot, to accept limits to the satisfactions in life. Maybe this surfeit business happens with those who nowadays are always looking upwards to greater things instead of sideways, around themselves? I mean, Soemini and Harjono only concerned with moving their own immediate family forward, while we were involved with the whole clan of them, beginning with Sri and Darmin, who were if anything too sweet and obedient, and Soenandar, who gnawed at our patience to the day of his death. And that's still our way: with Ngadiman getting on now, and his children become another charge on us. Yes, were Soemini and Harjono more concerned with the full meaning of kinship, instead of this new style of closing in on your own nest, well, there would be little time left in which to breed strife.

As expected, Bapaké Tolé had a hard time knowing what to make of such a wonder as a sulking daughter running back to her parents. I remembered how he dealt very solidly and intelligently with poor, distraught Hardojo that time when the boy couldn't marry Nunuk. Well, perhaps his uncertainty now about what to do with Soemini was due to the fact that this was a female, and a spoiled only-daughter, a pretty wilful one at that. Her attitude to her husband, as we judged from their argument, showed us that Soemini was still the young Soemini we had known. Best to keep father out of this, I decided; and he was happy to agree to my taking her aside for a good talk later.

'This can't go on, Pak, she can't expect to live here forever.'

7. The Wives

'Absolutely she can't. The thing, Buné, is how to make her understand that. I haven't worked out exactly how to do it yet. But it would be wrong to let her stay here, feeling sorry for yourself. And this daughter of yours can be stubborn. What a business. She's an adult, they both are. A grandmother, and wants to separate from her husband? I can't make it out.'

'Look, Pak, let me talk with her later. We'll work her around in a little while. I'm worried she'll expect to be pampered in the old way if you start talking to her.'

'H'm. Well, I'll leave it to you, Buné. Just be careful, is my advice. Catch the fish and don't muddy the water, that sort of thing.'

So it was left to me to melt Soemini's heart. Most days I got some exercise picking vegetables in the rear garden, and leaves from the hedges growing around it, and Soemini when she was little used to come with me. This was something she hadn't done in a long while, especially since they had begun living in Jakarta, but the old routine came back to her when we set off next morning.

'I see you're as fit and strong as ever, Bu.'

'Not nearly as much as I was, and I can't walk very quickly now.'

'You better be careful on this ground. This black soil here in Wanagalih is full of cracks, and it breaks up in lumps. You shouldn't come out by yourself at all, actually. You could fall. Tell Paerah or someone else to help you pick the vegetables.'

We checked the hedge that divided the kitchen garden from the rice field, picked cow peas and hyacinth beans, and various kinds of leaves growing on vines supported by a bamboo trellis. Then, among some black potato creepers spreading up the trellis I spotted a number of new yellowish fruit.

'What a lot of hairy dicks have gone ripe there, suddenly!'

'Mother! You mustn't call them that! How rude!'

'Oh, now, what's rude about it? They stick out like that, out of those fibres, and that's why they're called hairy dicks.'

'*Lho*, Bu. That's indecent. Someone will hear you.'

Then we both burst out laughing.

'Ho-ho, I didn't give them that name. It's what the children herding the buffaloes call them. It doesn't mean anything, Nduk. And anyway as long as there aren't any men around I can talk as I like.'

Soemini pinched my arm and we laughed and giggled together like a pair of young girls saying scandalous things out of earshot of their parents. We collected some of the disreputable fruit and walked on eating them towards the bund at the edge of the rice field, meaning to rest in the shelter where the children who guarded the rice from the birds usually sat. I noticed Trimo's boy was working among the rice. Since we had begun to get on and found ourselves unable to properly supervise the field labour we had gone into sharecropping with our old servant. I asked the boy to get some tea for us and something to eat from the house and bring the things to the shelter.

'The field seems so quiet, Bu. I remember there used to be parakeets up in the tops of the bamboos, and in that coral tree.'

'Yes, I know, Nduk. These last years, you hardly ever see parakeets around here anymore. Or any other birds much: pipits or rice finches or wood pigeons. Maybe the children have got them all with their catapults. They used to sell them, or roast and eat them themselves. Life's hard.'

We sat looking at our field, modest-sized but up to now enough for us. Trimo's boy came with hot tea and some boiled bananas. We sat there eating them and drinking tea, well-pleased.

'Have you thought about sending a letter to Harjono?'

'Not yet. Let him sit for a while.'

H'm. 'I feel a bit sad for him, Min, and the children too are probably in a turmoil at the moment. He'll be by himself and won't know where anything is in the house.'

'Won't do any harm, that, occasionally. I might get some appreciation.'

'You'll miss them all, you wait. And Wanagalih gets quiet, compared to Jakarta.'

Soemini said nothing. Then: 'I'm still angry with him.'

'I do understand that, but, you know, it's hard work to stay angry for very long.'

'And you know, I'm really disappointed in him. I've never felt so belittled in all our years together. To treat me like that, to be cast aside for a *keroncong* singer, a—what were they called in Dutch times, when that sort of thing used to go on?—a *zangeres*.'

'Yes, I can see you *are* very angry, Nduk.'

Soemini said nothing again, so I pressed on: 'I haven't had anything happen to us like this, but I understand your feelings and your attitude, and you're quite right to be angry. But you shouldn't be comparing yourself with a *sangres keroncong*, who's just a suit of clothes, after all. What's important is the woman inside and what your husband feels about that. Now did he say he's in love with her or anything of the sort?'

'Oh, he's made that clear enough. He said he needed a girlfriend.'

'Have you asked yourself why?'

There was a pause.

'I have, Bu. I couldn't answer that.'

'Goodness me, Nduk. Try again and don't be afraid of the answer.'

Soemini burst into tears.

'He's bored with me, Bu.'

'Maybe not so much with you as with the way you two live over there, or with himself too. Men are always getting bored, Nduk.'

7. The Wives

Soemini continued crying.

'Don't worry. He'll get bored with his new toy too, soon enough, as long as . . .'

'As long as what, Bu?'

'As long as you're patient and wise. Don't go drawing out your anger forever. I'll bet that Mas Har will come for you here in the next few days. And if not, then we'll send him a letter. Then, when he comes or writes, you mustn't hold a grudge or be proud towards him. Take him back in good spirit.'

'And if he won't come?'

'He'll come. Do you want to bet?'

Soemini smiled. Whether there was any value or sense in what I was saying, at least I had got that smile.

'Now, when he comes, take that as a sign of remorse, and so there won't be any need to demand an apology from him on top of that. Just attend to him as usual, and when he asks you to come back with him, do it. Easy.'

'It's a nice world for men.'

'Nduk, it's nice for all of us when we get along. Now, when you get back to Jakarta you try not to go out so much to those meetings of yours, just take care of your husband and home. I don't mean as a manager or whatever, but show that you are there to hold your little world together. Then you start to work slowly on your husband with whatever it takes to edge him away from that *sangres*. In fact, he'll probably drop her himself. Believe your old Ibu.'

Soemini grinned while she shook her head.

'You know the ways of men, Bu. But I thought Bapak never gave you much trouble, did he?'

'Oh Allah, your father? He's the son of hard-working peasants. There's never been a wild thought in his mind. For those games you need to go to the real gentry.'

Morning passed like that, until Paerah arrived to announce that Bapaké Tolé was waiting for us to join him at the midday meal.

My guess, thankfully, turned out to be right. Harjono arrived, and not on his own but with reinforcements: with Sumi, his oldest, leading my two-and-a-half-year-old great-grandson, and with other merry and noisy offspring, all students in the last stages of their university courses. We had universities now: nothing less for the new young! Anyway, a happy chaos filled our house on Setenan Road. I had reported to Bapaké Tolé on my talk with Soemini, and it had the effect straightaway of relaxing him. Now, surrounded and hugged by his grandchildren, kissed by a great-grandchild, he was clearly happy to give the crisis no more thought. I had to smile to myself, thinking how innocent was this good man who had reached the age of a father, grandfather and beyond, and yet imagined that because we two had had such a mild run as husband and wife, then Soemini's trouble could be fixed so easily. It probably hadn't entered his mind that time was now needed for them to approach each other and get back to their earlier closeness; much time, actually, in which misunderstandings and disorder might crop up again. But as to the present, it made the heart lighter to see them all together as a family; Soemini so happy in the company of her children and her grandchild, even though still a little unsure towards Harjono.

For some days the house was like the setting for a general honeymoon, a mood that touched the couple returning to each other—a bit shy, a bit awkward—and everyone else as well. And the pleasure that all those Jakarta-folk, as we now thought of them, got from Wanagalih, I also put to the rediscovering of what used to be familiar and had grown distant. Our modest kitchen-garden, its soil lumpy and cracked, and the rice-field beyond the trellises; the two great rivers, with their everlasting flow of chocolate water and sampans crowded with peasant passengers; the old fort, still out of sight and not easy to find—you would have thought that all those run-of-the-mill things were given a new colour or light by the present mood of relief at what had been averted. Maybe, too, there was some thoughtful looking at what time had taken away or given a new meaning to, a new appeal, to eyes more used now to the sights of a big city. It set me thinking about what causes someone to be hardly aware of a place one day and nostalgic for it the next. Who knows, it's probably God's way of making us more interesting to each other. Even some criminal boy like Soenandar is still interesting in that way; more so anyway than beasts being driven to the cattle market behind our house. Even Martokebo, not much cleverer than the animals he dealt in, was still in his time, if you thought about it, someone in his way amazing, if horribly so. Both Soenandar and Martokebo, with all the ugliness in their natures, were still capable of feelings only people have. Surely, even they had souls to sense something of what Mini and Harjono had come to feel with regret in Jakarta: that their lives were somehow out of order? Souls to feel pain and joy all mixed together in a moment of nostalgia for good things that had gone forever into the past? Those and other thoughts like them passed through my mind as I watched Soemini and her brood visiting again those old places, with the delight of children first finding meaning in what they saw around them. And warmth of family looked too to be one of the things they were finding again.

Finally, the time came for them to depart for the capital, and I thought Harjono kissed our hands with more than polite respect.

'Bapak, Ibu, we go with your permission and blessing.'

'Go, my son, go Nakmas. Go in good cheer all of you, and in harmony.'

Soemini then kissed Bapaké Tolé; and when she came to kiss me she hugged me tightly and whispered something in Dutch, of which of course I made out nothing, but I understood that it was her way of thanking me.

7. The Wives

'All right, Nduk, God be with you and with all of you. Take care.'

The young ones kissed their Embah Kakung's hands, but with me they kissed me several times in the modern fashion, on the cheeks.

'Good-bye, Mbah. Come and see us in Jakarta. Don't put it off.'

'Oh, I will someday. Good-bye.'

After Soemini had lifted her grandson to kiss Bapaké Tolé and then me, the party left, intending to travel back via Yogya and drop in on Hardojo, now living there.

The problems parents have with their children can sometimes seem never-ending. Even when we old ones become grandparents, or as in our case great-grandparents, we find ourselves never free of our children's trials. No sooner had we seen Soemini's crisis with Harjono end as satisfactorily as might be hoped, with Harjono finally disengaging from his singer, than now a letter came by express mail from Sus telling us that she was coming to Wanagalih. Something was up.

'What do you think has happened, Buné? Bit queer, her wanting to come alone. I hope it's not like that matter of Soemini's a while ago.'

'Oh, I don't think so, Pakné. Sus is different. She's attractive and as womanly as any man would want. Nothing like that assertive daughter of yours. No, Noegroho will stick close to her, I'm positive.'

I heard my husband give his old-man's laugh that sounded like a cackle nowadays.

'You, Bu, have got some pretty sharp opinions about people.'

'Ho, I'm only saying what's a fact. I'm very fond of Sus. I love them all, actually, our children-in-law and all their children as well. But you've often said you wanted to hear my view of things.'

'Ye-es.'

'Well, there! We better wait until Sus comes.'

She came a few days after the letter. Noegroho had now climbed up in life and was doing well in a way quite beyond the other two children, had become the director of a state company no less; so Sus hired a pirate taxi all the way to Wanagalih from Yogya. From Jakarta to Yogya she had taken a Garuda flight. Despite all that spending, she looked tired and rumpled when she arrived; however, she still managed to remain a good-looking woman. She kissed father's hands, then gave me a hug and kissed me on each cheek: with me she was easy and warm.

I thought I shouldn't try to hurry her too much into explaining this odd visit: 'There now, Nduk, so you've arrived. Come and sit down. Tea or coffee? Or would you like a glass of cool water from our earthenware *kendi*? People from the city seem to be always desperate for some *kendi* water.'

'Yes, Bu. I will have a glass of water, and then some hot coffee.'

'There, I knew it. Ra-ah! A glass of water from the *kendi*, Rah.'

While my attention was on that, Bapaké Tolé asked Sus straight out: 'How come you're here alone, Nduk? What's happened to Kamas?'

'Mas Noeg is in Europe at the moment, Pak.'

'Whew! That Kamas of yours flits about. Catches planes like we ride a buggy to Ngale. And your children? Couldn't any of them come with you?'

I saw Sus catch her breath and cloud over. A moment later her manner of a city-lady broke up and she was sobbing! I made a last effort to ease her into her explanation: 'There now, Sus, drink your coffee. Take your time and then you can tell us what happened.'

Sus sipped her coffee slowly, bringing herself back into some order to tell us her story.

It seems that the problem was her daughter, Marie. The young woman was now twenty-seven years of age. Normally, she should by this be married and with an armful of children; but Marie was a product of these new times, in no hurry to find a husband, although her parents had seen a line of young men pass from the rank of boyfriend to that of ex-boyfriend. Trying to press her to finally settle down and pick a serious prospect never got anyone very far. She had apparently become bored with her university course, dropped out, and neither Sus nor Noegroho could persuade her, let alone tell her, to get back to her studies. At some point, Marie's parents did admit that they were too soft in dealing with their children, that both were clearly growing up spoiled. After the death of Toni, Sus especially was never free of the thought that at any moment another of her children might be lost; she kept reliving the shock and grief of that loss, and the misery and feeling of emptiness after it. The result was that both parents, but Sus the most, never grudged the two children anything, protected them, gave way to them, and did everything to keep them happy. Noegroho coped sooner with Toni's death, but he understood his wife's pain and couldn't bring himself to criticise her, although they both had moments of worry about where this was leading, and particularly about Marie's behaviour. After she had been set up as a secretary in her father's office, Marie often left her work half-done; she went off on lunch dates with boyfriends and wasn't seen again for the rest of that day; or she might just not arrive at all, claiming a headache or the like, and afterwards be spotted around town with friends and going partying to all hours. It got to the point where Sus finally began to grow seriously uneasy and concerned that Marie might get into some kind of trouble. A number of times she almost talked to her daughter, but then drew back, frightened to irritate her or bring on one of her moods: Marie got huffy easily. Until one day Sus gathered herself to have a serious talk with her daughter, edging into the matter.

7. The Wives

'What's it like, Marie, since you started working in your father's office? Happy enough?'

'Eh, work? That's a funny question, Mama. Yeah, I'm happy. You're free enough there, can do what you like.'

'Oh? How can you be working and do what you like? Aren't there people there, superiors, to direct you and organise things for you to do?'

'Sure. There's Uncle Narto, there's Mbak Tri, they're my superiors, Ma. I'd like to see them pull rank on me, though.'

'Really now? Don't they bring you responsible work and expect you to deal with it? As I see it, you seem to have an awful amount of free time.'

Marie laughed. 'Mama dear. My job in Papa's office is of absolutely no importance. I type a letter or two, send them off to other offices, and they give me some outside work as well. That's about it.'

'Yes, but Marie, even if it's light work, surely you can't just do whatever you like there, can you?'

'Look, Ma, basically it's this way: I'm free there and I organise my own day.'

'Well, but Marie, I hope Bapak's office isn't losing out by employing you and paying you a salary?'

'Ha-ha-ha . . . Mama, let me tell you some facts. *Oom* Narto and Mbak Tri are under Bapak's thumb. Bapak is a retired colonel, right? Well, *Oom* Narto was only a major when he was in the army. Is he going to stir up problems with someone who out-ranks him, the boss of the company at that?'

Sus told us that she looked at her daughter with alarm. She said nothing, but wondered whether Noegroho was aware that Marie had this attitude towards her job. Sus must talk to him about it sometime.

'Let's drop it, Ma. Don't worry. Things are just fine with me at the office.'

Sus smiled weakly. She was an attractive delinquent this daughter of hers, knew how to impress people and get her way. Oh, well. . . . But there was still that other worry. Who were these acquaintances Marie went out with, stopping for a moment to pick up the girl and then bring her back home? One day Sus caught Noegroho at an opportune moment to discuss their daughter.

'Marie? What's there to worry about? She's an adult, she can look after herself, can't she?'

'Yes, I know. But these young men, who are they? Have you met them, Pak?'

'No, not all of them. One or two work somewhere in our company.'

'You seem to be pretty calm about Marie. But don't you think she's rather too free and easy in her life?'

'Well yes, I know that, and so do you. Wasn't that how we brought her up?'

'It's true that we spoiled her. But that doesn't mean she should be let live a disorganised life without any bearing to it. And, Bapak, do you happen to know that she does just whatever she likes at your office?'

'Yeah, I know. Poor Narto's always coming to me hat in hand to tell me about it. I've asked him go easy, but to keep an eye on her.'

'So in short you're not concerned about her?'

'No. She'll get tired and bored with that sort of life one day. She'll settled down and live quietly enough, with the regulation husband and children.'

Sus was pacified a little by her husband's confident view of the matter; only she kept wondering when that 'one day' would come, and at what point would Marie have had enough of sporting with boyfriends.

Then one of them made a more regular appearance. His name was Maridjan, and for once Marie had him stop in the house for more than the usual few minutes. She even went so far as to casually introduce him to her mother, and later her father. This Maridjan certainly was a male with appeal, could be described in the new language of students as *seksi*, and there was no doubt that he was handsome in the Javanese manner; but just by his name it was clear he was no scion of any priyayi line: it was a pure and unadorned village name. The boy interested Marie, that was clear: in a short space of time the other suitors disappeared and she was only seen around town with him. It seems he worked in another state enterprise, and Marie had met him when she was taking some papers there from her father's office. He might be handsome, but his manners were definitely unpolished. When he sat down, his feet and legs were everywhere, and he thought nothing of perching himself above those around him, apparently unaware of others' rank or his own social position. And his hair grew to an artistic length, not at all suited to a salaried employee in a government office, if indeed he was that and not just some messenger-boy.

'Marie, have you had a good look at this young man Maridjan of yours?'

Marie laughed lightly.

'Yes, all over actually. Why do you ask, Ma?'

'The boy seems to know very little about good manners.'

'Oh, for instance?'

'Why, he sits above people, doesn't stand up for me, flicks his cigarette ash everywhere.'

Marie's laugh was almost a guffaw.

'Oh, Ibu, really. What's important is this, and this. And this.'

She pointed to her forehead, her breast, and then lower.

'Marie! What sort of a girl are you turning out to be? That's obscene.'

Marie thought that remark even more hilarious, and Sus, shocked and horrified, could only invoke Allah in her heart.

'Marie, listen to me. Maridjan is not someone who is suitable for you.'

'Well now. What are we, Mama, that makes him not suitable?'

7. The Wives

'This family's background is well known to you, while he comes from some village, does he not? You are the daughter of a colonel who has had a Dutch education. We have brought you up, Marie, as an offspring of priyayi, of modern priyayi with *Europeesch* leanings.'

Sus watched her daughter laughing yet again. Was there an inkling of respect for a parent here, in the way Marie plainly found her words comical? The girl's attitude was wounding, painful.

'Mama, oh Mama . . . just what is our family, tell me. All right, Bapak's a colonel with a Dutch education. But who is Embah Kakung in Wanagalih the son of? Wasn't his father a village peasant too? You and Bapak may consider yourselves advanced gentry, *Eropis* as you say, can rattle off a Dutch sentence. But aren't we all, finally, descended from peasants and nothing more?'

'Maybe so, but I'm not very happy at how friendly you're getting to be with him. And on top of everything, he's so much younger than you. And he looks as though he hasn't got any money.'

Marie left the house, still laughing gaily, going who knows where, probably to meet Maridjan. Sus was not exaggerating when she thought the boy had no money, because since Marie had taken up with him she had asked her parents to increase the allowance they gave her on top of her salary at the office. It was easy to conclude that the money was going on entertainments which Maridjan himself was unable to pay for. Sus approached her husband again, to do something about this relationship, but he laughed the matter off as he had done in the past, telling her that this was precisely an example of her excessive concern for the children.

Then one day, while Sus was resting during the midday heat, Marie came into the room, threw herself on the bed and lay there sprawled beside her mother. At that time Noegroho was out of the country. Marie and Sus lay side by side for some moments without uttering a word. Sus, recovering from a doze in the stifling heat, waited for Marie to announce some matter: it was long now since as a pampered, cajoling young girl she had last come to her parents' bed like this.

'Ma . . .'

'Mm?'

Marie had perhaps hoped for some more encouraging response, and for some moments did not continue.

'Ma, I want to say something.'

'Yes, go on.'

Then Marie turned her face to her mother, and the young woman was an astonishing sight: she had a distracted look, her eyes were dark-ringed and tired, and, as Sus watched, she began to cry. Allah!—Marie crying?

'I'm in trouble, Ma. Here.'

Sus could not take her eyes away from her daughter's face.

'Ma, I'm . . . I think I might be pregnant.'

'Ha-ah?'

Sus could not utter more than that. It was as if a stone wall had risen up before her, blocking any useful delivery of comments, questions, or judgements. The wretched face of her daughter could only warrant one response: the two women hugged one another and cried.

By the time Sus had finished telling us what had happened, she was in tears again. I looked across at Bapaké Tolé sitting forward in his rocking-chair, clearly shaken and looking vaguely out into the street. I could imagine what he was feeling: surely grief for the plight of his daughter-in-law, but, with that, his own pain as the elder and hub of a Javanese clan that had been struck suddenly by an event threatening the self-respect and honour of all its members. I too felt that we had a bad situation here, although my thoughts went more directly towards how to save my granddaughter, and to worrying about such things as a safe pregnancy and the health of the little creature in her womb. Bapaké Tolé's immediate concern would be how to rescue the good name of Noegroho, retired colonel and director of a national business; what could be done for Marie would just have one part in the bigger problem.

'Bapak, Ibu, I beg you as humbly as I can, as sincerely as I can, to forgive me for not having taken proper care of your granddaughter. I'm at fault for having been so careless, for spoiling her. What's going to happen when Mas Noeg hears about this? He's just going to break out into the wildest fury at me!'

And she began sobbing again. Bapaké Tolé emerged from wherever he had been lost in thought, and his words were businesslike: 'That's enough, Sus, don't keep crying. The important things now are, firstly, do you know who your daughter is pregnant by?'

'Yes, Pak. It's that Maridjan, Pak.'

'Marie has told you that?'

'Yes, Pak.'

'In that case, don't waste any more time—call your husband home. Next, sort this matter out with Maridjan. That's important, Nduk. But, again, is he prepared to marry the girl?'

'Yes, it seems so.'

'*Lho*, it seems so, she says! You must find out quickly whether he will or won't. This is to do with the opinion people are going to have of this family. All of us, Nduk. Our name.'

Sus, who had begun to control her tears, now under Bapaké Tolé's urgent pressing started crying again.

'That's just it, Pak. Oh God, that he might . . .'

7. The Wives

'Might what, Sus?'

'Disappear.'

Bapaké Tolé said nothing. I hoped that he was not going over in his mind the history of Soenandar's absconding, leaving behind him poor fatherless Lantip. I quickly took my turn in this thing, trying to calm them both.

'There now, Sus. Let's settle down and not rush to all kinds of ideas about Maridjan. Bapak is quite right, you should call your husband back as quickly as possible. But for now, Nduk, do go and have a rest after your long trip.'

Sus took my advice, and after eating something went into one of the rooms, for she was indeed worn out. When Bapaké Tolé and I were alone we began talking again, quietly.

'H'm, Buné, we seem to be having a series of these trials this year. No sooner that matter with Soemini and Harjono got settled than this of the granddaughter arrives. There must be some great sin in our past.'

'Oh now, Bapakné, don't overdo your worry about this. It's something that can happen to anybody. When Noegroho comes, he'll set everything to rights, you'll see.'

I heard Bapaké Tolé give a little sigh and then draw in his breath.

'I don't know Buné. That Noegroho after he grew up and left here seemed to develop in some queer ways, you know.'

'How's that, Pakné?'

'He got to be, what, a general?'

'A colonel, Pakné. Retired.

'That's what I mean. Is it high, that rank?'

'Well, what about it?'

'He got to that high rank, and he can't manage his daughter and his wife?'

'Sh, not so loud. If Sus hears you we'll have more trouble.'

'He's let his wife and children roam free all this time, so now when he comes back what can we expect him to do?'

'Well, Sus herself has come to see that they've been too soft on the children. She sees that now and is sorry. People can change.'

'The thing that I regret when I look back is that Noegroho was staunch enough as a boy, and since then he's gone weak, limp, can't even control his own family. Did it happen after he became so well-off and got all those positions?'

'My regret, Pakné, is that they were never able to let go of Toni, as we're taught we must do when someone dies. With the result that the boy preyed on their minds and it affected the way they dealt with the other children. They overdid their care for them, gave them everything they wanted. As if you could ever guarantee life by having all the things of this world. Sus and Noegroho are as religious as any of us, and I suppose they do the daily prayers, yet they seemed to put out of mind that we're all mortal, finally. They neglected that side of their children's upbringing.'

'You know what I see, Buné? I see that all our lessons about values and principles from the *Wedhatama* and the *Wulangreh* and *Tripama* never had any effect on Noegroho, if all they led to was these barnyard capers. And now when an egg's broken in the coop, how's he going to make it whole again? There were two left, and now this one's broken. Women trouble: always a particularly bad business.'

Poor Bapaké Tolé, such an honest, straight man, still learning about life at his age, still having a parent's problems on his shoulders. All those lively get-togethers of the family in happy days, and in sad ones too, to share joys and sorrows, had kept us all close and harmonious. That was good, those were the old ways; but did they make the young ones too dependent on us when the new ways failed?

'Enough, Pakné. Let's go to bed. Tomorrow I'll work on Sus to make her a little happier, and we'll find the best way forward from here for all of them.'

Next day after talking some more with Sus we all decided that she should return to Jakarta, and that Lantip ought to go with her. He would be company for her during this distressing time when Noegroho was away, and he could meet Maridjan, get to know him, and perhaps see ways to bring some order into this thing. When Sus agreed we quickly got in touch with Lantip in Yogya, and a few days later he arrived in Wanagalih with Hari as well.

We could depend on Lantip. He was nearing thirty, had graduated from Gadjah Mada University and become a lecturer there, and now he had prospects of something higher in Jakarta. He was still unmarried, and even with his good position lived on with his foster father, Hardojo. We knew that for years he had been an upstanding member of that family, thoughtful and helpful, contributed to its affairs, was Hari's close friend and guide, and he could be relied on to give a hand in a ready, good-humoured and unforced spirit. This was the person we proposed to Sus as the fittest to help her. Tommi, Marie's younger brother, had little going for him. From what we learned, he looked to have been no less indulged than his sister. He had not, to this time, finished a degree, moving from one course to another as he pleased. Our hope was that stable, considerate Lantip would bring some calm to the Noegroho household, and that Sus and her husband when he returned would also get support from the other siblings and their families as needed.

As Hari, Sus, and Lantip depart and we wave to them from the front yard, Bapaké Tolé mutters to me that we should just about have enough energy left to attend Marie's wedding in Jakarta when the time comes. He sounds confident enough about that, but I have to smile. He might or might not be

7. The Wives

right about his own strength, but as for me, that young Dr Waluyo warned me not long ago to take care in my daily activities, that there was some problem with blood pressure, and I should use less salt, take more rest, and who knows what else of that kind of thing. And all these recent tensions in the family wouldn't have helped my nerves much either. Not that I've felt any particular problem in myself, not like a real illness. Only, my sleep has been broken a bit lately. But I suppose that that comes naturally with old age. And I've had this pain in the lower back, surely again something you can expect with the years. When I get dizzy and feel off-colour I've been going to an expert who does wonders by drawing the edge of a coin along the spine. And she does massages as well. Nothing like a good massage to spice up an old wife's body. The doctor says it's related to high blood pressure, that's all; and anyway I'm resigned to all that. Seventy years granted by the Lord Allah is a pretty long time, and I thank Him for every one of them; and for the way Bapaké Tolé remains healthy and nimble. More or less, anyway. He's on his way towards eighty but doesn't seem to have slowed much. That's what made me smile when he said something about our going to Jakarta for our granddaughter's wedding: he never takes the state of his health seriously because he's never ill. As for me, I have to be far more humble. When the doctor talks to me about my age, I understand he's saying kindly that my day is well and truly in its dusk. So be it, I'm happy to have lived long enough to help my children through some of their problems.

When I consider those children of mine, and their families, I just want to express my thanks to the Deity for the gift of them all, and I'm thankful that our three have been in His bestowal and mercy ever since they left our home. Yes, Soemini has had a bit of a trial with her husband, and Noegroho lost the son of his hopes, and now he'll have to confront some difficulties with that daughter of theirs. All that, I look on as the testing of His servants by an unfathomable God. They'll eventually pass those tests, I hope. And Bapaké Tolé and I have not been left out of those trials either. But everything, *alhamdulillah*, will work out in time. Only Hardojo alone has been unusually free of difficulties: his family living on steadily, calmly. Although of course there was that thing with the Christian girl, there was some unhappiness there. Since he met Sumarti and had Hari though, life has gone smoothly enough for them. And with Lantip there: always helpful, watchful. Whenever I think of Lantip I praise the Lord God, Allah the Just. A child born out of wedlock like that, to turn out so well, so loyal to us all.

But really, I don't think I'll be able to come to Marie's wedding. Never mind, I'll send my prayers from Wanagalih. I'll pray for her. For her happiness, poor girl.

8. LANTIP: from side to centre

Leaving Wanagalih to go with Budé Sus to Jakarta, I took away a distinct impression that Embah Putri was not well. Until then I had been happy, happy if somewhat astonished, that a woman of seventy could go on looking so fresh and pleasant, so healthily flushed; and that when she had so much to do by the side of her husband, Embah Kakung Sastrodarsono. With him she had to find time daily for an active social life, the land at the back had to be managed, and a still-large establishment in the house directed. I knew that she regularly dosed herself with the usual herbal tonics, but her energy and perseverance must also have had their source in the spirit with which she approached all her labours: contentedly, with tolerance, but vigorously and wholeheartedly. Market nostrums may or may not have some useful physical effects, but other, possibly inborn qualities are needed in any case: a predisposition to happiness and to accepting what life offers. But during this visit I was shocked to notice her diminished vitality, and had to ask myself if those problems concerning Bulik Soemini and Paklik Harjono, and now Marie, could have taken such a toll. I made a resolution to return as soon as possible to Wanagalih after I had done what I could to help out in Jakarta. I intended to stay close to Embah Putri and look after her; being there and relieving her of some of her work might bring back her old youthful spirits and energies.

We left Hari in Yogya, and on arriving in Jakarta I went straight to Pakdé Noegroho's house and had a meeting with Marie and Tommi. The description of them as vain and pampered was sadly accurate; and in addition I had to confront an old familiar attitude of coolness towards me. Apparently to them I was still Soenandar's son, Soenandar who had been the cause of so many difficulties for the family; and I was still the son of a Wanalawas tempeh-seller as well. It was obvious that they were reluctant to acknowledge me as a relative, which puzzled me after the length of time I had been accepted as a member of Bapak Hardojo's household, and otherwise of the Sastrodarsono clan in general. Budé Sus explained to her children that I had come to help out during Pakdé Noegroho's absence, to assist in such matters as locating and meeting Maridjan's family, and generally 'to deal with things'.

'Mama, why are we bothering Lantip? Don't you think Maridjan will come himself?'

'Allah, Marie, don't go putting on airs towards Mas Lantip. We've seen no sign of Maridjan till now, have we? And you're just as worried as the rest of

8. Lantip

us, so snap out of it; we will all have to work together for the best outcome here!'

I must say I was surprised at the sharp tone that Budé Sus used towards Marie; quite unlike her, and a sign that she must feel cornered and unnerved. I tried to relieve the stress in the room by turning to the matter in hand, with what I hoped was a quiet and positive manner.

'Let's try to talk calmly about this, Mbak Marie. The first thing we need to know, Mbak, is where Maridjan is. Would he be at his boarding house here, or has he gone home to his people?'

Marie had clearly been ill at ease in my presence, perhaps reluctant to put herself in a position where she would feel subordinate to me; and Tommi's discomfort was more probably with a situation that required decisions from him and one that he would rather have avoided; but once she felt that I was merely being practical, Marie's tone softened: 'I'm not really sure, Tip. He could be in his boarding house. If he's not there, I suppose he might have gone to Wonosari, to his parents.'

'In that case, we'll try his boarding house first. Mas Tommi, you ought to come with me, don't you think?'

'Oh, look, Tip, you better go by yourself. I'm really not very good when things get emotional. I'd probably put my foot in it and say something wrong.'

I had to smile at his nonchalance; but of course there could be no question of insisting. Marie's indifference to her brother's attitude was just slightly more surprising, she showed no annoyance or offence. Evidently I could be relied on to do that chore, and so her brother's unhappy services might be dispensed with. Never mind, I had come prepared to act alone.

'Very good. Mbak Marie can relax here at home while I go and look up Mas Maridjan. What's the address of his boarding house?'

That afternoon I went there and found Maridjan in his room. He turned out to be a very young man, some years younger than Marie, handsome, his bright eyes shining with self-confidence and fun; and it occurred to me that here was someone who was enjoying his youthful life far too much to have an easy transition into mature adulthood. His clothing was dishevelled, his hair uncombed, and I assumed that he had not washed that morning.

I introduced myself, and to clarify my connection with the Noegroho family I chatted with him about my own rural origins in Wanagalih and Wanalawas, spending a little time describing the poor quality of rice grown there, the regionally-famous tempeh, the buffaloes, the Madiun and Solo Rivers. He seemed content to be drawn into reminiscing in turn about Wonosari, equally infertile and dry, where folk apparently had to trudge kilometres to some small, red-clay spring. His parents' house was actually some distance from the town of Wonosari itself, their village being on the Baron Beach flank of Mount Kidul. I was familiar with the area, having known students from there when I was attending Gadjah Mada.

'And now, what would you like to do about this matter, Mas Maridjan?'

He fell silent, while his right hand went up to his head and began scratching there, and a finger of his left stroked the tip of his nose.

'You haven't told your parents yet, is that it, Mas?'

'No, not yet. But that won't be a problem, Mas, they'll agree. What can you expect, when I tell them the girl's father's a retired colonel, the director of a government enterprise?'

'So what's the reason for the delay, Mas?'

He smiled and began scratching at his head again. I wondered if these odd mannerisms and the frank, gay twinkle in his eyes, the boyish grin, were what had caught Marie.

'I suppose I am the reason, Mas.'

'Oh?'

'I've got to think how I'm going to feed Marie, and the baby later.'

'Oh, that? Is that all you've been worrying about? Take heart, man, take charge, go forward resolutely, as they say, and things will work out.'

'What you mean, Mas Lantip, is that things will work out with the help of my father-in-law. Bit indecent, isn't it? Here's some fellow drops in from nowhere and straight hangs his hooks into his wife's parents?'

'Whoa there now, Mas! We're got something of an emergency here. And the situation's been created by you and Marie, you'll allow. So it's a bit rich of you, Mas, to think of leaving it unrepaired to save your pride and self-respect. Pride and self-respect in fact require precisely mending what's done. Now, having said that, if the parents enter the picture to help out their children, is that so unnatural?'

Maridjan stopped to consider, forgetting to scratch.

'All right. I'll do whatever you think, Mas Lantip.'

I let off a small cheer in my mind. The first step had been taken.

'Good. Tomorrow morning I'll drop in here to pick you up and we'll have a meeting with Mbak Marie and her mother. Meanwhile, tonight you should write a serious and respectful letter to your parents, informing them of the current situation.'

And next morning the meeting went reasonably well, given a number of understandable tensions that needed to be smoothed over. Throughout her married life Budé Sus had passed on all difficulties to her husband, and now the strain on her was evident. Here was the prospective son-in-law she had waited so long for: only, he was at the furthest remove from anyone she herself would have chosen; and the wretch had impregnated her daughter! A young yokel from the backblocks of Wonosari, whose crudeness included neglecting even to properly introduce himself to the lady who was now to be his mother-in-law! As for Marie, coddled and self-willed child that she had

8. Lantip

been until lately, her constraint and embarrassment now were only mitigated somewhat by the hope of being rescued at the eleventh hour.

'So we understand each other then, Nak Maridjan? You have to be ready to marry Marie in a short while?'

'*Inggih*, Bu. I'm ready to do whatever you want, Bu.'

'It's not what *I* want at all. You, sir, must prepare yourself to marry my daughter!'

I grew somewhat alarmed at this new discovery of temper in Budé Sus.

'*Inggih*, Bu. I'm ready to marry Marie.'

The moment of strain passed, and I could see that Maridjan was quick on his feet. I caught sight of an unhappy, resigned smile on the face of Budé Sus, and something of the same on Marie's, and wondered if in the latter's case it had been forced there perhaps by the sad knowledge of how easy trifling answers came to the boy.

'You've contacted your parents in Wonosari?'

'I posted the letter this morning, Bu.'

At midday, Maridjan was invited to join the family for his first lunch with them.

Some days before Pakdé Noegroho was to return from overseas, things turned tense again: Budé Sus, who had calmed down and accepted the situation, with each day turned into an anxious woman again. She kept instructing her children in new ways of mollifying Pakdé Noeg, how they and she together should share in the inevitable storm, how to bear under it in such a way that it might not endure, and so on. I felt sorry for her, it was clear that she was shouldering a great burden, compounded evidently of pained sympathy for Marie and a sense of having failed her husband.

D-day came and we all, including Maridjan, went to Kemayoran airport to meet Pakdé Noegroho. When he finally emerged through the barrier, he was overwhelmed by the welcome of his wife and children, and while I probably felt as much relief as anyone at his finally arriving to take over the family's problems, it was painful to see that obviously forced expression of homecoming gladness on a face whose eyes at the same time moved with bewilderment and wretchedness from one welcomer to another.

His wife hurriedly introduced Maridjan, and here Pakdé's distress and indecision became even more evident: there was a frightening moment when he seemed to begin an attack, but it turned out that he could not make up his mind whether first to shake his future son-in-law's hand or clap him manfully on the shoulders, finally doing both together. Maridjan on his part submitted to whatever happened around him, grinned with boyish unease, and periodically scratched the back of his head. It appeared at least that there would be no explosion at the airport, and I could see Marie watched with relief this first meeting of her father with her future husband. The pall of anxiety which had lately been cast by Budé Sus over her household was for the moment lifted.

At home, Pakdé's frame of mind was not easy to interpret. The traveller's gifts were duly unpacked, even dinner passed oddly uneventfully, and it was only at the end of it that Pakdé showed signs of finally gathering together what I assumed was the manner of a family-head and retired commander. He began the awaited discussion. His attitude, at least while Maridjan was present that night, was businesslike, drawing on the brusqueness of a former colonel, if not indeed that of an interrogator from Military Intelligence.

'I've been led to understand, Nak Maridjan, that you've informed your parents?'

'I have, Pak.'

'Good. The proper thing now is for them to come here and make their request for Marie. A formality but important. Agreed?'

'Yes, Pak.'

'According to you, when can they be here?'

Maridjan, who had evidently not expected such a specific demand, tarried for a moment.

'When, Nak Maridjan? The sooner the better, agreed?'

'Yes Pak. I'll get in touch with them straight away.'

'Good. Maire, how long have you been pregnant?'

Marie and Budé Sus were both startled to find the questioning veering so directly to that topic, so publicly and at such a moment.

'Th-three months, Pak.'

'That's according to a doctor, or your own estimate?'

'According to a doctor, Pak.'

'So, Nak Maridjan, you see the situation yourself. We're pressed for time.'

'Yes, Pak. I understand.'

The meeting ended with everyone doing what was possible to maintain a controlled, polite tenor. Soon after, Maridjan left to go back to his boarding house. The moment he had departed, the atmosphere changed radically: Pakdé Noeg dropped his colonel's mask and revealed himself to be a very conventional father entrapped by circumstances; that is, in this case, as a sad, shamed man in mental turmoil.

'Oh, Allah, Nduk, Nduk! How could you let yourself get into this mess? And you, Bu . . . how could we fail so miserably to look after our only daughter? Oh God . . .'

I had never seen Pakdé Noeg with a face so flushed, and now it was streaked with tears which he had it seems heroically restrained until that moment. He seldom in my experience addressed his wife as *Bu*, normally calling her by some Dutch diminutive of 'Mother', and I took it as a sign of a desperate descent into the most profound origin of his being to have reverted in this way; and equally strange was it to hear him use the homely *Nduk* to his daughter.

8. Lantip

'How and where are we going to hide our faces, Bu? How am I going to feel when I meet people? . . .'

And for several minutes, his was the performance of an actor riven by tragedy, alone on a stage; only this was no act, and in fact his passion was not unshared, for Budé Sus sobbed with him as well, and Marie broke down too after a short show of self-control. Only Tommi, as usual unwilling or unable to partake in a crisis, disappeared without comment into his room.

I watched this scene with sadness, not caused primarily by Marie's trouble, which I considered to be sufficiently dealt with by Maridjan marrying her, but because in my imagination the figures of Embah Kakung and Embah Putri Sastrodarsono, the begetters of a line and of this family, stood before me: two noble souls who had with such perseverance, such vision and high ideals, raised and mentored their children to stand out in the eyes of other Javanese as examples of enlightened advancement. These before me at this moment were the offspring who if ever the Sastrodarsono couple had failed in their diligence would no doubt have been villagers now, scratching a living in the dirt. Now here sat Pakdé Noegroho, their first-born male whom they expected to entrust with bearing forward the Sastrodarsono name, this son who could find ways to advance to a high rank as an army officer and yet now blubbered at being humiliated by an undisciplined daughter's disgrace. I thought with melancholy of the house in Setenan Road, and images came into my mind: first, of the ferry-raft on which Embah Kakung crossed the river with me on his tireless passages to and from Karangdompol; then, of how we used to gather in an inner room to listen to the good teacher's homilies and object lessons; and suddenly I felt I could listen no longer to these sounds of grief, remorse, and reproaches around me. If those old aspirations were to be rescued, I must gather myself to do something.

And so in a kind of desperation I spoke: 'A thousand pardons, Pakdé, Budé and you too, Mbak Marie; please excuse me, but just dissolving into tears and regrets is not really very helpful in this situation, what we need . . .'

'Lantip . . .'

'No, forgive me, Pakdé, for taking the liberty, but you should really listen to my advice.'

The room fell into silence. Both Pakdé and Budé stared at me as if they had seen me for the first time. Apparently, not my unexceptional words but my speaking at all as a comforter revealed to them the measure of their descent into wretchedness. And that had the desired effect: they seemed to rally a little, and both nodded to me.

'Let's leave the past behind and consider the next steps. Mas Maridjan is willing to do his bit, and, if we accept that, then we should be looking at the coming arrangements for the wedding, a matter of celebration after all. We should be preparing for that, there is a lot to do, and the time is not unlimited.

So what do you say, shouldn't we get on with those practical matters then, Pakdé, Budé?'

Again, there was silence; at least that terrible grieving had stopped. Unexpectedly, Pakdé Noegroho reached out, put a hand on my shoulder and shook me.

'Lantip, my boy. Thank goodness you're here. And thank you for pointing out to your Pakdé and Budé that we're snivelling like children.'

'Yes, Lantip, I agree with your uncle here. And you must have thought I was acting so badly lately, isn't that so, Lé?'

I shook my head vigorously, touched by this sudden humbleness. It was a moment when I was very conscious that I, an illegitimate and never unanimously accepted member of this family, had my words listened to and noted.

'*Wah*, Pakdé and Budé. There's nothing bad in what's happening tonight. What I see is parents with great love for their children; and I see here the strength of self-respect, of family-respect; and these are wonderful things, Pakdé, Budé and Mbak Marie.'

The mood lightened and became considerably more agreeable.

'Excellent, Tip. Tomorrow we'll roll up our shirt-sleeves and our jacket-sleeves as well. We are going to send this daughter of ours off with one giant of a wedding party!'

And so we were now in more jovial, cordial spirits, a sparkle had returned to Marie's eyes, when—in the name of Allah!—there was a loud ring from the doorbell, someone brought in a telegram: Embah Putri Sastrodarsono had died in Wanagalih.

When we arrived in Setenan Road, the marquee had been set up in the front yard, there were rows of chairs, and people were coming and going in the act of paying their last respects. Our group hurried into the house. We had been driving almost non-stop all night, accompanied in the later stage by Bulik Soemini and Paklik Harjono in their car. Having taken the coastal route, we had only paused for a quick meal at Semarang; but now that we were finally here there could be no question of succumbing to tiredness or lack of sleep. Inside, we saw Embah Kakung sitting in his rocking chair, lost in a muse, while around him moved the figures of my foster parents and Gus Hari. Having arrived earlier from Yogya, they had taken in hand the organising of the poignant event. We kissed Embah Kakung's hands, and some unable to restrain themselves embraced him, and thus discovered how physically frail he had become lately. He looked worn in fact: past eighty now, with the wrinkles that had appeared during these last years, his tiredness and diminishing robustness were unmistakeable. And yet, only recently, when I had come to take

8. Lantip

Budé Sus back to Jakarta, he had seemed reasonably lively and strong, his frame still durable. That morning I saw that much had changed. Everyone there tried to engage him with something cheerful, and he responded with an agreeing nod or shook his head, but from his mouth only issued the murmur: 'Dik Ngaisah . . . Dik Ngaisah . . .'

Embah Putri's body was given to the adult females in our party to be ritually washed, the young children sprinkling a little water on it in their turn. Enfolded in a shroud, her face alone visible, Embah Putri seemed now to have regained much of her previous youth and pleasant looks in the repose of her countenance. I felt at fault for not fulfilling my resolution to come back to Wanagalih and spend some time with her. It seems that the disturbing signs in her appearance which I had detected last time had been indeed a serious warning. Gus Hari heard from Bapak that Embah Putri had been suffering for some time from a problem with her liver. We had not known until now, because Dr Waluyo had recommended to Bapak and to Pakdé Noeg and others that they keep the matter quiet, so that Embah Kakung should not worry. The visible effect of her death on Embah Kakung showed how well-judged had been the doctor's sensitive advice.

About two in the afternoon, we began transporting Embah Putri's body to the cemetery. It was evident by the number of mourners how widely the good lady had been known and honoured in Wanagalih. The road to the cemetery passed over the Jamus Bridge and out of the town, a well-known road to me, for it went in the direction of Wanalawas, and it was a reminder that I had too long neglected to visit the grave of my own mother and grandmother. I decided I would find some time to do that on this occasion. We arrived at the cemetery, finding Embah Kakung there already, brought ahead in Pakdé Noeg's car. Bulik Soemini and the others had tried to talk him into remaining at home, but he insisted on going. He said he wanted to spread flowers on Dik Ngaisah's grave. I was strangely affected by hearing again that long-disused diminutive, and it took me back to earlier days when I was still attending school in Karangdompol, to a time when even then 'Dik Ngaisah' evoked the youthful tenderness of their marriage. Perhaps her departure, all the saddening transformations which it entailed, had jolted him back to the time of that earlier change in his life occasioned by her entry into it, when she had arrived to take her place beside him and share the joys and sorrows of the years to come. He spread the flowers very carefully over the length of the mound, with slow rhythmic gestures of his hand, beginning from the northern end where her head rested and ending at the feet. He seemed to be muttering something while he did that, and we who stood waiting respectfully a little distance from the grave tried to hear what he was saying, but could not.

That afternoon, after we had returned and were sitting about and resting, Embah Kakung strangely regained his spirits. While he drank his coffee with evident pleasure, a flush and a livelier expression slowly spread over his face. He turned a firm gaze on those around him and smiled. We returned his smile.

'Well, here we are, my children and grandchildren. Embah Putri has been called back by Allah Almighty and no one can resist that call. Therefore we must let her go with resignation. Agreed? All of us?'

We did not delay in chorusing: '*Inggih!*'

'Good. That's as it should be. So that ends our lamenting, yes?'

'Oh, *inggih!*'

'Let's now instead bring out our best memories of Embah Putri, the funny things and the happy things that we can recall.'

'*Inggi-ih!*'

Then there was silence. Perhaps those of us there at such a moment were indeed thinking of some good time they had shared with Embah Putri; but it was Embah Kakung himself who suddenly chuckled, and we knew that we must leave it to him to lead us.

'Hee-hee-hee . . . that Embah Putri of ours, I tell you . . . hee-hee-hee . . .'

We remained silent, wondering what on earth had been such an amusing recollection to Embah Kakung.

'Embah Putri, oh dear . . . hee-hee-hee . . .'

We went on waiting.

'When I brought her home to my parents in Kedungsimo, they served us a meal of roasted herring in banana leaf. Embah Putri had expected something steamed in coconut, those little sea-fish, *teri*, and when she unwrapped the leaf and saw that it was herring, all covered in black sesame seed, she was revolted. Oh, our Embah Putri had no end of a shock . . . hee-hee-hee . . . you should have seen her face, it was a sight. She pushed her plate away. My mother thought she had cooked a particularly delicious meal, peasant stuff but good, and she couldn't understand. So she kept urging, forcing you might say, Embah Putri, her daughter-in-law of one day, to eat. And I remember that expression on Embah Putri's face . . . hee-hee-hee . . . I know I should have done something, but it was so funny, she was so comical. Her eyes were popped wide open, she was just so shocked by the taste, repelled by that black mess. And . . . hee-hee-hee . . . she couldn't do a thing except swallow the lot of it, to the end. Oh, how she tried to get rid of it as quickly as she could, down her throat! Her face—I'll never forget it!'

We laughed appropriately with Embah Kakung at his story of Embah Putri and the incident of the herring; but where there was anything amusing in a person being forced to eat like that, I could not see. But we laughed with Embah Kakung since he seemed in such good spirits, and we, I am sure, all tried too to remember some comic story, while Embah Kakung continued chuckling and laughing his cackling old-man's laugh: 'Hee-hee-hee . . . Embah Putri . . . hee-hee-hee . . .'

8. Lantip

I became concerned. It was going on too long. And there was something in his eyes that was in conflict with that happy noise, the expression there was of a soul in turmoil. Poor man.

'Hee-hee-hee . . . Embah Putri, Embah Putri . . . Dik Ngaisah . . . Dik Ngaisah . . .'

And Embah Kakung began crying, and to bring up sobs which seemed to erupt from the depths of his old frame.

We were stunned. I saw Soemini and the other women look at each other in dismay, and then in something verging on panic, while the men rose quickly to half-escort, half-carry Embah Kakung to his room and help him onto his bed. I brought the *kendi*, and he gulped some water down, once, twice. Budé Sus and Bulik Soemini fanned him, because the room was stuffy; and gradually he fell asleep and we quietly left him.

We remained a week in Wanagalih and then most of us left, the exceptions being Bulik Soemini and my foster mother and Gus Hari. I would have liked to remain with them to attend to Embah Kakung a little longer, but I needed to return to Jakarta to help out in the coming wedding of Marie with Maridjan.

The willingness of Gus Hari to give up time to comfort his grandfather was noted approvingly by everybody, but it did not surprise me in the least, nor I doubt would have surprised his parents. They knew, as I did, who had had him under my wing from boyhood, that he was endowed with exceptional generosity and sensitivity to the misfortunes of others. And here, of course, was the matter of a particularly well-loved grandmother and grandfather. I had to wonder, nevertheless, how he would manage to temporarily withdraw from all those commitments of his, for he was involved with *Lekra*, the left-wing People's Cultural Association, had raised a number of dramatic groups both in Central Java and in the Yogya Special District, and he ran choirs and discussion groups. Despite all this 'progressivism' of his, a very traditional closeness with the Sastrodarsono family evidently still remained important to him.

When we were about to leave, and had collected in Embah Kakung's room to kiss his hands and embrace him, he gathered himself sufficiently to deliver a farewell homily to Pakdé Noeg and Budé Sus: 'Noegroho, and you, Nduk Sus. You two have a serious matter before you, giving away Marie, my first grandchild to be married. Do it with care and honourably, be brave in parting with your girl. I won't be there to be beside you. I don't think I can travel so far now. But carry my blessing with you.'

Then to Marie: 'Nduk Marie, child. You'll be a wife soon, a mother too. Be good and conscientious in both those roles, be faithful to your husband and do all that's necessary to ensure he will be faithful to you. Set the most important goal before you that of creating a harmonious and prosperous family. My blessing go with you.'

When the others were leaving and it was my turn to bid him good-bye, he whispered to me: 'Keep an eye on them. See that the wedding goes well. You understand.'

And I, head bowed to hide my surprise, whispered back: 'Embah, I'll do everything in my power.'

We departed: I, weighed down on the one hand by concern about the deteriorating state of Embah Kakung's health, and on the other by the responsibility placed on me to make Marie's wedding a success.

About two weeks before the day of the wedding, the Noegroho house was again in an uproar. It had been some time since Maridjan had called in, and I was sent to inquire at his boarding house to see what the matter was. The landlady informed me that he had vacated his room over a week earlier, taking his things with him, and she had not been told where exactly he was going, apparently to some friend. When I asked her whether she had heard from Maridjan that he was getting married, the woman stared at me.

'Eh? Getting married? What's he want to get married again for?'

It was my turn to stand rooted to the spot, virtually open-mouthed.

'Again? How can that be, Bu? In a week or so Maridjan is marrying a relative of mine. The daughter of a retired army officer.'

'Well, he might well do that, marry your relative, the daughter of a general or whatever. All I know is, he's already married to one of the girls who used to work as a domestic here. And he's got a kid. The wife's stashed back with her parents, wherever in Java they all live.'

Masya Allah! . . . A fine young rooster! And Marie . . . picking up someone like that and then expecting a wedding from him next! I said a hurried good-bye to the landlady and left, wondering on the way back how I was going to break the news to Marie's father and family. I cudgelled my brain, even considered covering up the situation, deceiving them in fact; but it would have been hopeless to tell them anything other than the truth, it would have been revealed eventually in some even more disastrous way. I did the best I possibly could to present my report sensitively, but it was a hopeless task, Pakdé Noegroho's face flushed deep red.

'Wha-at! Maridjan's got a wife and a child? Dog! Bastard! Putrid son of a bitch!'

Budé Sus nearly fainted; Marie paled, and above the tenseness of her jaw and lower face her eyes wandered off somewhere into the distance; vague signs of disturbance even passed over Tommi's usual indifference; while in the background of these impressions I could hear Pakdés continuing bellow reverberating: '. . . such a nice country lad, what? Turns out a crook! Butter

8. Lantip

wouldn't melt... Well, Marie? That's what you get for alley-cattying all over the city, young woman. Wilful, wanton girl! *Now* what are we going to do? Where are your mother and father to hide their faces *now*? *Where*?'

Marie suddenly shrieked and started sobbing hysterically, an act which seemed to send her parents into further paroxysms: one of fury, the other of anguish. I saw that calming the situation needed first some effort to quieten Marie, and I quickly set about as best I could to comfort her, begging her to sit down, to drink some tea.

'Paké, Budé, I'm sorry to have had to bring you such news, but now, from this point, what do you think is the best way forward?'

Pakdé was in the grip of his rage, and if anything was left in him beyond that it was clearly not the ability to decide anything; Budé seemed strengthless and beyond speech; no hope lay in Tommi. It was left to me to take some initiative, and I brought out the suggestion that we could begin to do something by tracing Maridjan to the village of his parents, hoping he had gone to them. I offered to travel to Wonosari to see what the state of affairs was there, to ask them directly for an explanation. I requested from Pakdé and Budé the authority to carry out this errand and to arrange things the best way I could.

Pakdé immediately agreed: 'Go, Lé, do it. I should be the one going, to lay into that Maridjan if he's there. But if I lost control of myself it would be the end of everything.'

I nodded in acceptance, but did feel disappointed. In proposing to go to Wonosari I had not been prepared for such a complete abdication by Pakdé, having rather expected he would want to come with me if not actually overruling me and going alone. Had he always had such a limited ability to carry things through, such volatility in his nature? Nevertheless, I willingly accepted this duty, accepted it in dedication to Embah Putri and Embah Kakung and in response to what would have been their desire.

On the way to Wonosari I stopped at my foster parents' home to tell them of these latest events. Since Gus Hari had returned from Wanagalih, I invited him to accompany me onwards to Maridjan's village.

My news was received with general astonishment: 'But what about Tommi, didn't you ask him to go with you, Lé?'

'*Wah*, Bapak, surely you know what that boy's like. Even if he'd agreed to come, he would have been more trouble than he's worth.'

'H'm. Heaven has sent some trials to that family. First they lose the eldest son, then Marie has these problems. Well then, take care you two, go with our hopes that you'll do some good.'

We left for Wonosari. Hari, as it happened, had gone to the Mount Kidul area a number of times with a *Lekra* troupe and knew the area well. The troupe was a 'folk-cultural' group called Mardi Budaya, then popular in the

Gentry

Yogya Special District, consisting of school and university students and amateur 'people's artists'. The village we were looking for, not far from Baron Beach, proved therefore relatively easy to locate. And there indeed we found Maridjan with his parents. Gus Hari and I paid our due salaams to the couple, whom I had already met once when they came to formally request Marie for their son. I introduced Gus Hari, and without further niceties asked for an explanation of Maridjan's latest escapade. It was obvious, from the moment we had appeared, that all three of them were in some considerable discomfort.

'A thousand pardons, Nak Lantip and Nak Hari. We've been a great trouble to Bapak Noegroho's family. There is a reason why we have not appeared again since the time we came to propose in Jakarta.'

We two remained silent. Maridjan's father, Bapak Wongsokarjo, should be allowed to explain in his own time.

'By now you, Nak Lantip, and all Pak Noegroho's family will have heard that Maridjan was married once?'

'Was once? Not still, Pak Wongso?'

Maridjan's father said nothing for a moment and looked at his son, whose expression, as they say, spoke in a thousand tongues, not two in accord.

'That is so, Nak. Was once, not still.'

'Oh?'

'Maridjan was married to a girl called Suminten, a girl from Sleman, and they had a child. But he divorced her. That's how it is, Nak.'

Gus Hari and I looked at each other. I thought this new information about a divorce sounded highly suspicious, and the same doubt was evidently passing through Gus Hari's mind too.

'Mas Maridjan, when did you divorce Suminten?'

Before answering, Maridjan looked at his parents, and then his father began to speak on Maridjan's behalf: 'Well it's like this, Nak Lantip. The intention had been around for some time, but . . .'

'One moment, Pak Wongso. Please let Maridjan tell us himself.'

This interruption by Gus Hari startled me a little, particularly the no-nonsense tone of it, but it accorded with my own mood. I too wanted to see how Maridjan would stand up for himself in this situation, having by now become more than a little irritated by the ways of this young man. He had recently said to me and to Pakdé and Budé that he would willingly wed Marie, and I had taken that statement as something that would fly, was genuine. Now it seemed that he was able to maintain such a thing and simultaneously the secret that he was or had been married and had a child. And he was visibly nervous.

'I can only beg both of you most humbly for your understanding, Mas Hari and Mas Lantip. I can see how you and Bapak and Ibu Noegroho, and

8. Lantip

especially Marie, must see me just now: a pretty poor sort, I guess, or even something worse. I can understand that. But I didn't say anything earlier about being married because at the time I was divorcing my wife, Suminten. I was worried about bringing that out because it would have added to all the trouble going on then in Bapak Noegroho's house.'

'Yes, but really, you can't keep that kind of thing secret. And the house is now in turmoil anyway. So how do things stand with you at this point?'

'The divorce has gone through the religious affairs office, it's official. I assure you I was about to return to Jakarta, to marry Marie, as I said I would.'

'So all your affairs with your ex-wife—concerning the child, and so forth— have been settled?'

'Yes, they have, Mas.'

'Because, look, this is not our business, Mas Maridjan, but you'd be advised to have a good talk with Mbak Marie at the earliest opportunity. About all that, but especially the child: whose name it takes, for example. At some point the kid will want to know who its father was.'

'Of course, Mas. I've been planning to talk all that over with her.'

'Very well, then. I think you better come with us to Yogya tomorrow. We'll stay the night there and leave next morning for Jakarta.'

Once more, as we travelled back to the capital, I felt a measure of relief. Things appeared to be not as bad as they seemed, not beyond rescue, at least as regards the immediate future and the marriage. How those two would conduct their lives after the wedding was a matter for fate. My remaining concern was with Suminten: there was something there that reflected on my own abandoned mother, and myself in my earliest childhood. Well, at least Maridjan, scapegrace that he was, had dealt correctly by his wife in the matter of the divorce; but what about the child? Would it be as fortunate as I had been, to be fostered by such kindly people as those who had raised me and encouraged me through so many years of school and university education? I had been exceptionally lucky there.

Gus Hari had long ago heard my story, and at some point on our way westward now, while I was dwelling on such thoughts and Maridjan sat some distance from us in the carriage, he looked into my face and said: 'It's your mother you're thinking about, isn't it?'

'Yes, Gus. You can read minds.'

'Oh, no, it's not hard. Here we are, convoying Maridjan, shepherding him over there to do his duty. Life repeats itself more or less. But I agree with your way of doing things, Kang. You don't lay down the law. Hopefully, Marie is daily growing more mature, enough to deal with what's coming. I think she'll cope. Call it my woman's intuition.'

We arrived in Jakarta to convene once more in the Noegroho living room. The humble tone with which Maridjan told his tale confirmed his shrewd intelligence to those of us who were beginning to become familiar with him. Yes, he accepted his fate; yes, he submitted happily to the coming wedding; his previous marriage was not an issue. Such repeated assurances finally satisfied Pakdé and Budé Noeg, who had met our arrival prepared to crush the boy utterly.

But Marie, after listening tight-lipped to Maridjan, unexpectedly launched a new difficulty, a surprising one, coming from an indulged girl who had always thought of no one but herself: 'Bapak, Mama, this is dreadful about Suminten. If it wasn't that I'm bearing Maridjan's child, I would refuse to marry him. He obviously divorced her to marry me. All right, divorces happen all the time, but this is some village girl being cast aside to let the man marry into a city priyayi family. I understand my marriage must take place; then, Bapak, Mama, let me be Maridjan's second wife. Second to Suminten.'

The immediate effect of this missile was shocked silence. We turned to Pakdé and Budé, but they were speechless. Maridjan entered the vacuum.

'But Marie, Suminten and I were divorcing before any of this happened here. You don't have to feel responsible for our divorce or in debt to Suminten.'

'I won't believe it! You divorced her to marry me, you must have! Cancel the divorce!'

'Marie, child, you're becoming sentimental, irrational. What Maridjan says is right. You've got no debt whatsoever to Suminten. Let's get on with things! It's not long to the wedding!'

'Oh Bapak, all you can think of is the wedding. So that you and Ibu and all the family don't have to feel embarrassed. But here is a blameless woman who's being sacrificed!'

Pakdé put his head in his hands. Marie's stubbornness was increasing by the minute.

A burst of frantic Dutch had already issued from Budé, amid which *koppig*—mulish, pig-headed—was heard repeated several times; now came her own attempt to reason with the girl: 'Marie, listen to your father and Maridjan, they are totally right. What's this about being a second wife? What are you complicating everything for? And think of how it will look if your *Tante* Mini hears of it! She's a leading member in *Perwari*, the Association of Indonesian Women no less! She'll absolutely pour scorn on all of us and be embarrassed to have you as a relative! In *Perwari* they want to modernise families and the role of women, and you . . . Marie, don't you realise that you're talking about concubinage?'

'Oh, come Mama. Fancy bringing *Tante* Mini into this. She who panicked when *Oom* Harjono was ready enough to get himself a number two on the side! Panicked at being displaced by a kampong singer! Well, here it's I who's standing back, giving up my place to bring justice to a situation. Isn't that so?'

8. Lantip

Marie's tone brooked no opposition. A long moment of silence ensued. Looking around, I noted the darkening expression of Pakdé Noeg preparing himself for a new explosion, and Budé about to burst into tears. Tommi was playing with a pencil on the table-top, while Gus Hari, come to Jakarta to assist in the wedding, sat calm but inactive. I felt the unspoken mandate of the old teacher and his wife weighing on me. I must try to move things through this impasse somehow.

'Pakdé, Budé. With your permission, might I suggest something at this point, a possible solution?'

'Well, Tip, let's hear it! By God, let's hear it!'

'Look, Mbak Marie. The divorce procedure has been completed, the formula's uttered. So Suminten according to religious law is no longer married to Maridjan. Now I can understand and sympathise with your concern. You want to help her and her baby. All right, what about if that help takes the form of some support for her up to the time when she remarries? And the child might be allowed to meet and stay with the father from time to time? This perhaps sounds too rational, but we ought to meet these problems with some common sense too, no? Sentiment now is all very well, but the emotional cost later, of living as a second wife, Mbak Marie, can be very, very heavy. You should think about that.'

Marie's grim look melted slowly, and a moment later she smiled at me.

'How many wives have you got hidden away, Tip? It sounds as though you've had some experience there. But I suppose you're right. And Maridjan, I think you should agree too. In fact, you better agree!'

'Yes, yes, I do, Marie.'

So that seemed to be that. My suggestion was accepted, and everybody began to breathe again. Naturally such an important convocation, and one so fraught with ambushes and flounderings, had to be ended in a common meal; and as we were all moving to the dining room I saw Gus Hari approach Marie and give her cheek a quick peck.

'Mbak Marie, you were wonderful. I'm so proud of you.'

Whether there was a touch of irony there, I could not be sure, but that gesture launched the lightening mood which soon had all the company around Pakdé and Budé Noegroho's table revived and considerably happier. I found the food especially good.

The wedding ceremony was conducted by an imam from the Office of Religious Affairs on a day when rain fell in such noisy torrents that the contractual phrases needed to be repeated so that Maridjan might recognize them and declare his acceptance. So too when the cleric gave his sermon addressed to the wedded couple: hardly a word was understood by anyone until suddenly those assembled there realised they were hearing the formula *wassal-amualaikum warohmatullahi wabarokatuh*, the closing 'peace be with you and God's blessing.' With that, someone acting as MC invited the crowd of guests to the three tables that had been set up under marquees outside the house. There, under a deluge of water assaulting the canvas, people sheltered as best they could, holding plates of food in their hands.

Ignoring the discomforts of the occasion, Pakdé and Budé Noegroho glowed with satisfaction that the main business had been concluded at last without further difficulties or perils, had been irrevocably recognised and blessed by the attendance of so many guests and family members. They went about smiling and urging people to take more food, stopping to have a word with someone here, trading the conventional wedding-jokes with someone else there, and all in all the sorrow of losing a daughter was hardly noted in a day that delivered them at last from further care. There was, admittedly, one exception, one moment unavoidably sad. In a Javanese family, at the point in a wedding ceremony when the young couple press their faces and lips to the knees of the parents, the relinquishing elders almost always have difficulty restraining some sign of agitation at the imminence of parting with their children. As could be expected here, where the parental relationship with the girl had been emotionally fraught and close, Marie kneeling before her father and mother—an act recalling childhood dependence and evoking the whole history of that minority—did draw on the parent's faces an expression of sudden pain and loss.

The reception that night was held at the Duta Indonesia Hotel and represented the pinnacle of the day's celebrations. Pakdé Noeg must have mobilised all the power which his prestige and official position availed him, to make the party so incontestably '*Wah!*' Some five hundred invitations were sent out, meaning that about a thousand guests filled the hotel's reception hall. Entertaining this illustrious mêlée were both a Western band and a gamelan orchestra with singers and dancers performing in the Javanese style, while numerous tables loaded with delicacies were ceaselessly surrounded by shuffling ranks. We of the family, acting as a committee of welcome and as guides, found time occasionally to look around ourselves with some wonder at the splendour of it all. Only Gus Hari seemed to grow more and more troubled.

'Unbelievable. This party of Pakdé's—where did the money come from?'

Tommi, overhearing, shot back peevishly: 'His own sweat, what do you think? It's his only daughter, isn't it?'

I thought Gus Hari smiled strangely.

'Ah yes, from his modest salary. And I'm a turkey's son. Every up-river tree-ape knows about these parties our new magnates hold here in Jakarta.'

Gus Hari seemed to make his displeasure and cynicism towards those

8. Lantip

with wealth heard more frequently lately. Apart from being close to people in *Lekra*, he also had some connection with the *Himpunan Sarjana Indonesia*, an association of radical academics, and both those groups at this stage of the mid-1960s were increasingly active and belligerent. Fortunately, Tommi made nothing out of Gus Hari's allusions, and I quickly took the latter's arm and we set off to see if anything was lacking around the hall.

Some days after the wedding, my foster parents, Gus Hari, and I left for Yogya.

Gus Hari had grown into a considerate young man, sensitive to those compelled to live a hard, deprived life. This was a part of his character which was noticeable from the days of his earliest boyhood. Another part reflected his intelligence and love of the arts. Embah Kakung Sastrodarsono often regretted his own inadequacy in the Javanese arts, and how little of that sphere he could pass on to his children. If this was indeed a true statement of the facts, then my foster father must have acquired his love of our arts intuitively; and moreover he was determined that Gus Hari and I should possess and enjoy whatever he might yet lack. When before the revolution he was still an employee of the Mangkunegaran palace, Bapak often took Gus Hari and me to watch presentations of classical Javanese dancing in the Solo style. Later, he encouraged us to learn dancing with the Anggana Raras group, active in promoting that skill among the local youth of the princedom. We two were also obliged to learn to play such gamelan instruments as the xylophone and the metalophone. Now while I was acquainted with the various percussion instruments of the gamelan orchestra since my time at village school at least, it was quite evident from Gus Hari's earliest attempts that his proficiency would far surpass mine. He became very quickly an excellent dancer as well, and was included in a number of presentations held in the Mangkunegaran court. One particular role he was adept in, while he was still attending secondary school, was that of Gatutkaca Gandrung, the lovelorn Pendawa figure from the *Mahabharata*, choreographed in the specifically Mangkunegaran style. Among the instruments of the gamelan, his own favourites were the xylophone and the *kendang*, a type of small, double-ended drum. Whenever Gus Hari set himself to practice the xylophone at home in the evenings, and sometimes well into the night, a pleasant feeling as if the atmosphere had been refreshed by a cooling rain permeated the house and all the neighbourhood within earshot. I could only sigh at my own inadequate sensitivity of touch compared to his, and at the fact that all I had found my talent availed me to learn of music and of dancing was really only good enough for the untutored, simple pleasures of village nights.

Gentry

When in 1950 the major part of the civil service of the newly-sovereign Republic migrated to Jakarta, my foster father chose to work in Yogya, in one of the departments of its Special District. It seems that while he had been disappointed with the Solo princedom's behaviour in disfavouring the Republic and sympathising with the Dutch, nevertheless he continued to prefer living under a system which retained monarchic overtones. The compromise achieved by working for the new Indonesia, yet within a traditional Javanese cultural milieu headed by a sultan—if nevertheless a modernising and temperamentally republican figure—suited him admirably. He could see much of worth to the new nation in the old traditions, in their richness, beauty, and stability, and all who lived in his home were inculcated with this spirit. And it was noteworthy that the Hardojo household, more conservative than the Noegroho family or Harjono's, never in all the time I lived there had domestic problems of the sort just recounted. All our relatives and all who knew my foster parents described us as an uncomplicated and harmonious family. Such, at least, was an acceptable description up to the time Gus Hari attained a new independence with his arrival into adulthood and his completion of a degree in sociology and politics.

As said, he was a very bright young man, and he found little difficulty in absorbing what he was taught of those subjects; while I, on the other hand, who attended the same lectures in the same faculty, seemed to require twice as much time in considering and accepting the same material. Mostly, while I was doing that, he would be found enjoying himself watching stage performances, usually of a traditional character, or taking part in them himself. To his skill in Mangkunegaran dance-forms was now added those of the Mataram variant; so too did his gamelan technique further broaden here in Yogya. I watched all these conquests and triumphs by my charge—as in a sense I considered him—with admiration and astonishment, and so did his father; until we two students met Sunaryo, and certain things changed.

He was a couple of years ahead of us, in an advanced course of studies, a pleasant, sociable chap, just returned from a tour of socialist countries in Eastern Europe where he had attended a youth festival of drama held in Prague. Gus Hari was immediately drawn to Sunaryo as to a soul-fellow, someone intelligent and attracted to the arts, principally to the same forms: dance, theatre, and gamelan music. They quickly became good friends and were often seen together, active in university theatrical events, into the time when Gus Hari and I were approaching the completion of our basic degree. Not being involved myself in those extracurricular interests, I pressed onwards to finish my course as quickly as possible, being very conscious that my foster parents were supporting me, and so during that last period I did not follow very carefully what Gus Hari, Sunaryo and others of that circle were doing. Then suddenly I began to notice a shift in Gus Hari's attitude towards the arts.

8. Lantip

It seemed that now those had become for him an inseparable part of politics, were subservient to and an instrument of politics. It was only then, too, that I became truly aware that Sunaryo was a Marxist, was associated with Marxists, and seriously involved in Marxist studies. He had all sorts of connections with people belonging to *Lekra*, as well as to a left-wing student organization called the Indonesian Student Movements' Central Directory, its title contracted from *Central Gerakan Mahasiswa Indonesia* to CGMI, and also to an association of academics, the *Himpunan Sarjana Indonesia*.

One afternoon while we were at home relaxing, Gus Hari came out with: 'Say, Tip, I'd better tell you. I'm involved with *Lekra* and with CGMI. You don't mind, do you?'

'No one stops you joining any organisation whatever, Gus.'

'Yes, all right, but I'd like to know your view on that.'

'Well, obviously I'm not opposing it. It's your choice and you have a right to it.'

Gus Hari laughed, and I could see he was happy to start a conversation, for he continued: 'You're going to have to make up your mind about joining something or other yourself soon, Tip. You can't be an educated person today and remain neutral. And you're aspiring for an academic life.'

'Who says I'm neutral? At the moment I'm not particularly attracted to any group. I've only just got an assistantship. That takes up enough of my time, Gus.'

'Now take me. Since I've been around those *Lekra* pals of mine I've got a bit wiser about the true function of the dramatic arts. I always thought of them as just that, art, that they hadn't any function really, not as we understand function. As far as I was concerned they were something of beauty, simply to enjoy.'

'Mm? And now?'

'Now I see to what extent they've been instruments of class ascendancy. What we understood until now as simply 'the arts', have been devices serving the interests of a feudal and then a bourgeois class, Tip.'

I made no comment. The left did talk like that. What could I say?

'So, Tip? You know what I'm saying. Do you agree with that?'

'No, Gus. I take the old-fashioned view that artistic experiences are given us just to be enjoyed. Whether it's a villager tapping a gong or chanting a *macapat* to himself out in the fields, or his wife humming something while plaiting a mat at home, there's nothing more in it than happy enjoyment. Of course your priyayi sitting in a grand hall attending some performance has his own level of enjoyment, but it's not a difference to fashion a sinister divisiveness out of.'

'*Wah*, typical liberal bourgeois stuff, Tip. Who's been forcing that into you?'

'Oh, Gus, really now. We've gone to school and read the same books and discussed the same ideas. You should go and talk to your father and mother if you want a debate with those of a different upbringing.'

'Very amusing, Tip, discussing matters of this sort with people like Bapak and Ibu. They're priyayi, and of course with a feudal standpoint. Their party, if they joined one, would be the Nationals, the party of the upper classes. What's the good of arguing with them? It would be a disaster.'

And there the talking petered out, suppressed by the influences of a drowsy afternoon more than anything else. But what developed further from there was that Gus Hari's relations with *Lekra* grew keener, while his interest in acting the classics, in the mythological fare of shadow-puppetry, and in concert-hall gamelan, waned; because, as he said, they represented high-brow, great-tradition, feudalistic culture. What occupied him, from this period on, were the presentations of travelling troupes, the semi-historical fare of folk-theatre and the gamelan of 'the social margins'. These were the more truly universal theatrical arts, he told me; they were by the folk and for the folk. If the feudal class could use art for their suppressive purposes, then the *wong cilik* could do so too in countervailing them.

I noticed, too, that at this time Gus Hari had got himself a girlfriend, and *that* at least I found definitely pleasing. She was a poetess, and of course belonged to *Lekra*. Her name was Retno Dumilah, but she preferred to be called by her penname Gadis Pari—literally, 'girl of the paddies'—distancing herself thus from an excessively 'feudal-sounding' given name. And her verse was indeed sharp and full of allusive and sardonic attacks on the aristocrats.

As for myself, life went on, and as I approached thirty I still had not met anyone. The field was diminishing; but I did have a good friend, Halimah, an assistant lecturer and colleague, a Pariaman girl from West Sumatra. Sometimes lately I had been thinking that she might be the one.

9. HARIMURTI: third variation: over-reach

That night Gadis wanted to pay. I remember the day well, the date was 8 May 1964, the occasion when the Great Leader of the Revolution—we used such mouthfuls—announced the suppression of the *Manifesto Kebudayaan*, the anticommunist declaration known as *Manikebu* for short, that had been proclaimed the previous year by reactionary writers opposed to the socialist realism and political activism of *Lekra*. Gadis said she wanted to celebrate with me alone.

We went down Malioboro Road, southwards all the way until we came to a left turn in the direction of Sentul. Our goal was the stall of Yu Marsinem, if you could call it a stall, it was really just an awning-covered porch attached to a building. There, a famous Yogya specialty, the *gudeg*, could be had: a concoction of young jackfruit cooked with spices in coconut milk. The rash of *gudeg*-selling all over the city meant that the name of this great delicacy had become transferred to the places where it and similar dainties were to be had. What distinguished Yu Marsinem's *gudeg*—the place—from scores of others was not any special culinary talents the lady possessed, but the fact that her establishment was the preferred hangout of *Lekra* artists and writers. No, Yu Marsinem's was very ordinary, not to say squalid, in comparison with the *gudegs* patronised by office workers in the central district, such as those setups clustered about the corner of Wijilan Street, or even with the *gudegs* in the Kranggan market. Yu Marsinem might also serve you eggs, tofu and tempeh, and on occasion she could cook up a chicken, but that was about it. Yu had no hope of accumulating the funds to compete with the big operators in that line with what she earned from her usually straitened and forgetful *Lekra* clients.

The way the Marsinem *gudeg* became the resort of many in *Lekra* is a story in itself. The woman had once been a servant in some government official's home in the Sentul area, had fallen pregnant to who knows whom, been thrown out by her employer, and then rescued by a painter belonging to the Brotherhood of People's Artists. He had married her, set her up in her stall, and regularly brought his colleagues there as customers; where they, he, and many *Lekra* people habitually spent the whole night talking. Gadis too, despite being the daughter of a primary-school inspector and therefore herself of the gentry, liked to come to the wretched place and take part in endless sessions about art and politics, arguing with the best of them. And that was where I met her. To be frank, at first I was more inclined to sit mute and restrained than think about falling in love with her. A girl of her age, with such authoritative views on culture and society, such a direct way of stating them! I had never before come into contact with any young Javanese—a priyayi at that—who readily and without any verbal finesse issued forth all kinds of opinions and decisive pronouncements in the way she did. The girls I had known up to then, and some I had taken out, came from good families and were well-versed in the manners expected of their class. I don't dislike such girls and don't see any problem in women being modest and good-mannered. Those, understandably, are very acceptable qualities to any male. It's just that so often girls of that background never went beyond carefully limiting themselves to those qualities; and when I wanted to exchange intelligent ideas with them about any controversial matter, they invariable were unwilling or were startled into silence or perhaps were just unable to respond. Discussions with them were never carried through to a conclusion: the girl would give up and leave the field to me and turn to some ordinary, dull, and harmless subject.

Gadis was altogether different. During our first conversation she challenged spiritedly my outlook on mytho-historical drama. Since it was typically presented by back-country troupes and was therefore clearly of the people, I had become actively involved in it; and now Gadis delivered me a sharp lecture on my too-neutral understanding of the genre. Apparently I had been viewing it through the lens of a feudal aesthetic: that is, ostensibly apolitically despite my sympathy for those it entertained. She criticised me for being frightened to deconstruct the popular and unrealistic stories to emphasise aspects which breathed more with socialist realism: in other words, those that made more prominent the historical status of the labouring masses. People's drama for its own sake?—where was the polemic? Now, I was quite prepared to accept such critiques or to react to them in some way when heard from a male, but not when delivered off the cuff and yet with such argumentative force by a young woman. From being taken aback, I grew drawn to this unusual person, came in time to be somewhat in awe of her. We became friends and our friendship deepened; until one night, after we had been talking about something or other over a glass of ginger tea in Bu Amanat's booth—I'll always remember it, behind the big clock of the National Building on the road to Beringhardjo market—we, well, we suddenly kissed. It was a long kiss, and a startling preface to our becoming lovers.

At Yu Marsinem's we found things strangely quiet, considering the significance of that day for our side; but Yu told us that some artists known to us had just left, after having had *gudeg* and coffee on tick. We asked for the same; then, in thanksgiving for the great victory, Gadis ordered a complete meal of breast of chicken, eggs, and as an afterthought called for more syrup of coco-nut milk for her *gudeg*.

9. Harimurti

'Say, Dis, where's the money coming from for all this stuff? I see some serious *kapitalis-birokratis* spending here, no?'

'Don't worry, I've just got something from *The Lantern*. And there's a bunch of my poems being published in *Renewal* that'll pay too, eventually.'

'You don't think we're overdoing it?'

'Alla-ah, the food's edible and you'll eat it, so don't be such a hypocrite. What's wrong if the people's artists have an occasional binge? What's more, I've earned this money, it's halal; what's more . . .'

'Looks a bit like a victor's spree.'

'It is, my friend. And I'll start by annihilating this *gudeg*.'

And we got on with the meal. I had never seen Gadis eat so much and so heartily. The defeat of the *Manikebu* crowd clearly meant a great deal to her.

'I'm delighted. They've been blocked. That's the end of them. Their bunkers in the arts faculties have been demolished. Where do they think they'll go now? Where and what can they write?'

I was hungry too, and kept eating and looking up at her while she talked; with a mouth full of chicken I almost laughed at her excitement. Yet, sometimes catching that bright bitterness in her eyes I was a little troubled too. Could she really hate those opposition writers so much? To start a discussion, between chewing I asked for her opinion about the piece by Chairil Anwar entitled 'Nightfall at the Anchorage'. The question brought a pause in her harangue. Then she smiled.

'Aha, I see you want to provoke me into declaring that it's a poor poem, mm? You'll be disappointed there, Mas Hari. It's a beautiful poem.'

'Beautiful? Haven't we just denounced his crowd of humanist universalists?'

'One moment! Beautiful according to the aesthetic understanding of our bourgeois liberals. The work succeeds in calling up an atmosphere of desertion, stillness, an emptiness of the heart. Beyond that there's nothing. Chairil is of no use in our struggle. In fact his effect is negative, there's nil optimism in it. Where's its practical value for the masses?'

And we proceeded loudly and happily to argue about that and all kinds of other matter. I felt glad to see her so flushed with her victory, and so enthused with energy by it that she would now be inspired to write many more of her things. Nevertheless, her passion rather worried me too, her extraordinary desire to crush the enemy, which ultimately she meant in all senses. In my own view, our enemies were immaterial, existing in the realm of ideas and ideology only, nothing more.

We extended our extravagance that night by riding to her boarding house in a pedicab. It was late and the air of the approaching cooler season was fresh. In the pedicab Gadis wanted to be hugged for warmth and I happily obliged her, first with my arm around her shoulders and then slipping it down to her waist. And so we rode, with the creak of the chain and our own breathing audible to us in the dark. At the boarding house the lights were all out.

Gentry

Gadis said that there would be no one else there that night. The landlady and her family had gone to Solo for the wedding of some relative, and so I might see her up to her room. We entered and she switched on a lamp in the corner.

'What will the neighbours say?'

'They've gone to bed.'

'What about the help?'

'Who? Mbok Nah? She's asleep in her room at the back. Stop fretting, priyayi.'

We sat on the bed and giggled. I patted the head of the mattress.

'All right. But no discussions now,' I said. 'I know you, once you start you'll wake the neighbours.'

'Who's discussing?'

Again we laughed softly together, sitting there on the edge of her bed. It was a big old four-poster with iron ornaments at both ends, and there was a mosquito net over it, fastened at each post with some sort of silvery clasp in the form of a flower. The coverlet was white and clean and fringed with lace, all those details unexpected. After having taken stock of the room, of its atmosphere, and the meaning of our presence there together, I chuckled.

'You're laughing? What's up, Mas?'

But her question only made our situation there more amusing to me.

'No, it's just that I remembered that painting by Otto Djaja, with a fellow and girl sitting on the edge of a bed like this. There's even a mosquito net in it.'

'I see. A brothel-scene, as I recall. And it brought out the snob in you? You insolent wretch!'

'No, no, I'd even forgotten that it was what Otto Djaja did actually paint. All that came to me from it just now was the romantic aspect, and the amusing thought that there were two people in it about to make love, and everything else that those two considered of immense importance was making way for something which is so simply human and natural. I'm very grateful to Otto for giving me that amusing insight.'

Gadis's moment of touchiness passed and she softened. And we kissed. Then we were suddenly undressed and making love in that old bed of hers, which turned out to be very soft and very homey; we whispered to each other for a long time, talking mostly nonsense, until at last we both drifted off to sleep. We slept soundly until dawn and were awakened by roosters and the cooing of some white pigeons in a cage hanging nearby outside. I leapt out of the bed, got my clothing together and prepared to make a tiptoe departure. Everything I had worn when I came the previous night, from shirt to shoes, was in my hands, and I saw Gadis smiling at me with an amused and incredulous expression from the bed.

'Where are you going like that? You haven't combed your hair.'

9. Harimurti

'Would you lend me your comb, please?'

'That's not going to help you much either, Bung. Have a splash. The bathroom's over there.'

Her room fortunately had such an amenity, where I could gather myself and take care of the decencies.

After that night we were together all the time. We went to all kinds of meetings and discussions, attended exhibitions of paintings, listened to poetry readings, went to see folk dramas, and sometimes modern theatre as well. In general, the various arts we liked and understood best were those which seemed to open new prospects for the suffering masses and which promised them freedom.

Alas, while my attitude and zeal in those areas matured, it pained me to notice that my parents appeared uneasy with that development; nor was Lantip, whom I loved like an elder brother, very happy. I should have expected my father would eventually question my way of life at that time, but when he and my mother did, I was still unprepared for the depressing gap revealed between us.

'Hari, you've got your degree, but all we seem to see you doing these days is happily running off to this or that exhibition or dramatic night. And this involvement with those people on the left . . . Isn't it time you should be thinking seriously about a career?'

'Well, you know, Pak, Bu—this *is* my career.'

'Oh, come now. Managing travelling troupes, attending discussions, poetry recitals: do you call that a career? What was the point of graduating with that degree in sociology and politics then?'

'It's like this, Pak. Travelling troupes, discussions, poetry recitals, and my degree, those are not unconnected things. The first relate to art and bear on the class struggle. Now, the class whose struggle I partake in is that of the *wong cilik*, and I do that by identifying the political component in various fields of art and then turn that component to advantage the *wong cilik*. There, Pak, is where my degree in politics and sociology meets art.'

My father and mother remained silent. Lantip heard me calmly because these things had been long talked about between us.

Then my mother spoke: 'But how are you, at some point, going to raise a family on such a career, Lé? It's 1964, and you're twenty-nine years old. Are you thinking of devoting yourself to those things forever and become an old bachelor, or what?'

'Your mother wants to dandle grandchildren on her knees, Lé. It's time you took life seriously and looked for a good job and a girl.'

I felt sad for them. To put it mildly, they were disappointed in me; and I had seen this unhappiness of theirs growing, their hopes in me diminishing. I had been afraid for some time that I was causing them pain.

Gentry

'Bapak, Ibu, I'm truly sorry to upset you. I understand that both of you think, and perhaps everyone else in our Sastrodarsono circle thinks, that I'm doing something inappropriate. All right, I've gone and chosen my own path, but I'm afraid I feel firmly about that choice. I'm determined in it and I beg to be allowed to go that way. If it turns out to have been the wrong choice, I'll certainly return to ask you all humbly for a better direction.'

'If that's your choice, so be it. But what I want to know is when you're going to marry, Lé. How can someone at your age not even have a girl in mind?'

I had to smile at my mother's insistence. The family's continuance was her priority. Well, father's too, of course; only I could see that in addition he was also uncomfortable with my ideas, with my choice of an ideology. He was a priyayi, a member, I had in fact recently learned, of the *Partai Nasional Indonesia*; a not very active member perhaps, but in any case far too moderate, I felt, in his views on the need for social change, and so my leaning towards Marxism would certainly not be to his taste.

'Now, mother, don't go worrying about that, I'll find myself a girl.'

'Well I'm glad to hear it, but who? Have you got someone?'

Even my father and Lantip smiled at her persistence.

'Didn't I bring Gadis here and introduced her to you? She might be the one.'

'Gadis? Don't you think she's rather independent?'

'Oh? How?'

'I mean, just to hear how she talks. She's so emphatic, it's all *tas-tes*, one point after another...'

'*Tas-tes?* What's that now, dear?'

'Oh, Allah, *Meneer* Hardojo, *Meneer* Hardojo. *Tas-tes* means someone who's just too clever, too quick and too sharp. And Hari, you should look out that she doesn't leave you behind, that you don't find yourself unable to keep up with her ways and with what she thinks. She sounds like someone who could easily go to extremes.'

'You don't need to worry, Bu. We'll manage fine.'

'This Gadis, she's of the same political orientation as yourself?'

'Ye-es, Pak. You could say that.'

'H'm.'

'Sound like you aren't too happy about her politics either, Pak.'

'Yes, no. Only I had imagined that any woman who took up politics wouldn't be quite so fierce.'

'Oh you don't know her, Pak. She's got some strong opinions, but she's just an honest kid. Only she sometimes sounds a bit unyielding, a bit prickly.'

'Yes, but that's the trouble, Lé. No one objects to women going into politics if they don't forget they're still women. The light touch, you know:

manners, sociability, a bit of elegance, politeness, modesty. Only women do or show those things to us well. If those social virtues go out of the window, *wah*, it's going to be one unattractive, grey world, Lé, that's all I can say.'

There I surrendered the debate to my father. Obviously, we had different views, the usual clash of generations no doubt. For them, what was on the surface was most important: shows and appearances were an expression of the soul within. I felt differently about that. I thought that one should determine a person's honesty and sincerity directly. Superficial manners and mannerisms were something which could be picked up any time along life's journey.

But my father soothed our differences with some concluding words intended to comfort me: 'But Hari, don't misunderstand us, lad. Whoever you choose to marry, we wouldn't interfere in that. You're well into adulthood. If you decide it's to be Gadis, you would by then have given it a lot of thought. All we want is to see you happy, with your own home and family soon.'

And I bowed my head as a dutiful Javanese son should. Poor father. Could I possibly have any real conflict with such a good man?

One night Gadis and I were absorbed in our preparations for staging a play to be taken around the Yogya Special District. It was *Ki Ageng Mangir*, the tragedy of a democratic village leader, one Ageng of Mangir, succumbing to Senapati's centralising despotism during a time of instability after the collapse of Majapahit in the early 1500s. If we were successful in the YSD, we would tour other areas. We were discussing the play after having just practised some of its scenes with the troupe. A number of the actors had until recently been members of the renowned Radio Republik Indonesia dramatic group; they were the very nucleus of that group in fact, and we felt privileged to have them join us. Among them were two who would take leading parts, Pak Dadi and Bu Kadarwati, and they with some others had in the rehearsal just ended given us a fine display of their talents, particularly in the three central scenes of the play. The first scene showed Senapati instructing his daughter to masquerade as a *ronggeng* girl and win the heart of Ki Ageng. In the second, Ki Ageng after marrying the girl and discovering her identity reluctantly agrees to submit to Senapati and go to the latter's new capital, Mataram. The last is the scene in which Ki Ageng is killed in the act of kissing Senapati's foot. As I said, the rehearsal went very well, and the acting was professional and elegant: Bu Kadarwati portrayed the role of the seductress very creditably, as did Pak Dadi that of the power-thirsty Senapati. Mas Guno made well for a handsome, luckless Ki Ageng. The confrontation between the two men was fascinating. When we set to analysing the performance, Bung Naryo was there to join in and make some critical remarks directed specifically to me as the writer of the scenario.

'Bung Hari, just a few words to you, if I may. Naturally, the main thing is that the play should succeed as a political vehicle and also as spectacle. Good people's theatre, in other words.'

I smiled. He was ultimately a kindly, well-mannered person and always tried to soften his sharpest criticisms.

'Surely, Bung, go ahead.'

'As far as the acting goes, its thumbs up. Bu Kadarwati, Pak Dadi, Mas Guno, all of you—first rate!'

'Well, thank you, Bung Naryo.'

'But the tale, Bung Hari, as you've represented it, has grown too romantic by far. The part where Senapati's daughter and Mangir fall in love is too well done, overdone, there's too much stress on that, it distracts from the point of everything. The dialogue is good, rather literary but good. However, you've led us into a mere drama of a couple's love, and not one about power, about ruthless, arbitrary power wielded by feudal overlords. That's where the emphasis should fall. People's theatre is a political instrument promoting the interests of the masses, don't forget its purpose. So I have these suggestions: that Senapati's character, his haughtiness and hunger for power, should be enlarged on; and so too the character of Mangir, not as lover but as a tragic hero struggling to further a people's democracy.'

'Thank you, Bung Naryo. I had actually hoped to present in *Ki Ageng Mangir* a story of human beings caught up in, tragically affected by, power-machinations. I saw all three figures—Mangir, Senapati, and his daughter—in that light. Maybe I stressed the romantic aspect of the story, but the fact remains that those two were indeed in love. I had intended the spectators to be actually more affected by the evil of insatiable power by witnessing the way it destroys something as pure and beautiful as human love.'

'Permit me to point out, Bung Hari, that love may indeed be beautiful, etcetera, but in this story it's merely a detail in a strategy to consolidate power. A very ugly strategy. This beautiful love of yours only came into being as an accessory to that strategy. You do agree? Don't you?'

'*Wah*, I'm somewhat fazed to hear you dismiss the role of love here as a mere detail, Bung. Their love was genuine and touching. I agree that Senapati's daughter went consciously to Mangir on a mission of entrapment set by her father; but they met and fell in love, just like that, fell in love. Is that a detail? No, Bung, it's a new situation independent of what came previously. It needs to be considered on its own, admittedly juxtaposed with the other.'

'Dear me. This is what results when you neglect us, Bung, when we don't see you at Party meetings. I'm afraid that your idea of what constitutes socialist realism gets somewhat tangled up with the liberal theories of universal humanism which we've just recently seen liquidated in this country.'

And we continued debating into the night. Naturally, I had to declare defeat; Bung Naryo was a formidable theoretician, as well as eloquent and

9. Harimurti

witty. How could I stand up to his vast store of experience acquired in and out of our country? The play *Ki Ageng Mangir* was dismantled and remodelled to accord with his propositions. Yet, a splinter of doubt, of dissatisfaction, continued to nag at me. Love—a mere detail?

Gadis invited me to go to Wates and meet her parents, where they lived not far from the Kulon Progo kabupaten office. Their modest house was well-cared for and neat, the furniture old, the floor laid with tiles of a bygone style, and the walls were decorated with inexpensive landscapes and framed reproductions of pre-war Hollywood film-stars. Everything was spotless in a way that spoke of regular supervised attention; and I was immediately reminded of my grandmother's house in Wanagalih, of that same atmosphere of petit bourgeois cleanliness and order, bless her. At least that had been so in her day, when she was still alive.

'Come in, come in, Nak. Come and sit here.'

I took a chair in their front veranda, looking out on a quiet street. There was hardly any traffic, and the sound of a turtledove somewhere made the general silence more noticeable.

'Yes, this is our home, Nak Hari. A pensioner's, rather forlorn I suppose. You know how it is with us in the country.'

'Why, not at all, Pak, it's very peaceful here. This is the main town in your kabupaten, and yet it still hasn't become noisy and crowded. Yogya is all chaos with those pupils and students whizzing about on their bikes.'

Gadis's father laughed politely, and just at that moment a young man appeared in the room; or a boy, I thought, for I had difficulty in placing his age. He had a large, shaven head and his expression showed the usual sad signs of mental retardation. He shuffled towards me, giggling, swaying, his hand extended. I gripped it without hesitation.

'Hee-hee . . . Mas. I'm Kentus. Who you, ha?'

'Hello, I'm Hari. A friend of Gadis.'

'Gadis? Who Gadis?'

There was a patient interjection from Gadis's mother: 'It's Mbak Dumilah, dear, Mbak Dum. Now you go to the back and play. Be off with you now.'

'Mas Hari got hamonica?'

'A . . . what?'

'Ha-mo-ni-ca. Hamonica.'

'Oh yes, I do have one. But I left it at home. I'll bring it with me next time, all right?'

'Will you play wiv me then?'

'Yes, surely, Kentus.'

'Horee. I get my hamonica.'

Gentry

He ran off, and I saw that Gadis was red with embarrassment. She hadn't told me about Kentus. Her parents quickly informed me now that he was the son of a departed relative on the mother's side and was considered a younger brother to Gadis.

'We feel so sorry for him, Nak. Something happened to him and he won't develop any further. At least he can talk a little.'

I wondered if his situation was really hopeless, for I found him pleasant enough to talk to. Perhaps people gave up too soon in these cases. Then I was invited to eat, with the usual warning not to expect too much from the meal; and when we sat down at the table within, the meal did consist largely of vegetables and tempeh with a little fish. But although I was eating in Gadis's home for the first time, the modest fare only served to make me feel even more at ease: the atmosphere was undemanding and calm and her parents were kindly and in no way overwhelming.

In the later stages of the meal we were entertained by the harmonica of Kentus, his piece of choice being 'The Cockatoo', played with brow-wrinkling concentration inversely proportionate to accuracy. Then it turned out that this was the only tune he knew, and we had to hear it again, without any improvements. But I did my best to show appreciation, and at the end Gadis and I laid down fork and spoon and clapped Kentus heartily. Gadis stroked his head and leant over to kiss his cheek.

'*Wah*, what a musician we have here.'

'Really? I good, Mbak?'

'Very good.'

'Horee, I can play hamonica. Mas Hari, you come, bring hamonica. Teach me more songs.'

'Certainly.'

'What songs?'

'Oh, many. There's "Our Archipelago", and "Advance! My Nation's Precepts Five", and "Country, Creed, and Communism Leagued" . . . lots more.'

'That's enough now, Kentus. Let your Mbak and Mas Hari finish eating. You go out and play.'

Gadis brought up the matter of my staying overnight, and her parents insisted on it: 'Let Nak Hari have an opportunity to hear how quiet life here is after dark.'

I had to smile. I had spent enough nights in Wanagalih to be familiar with country silence. The small guest-room I was led to was in the forward area of the house, and its furnishings consisted solely of a divan and a wardrobe. I was drowsy and glad to collapse on the divan, and I lay there asleep for I don't know how long before suddenly becoming conscious of a hand patting my chest and then my hair. I heard Gadis whisper: 'Bung, are you asleep, Bung?'

Hell, I thought, she's taking a chance, her parents will hear us! 'You're

9. Harimurti

mad!' I hissed to her.

'You'll have to put up with that. Move over.'

'Shush!'

'Shush what?'

'Just shush.'

There was a chortle from her.

'If your folks wake, what then?'

'Hee-hee. You direct plays, don't you, priyayi?'

We kept quiet for a while. Gadis was sniffing at my cheeks and mouth, and from her own mouth wafted an odour of toothpaste.

'Gadis.'

'Mm?'

'Why didn't you tell me about Kentus before? Ashamed, were you?'

'No, I just wanted you to come here and see for yourself how my family too has suffered as members of a downtrodden class.'

'Oh now, downtrodden. How?'

'With your own priyayi family everything's been great, you've all had your comfortable life. Well, my father's a priyayi too, of a low level, who's lived on his wages only. Kentus was born to my mother's cousin who was an even lower priyayi and had a bad time. Her husband was a village teacher with a small plot of land. He mortgaged it to some haji of a landlord to get money for Kentus. My father spent it all on village healers and then on a doctor. It had no effect and the land was forfeited. They lived miserably after that, until both the parents died of TB, one after the other. So we took on the raising of Kentus. If that's not an example of a downtrodden class, then what do you call what happened to my family?'

While I was listening to Gadis, the memory of my own youth in Solo and Wanagalih passed through my mind, and I could of course see that the Sastrodarsono family had been far more fortunate than that of Gadis. But could it be truthfully said that Kentus and his mother and father were examples of a downtrodden class? Was there no room for the play or the vagaries of fortune in their life-experience? It seemed to me that the sorrows of that family had begun earlier than in the unhappy story I had just heard, that it had begun in a mother's womb.

'Bung Hari, you remember that debate with Bung Naryo, don't you? When he said that in an unjust society everything, even love, is conditioned by the greed of a dominant class? Well, the tale of Kentus and what followed with his father and mother is all part of that: their misery resulted from the oppressive economy of a dominant class.'

'Sorry, Gadis, but it resulted from some mishap in the womb of a particular mother, and not from the actions of any class.'

'Oh come now, you're being obtuse. You've got to go back and back. If his family had not had to lead a miserable life, had lived in moderately just economic conditions, would his mother have been prone to give birth to a defective son? Ay?'

'But isn't it true that the most wretched beggars produce healthy children, while plenty of middle-class families have those like Kentus or worse?'

The hisses and whispers of this debate continued through a good part of the night, until we concluded it with something more satisfying to us both. Not that there remained much time for that, because by then dawn was near.

Kang Lantip finally got engaged to Halimah, and I was happy for him. It was well past the normal time when he should have made that decision, but better late than never of course. And as for myself? The way things were going I wondered sometimes whether I too would slip into old-bachelorhood. The problem was that although Gadis and I had agreed to one day become officially engaged and then to marry, our commitments just went on and got into the way of such things. We even barely made it to my home for Kang Lantip's engagement party, because I had been away in Temanggung putting on *Ki Ageng Mangir*. The production which toured around Temanggung and Wonosobo and other places was such a success and excited so much talk and so many meetings that I almost forgot that my father was having the party for Kang Lantip and Halimah. Gadis and I had to rush back for it.

It was a small celebration for the closer relatives and friends on both sides, including those representing Halimah's parents, who couldn't leave their kampong in West Sumatra because that province had still not fully settled down after the regional rebellions of the late 1950s. When I entered my home I had a joyous moment, seeing before me the collected faces of all my relatives; but, alas, absent was Embah Kakung Sastrodarsono, now past travelling. Apart from my own pleasure at once again meeting with all those dear people, I was touched too by this visible confirmation of Kang Lantip's place well and truly in the bosom of our greater family. Pakdé and Budé Noegroho, who had once taken a slightly distant attitude to Kang Lantip and shown themselves not fully content when my father took him in, now had changed completely. They were clearly grateful to him for his services in resolving the difficulties surrounding the marriage of Marie and Maridjan. Those two now had two children, and their marriage was going well.

I also found the continuing closeness and shared views of this clan of ours more than affecting, it was thought-provoking. I had to admit to myself I was happy to see that our ties overall still held well and that there was a sense here that whatever might happen to oneself, kinship would always be something to fall back on. All of which made me feel uncomfortable, remembering how often I had laughingly referred to priyayi families as feudal coteries of

9. Harimurti

little use in modern Indonesia's advancement.

'Hallo, here comes the grasping landlord to throw us out of our home. Where are you from this time, Lé?'

'Phew, just got back from a tour, Pakdé.'

'What do you think of him, Mas? This son of mine's promotion? From university graduate to the crowned *bas* of a travelling troupe?'

'We-ell now. Seems the boy's been all this time a quiet admirer of Grandfather Kusumo Lakubroto. *There* was a famous *bas*. Got your gold teeth yet, Lé?'

Gadis could not join the ragging, not knowing the family chronicle of that alternately peripatetic and clam-like Eyang who had regularly frozen in the waters of the Ketangga and at one point bossed a failing troupe.

'But are you going to get engaged yourself one day, or what, Lé?'

'*Wah*, give me a chance, Bulik Mini. I've got to get into the correct state of mind first.'

'Ah, but you've got someone then? So where is she, this lucky candidate you've been hiding from your aunt?'

'*Ayo*, Hari, introduce Gadis to your Bulik, Paklik, Budé, Pakdé—everyone!'

So I had to drag Gadis around the whole company, and they all received and accepted her with good nature and humour.

'That's a nice name you have, Gadis. But after you marry won't it sound a bit strange, a bit youthful?'

'It's not my real name, Mbak Sus. It's my pen-name.'

'My, a writer daughter-in-law, and with a *schuilnaam*. So what *is* your name, Nak?'

Gadis, who was normally so quick-witted, suddenly hesitated, and then replied shyly: 'Retno Dumilah, *Tante*.'

'*Wat een prachtige naam, Meis*! It's a splendid name, young lady. Did you know it was borne by the daughter of the high bupati of Madiun, she who became wife to Senapati, the founder of the Mataram dynasty?'

I saw out of the corner of my eye a red-faced Gadis who I could tell was having some difficulty with contrary feelings: a girlish pleased embarrassment, and on the other hand chagrin at being reminded that she had been bestowed the name of the hated consort of a Javanese tyrant.

'Thank you, *Tante*. Very kind of you.'

The affiancing ceremony was quite modest. My father and the representative who was acting for Halimah's family each gave a short speech; each of the couple fitted in turn a gold ring on the other's finger; and then my father invited everyone to recite the Koranic exordium: *Al-Fatihah*. When we queued up to offer our congratulations, Kang Lantip and I embraced for such a long time that those behind us had to demand their turn. We all then surrounded the traditional cone of yellow rice and took our pinch, a preamble to a larger, gay dinner extending long into the night. In the mood of the occasion, I sat Gadis beside Kang Lantip, with a warning that she should know he was a brother whom I loved dearly but a frightful right-wing liberal: and they both laughed. But in fact they knew each other well by then, and Gadis had lectured him not a few times already. It was that kind of a night, the glow of the occasion could hardly lend to any sort of confrontation, and anyway Gadis liked him. Probably, to nurture any sort of real hostility towards my foster-brother would have needed a hopelessly hard-hearted nature.

In a pedicab riding back to her boarding house, Gadis said suddenly to me:

'So you can recite the *Al-Fatihah* then.'

'I can, sure. Father had me study gamelan and dancing, but also to recite the Koran and memorise prayers. That was with Pak Kaji Ngaliman, in Solo.'

'And you pray now?'

'Well, yes, occasionally.'

'Like, even nowadays, as well?'

'I actually haven't prayed for quite a while. But it's something that comes out fairly spontaneously. As with that *Al-Fatihah*.'

The pedicab creaked to a halt and I followed Gadis to the gate of her fence. I stopped there and kissed her on the forehead.

'What about you? Have you ever prayed?'

'No. We're small priyayi of a strictly *abangan* persuasion.'

'Heavens! That's a mighty long title for it.'

'Whereas your priyayi family are fake *santri*. But never mind. I like them. Good-hearted feudal folk.'

'In that case, I better give you another kiss. Hold there.'

We only separated after Gadis had slapped my arm to remind me that the patient pedicab driver was waiting.

Then that day broke on us. I was visiting Wates again, where my presence and good standing with Gadis's family was now habitual. I had by this time had many a hint from them that they would have nothing against it if in the near future Gadis and I should take steps towards matrimony. That afternoon we two were sitting under the rose-apple tree in their front yard. Kentus was there, showing off his playing. As promised, I had taught him, or tried to teach him, a number of tunes, and now he wanted to demonstrate that he had them pat. We listened with serious and encouraging looks while he blew away energetically at three of those songs. And how could one not be moved to see with what effort of his poor strength and ability he tried to bring out those simple tunes? Of course, from 'Precepts Five', 'Archipelago', or 'Country, Creed, and Communism Leagued' it was possible to catch

9. Harimurti

something of the original, but not much. We applauded, and he accepted ecstatically every sign that he was doing well, even asking us to join him in his success by singing along. And so we sang. The yard rang with the *Garuda Pancasila* march: 'Advance! my nation's precepts five; I'll e'er proclaim them while alive . . .' then: 'Our archipelago far-flung, home of one nation and one tongue . . .' and, inevitably: 'With country, creed, and communism fast, we'll free ourselves of blockhead-rule at last! . . .' Kentus blew spiritedly, blew with his usual pathetic gusto, while we two had difficulty keeping up with him, for our singing was as disjointed as his playing: try as we did, it was difficult not to laugh.

Then suddenly a motorbike arrived bearing two of our colleagues from *Lekra*, and we were told to return quickly to the Association's office. Things had turned bad in the country. The Council of Generals had launched a coup, they said. The two rode off without further words, except for a shout of '*merdeka!*' from one of them. Freedom. Freedom seemed indeed once again under threat.

That night we were instructed to gather next day with other elements of the progressive masses in a parade of support for the Revolutionary Council. Gadis and I left the Association meeting and went to her boarding house. Once again it was empty, and we thought we might try inside to come at some understanding of what those confused reports from Jakarta meant. We were troubled by the feeling that there were aspects to these events which we didn't know, possibly were deliberately not being informed about by those of our colleagues who were in the Party. Bung Naryo, close to the Party, probably a member himself for some time, only appeared briefly at the office, to say that there was indeed a crisis but we should all stay calm and take our instructions only from the Party, because what arrived through other means, including the radio, would be unreliable.

In Gadis's room we couldn't hide our concern and alarm from each other. Events were occurring which were so far outside my own areas of practical interest that I had difficulty in imagining an explanation for them.

'Gadis, what do you think is happening?'

'I'm very frightened. I think there's going to be a huge fight to the death between us and the reactionaries.'

'I too have that feeling. Like something vast and terrible is about to happen, but I don't know what.'

'We've outdone them in every field. In the cities, in the villages, in everything, politics, education, the arts. Now they're asking the military to help them.'

And so in that room, lying on her bed, we tried to guess what was occurring and what would occur next. We were very aware that in *Lekra* we were only concerned with how the arts and drama might be made to further social development in a progressive direction; but what the intentions of the Party were in the arena of applied, real politics—well, most of that was a mystery to us. So now that we were told a crisis was upon us, all we could make out was that it concerned the Revolutionary Council and the Council of Generals, but into what this might develop we were free to conjecture at will. Beyond that, we should, as bidden, present ourselves at some parade or demonstration on the morrow. It was going to be a long night. Although at least there were pleasant ways to spend some of that time in Gadis's bed.

'Bung, if I wax a bit sentimental tonight, is that all right?'

'You may.'

'I'm madly in love with you.'

'I like that. What else?'

'Listen, I'm serious.'

'Yes, I know. And I feel the same. When all this nonsense out there is over, would you like to marry me?'

'That's what I was getting at. Yes!'

'Sh. Not so loud.'

'Yes, Bung. And I'm late with my monthlies.'

'Oh? What's that mean?'

'If I don't have them it means I'm pregnant, what d'you think it means? Do you have any other explanation?'

'*Wah!*'

'Just what I thought, priyayi. You're frightened, ay? You're frightened!'

I kissed her. Then she kissed me, and we embraced very tightly. Then we made love again.

The parade went well enough, everyone shouted support for the Revolutionary Council, while people standing at the side looked on with amazed interest at us; but at its conclusion we heard that the military had taken full control and was commencing a general repression of the PKI and its mass organizations. We were hurriedly advised to disperse, hole up and await developments. I went home, and Gadis returned to Wates. My father soon confirmed that the situation was deteriorating rapidly for people on my side of politics.

'Hari, you are in danger. We think that you shouldn't try to run for it. Just keep your head down for the time being and we'll try to find the best way to get you out of this.'

'But why should I run? If they come for me, I'll explain exactly where I stand. I'm not a Party member, am I?'

'True enough, but until things settle down you better stay here with us. We'll get your Pakdé Noegroho onto this to give us a hand.'

'Gus, father is right. I've been out there seeing people being arrested everywhere. If they catch you running, you'll be in trouble.'

9. Harimurti

'If I stay here for any length of time I'll be found out and picked up.'

'Yes, but if you'll all listen, I've got a suggestion for you, Gus. Now I don't want to be misunderstood by anyone, however.'

'Well, what is it, Lé?'

'It's this, Pak. I know some people in the army pretty well. Officers. We could put Gus Hari and his case in their hands.'

'What—you'd turn him over to the tigers?'

'There, Pak. You *have* misunderstood me. I'm not talking about dropping Gus Hari in any tiger cage. I would ask them to keep him in protective custody. Here, he might be mobbed at any time. There are gangs going around grabbing people. If they drag him away they've got bruisers, those gangs, who would beat him black and blue and we wouldn't hear any more about him. If we surrender him to some known authority, I mean people known to us, they might interrogate him, but at least that would be in a formal, regular setting. And meanwhile with Pakdé Noegroho's influence we'd be investigating all avenues to assist Gus Hari.'

We thought this over. It made sense, but I remained unhappy. Kakak Lantip would be giving me up to those who considered me an enemy; but on the other hand things were indeed going bad, turning frightful. And then I had Gadis on my mind. I regretted not going with her to Wates after the demonstration. What was happening to her? Was anyone protecting *her*?

'All right then, Kang. I'll go along with whatever you think best.'

With that, my mother burst into tears: 'Oh, Allah, boy. What a disaster. How could you have got into this mess?'

'There, Bu, everything's all right. I'm still here with you, aren't I?'

'Yes, but your brother is going to give you up. Oh, dear. Do be careful, Lé.'

'Don't worry, Bu. Nothing will happen to me. But I do want to ask Kang Lantip for something else.'

'Yes, Gus.'

'It's Gadis, Kang. Try to find out what's happening to her. It would be really good if you could help her in some way, maybe as you're doing with me.'

'Absolutely, Gus. I'll get on to that immediately.'

'You're a brother in a thousand.'

I embraced him, and a whole mix of emotions met inside me at that moment. The least important was fear of going to jail or some other form of detention; far more than by such a concern, I was stirred once again by the love that this honest, sincere man had for us, stirred also by the resolution and devotion of all our family; and of course I was in pain for Gadis, who at this moment carried the daily-growing product of our love. Should I speak to them about that now? No, my parents' distress was deep enough already.

A few days later, I went with Lantip to a building in Kotabaru where investigations were being conducted into those suspected of having been involved in the great *Gestapu* plot: the *Gerakan September Tiga Puluh*, the apparent attempt on 30 September 1965 to seize control of the government.

In prison I had ample opportunity to consider my life, my past and my future. One would think that until the day I entered that cell I had been denied the ability to make such a review, had no time to ponder over and weigh up each step I had taken to that point; as if my life had been solely motivated by impulses and the necessities of the work I set myself. I mulled over that thought until I could almost have submitted a report on what I concluded, a statement to an interrogator, as it were.

A statement, or a litany of further questions? Surely, I would begin, there must have been some reasoning and choice, however unclear, in everything I did: to explain why I decided to join *Lekra*, had happily directed theatre troupes, had fallen in love with Gadis? Were those reasons and choices influenced by my childhood and youth, were they formed in my early associations with neighbourhood children, in my upbringing by my father, or my education by teachers? I only know that since I was very young I had been aware of being sustained and directed in all things by my father; aware of being the only child that my parents would have. Although I was by no means spoiled, as happened with sole children, I knew that my father was always considering how to provide the best conditions for my development, and he expected a lot from me. Even in the selection of a name, Harimurti, he had looked deep into the future and seen splendid possibilities there. Mine is one of the alternative names of Krishna, wise and all-knowing ruler of the idyllic kingdom of Dwarawati. So when from time to time I was behaving badly, he would remind me of my illustrious other name. He would point out to me the impossibility and incongruity of someone called Krishna being naughty. Later, at university, I read the original Indian descriptions of Krishna, which showed him to possess not only noble qualities and great sacral powers, but among the attributes of his godhead there were more human traits as well, even some akin to those of a village playboy and prankster. Thus, the weight of that name began to have less effect on my outlook, which up till then was that of a normally-developing young priyayi; and in fact I felt more and more inclined to shrug that weight off. What mainly remained, I think, was the impression left by my first playmates, the kampong children, and by Kakang Lantip, and by small-town Wanagalih, more than the sway of any Hindu mythologies or the time I spent about the Mangkunegaran court, pleasant and pretty as that was. Rather, I remembered best from Solo the tours among back-country villages with my father, the sight of those strong, clumsy adults struggling to get their fragments of an education, my games with the village children, and the scenery of the countryside itself: rice-fields, peasant

9. Harimurti

hovels, cattle. And it was Kakang Lantip too who really taught me a lot; not in the sense of school-teaching but by being what he was: modest, good-hearted, honest. I know I felt a brotherly love for him from the start, since our earliest days in Wanagalih and when we visited Wanalawas. None of the wretchedness and poverty of his origins, or his standing as an adopted outsider during his time in Setenan Road, caused him to grow dispirited or to harbor that poisonous sense of feeling oneself a lesser being—*minder*, to use the colonial-era term—which should have been engendered in his case. His guileless, calm, accepting nature caused no end of perturbation in me, almost panic, whenever I thought about it later at university. How could someone who when considered from the perspective of class struggle ought to be boiling with anger, remain so collected? Surely his was an imposed fate, if understood in terms satisfying to Gadis and Sunaryo, even to Pak Lurah Wanalwas: an unjust distribution of this world's goods doomed in sequential progression the lives of people such as Sunandar and Kentus, innumerable people. Yet on the contrary Lantip confronted his lot, and the inequities of the wider situation, with an unfeigned acceptance which in no way demeaned him. Yes, and Wanagalih, the ways of that house on Setenan Road, of Embah Kakung and Embah Putri, founders of this so-called dynasty of ours, its returning assemblies during crises and gay occasions: all those had left their question mark as well somewhere inside me. My comings and goings among the village-world in the hinterland of the princedom, and between Wanagalih and Wanalawas—settings for countless small epics unlikely to have been noticed by me were it not that they occurred in the world of Kang Lantip's origins—had bent me towards a concern for the small folk, for the lives of the *wong cilik*. And so too did those opportunities to contrast the high culture of the palace with the humbler one of my up-and-coming kin predispose me to appreciate the remnant peasantry in the nature of the latter. I became a person swayed by sympathy and solidarity in two directions: on the one hand towards the *wong cilik* as the unfortunate counterpart of those with power—and also as folk of the same blood as myself—and on the other towards the lower, ascending gentry, dragging itself out of the paddy mud and dragging as best they could their kith and kin with them, up to the surface, to finally grasp and enjoy a cantle of the higher civilisation of their race, to shape that civilisation, too, and contribute to its form, whatever that might take. I had turned my back on the Krishna of the high traditions; but had not my family by their noble exertions become inseparable from that ancient order, all that feudalism I scoffed at? And it seems, I don't now know how myself, that in this time of void, confusion and novelty *Lekra* and its apparent certainties and explanations, and the inextinguishable remnants of those old Javanese arts I loved, provided together a direction, accommodated all contradictions. And Gadis? At least there one certainty truly did exist and remains: my love for her. How should it have happened that I became attracted to her, had intended to marry her? Well, she was as much as I an embodiment of doubts and contradictory pulls. A kindred spirit, I suppose. The only difference in our circumstancesl being that my family appeared to her to have been denied what she would have called the life-educational taste of misfortune hers had known.

But what was the importance of such soliloquies now, when I was torn by all kinds of despair, not knowing where Gadis might be, lost and pregnant, carrying our child! Could all this nightmare be real? Would it end?

One morning, four months later, I was called to the head-warden's office, and my surprise might be imagined when I saw gathered there my parents, Pakdé Noegroho and Kang Lantip. I was informed that I could go home and remain there under conditions of house arrest. I left my cell carrying a small bag that had in it a change of clothes, some underwear and a toothbrush; and on the way across the quadrangle, towards the exit where the rest of my people waited, I had a distinct feeling of discomfort. I moved quickly with my head down, knowing that I was being watched through grilles by those who had been arrested with me and were remaining in their cells.

I heard one of them shout: 'Stepping out, are we? Hey, he's on his way to Malioboro! Be sure to get an eyeful for your mates here!'

'Right, I will!' I shouted back.

'And our love to the ladies at Balokan!'

'The hell with you!'

The last I heard behind me was a general roar of hoots and bitter laughter. I waved behind me without turning and passed through the portals. I didn't really know who those in the neighbouring cells had been, but I still felt guilty at be singled out and favoured like this. Bung Naryo, I knew, had definitely not been in that prison, and in fact I had no way of even knowing if he had been caught. Gadis too was not there, the rumour being that female prisoners were kept in special detention somewhere near Semarang; but for all I knew she could still be in hiding.

We arrived home, and as I expected there was the ceremonial dish of yellow rice on the table; I could see that all the other welcoming to-do was also going to be unavoidable. A short speech by my father explained what was clear enough to everyone there: all this procedure was celebrating the return of a stray to the fold.

We recited the *Al-Fatihah*, began eating, and my father opened the conversation: 'Allah be thanked, Hari, boy. You passed through the eye of the needle there.'

'Yes, Pak.'

9. Harimurti

I bobbed my head and continued eating. It would be a while before I re-educated my palate to the taste of proper food. The memory of ration-rice was going to be with me for some time.

'Without your Pakdé Noegroho's help, I don't know how we might have got you back. You're still under house arrest, but that's better than the cells, isn't it?'

I turned to my uncle: 'I'm very, very grateful, Pakdé. I'm very indebted to you.'

Pakdé nodded and went on cleaning up the last of the rice and a scrap of roast chicken on his plate. Finally satisfied and pushing the plate away he turned his attention to me and began speaking: 'Hari my boy, there's nothing that gives an uncle more pleasure than helping his nephews. It's a happy duty done to the lineage, a service to the greater family which encompasses us all.'

'Indeed, Pakdé.'

'What's important now, Hari, is for you to give some thought to your position and make a few small corrections to some of your past ways. You've been, forgive me, a little confused lately. Those commie dogmas do that to people. You took the wrong road there, Lé. Now you stay here in this house and begin re-reading and studying the *Pancasila*, the five principles on which this great country of ours is constituted. H'm, let me see, what are they: God, humanity, unity, democracy, justice: is that five? Anyway, those are all that Indonesia needs. Why, Hari, without the *Pancasila* all your other ideologies, movements, parties, your *komunisme*, even if they succeeded in taking power, it would be like a thief breaking into an empty house.'

'Indeed, Pakdé.'

'Now, if you go carefully, show that you're absorbing your *Pancasila* nicely: well, I might be able to work something more for you, something that sets you a bit freer. Know what I mean?'

'I do, Pakdé. Thank you again. Very much.'

'Excellent, Hari. You can rest assured that I would never dream of letting you drop off the edge. A little pain for the sake of your education is one thing, but we won't let anything more serious than that happen to you. Not our Javanese way, that. Not my way, your Pakdé, who after all has to consider the standing of our name. No, no. And then you yourself, together with your brother Lantip here, acted from the very same standpoint in that matter of the little difficulty with Marie. Yes, we have principles, we have solidarity in this family.'

It had been an exhausting day and I could do no more than bow my head. We dispersed and went to our rooms. The one which I shared with Kang Lantip seemed after months in obscenely filthy cells astonishingly clean and spacious, even foreign. But then, also, for some time before being taken to prison I had not used the room very much, my affairs with *Lekra* and the management of troupes and whatnot meant that I slept often at the houses of friends, at the *Lekra* office, or of course at the boarding house with Gadis. The shelves here were neatly stacked with books of my student days, the table was clear of papers, my clothes were folded away in their place in the wardrobe. Thoughtful, thoughtful mother. And Kang Lantip too. He was always by far the more orderly and organized of us two, while I, to put it mildly, had been careless. I could see he wanted to talk.

'Now Gus, don't look like that. It's just our room, you know.'

I had to smile. Good old Lantip, brimming even more than usual with warmth and friendliness.

'Yeah, I know, Kang. I've been on a *rantau*, came back from my travels and everything is so well-cared for. Is that some scent I can smell, something mother has spread around here?'

'Very good, that, Gus—a *rantau*. But you know, you shouldn't be too cynical over what happened. Enjoy being out and let's be grateful.'

'Yes, I'm sorry, Kang. I should apologise for sounding unappreciative and less than truly thankful to you all. No, it's a blessing to be back.'

Kang Lantip chuckled.

'You hardly sounded ecstatic with your ". . . indeed, indeed, Pakdé", a little while ago.'

I laughed with him: 'What else could I say? Everything he laid out was true, wasn't it?'

'Ha, now you're being cynical again, if you're alluding to the deep knowledge our uncle has of the *Pancasila*.'

'As to that you'd know best. It's some time since I followed the way his mind moves. Maybe some natures are best measured for width rather than depth, I don't know. But at least what he said about the need for family solidarity is certainly appropriate. I have to admit that I'd turned away from that simple truth of our fathers. I was a bit startled to hear how positive Pakdé sounded when he was referring to the need for that loyalty and cooperation. I'd heard it a hundred times before, but it really sunk in today.'

Kang Lantip looked at me quietly for a moment and then broke into a wide grin.

'Gus, let me say that I'm very, very happy that you're back among us. Just rest here quietly to your heart's content; and as for what happens next, don't you worry. We'll discuss it all tomorrow and decide for the best.'

I changed my clothes and then collapsed on my bed. For a while I stared at the ceiling, thinking of Gadis, of Bung Naryo, of the possible things which might have happened to them; Gadis pregnant and pursued, Bung Naryo perhaps in hiding or worse. But I was very tired and soon dropped off.

9. Harimurti

It didn't take me long to become comfortable again in the surroundings of my home, with everyone doing all they could to let me recover and return more or less to the life I had there when I was a boy. My mother fussed over me, made my favourite meals, all that kind of thing; not that it would have been difficult to please my stomach just then. Father, unlike Pakdé Noegroho, avoided lecturing me, least of all on the merits of *Pancasila*, probably because he too was vague about our national text, but mainly from his natural delicacy which I knew would have him want to avoid any more battles of ideas. Quite obviously his main concern was simply to make me feel comfortable in an atmosphere soothed by small talk, family talk: about Embah Kakung for example, now living alone in Wanagalih, although Pakdé Ngadiman and his family kept an eye on him; about Bulik Soemini and Paklik Harjono and their children, thankfully living without any further incidents; and, of course, since my circumstances much dependent on Pakdé Noegroho, he and his family were often in our conversations. I was determined that whenever the authorities finally allowed me freedom to travel, I would go to Wanagalih as a priority. The old man must by now have become quite frail and past moving much beyond his house.

Warmly pleasant as it was to talk about such plans and to imagine all sorts of things to do in other circumstances, the sharp reality of my status as a prisoner under house arrest never faded. And the fact that I had selected a choice of direction in my life that had brought me to my present situation, made for bitter contemplation. Wry contemplation, usually, when I considered that while my convictions had never properly settled, were even kindly derided by real Marxists, were practically only ever applied in the sphere of the arts, and I had yet to be persuaded about the necessity of radical action in their fulfilment in any wider sphere, yet I had fallen by mere tendency into the ambient of those who were indeed prepared to turn this new nation of ours inside out. And the result was all this that had occurred. These thoughts more than once suddenly agitated the long tranquil spells of virtual convalescence in my parents' home; and when they did, they pricked my imagination into once again envisaging the possible fate of Gadis, of her parents and even poor Kentus in Wates, of Bung Naryo and our other friends, by now dispersed Allah knew where. I could now listen to the radio and read newspapers, and Kang Lantip brought back reports of the continuing daily consequences of what seemed to have been an attempted coup, and I understood that thousands were falling victims in the widening reaction, perhaps tens of thousands, hundreds of thousands. The horror of those accounts made one's hair stand on end, the collective cruelty seemed like a wave which grew as it rolled onwards towards who knew what conclusion or with what purpose; and people lived on as if under some evil spell, transfixed, insensitive as stones, incapable of stopping the madness.

Gentry

Then one afternoon, while I sat reading on the veranda, Kang Lantip came back from work, subdued I could see, and he sat down beside me. He gulped down some tea which my mother nowadays brought out there for us at this time, looked speculatively at me, and began: 'I've got news about Mas Naryo, Gus.'

'And Gadis?'

'No, nothing yet about her. But as to Mas Naryo, I got the full story from a witness.'

'Well?'

'Gus, I have to tell you that he's dead. Killed by a mob. Executed, as they say, by the masses stirred to justifiable anger. In the Boko area, around Prambanan.'

Bung Naryo had been hiding in a local villager's house, was spotted, and a crowd arrived to surround the place; but he managed to wriggle through a kitchen window and escape into the paddies. He ducked and weaved from one field to another, got to the edge of the hill near the remains of the Boko temple, and there they caught him, at the edge of a canal. The mob beat him without mercy, kicked him about, until someone with a pistol ordered them to stand aside. He was going to finish him off, but then Bung Naryo unbelievably asked to be allowed to make a farewell speech! So they let him. The pity of it was that nobody remembers what he said, and of course there would hardly have been anyone there taking notes. These were all *santri* villagers, with little time for anyone who had the slightest stink of the PKI about him, and they obviously wouldn't have been in a mood to listen attentively to all that.

But I hardly needed a transcript, I knew Bung Naryo's style, had known his patient brotherly ways and could imagine how he had gone about the matter: probably smiling in the very presence of death; probably smiling and fearful, far from heroic or brave, as who could be, pursued and beaten like that? He would have smiled, I supposed, in acknowledgement that his life's gamble, in which the tokens and stakes were ideas and convictions, had come to an end. And he needed to end it in a fine speech, because like most politicians he looked on the world as a stage where every actor must try to make as memorable an exit as possible. It would have been a fine speech, an oration full of assurances to invisible comrades, urgings to not be downhearted or lose faith because of this momentary reversal, full of rhetoric about silver linings, a polemic but also undoubtedly clever and convincing, he himself in those last moments fervently needing conviction. Poor Bung Naryo, goodbye, then. We had argued, clashed, I had disagreed with him and could not accept many of his opinions; but, never mind, I remained grateful for having known him, and now I felt kindly towards him as he departed my life.

Kang Lantip, who had known him too of course, sighed unhappily and said: 'It happened some months ago, Gus. I just heard about it today. As for Gadis, try not to worry. We're sure to come across news of her soon.'

I returned to thinking about Bung Naryo. It would take some time to forget him. I had been so long involved with all the stand-bys of folk theatre, and now I kept imagining him dying before such a stagy background as the ruined Boko temple. It resonated with that episode in the legend of Lara Jonggrang, where Bandung Bondowoso is convinced he can raise a mighty temple in the course of one night, and Lara Jonggrang commands the day to dawn early. End of story.

'You know, Gus, I wasn't one of those who accepted all the views of Mas Naryo, but there was a lot attractive about the man. I liked him and I respected the strength with which he held his ideas. And he was very clever, very sharp. And yet he was in error when he gave his talents to that system, that's the pity of it. A pity that he should die so barbarously for it.'

'What about yourself, Kang, you were born in a poor village; why weren't you attracted to the PKI, or at least the Socialists, or to something like *Lekra*?'

He looked at me and smiled.

'It's probably because I couldn't bring myself to believe in a system that could give rise to a potentate like Stalin. As I couldn't believe in systems that produced a Hitler or Mussolini. And of course, equally, an Amangkurat in the old days, a butcher of the *santri*. Such systems always contain the seeds of later ruthlessness that claims countless helpless victims.'

I was surprised at Lantip's clipped tone. This was my brother, a kind, polite man, follower of the formalities, in one sweep mowing down three and more political economies of historically immense moment.

'But can we dispense with systems, Kang? Without one or another will we ever be able to better the lives of vulnerable people?'

'Well, I guess we will always need some system, and people's lives need bettering, that's for sure. But those who promote ruthless, cruel systems at all cost will never do much good for the underclass, no matter how much they might claim that to be their goal. The problem is that in fact your potentates, your totally committed seekers after power, seldom have any practical knowledge of how the *wong cilik* live.'

'But you do say we can't dispense with some system or other. How do we create one which doesn't produce ruthless leaders and give us those who really know the people's miseries?'

'I guess we have to try harder to create one in which those leaders believe in the people.'

'Mm. Believe in the people.'

'Yeah, I mean they believe, accept, that other people are like themselves, instead of going around dividing and separating everyone into contrasting classes or blocs or whatever. Believe that we all have opinions and wants and needs and choices and dreams and rights. Basically, that we are all equal in those. Once we have that foundation, we develop a clear and open system on it capable of giving everyone an opportunity to speak out, declare each person's opinions and aspirations. And because we've decided to grant that everyone is capable of thinking and can formulate opinions, then it follows that we must listen to others with sympathy, unburdened by all those theoretical preconceptions, those weighty ideas which imply to our own great satisfaction that we are cleverer than they, clever than the masses, who can't think, that we know the nature of their needs and their wants better than they do. Why—it would probably prove a positive relief to thus unburden one's mind, one's heart, if only we tried it, Gus!'

'That's hard, that inclusive *we*, Kang.'

'But I'm only talking after all about me, you, my friends, yours, all of us. And suddenly there's your system. One which does away with the notion that to improve people's lives you have to murder untold numbers of them. I'm tired of seeing where that leads: Madiun, this business now, and who knows how many more still to come. No, we should turn more humbly to simple discussion and dialogue. You want revolutionary change? Let it be through peaceful transformation: *there's* a revolutionary idea these days!'

We continued trading notions of greater or lesser practicality late into the afternoon, until the time arrived when good priyayi need to part to take their pre-dinner siestas.

About two months later, Kang Lantip finally came home with news of Gadis. My parents and I were sitting at the table having just finished lunch when he hurried into the room and began speaking: 'We were right. Gadis is being held in Plantungan. She was caught in a hide near Magelang, together with some friends of hers who were in that women's movement, *Gerwani*. Plantungan is a detention centre for female prisoners. However . . .'

'What, Kang?'

I was in a turmoil, and Lantip seemed to be looking at me carefully.

'Well, there's something peculiar that I can't understand. About her condition.'

'What, Kang?'

'Well, according to my source, a certain *Gerwani* prisoner called Retno Dumilah who's being held over there, happens to be seven months pregnant. How could that be?'

My mother instantly dismissed the information: 'It can't be Gadis then, Tip. Probably another *Gerwani* woman with that name. Lots of Javanese are called that.'

9. Harimurti

'Oh well, I suppose it can't be your Gadis then, Gus. Wrong person.'

'No, wait!'

Everyone turned away from Kang Lantip to look at me. I was aware that I had spoken sharply.

'Look, I'm certain, or almost certain, that it must be Gadis.'

'How could that be, Lé?'

'I'm sorry, Pak. And I have to ask your pardon, Bu and Kang Lantip. There was more to my relations with Gadis than I told you. But at the time there just wasn't an opportunity to say more about it, and since then there were so many other problems. Gadis and I were very close right up to the time when the crisis broke, and just before it she told me she had missed a month's menstruation. If Kang Lantip says the *Gerwani* prisoner is seven months pregnant, and her name is Retno Dumilah, then it tallies and must surely be Gadis. And the child she's carrying is mine.'

My father, and particularly my mother, continued sitting obviously shaken and seemed to have difficulty finding a target in the room to fix their eyes on. Only Lantip appeared calm in his chair, waiting for whatever else I might next divulge. But I was preoccupied with trying to control my own sensations. I imagined Gadis in her condition, bent over in a confined, airless cell, possibly crowded with other unfortunates, the unborn in her belly daily under threat.

I tore myself away from that nightmare and turned to the others; it was all I could do to keep from breaking down: 'Bapak, Ibu, Kang Lantip, can I ask you again to forgive me? Forcing more pain on you, and now I suppose shame as well?'

My mother, good, noble-natured woman, came over and hugged me, tried to comfort me, to console me, as she had done when I was little and had come home in trouble or after some accident: 'There, now, Lé, calm yourself, there's no question of shame here. The important thing for us is to find the best way forward in this.'

'Kang Lantip, help me get to Plantungan. And to Wates, so I can tell her parents, poor people. O what a sorrowful time it's been for them! Help me Kang.'

'Easy, Lé, take it easy. Don't let your feelings complicate matters. You're still under house arrest. You can't leave here. Let's give this some cool, quiet thinking.'

'Father is right, Gus. I'm sorry but you'll have to stay here. We all understand how hard that must be for you. It's a sad thing, but if you were to insist and went to Plantungan it would just make everything worse, it would all just turn hopeless. You understand that, Gus, don't you?'

I could only nod and curse fate in my mind, curse the turn of events and my helplessness.

'Good, that's the way. Listen, Gus. Let me go to Plantungan and see if they'll allow me to meet Gadis. I'm hopeful they'll let me in. I've got contacts all over and I'll find someone or other who will help. Next, I'll go to Wates, to her people, and tell them the news. Well, what do you think? And while I'm doing that, Bapak here can get in touch with Pakdé Noeg in Jakarta. He should be able to start something now that we've discovered Gadis.'

We fell in with Lantip's suggestions, and he left for Plantungan. He was away four days while we waited anxiously for his return. My father sent Pakdé Noeg a letter giving him the news about Gadis. Finally, on the fifth day, Lantip arrived looking tired and dishevelled, evidence that he had covered a lot of ground and with little rest.

'Have some tea first, Tip, or go and have a bath and then we'll talk. Or would you rather go to bed? You look tired.'

'Just let me have a gulp of tea and a wash, Bu. I'll tell you what happened and then sleep.'

He returned from the bathroom looking fresh and a lot livelier, having miraculously cast off the signs of his journey. He was always resilient, Lantip. He described his meeting with Gadis.

Yes, the *Gerwani* person held at Plantungan under the name Retno Dumilah was she. When they saw each other in the head-warden's office, each was stunned: Gadis, because of the unexpectedness of Lantip's arrival, and he on his part by the sight of the slim girl he had known in the recent past now standing before him in the shape of one far gone in pregnancy. They embraced, Gadis burst into tears and cried on his shoulder, and Lantip too admitted that it was a difficult moment for him as well.

'Yes, it's what you see, Kang,' she said to him after calming down a little. 'A wretched prisoner, and pregnant as well. I go around half-dead with shame. Every warden and picket-private torments me and flings obscenities at me.'

'Be brave, Gadis. The whole family is looking for a way to get you out of here.'

'How can they, Kang? They've decided that I'm a *Gerwani* rabble-rouser. I wasn't in *Gerwani*, I wrote poems for *Lekra*! I was a member of *Lestra*, the *Lembaga Sastra Indonesia*, *Lekra's* literary wing. But I can't make them see sense. We're all *Gerwani* to them here. And then when they take me over for their interrogations they decide that I'm contrary. I argue with them, talk back, they say.'

'All right now, Gadis. You're in this place and carrying a child, so save your energy, try to keep healthy for its sake and your own. And you have to be wise and control yourself when you deal with the authorities here.'

She calmed down, switching her attention to what Lantip might do to get

9. Harimurti

her out; and he said he thought that Pakdé Noegroho could be relied on to move things much as he had managed to do before in my case. She wrinkled her lips.

'A fine thing, having an uncle in the army. Very desirable, every family should have one, a colonel preferably. Bung Hari's sitting comfortably at home now, while I rot here on my own with this belly. How reasonable is that, Kang? He should be here with me!'

'Now Gadis, don't go flaying yourself with such thoughts and saying silly things. You know very well that Hari is suffering too, unable to come to you and comfort you and plan with you the future of your baby. He loves you very much. He worries all the time about you and your family.'

Lantip's firmness and good temper finally had its usual effect, and also Gadis in her physical state could not long stoke her passion for argument.

Suddenly, rather weakly, she said to him: 'Kang Lantip, all I want at this moment is to find a clean, quiet corner where I can give birth to this baby when the time comes.'

'That's among the things we're looking into. If Pakdé Noegroho can't free you in time, we'll at least try to have them let you have your confinement in a hospital.'

'If it happens here, in this crowded, stifling dump . . . well, all I can say is poor me, poor baby.'

'We'll hope for the best. Trust in God, Gadis. *Insya Allah.*'

'You know, I've thought of a name for the baby. If it's a boy it'll be Sungkowo; a girl, then Prihatin. Solace and Mercy are in great demand these days.'

'That's very good, Gadis. Just leave it to us to deal with this. The most important thing is for you to look after your health. If you can keep up your spirits that would help you too.'

Lantip left her, both of them hoping that the next time they met would be when he came with Pakdé Noegroho to take her away from Plantungan.

Then Lantip went to Wates to see the parents. As he described it, from the street there was a stillness about the house, and he wondered if the people had gone, or been taken away; but as he entered the front yard he became aware of a queer, discordant music, and then barely recognised sounds corresponding to the words 'One Archipelago, One Land' coming from a mouth organ. The couple emerged from the back, and he introduced himself, was asked inside, and soon was recounting to them the situation and condition of their daughter. They were shocked to hear that she was far gone in pregnancy, but Lantip quickly relieved their minds by assuring them that our family accepted Gadis, would accept the child, and were even then trying to have her status improved to one of house detention. Lantip's reassurances apparently composed the parents, and when he mentioned that Gadis had already provisionally decided on a name for the baby, their last worries gave way to broad smiles and chuckles.

We listened with a mixture of feelings to Lantip's report: happy and relieved to have at last a clear picture of Gadis's situation, but concerned about her state of health and what it might mean for the unborn baby. We now waited in hope and apprehension for news from Pakdé Noeg. A week passed, then two, then three: nothing. We grew worried and speculated about all kinds of things: surely, he wouldn't refuse to help, wouldn't look on Gadis as an outsider, unrelated to us? But he finally arrived at our home in the fourth week, spotless and full of cheer, looking younger and more dashing than last time we had seen him. We had been suffering agonies of impatience, and my father in particular looked worn; but Pakdé's world was evidently rosy, and he might have been taken as my father's junior.

Father met his bouncing arrival with poorly-suppressed exasperation: 'We've been watching a coconut tree growing, Mas, waiting for you!'

'Heh-heh-heh. Sorry, sorry. Didn't have a chance to send you the news. Got a lot of affairs to attend to these days. Anyway, I'm here now, and I bear happy tidings.'

There was an immediate lightening of spirits, mine in particular.

'Firstly, thanks to your prayers, I'm sure, and to the virtues of Bapak in Wanagalih being recognised by heaven, I can report that I've been given a new position: promoted to Director General of the Department of Trade.'

There was a chorus of happy screams and shouts: '*Waaah*! Terrific!'

Pakdé Noeg nodded graciously to everyone.

'The second matter, I'm glad to say, concerns our Hari here.'

I couldn't control myself and broke across what was going to be a long preamble by Pakdé: 'What—Pakdé Noeg—what news is there about Gadis?'

'Heh-heh-heh. Wait, wait. No frontal assaults please, your poor old Pakdé's retired from that now.'

While the others laughed I bit my lip and waited as my uncle reclaimed the floor.

'Yes, things went as follows. I looked up a few mates who are still in Army Headquarters, and then a few more in Military Intelligence, and came away with all the necessary paperwork. So now Gadis is being reclassified, her status as a detainee changes. Then on the way here I dropped in at Semarang for a permit that allows us all, minus Hari, to go and pick up Gadis in Plantungan. There. It's all official, *alhamdulillah*; and so, Hari, you'll soon be seeing your girl again. Heh-heh.'

We were overjoyed. In my happiness, I ran over to Pakdé and threw my arms around him, then giving thought to the proprieties I also took his hand and kissed it.

9. Harimurti

'Heh-heh-heh... Hari-i, Hari lad, you certainly put your foot in it at every turn, hey? Plays politics, he picks the PKI; chooses a wife, and she's a *Gerwani* spitfire, what?'

But I couldn't be provoked or protest at such a moment, I was so full of joy and relief, so overflowing with gratitude to Pakdé Noegroho. One after another, my mother and father raised their voices in thanksgiving: 'There, Hari. What did I tell you? Be patient, resign yourself to the mercy of Great Allah. Appeal to Him and, *lha*, He answers your prayers. Be grateful to Him, and to your Pakdé Noeg.'

'It's nothing short of a miracle, Lé. Who could have thought God would solve all your problems like this? And you should indeed be eternally grateful to Pakdé.'

Pakdé waved his hand: 'All right, all right, that's enough. I repeat what I said on the other occasion, that it's just one's duty to the family, the Sastrodarsono family. Who else, if not I, ought to have taken responsibility for dealing with these matters? Can one watch a family member suffer and do nothing to help? Well, it would be a poor sort of family where that was allowed. So let's leave it there. I'm repaid by the pleasure I have in seeing you all happy. Tomorrow we'll gather ourselves and go forth to see Gadis. Except you of course, Hari. You can't come. You're still under house arrest. But that's no matter, is it, Hari?'

'So be it, Pakdé, if that's the way it must be. I can do nothing.'

'That's it, there's nothing for it, Lé. And don't worry, you can rely on it that I'll be around to help out with the little kiddy after it's born. Won't be too long now, either.'

'Yes, don't delay, go all of you, get Gadis. I'll stay here and tidy the room for her, make it ready for her and the child.'

They left early next morning, headed for Plantungan in two cars. And that was exactly what I did while they were gone: cleaned the whole room from top to bottom. It had been Lantip's room too, but he had willingly given it up to us, had moved with his bed to the back of the house where the servants were and the kitchen. I dragged in a larger bed from the guest room in exchange for mine; there seemed to be fewer guests visiting us anyway in this unsettled and uncertain period. I mopped the floor, then on second thoughts scrubbed it with Creoline to disinfect it, until the room smelled like a hospital. There were positive things in being under house arrest: I had become something of an artist with the mop. I weighed up the merits of pictures that hung in various places, trying to select one which might look suitable in a room where there was going to be a mother and baby: flowers perhaps, or scenery that Gadis might like. I knew there was a painting of Mount Merapi by Trubus somewhere, and I wondered what had happened to it and what might please a newborn child. Would it be Sungkowo or Prihatin? I would know soon enough, any time now. I put off the matter of the pictures until they were here.

By late afternoon, I had washed and dressed, donned my best jacket, looked, I thought, very clean and smart. I sat on the veranda, on the low bamboo bench where I could look out on the road beyond the yard. I found myself with something of the feeling that I had when as a boy I waited for my mother to return home from the market. Lantip had described the same kind of timid hope and excitement when he had been alone and waiting in Wanalawas. Then, finally, when darkness was already approaching, the first car entered the front yard and I sprang up and walked quickly towards it. The doors for some reason were not immediately thrown open, and when they opened I heard my mother crying inside. She came out, and others then followed her. She was sobbing and she threw her arms around me.

'Oh, God, Lé. It's fate, it's fate. It's your wife, child. Your wife's gone, died . . .'

I turned to stone. I couldn't cry, couldn't do anything. I stood and listened to my parents telling me that Gadis had died some days earlier in giving premature birth to twins, a boy and a girl.

'Try to be strong, be firm, Lé, won't you? We'll do all we can to help you. Nothing can be done about it. Allah decided so. A terrible trial for you. But be resigned, resign yourself, boy.'

That was my father's voice, and I heard it as if coming from a distance, an echo. Like a sound coming from an empty, uninhabited room.

'There now, Hari. There. Come inside. Let's all go in.'

I don't remember who it was urging me to come into the house, only that I asked to be left outside; and there I paced about alone within that small yard. The last of the sunset was red and low in the sky, and a moment later the light had gone and everything was swallowed by the evening darkness: the neighbouring houses, the trees, all disappeared. I found myself turned to where the sun had gone, and I was telling Gadis that she had given life to solace and mercy both; and that I hoped she would find things good over there. I could hear her reading one of those poems of hers: political of course, as usual. It was morning in that poem, and a peasant had stopped working to wipe his face and sigh: 'O land that gives me life, will you be mine at last?' That was what he was asking, something like that. I heard Kentus, blowing on his harmonica the mixed-together ditties that had been our great hymns of that time: great hymns to unity, to the nation, and heaven knows what else. When I turned back to go to the house a little later, it was black night.

10. LANTIP: end and succession

The jackfruit tree at the corner of the front yard in Setenan Road finally broke and came down. Who knows how old it was, quite a few decades certainly, for people said it had been growing before Embah Kakung and Embah Putri Sastrodarsono had come to live at that address. The tree came down, and there ended its service to the Sastrodarsono family; and actually to the whole street, for it had been a famous tree and its generous fruiting had given enjoyment to folk of every level in the neighbourhood. Everyone around was familiar with its juicy segments and its special flavour, either when a pod had been freshly cut down or afterwards in the form of candy or puddings. The tree had given equally of its bounty to such people as the cattle dealer Pak Martokebo, who had figured in the Madiun uprising as a local member of the PKI, and to Pak Haji Mansoer, killed by the same insurgents.

I had been two weeks in Wanagalih with Gus Hari. Not long after the death of Gadis he had been informed that his status as a detainee under house arrest had been relaxed to one restricted to his town. With that came a concession allowing him to travel on family matters: undoubtedly more evidence of Pakdé Noegroho's operating behind the scenes among his shadowy acquaintances in Jakarta. Hari had been enjoying that freedom now for a year, and it had gradually had an effect on him like a slow-acting tonic, while we at home were relieved to see how he regained his spirits over that time. We had been worried when he seemed to spend so much of his day sitting abstracted on the veranda bench; but, thankfully, he had pulled out of that at last. The first step in his recovery occurred probably when he decided to ask father for some money and the use of our empty garage to establish a small library for the younger schoolchildren of the area. We all responded readily and helped him set things up, so that in a short time his modest collection of books was attracting young borrowers from the neighbourhood and some beyond it. It was pleasing and touching to see the growth in him of this new enthusiasm. Hari then extended his activities as a librarian to include teaching English to primary and lower-secondary schoolchildren. That also went well, without any difficulties raised by the officials overseeing his case, once father and I had lodged guarantees that those projects would not be transformed into hives of subversion.

Then, suddenly, an express letter arrived from Paklik Ngadiman alerting us to the fact that Embah Kakung's health was declining rapidly. He had aged markedly by this, and we all knew that often now his speech was difficult to follow. Hari and I were requested by Bapak and Ibu to leave quickly for Wanagalih and assist Paklik Ngadiman and his children in keeping an eye on Embah Kakung and be of service to the old man in any way possible. It was 1967, meaning that he was somewhere in the region of eighty-three years of age, given the imprecision with which people of that generation knew their date of birth. Whatever the exact age, it certainly approached an unusual sum of years for a Javanese, and we and the whole family had been concerned for some time now, expecting the worst news about Embah Kakung's health.

Thus it was that on that afternoon Hari and I were there to stand watching a crowd of people chopping up and dividing among themselves the trunk, the branches and even the smaller twigs of our beloved jackfruit tree. The very children and their goats had come to share in what they could by its fall: the first collecting, the second eating on the spot the leaves which had been brought down and were lying scattered about the ground. All this was being done by the wish and approval of Embah Kakung himself. When Paklik Ngadiman, Gus Hari and I came in to tell Embah Kakung that the tree had come down, the old man had been dozing on a divan in one of the inner rooms. He virtually sprang into a sitting position, his face grew quite radiant, and we saw in it a degree of alertness that had been absent in recent times.

Having had confirmed to him the truth of what we reported, he turned to us and with total clarity of speech, controlled and aware, he pronounced the following: 'Young people, hear me! The jackfruit tree which now lies broken was the spirit of this house and of the family that lived here. It guarded the wellbeing of our home, of all things and all people inside these walls. With its fall the tree has ended that guardian duty. I desire that it be donated to our people, its soul be shared by all. Anyone may take of its wood, its leaves, and if there still be any fruit, of that.'

Such was the command we received from the ancestral source of the Sastrodarsono dynasty, and, hearing it, we could do no other than heed it without question. That afternoon Paklik Ngadiman and Marman were sent out, and while from the elevation of the front veranda we two and others watched those who had been invited by them dividing in a spirit of celebration the body of the tree, suddenly we heard behind us the *srek-srek* of sandals scraping slowly towards us. *Masya Allah*—Embah Kakung, so frail, had appeared and was shuffling towards his old rocking chair! We hurriedly turned to help him into it.

'I just wanted to see it. How the people have come, happy to share our tree and its soul. He-he-he . . . enjoy yourselves! Welcome all!'

And we, his descendants, smiled and were happy too to see Embah Kakung in good spirits again. When the last of the tree was gone and all those who had come for a portion had left our yard, Embah Kakung made a sign

10. Lantip

that he wanted to be assisted back into the house. Gus Hari and I quickly supported him under the arms and we slowly returned him inside, hearing below us again the slow scrape of his sandals: *srek-srek* . . . *srek-srek* . . . Suddenly, Embah Kakung's body sagged between us. Dear God—he had fainted! We carried him quickly into his bedroom and called Doctor Waluyo.

The examination went on while we surrounded the bed and waited in silent common apprehension; then the doctor motioned us out of the room and quietly informed us that Embah Kakung's condition was such that we were advised to call all the family quickly.

We sent telegrams and made phone calls, and one by one in the ensuing days parents, spouses, and children arrived in Wanagalih. Halimah too accompanied my foster father and mother. Just as the last members appeared—Mbak Marie and Mas Maridjan—Embah Kakung passed away. Yes, he died just then, as if he had waited for his complete earthly family to attend him before he moved on to the hereafter. No one cried. We all knew that the time had come for him to follow Embah Putri. No one cried, but each of us in that room was certainly gripped by some private emotion. I stood there and remembered the first time I had gone into that room to be instructed by Embah Putri on the technique of mopping its floor. I had been astonished then by the splendour of this room. Well, to me it still was splendid.

We decided to have the funeral and then we would disperse; but first we gathered to choose the one who would make the final farewell speech over the grave of Embah Kakung. I assumed that there could be none more appropriate than Pakdé Noegroho to give it, the first of Embah's sons and who now had taken up the role of elder and head of the Sastrodarsono line. But in fact he determined otherwise. He thought that one of the younger members should have that honour, to express the family's continuity and the distance its flourishing had taken it from its origins in Kedungsimo. We all nodded in agreement with Pakdé's very apt and original idea. The other men, their wives and adult children chose, interestingly, Gus Hari for that duty.

But he slowly and reluctantly rose to speak to the assembly, in a quiet, firm voice: 'Dear relatives all. Dear members of the greater Sastrodarsono family, within whose Javanese hierarchies—Pakdé and Paklik, Budé and Bulik, Kakak, Adik and others—I have once more been learning to feel included, after having wandered from you and given you cause for unease and shame. Permit me to decline this honour. I understand Pakdé Noegroho's intention to symbolise the comprehensiveness and the reach of our family system, our Javanese family, specifically this family, by honouring such a junior member as myself, who in addition has sinned against that system; but there is one here we have embraced, someone who once stood even further at the margins of this great family of ours, who by our welcome and our receiving him represents this family's generous inclusiveness even better than my case could represent it: Lantip. I propose my brother Lantip should give the speech. Honest, sincere Lantip, always devoted to us all, never seeking a reward for his numberless services, a true priyayi.'

Well! I felt as if I had been struck by lightning. Confusion and panic overwhelmed me for a moment. I shook my head. I was an adopted child, the illegitimate offspring of a criminal who had once sullied the good name of these people, had shattered the lives of my grandmother and mother—now, at such a moment of unparalleled significance as this, I was being proposed as the Sastrodarsono clan's most fitting spokesman! . . .

Pakdé Noegroho nodded and said simply: 'Very good, Hari. I agree with you. Lantip, you must speak for us.'

There was authority in Pakdé's short sentences, and they were followed by a series of approving murmurs around the room: 'Agreed, agreed . . .' I bowed my head, both in powerless acceptance and to hide the effect of a sudden stinging sensation in my eyes.

The funeral procession set off, and on that very road to the cemetery I saw again in my mind my mother lurching under the weight of her basket, stopping first to one side, then the other, investigating the possibility of buyers where lanes led to outlying corners of the town. And I saw again Wanalawas and the shabby hut where she had lived; and then my grandmother and Pak Dukuh appeared to me, and I wondered how all those departed figures of my youth would have understood this astonishing commision, that I should act for the Sastrodarsono family like this, and what on earth they would have made of it, would have said to each other. I remembered my mother that evening of the splendid, eerie sunset, when she told me she was sending me into service with Ndoro Sastrodarsono, and then comforted me in my bewildered sorrow; and how she had shed tears hearing that I would pass even further from her reach by my receiving an education, her own hope for me.

And in that frame of mind I arrived with the procession at the site of the grave. *Masya Allah*, what could I possibly say?

I began: 'Peace be unto you, and Allah's mercy be upon us. Dear mourners gathered here, you whom I honour and love. A few days before Embah Kakung Sastrodarsono passed away, an old jackfruit tree growing in the front yard of his Setenan Road home toppled to the ground. I had no inkling that this might be a divine signal, an omen and a sign. Yes, a sign sent by Allah—praise unto Him—to be understood as meaning that someone of distinction, someone who had rendered much service and received the love of many, was being summoned back into God's mercy. I had not caught the import of that omen, for I am illiterate in the matter of signs and imports from Allah, I'm dull and insensitive there, and tend to take more notice of meanings on the surface of worldly things. It was only when that sign sent to us by Allah had been interpreted for me by Embah Kakung himself, when he willed that the jackfruit tree should be shared among all who had need of its components, that its remnant bounty be gathered by all, it was only then that I grew a little enlightened. Embah Kakung had decided that as he departed on his way to the hereafter he would leave with his children, grandchildren and great-grandchildren a legacy. It was not a legacy of dazzling goods which might swell us with pride in possessing them: Embah Kakung never valued worldly goods. What he left us was a vision of beneficence and service to the last, and those directed to as wide a compass of humanity as possible. Let us ponder on this episode of the tree in a spirit of loving-kindness and brotherhood, for heeding that parable, in that spirit, we will grow daily better as men and women advancing the will of God in His earthly realm.

'Dear mourners gathered here, you whom I honour and love. Embah Kakung began his long journey in this life by taking all those years ago a first step on what he knew was the path to priyayi advancement, that journey which began with his acquiring enough education to become an assistant teacher at a village far from here before we knew him as school-head at Karangdompol across the Madiun River. Then was it in those early days that he planted the first seeds which would grow into this family we have around us now. He wanted to see his family grow strong like that jackfruit tree, staunch, with a sturdy central core that supported the variously-grained layers around it. That core with its layers was really a principle, the priyayi principle of service. Yes, he, a descendant of peasantry, wanted no less than to make that gigantic effort to nurture in himself, and display as an example to others, the spirit of a priyayi, something which had been forever considered could rarely be successfully done except by those born into that class. And since what effectively distinguished the bearers of that high ideal from workaday people was the literacy of the former and the illiteracy of the latter, Embah Kakung ceaselessly emphasised the need for wider opportunities in education; yes, to give others among the *wong cilik* a chance to share in that ideal. Not primarily to enjoy the good life of the gentry, its refinement and manners, its elegance and complex culture, which for many, including a great number of priyayi themselves, is all by which that class is characterised; no, but to engage in a more exalted perception of that class, as duty-bound to serve others, particularly the most vulnerable, serve without reward beyond the satisfaction of serving, in a spirit of harmony and brotherhood. This ultimately democratic idea was what he wanted to instill into his widening family, even as its extending generations learned by their own experiences the necessity of harmony and brotherhood.

'Dear relatives all, honoured and loved. I was chosen to recall Embah Sastrodarsono's mission of service, and to wish him this day God's speed on his second long journey, a journey which not one of us here is truly capable of envisaging. We can only pray that it is a journey whose goal will recompense, and more, Embah's exertions on his terrestrial voyage. I was chosen by you to present to the younger generations of this family our understanding of Embah Kakung's life. He lived, as I said, by a vision, of priyayi submission to an ideal for the sake of those less fortunate, and he wished to inculcate in his descendants—who by his efforts have now been born priyayi—that noble view. That is my understanding of the meaning of Embah Kakung's life.

'Dear relatives, old and young. Forgive me if I'm unable to interpret to you the full sense of that service and obligation which was deeply imbedded in one whom we all loved. Ours are generations which have grown in an era of great changes and the signs of more great changes to come. We have seen one crisis follow another, right up to these times, and we should in fact be growing more capable of reading the omens and signals sent to us by God. If we sometimes still have difficulty in interpreting the meaning of things around us, well, dealing with that perplexity is part of education, and life is a school, learning is a journey through life, and while we live we have no choice but to go on learning. Let us all, dear relatives, take that journey bravely and with resolution and with concern for others, in the spirit that dwelt in him whom we have come to lay to rest.

'And now let us recite the *Al-Fatihah*, the epistle at the core of our religion. In the name of Allah, the compassionate, the merciful...'

On the way back to the vehicles, Pakdé Noeg, Budé Sus, Bulik Soemini and Paklik Harjono walked beside me in silence, and after some time I heard Pakdé addressing me, sounding puzzled: 'Tip, that was a fine speech. But, you know, there were things in it we didn't quite follow. What actually was the point you were making?'

I gave a quick glance around and noted that Hari and his parents broke into smiles. Some of the others seemed tired and were perspiring in the heat and looked only concerned with returning to the vehicles, yet others were tapping loose the grave-soil adhering to their shoes. Halimah, I was glad to see, smiled at me too.

'I must say, Pakdé, that it wasn't altogether clear in my own mind. I'm sorry if it sounded confused.'

'No, but . . . according to you, Tip, what really then is the meaning of *priyayi*?'

I did not reply immediately and lowered my head. Then, still looking down at the ground I said: 'To tell the truth, I don't know any longer myself, Pakdé. It's a word that has been losing its meaning and its importance in these times.'

I had spoken without looking up, and so could not see what effect my

10. Lantip

words had on Pakdé Noeg. In fact, considering the full implication of what I had just murmured—that I could see the prospect of extinction for the class of priyayi—I had not dared to look up at him. I soon moved away and walked beside Halimah, then took her hand in mine and steered her away from the others. Suddenly, I felt an urge to go back once again to Wanalawas: it was not far from the cemetery. I wanted Halimah to join me in saying a prayer over the graves of my mother and grandmother. Then someone behind me plucked at my arm.

'I'm coming too, Kang.'

I turned and saw that it was Hari.

'We're going to Wanalawas on foot, Gus.'

'Fine, I want to have a walk. And to talk with you two.'

'You're very welcome.'

We went and we talked about all kinds of things, our childhood and growing up, our future now that we had grown up. We found things to laugh about in remembering the better days of our youth, and became thoughtful when we considered the unpredictability of our lives in these times. We walked and talked, and the Javanese setting now surrounding our recollections and concerns alternated with Halimah's depictions of her own native kampong, in what she made sound like a fine, attractive West Sumatran town, quiet and well-to-do.

'Is it much different there to Wanagalih, Mbak Halimah?'

'Oh, yes, it's quite different. But then again, it's not. Is that an important question, Dik Hari, about how different we Sumatrans are?'

'See, Gus, you're under attack! You've got to be very careful when you speak to these matriarchs from the Pariaman.'

We all laughed, young citizens of this new Indonesia. Young, but probably already being overtaken by even newer cohorts behind us. I suddenly began to recite aloud a stanza of Javanese song-poetry that came into my mind, one of those composed by Subokastowo. I had seen in the distance Mount Kendeng rising above the skirting of forest around it, and the lines suited that sight. Gus Hari immediately joined me, and we three walked on, slowing our pace now to the rhythm of the verses. They described the poignant episode in the *Ramayana* when the three exiles, Rama, Sita and Laksmana first enter the dark forest of their banishment, to begin there their far wanderings over land and sea:

Wide to awed wanderers the world extends:
Lands, oceans, cities pass, and grief ne'er mends . . .

Not to be outdone, Halimah followed our song with some lyrics from her own region, whose tradition of itinerancy long ago gave rise to many ballads

Gentry
of longing, of remembered scenes, and atmospheric impressions of place:

Sunrise, where Mandalian springs;
Wading days for shrimp and eel,
Drunk on dusk and morning's feel,
And the arrack-coin night brings.

Bailed out Padang Bay by tin;
Waded seas of paddy mud;
Bought the bride by sweat and blood:
Nothing suits her mother-kin.

Minang man dies dry or drowns;
Tart his tears, like peppers' ooze.
Sun's descending, time to muse
On rantau treks and other towns.

Not a rendering of an imported and domesticated grand legend, but of simpler, unstudied moods, returning the heart more than the mind to some longed-for lost beginning of things. There were but those three short stanzas in Halimah's song, dwelling with sad humour on retrospections, and each ended with the awed exclamation: *'See how the twilight comes!'*

And we walked on, while the sky indeed coloured around the slopes of Kendeng, and the evening settled about us.

www.ingramcontent.com/pod-product-compliance
Lightning Source LLC
Chambersburg PA
CBHW061427040426
42450CB00007B/934